CADOGAN

Alex and Gardênia Robinson

with additional accounts
by David Stott and Helen Laird

the Amazon

YO-CAS-369

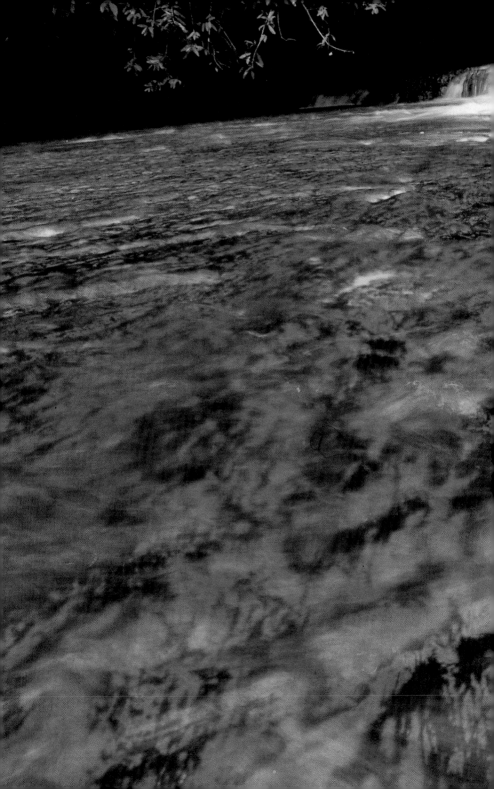

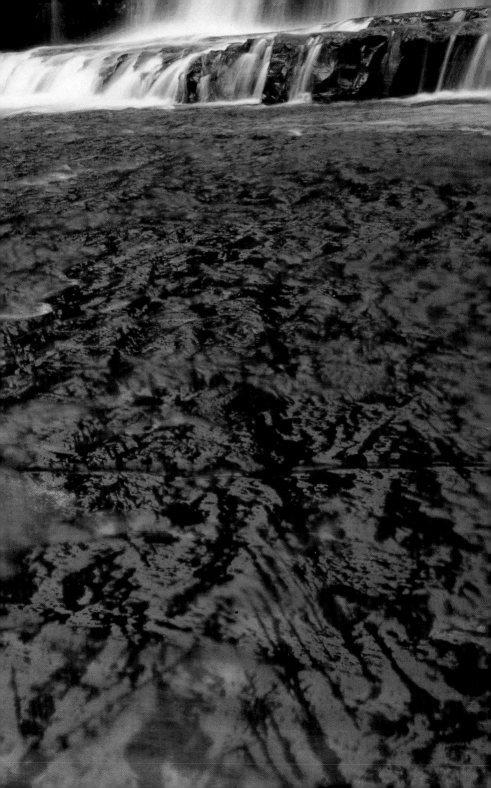

Noel Kempff Mercado National Park, Bolivia

The cathedral and plaza, Cusco, Peru

Terraces of Machu Picchu, Peru

Cusco streetlife, Peru

2   3   4   5   6   7

Quebrada de Jasper Falls, Venezuela

Petals, Brazil

Caiman, Pantanal, Brazil

Sunset near Iquitos, Peru

8   9   10   11   12   13

Belém, Peru

Shoal of silver dorado, Bonito, Brazil

Ticuna Indian dug-out canoes, Brazil

Kaieteur Falls, Guyana

14   15   16   17   18   19-

Blood flower, Brazil

Black caiman, Pantanal

Caboclo houses/Ticuna Indian peeling manioc

Fishing on the Río Javari/ Peruvian woman

Blue and yellow macaw

City Hall, Georgetown, Guyana

20   21   22   23   24   25

King Island Hotel, São Gabriel, Brazil

Victoria Regia waterlily

Wild pineapple

Tambopata-Candamo National Park, Peru

26   27   28   29   30   31

Foreword

by Manoel Fernandes Moura (Axketo)
son of seven generations of Tucano Indian shamans
and President of FIUPAM, Tabatinga, Brazilian Amazon

'For non-Indians, the Amazon is the world's largest well of natural resources, and a guarantee of an oasis in the desert the world will become. It is the lungs of the world.

'For we Indians the Amazon is much more than this. It is the greatest university and living model of the universal mother of our Earth. Through it, she teaches us, gives us examples, shows us her truths and feeds us her fruits. She offers a physical and spiritual cradle. Her knowledge and wisdom is given little by little throughout our human development, and all of her elements work together in faultless, divine clockwork within which Man is sheltered and provided for from the cradle to the tomb of eternal rest. And all is given free of charge.

'This sublime university doesn't demand a matriculation fee, but the criteria for entrance are nonetheless very demanding. Her fee is true love and tolerance, unselfishness and a deep sense of gratitude for all. For this reason, the graduates of this university are greater than others, and emerge richer in true love, in tolerance, in generosity and in gratitude than any who graduate as doctors of the arts or the sciences from other universities throughout the world.

'We have been asking Tupa (God) to accept our request that non-Indians enter this university. After successful graduation, all our brothers throughout the world will be able to put into practice what they have learned, and thus prevent the extinction of this sacred university; this university devoted to the mathematically and magically perfect forge of our characters, our spirits and our collective consciousness; mathematical because all within it has its harmonious place (and human technology too should find its part within this); magical because our ancestors have preserved the teachings of the old ones, of the Sun, of the Moon, of the stones, of the soil and the air, of the waters, of vibration, and of all the voices that only we Indians can hear and understand.'

1

Cadogan Guides
West End House, 11 Hills Place, London W1R 1AG,
cadoganguides@morrispub.co.uk

The Globe Pequot Press
246 Goose Lane, PO Box 480, Guilford, Connecticut 06347–0480

Wildlife illustrations © Anni Jenkins

Editorial Director: Vicki Ingle
Series Editor: Linda McQueen

Editor: Mary-Ann Gallagher
Proofreading: Vivienne Richardson
Indexing: Isobel McLean
Production: Book Production Services

A catalogue record for this book is available from the British Library ISBN 1-86011-983-2
Printed and bound in Italy by LEGOPRINT

The author and publishers have made every effort to ensure the accuracy of the information in the book at the time of going to press. However, they cannot accept any responsibility for any loss, injury or inconvenience resulting from the use of information contained in this guide.

About the Authors

Gardênia Robinson was born in Belo Horizonte, Minas Gerais, Brazil, and though she lives in England and likes tea, it only makes her feel more Brazilian. She graduated in Business Administration from the University of São Paulo's FEA School of Economics, and became a merchant banker. She now works for non-governmental organisations and as a travel researcher and photographer. She is a Nicheren Daishonin Buddhist.

Alex Robinson feels Latin American and tries not to be too British, but even after visiting 48 countries, most of them hot, he still goes bright red in the sun. He has a first class honours degree in theology from Bristol University, and was a postgraduate student at Emmanuel College, Cambridge. He has worked in television production and is now a travel writer and photographer. He also contributes regular articles on World Music to a variety of publications.

With special remembrance for Alice Robinson

Contents

Brazil and Colombia

Venezuela

The Guianas

Language and Glossary

Further Reading

Maps

Acknowledgments

Much thanks to David and Helen Stott for their thorough and dedicated work; Mary-Ann for always being cheerful and human; Rachel Fielding for commissioning the book; Vicki Ingle for believing in us; Dr E Robinson for the house; Dr M Robinson for the encouragement; Daniel Counihan for inspiration; the França Family for abundant love; Kicca Tommasi for liking our photos; Manuel and Veronica Moura for wonderful hospitality; George Lyons for always believing in us; Gerardo Reichel Dolmatoff for his inspiring books; Daisaku Ikeda for the poem 'The Long and Distant Amazon Current'; Silvana Vicente and Kate McAusland for kind encouragement; Hugo Pepper; Marianne van Vlaardingen; Barry Walker; Maria Emilia de Cabrera; everyone at Tabatinga Town Hall; Hitoma; Sacambu Lodge; Sr. Chagas from Rico Linhas Aéreas; Akira Tanaka; Estevão Lemos Barreto; Marcelo and family (boat driver) Rio Uaupés; Tarcisio, Balbina, Francisco, Claudio, Domingos, Olvide and São Domingos Community in general; João Bosco from Assumpção Community; the army doctor who helped us in Pari Cachoeira; Tenente Alberto from Cucuy; Eugenio and Caetano from Saude e Alegria; Professor, Capitão and Ia Mirim Community in general; Joel Souza; Cuiabá Tourist Office; Helio Brun from Campo Grande Tourist Office; Andre Thuyarani, Explorer Expeditur; Green Track; Walter Ley and Santa Clara Lodge; the Colombian Consul in São Gabriel; Maria and Antonio Gavani and Carlos Israel Tovar from San Carlos de Rio Negro; Ivan Artal from Ruta Salvaje; Luis and Vadim from Z Café in Santa Elena; Capt. Gouveia from Roraima Airways; Colette McDermott; Diane McTurk from Karanambu Ranch (and her wonderful otter friends); Cristina Fuentes La Roche; Cesar and Franco at Varig; Becky Jump at Karrimor.

With special thanks to the guest essay writers

Manoel Fernandes Moura (Axketo), President of FIUPAM, (Foreword)
Marianne Von Vlaardingen and **Miles Cohen** of Pantiacolla Tours (Amazon Fauna)
Simon Boyes of Ornitholidays (Birds of the Pantanal)
Barry Walker of Manu Expeditions (Birds and Bird-watching in the Western Amazon)
Professor Ghillean Prance of The Eden Project (Amazon Flora)
Jane Wilson-Howarth (Amazon Health)
Marcus Colchester of the Forest People's Programme (Indigenous Peoples of the Amazon Basin)

The Amazon is not a river: it is myriad rivers. Together they form an inland sea that holds more than one fifth of the world's fresh water; a living, flowing pattern as intricate as the labyrinth of blood vessels that fill the human body. Its span is

Introduction

literally that of an ocean. The Orinoco in Venezuela and Rio Plata in Argentina are linked through navigable waterways as long as the Pacific Ocean is broad. Passenger and cargo boats, dug-out canoes and dinghies ply these waters. Villages, towns and even cities have grown up on river banks. These are often named after the tribal nations they have destroyed or displaced to the depths of the forest. Hundreds of small nations still live here, such as the Shipibo, Ticuna, Tucano and Yanomami. Others choose to remain remote in the upper reaches of the Javari, or in Manu or Amapá. Dozens of Indian nations have never seen a white face. Some tribes welcome visitors, and see tourism as a tool in their fight to become masters of their own destiny. A stay with the Huaorani, Shuar, Ticuna or Tucano will be rough for those used to western comforts, but it can be a life-changing experience.

The Amazon itself is a rainbow river. The waters that fill it flow in from rivers of many colours. The Rio Negro is as black as espresso coffee; the Madeira the colour of drinking chocolate, and the Tapajos ocean-blue. The Rio Cristalino runs clear as glass; the Urubamba foams like cappuccino. The Mamoré and Madre de Dios are slow and sluggish, meandering through steamy tropical forest for hundreds and hundreds of unchanging miles. The Apurimac rushes headlong over fierce rapids, through the deepest gorges in the world. Many of these rivers are lined by beaches whose white sand is as fine and soft as any in the Caribbean, and in places rain-forest lodges have been built on their banks, with paths leading into the surrounding forest. Some are very comfortable, with all the luxury for which one could hope in the hot, damp, insect-riven rainforest. Others are tougher and more remote, but those who yearn for adventure, who love Thoreau or who yearn to see wildlife will find the rewards of visiting them are correspondingly greater.

7

The Amazon herself, in whom all colours mingle, dwarfs all other rivers in the world. The Nile may claim to be longer, but she cannot hold an island the size of Denmark in her mouth. The Yangtze and Volga are garden streams next to her; at Santarém, 800 miles inland, her waters are broader than the distance between London and Paris. Her annual floods rise to the tops of the highest rainforest trees, allowing vegetarian fish to graze in the canopy. Dolphins, sharks, stingrays and giant turtles swim in her waters, together with fish twice the size of a man.

The forests of the Amazon are as diverse and rich as her rivers, and only the Taiga in Siberia is larger. Without the forest, the Guyana Shield in the north would be a huge desert: its vast swathes of giant trees survive on bone-dry sand and the forest floor is a filigree of tiny rootlets that recycle over 98% of rainwater and nutrients. Slabs of ancient sandstone burst through the seemingly infinite flatness of the forest canopy, rising to over 3,000 metres in the remote Pico da Neblina range of northern Brazil. Further to the east, in Venezuela, these slabs turn into hulking table-top mountains battered by lightning storms, and watching over a sea of grass and scrub known as the Gran Sabana. Waterfalls pour from their sides, flowing over sandstone, quartzite and bright red jasper.

The forests further south grow thick and lush on red, leached soil that is almost as nutrient-poor as the Guyana Shield sands. These forests also break into grasslands, the largest of which is the Pantanal, whose flat expanse forms a causeway of lakes and rivers in the wet, stretching across central Brazil and the corners of Bolivia, Paraguay and Argentina. These attract hordes of clamouring birds and are a haven for many Amazonian mammals and larger reptiles. Of all the vast Amazon lands, only the seasonally flooded river banks are nutrient-rich and, as is true throughout the region, only the Indians have ever succeeded in farming them efficiently. If you have the time, it is worth visiting all these environments, travelling between them by plane, boat and road. Only then will you begin to get a feel for the Amazon's primordial vastness and the astonishing diversity of its scenery.

Wildlife

Animals are difficult to see in the Amazon forest. At times the gallery of trees can be unnervingly quiet and still: a vast cathedral of giant trees and dripping mosses. Only birds and butterflies are easy to see, descending in a riot of noise and colour, or flashing past in electric blue or iridescent green. Animals are easiest to see in the Pantanal, South America's Serengeti, where long, orange sunsets silhouette huge flocks of birds and the Amazon's wildlife is out in the open. But, magnificent though it may be, the Pantanal never captures the mystery and enigma of the Amazon rainforest. A night under the trees or floating in a dug-out on the river will raise the hairs on your neck and remain in your subconscious forever.

For all its power and immensity, the **Amazon urgently needs your help**. Brazil has long had plans to chop half the forest down and replace it with eucalyptus groves and cattle ranches and Ecuador, Colombia and the Guianas are increasingly threatened by the petrochemical, timber and mining industries. By visiting the Amazon, you are helping to save it. Your money will help convince local people that a live jaguar is worth far more in tourist dollars than a dead jaguar's skin, and your visit will show governments that the forest can earn them money over the long and not just the short term. A visit here is no more difficult than a visit to Alaska, the Yukon or outback Australia. It is possible to fly direct to the heart of the Amazon with only one change of plane; there is plenty of tourist infrastructure, and you will be far safer here than on the streets of New York or London.

Travel

By Air

Prices vary dramatically, depending on when, where and how you're going. The peak season is May–September, the first week of December until 15 January and, in Brazil, the Carnaval (the week before Ash Wednesday, in February or March); (during these periods try to book as far ahead as possible. Flights taking in a stopover (e.g. New York or Miami) may be slightly more expensive. Excursion fares are valid from 5 to 90 days; year-long fares are more flexible and return dates can be kept open (one-way tickets are possible but bear in mind that international tickets purchased in Latin America will be more expensive). 'Open-jaw' tickets allow passengers to touch down in one country and leave from another (travel from jaw to jaw is at your own expense). Specialist travel agents (e.g. Journey Latin America, Trailfinders, STA, eXito) have some of the best deals on scheduled flights, and are especially useful for organizing multi-stop itineraries. For last minute discounts have a trawl through the Internet, or consult the travel sections in the Sunday papers, or in London try *Time Out* and the *Evening Standard*. You'll find the cheapest deals in the spring (February–May) and autumn (September–November). Make sure your travel insurance covers re-issue of lost or stolen tickets. Always reconfirm your flight 72 hours before leaving and get to the airport at least two hours before departure. All South American countries levy a departure tax (around $20–$50). This is payable in hard currency, so don't forget to keep some dollars back at the airport. Baggage allowances are mostly 30kg first class, and 20kg second class. *See* also Airpasses, below. Some of the best last-minute bargains are posted on the Internet. Try *www.cheapflights.com, www.lastminute.com, www.travelselect.com, www.airtickets.co.uk.*

From the UK and Europe

Unless you are flying direct from Paris to Cayenne in French Guiana, you need to get a connecting flight at Miami to fly right into the heart of the Amazon (Manaus or Belém in Brazil). Alternatively, there are also connections via Miami to Quito in Ecuador, Santa Cruz in Bolivia or Bogotá in Colombia (from Bogotá there are direct air connections to Leticia). Flights from Miami also connect to Georgetown in Guyana, Paramaribo in Suriname and Cayenne in French Guiana. Fares from Paris to Cayenne are generally the cheapest available to anywhere in the Amazon Basin, as this is regarded as an internal French flight. Cheapest low season fares to Belém and Manaus cost around £590 and tickets to Rio, Lima, Quito, Caracas and Bogotá can go as low as £240–£388.

Airlines

Aerolineas Argentinas, ✆ (020) 7494 1001, ✉ (020) 7494 1002. Argentinian national airline. Flights to several South American destinations.

Avianca, ✆ (08705) 767 747. Colombian national airline with flights to Bogotá and Quito.

Air France, ✆ (020) 8742 6600, *www.airfrance.com*. Fifty-one flights a week to South America (all flights connect via Paris), also Miami to Bogotá (Colombia), Quito (Ecuador) and Paris to Cayenne (French Guiana/Guyane).

Alitalia, ✆ (08705) 448 259, *www.klm-alitalia.com*. Direct flights to Bogotá and Lima.

British Airways, ✆ (0345) 222 111, *www.british-airways.com*. Fights to Caracas and Bogotá.

Iberia, ✆ (020) 7830 9911, *www.iberia.com.* Flies via Miami to Quito and Caracas.

KLM Direct, ✆ (08705) 074 074, ✆ 0990 750 900, *www.klmuk.com.* Direct flights to Quito, Lima and Paramaribo (and onwards to Belém via Suriname Airways).

Lufthansa, ✆ (0845) 773 7747, *www.lufthansa.com.* Direct flights to Bogotá and Quito.

TAM (Brazil), ✆ (020) 7707 4586. Flights to and within Brazil.

TAP Air Portugal, ✆ (0845) 601 0932. Good fares to Caracas and Rio de Janeiro.

Varig, ✆ (0845) 603 7601, *www.varig.co.uk.* Flights from Miami to Manaus and Belém.

Specialist Agencies in the UK and Ireland

Journey Latin America, 12–13 Heathfield Terrace, Chiswick, London W4 4JE, ✆ (020) 8747 3108, ✉ (020) 8742 1312, *www.journeylatinamerica.co.uk.* Comprehensive range of flight options to the whole of Latin America.

Trailfinders, 194 Kensington High Street, London W8 7RG, ✆ (020) 7938 3939.

Austral Tours, 20 Upper Tachbrook Street, London SW1V 1SH, ✆ (020) 7233 5384, *www.latin-america.co.uk.*

Bridge the World, 47 Chalk Farm Road, London NW1 8AW, ✆ (020) 7911 0900.

Last Frontiers, Swan House, High St, Long Crandon, Bucks HP18 9AF, ✆ (01844) 208 405.

See also the agencies listed in the 'Specialist Tour Operators', p.16

From the USA and Canada

There are direct flights to Rio and São Paulo in Brazil from Newark New Jersey on Continental. From Miami there are direct flights (American Airlines, LAB, Varig) to Manaus and Belém in the heart of the Amazon. Alternatively you can fly via Miami to Caracas in Venezuela, Quito in Ecuador, Santa Cruz in Bolivia or Bogotá in Colombia (from Bogotá there is a direct air connection to Leticia in the Colombian Amazon).

Airlines

American Airlines, ✆ (0800) 433 7300. Flights to Caracas, Venezuela (four hours from Miami), and a direct service between Miami and La Paz or Santa Cruz.

British Airways, ✆ (0800) 247 9297, *www.british-airways.com.*

Continental Airlines, ✆ (0800) 231 0856, *www.continental.com.*

KLM, ✆ (0800) 361 5330, *www.klm.com.*

Lloyd Aéreo Boliviano, ✆ (0800) 327 7407. The national Bolivian airline with direct flights Miami–Manaus, and Miami–La Paz/Santa Cruz.

Lufthansa, ✆ (0800) 645 3880, *www.lufthansa.com.*

SAETA, ✆ (0800) 827 2382, *www.saeta.com.ec* (under construction), email for information to *ehbuzon@saeta.com.ec.* Ecuadorean airlines.

Varig, ✆ (0800) GO VARIG. Brazilian airline with connections to Manaus and Belém.

Specialist Agencies in the USA and Canada

Air Brokers International, USA, ✆ (0800) 883 3273. Discounts.

Council Travel, 205 E 42nd Street, New York, NY 10017, ✆ (0800) 743 1823. Major specialist in student and charter flights; branches all over the USA.

Encore Travel Club, USA, ✆ (0800) 444 9800. Scheduled flight discount club.

Last Minute Travel Club, USA, ✆ (0800) 527 8646.

New Frontiers, USA, ✆ (0800) 366 6387. Canada, in Montreal, ✆ (514) 526 8444.

STA Travel, in the USA, New York, ✆ (212) 627 3111, or toll-free ✆ (0800) 777 0112.

Travel Avenue, USA, ✆ (0800) 333 3335.

Travel Cuts, 187 College Street, Toronto, Ontario M5T 1P7, ✆ (416) 979 2406. Canada's largest student travel specialists; branches in most provinces.

See also under US specialist tour operators, p.18

From Australasia and Asia

There are no direct flights from Australia or New Zealand to Rio or São Paulo, or to other Amazon Basin destinations. Qantas, Aerolineas Argentinas and Lan Chile all fly between Australia/New Zealand and Argentina or Chile, with onward connections to the Amazon.

Airlines

Qantas, ✆ 131313 (within Australia), *www.qantas.com.au*. Flights to Buenos Aires via Auckland and South Pacific from Sydney.

Lan Chile, ✆ (02) 9244 2333. Two flights a week to Santiago via Auckland and Tahiti.

Aerolineas Argentinas, 580 George St, Sydney, ✆ (02) 9283 3660; ASB Centre, 135 Albert St, Auckland, ✆ (09) 3793 076. Two flights a week to Buenos Aires via New Zealand.

Trailfinders, ✆ (02) 9247 7666, 8 Spring Street, Sydney.

All other Asian flights (from Singapore, Hong Kong and Bangkok) go via Europe.

By Boat

Travelling by cargo or banana boat from Europe will cost in the region of £2,000. It takes around three weeks to cross the Atlantic or around 40–80 days for a round trip. A 14-day passage from Florida costs around $1,500. Contact:

Strand Voyages, Charing Cross Shopping Concourse, The Strand, London WC2N 4HZ, ✆ (020) 7836 6363.

Cargo Ship Voyages Ltd., Hemley, Woodbridge, Suffolk IP12 4QF, ✆ (01473) 736 265. Booking agents for Fyffes banana boats sailing to Suriname and Guyana.

Traveltips Cruise and Freighter Travel Association, 163-07 Depot Road, PO Box 188, Flushing NY 11358, ✆ (0800) 872 8584.

Entry Formalities and Customs

All travellers need a full passport valid for a minimum of six months. Visitors from the UK staying 90 days or less do not need a visa for any of the Amazonian countries except Suriname. These can be obtained in Amsterdam or Guyana (*see* p.272). There is no Surinamese consulate in the UK. If you want to stay in any Amazon country longer than 90 days, apply for a visa in your home country well before travelling or extend your visa at immigration in the country in question. If you plan on staying longer than 30 days in either Bolivia or Colombia ask for an extended 90-day visa at your point of entry. Citizens of the USA and Japan require visas for Brazil and Suriname. Canadians need visas for Brazil, and Australians and New Zealanders need visas for Brazil, French Guiana and Suriname. If you plan to stay in any of the

Amazon countries longer than 90 days, apply for a full visa in your home country well before travelling (visas must be applied for in person at the embassy). Brazilians need visas for Guyane (even though they are not required for France itself). These must be obtained in Brazil.

Overland travellers from everywhere except Brazil (and most other Latin American republics) need visas to enter Venezuela. If you have not got a visa in advance you should get these from the consulate in Manaus (*see* p.208), whether you intend to travel into Venezuela through Boa Vista or São Gabriel da Cachoeira. The Amazon border between Peru and Ecuador is closed both to boats and overland travellers.

Visa requirements in South America can change at short notice, so check with embassies or your tour operator before you go. If you overstay your visa without extending it at least two weeks before its expiry you risk being arrested and fined. Keep a record of your passport details, in case of loss or theft, plus photocopies of any entry cards or stamps.

Customs: A Few Words of Warning

It is not a good idea to buy any pelts or materials made from the skin of any Amazonian animal. Aside from encouraging illicit slaughter, you will be very heavily fined if you are caught by customs either within South America or back home. Customs in Tabatinga (Brazil) and Leticia (Colombia) are particularly vigilant.

Getting Around

Getting around towns in the Amazon Basin is straightforward. There's a fairly extensive network of jet and turbo-prop flights and passenger and cargo boats ply all the major rivers, particularly within Brazil, Peru and Ecuador; where they don't, it is often possible to hitch a ride on a cargo boat. Efficient, air-conditioned buses and rickety old crates brave dirt roads, and it is possible to hire cars and 4x4s. Full details are given within the country chapters.

By Air

Flying within Latin America is an affordable option (flying over the Andes from Lima to Iquitos in the heart of the Amazon can cost as little as $60). There are good connections between most of the major cities and towns; and sometimes flying is the only way to reach the more remote areas and settlements. It is not necessary to fix up internal air flights before you leave; visit the local airlines in the airport or relevant town, or book through a street travel agent. Full details are given in the country chapters.

Airpasses

For those leap-frogging their way across the South American continent, there are various airpasses available which work out cheaper than buying individual flights. Brazil, Colombia, Venezuela, Peru and Bolivia are linked in airpass schemes: between four and eight stops costs around US$500–$1,000. Avensa, the national Venezuelan airline, has a 45-day four-coupon airpass (minimum US$200), taking in Miami as well as Latin America. Varig, the Brazilian airline, have a new 30-day Brazil Airpass 500 offering unlimited travel in the whole of Brazil (including Manaus, Santarém, Belém and Tabatinga) for US$450. The Mercosur Airpass gives hefty discounts on air miles flown in Brazil (Manaus), Argentina, Uruguay, Paraguay and Chile. Most airpasses should be purchased outside Latin America or the Caribbean. Check the latest offers with your travel agent or contact one of the Latin American national airlines.

There are plenty of passenger and cargo boats on the rivers of the Amazon, and in Peru and Brazil you will rarely have to wait more than a few days for a service, even in little places like Tabatinga. A hammock is an absolute necessity for this type of travel. You should also buy a couple of pieces of rope (about 1m long each), for tying up your hammock. The rivers can get surprisingly cold at night-time so be sure to have a light fleece, socks and a sheet sleeping bag. River boats usually have communal showers and a communal dining area. Food can be a little bland, bu it's generally safe to eat. Bring plenty of bottled water, some snacks, water purification tablets or iodine and some very large novels; watching endless, unchanging forest can get a little boring after a while. If you'd rather have a stuffy cabin, it'll cost you extra. In the pricier public boats, you may get a private shower and bathroom. But life is more fun in a hammock.

A more expensive, altogether smarter alternative is to take a luxury cruise upstream from Belém or Manaus in Brazil, Iquitos in Peru, Puerto Ayacucho in Venezuela, or Trinidad in Bolivia (*see* the relevant chapter information). It is even possible to journey from Belém all the way to Iquitos. This 3,000km route is navigable all the way by ocean-going ships and takes around 18 days (including stops for exploration by dinghy). Prices are expensive (in the region of US$5,000–$6,000; to cut them you could opt for a half trip (Belém to Manaus or Manaus to Iquitos). Be sure to check that your boat doesn't flush its rubbish straight into the river, or the sea. Most liners, even the most luxurious, do so.

Full details of such services are given in the country chapters.

Canoeing or kayaking down the Amazon is also possible, along any of its myriad tributaries. South American Explorers (*see* pp.113 and 298) can advise on this. Joe Kane's *Running the Amazon* is a thrilling account of such a journey.

Cruise Operators

Amazon Clipper Cruises, Rua Sucupira 274, Kíssia, 69.040-350, Manaus, ✆ (92) 656 1246, ✉ (92) 656 3583. All mod cons including salon and bar, video and library.

Amazon Explorers, Rua Nhamundá 21, Praça Auxiliadora, 69.025-190, Manaus, ✆ (92) 633 3319, ✉ (92) 234 5753. Available for charter with all mod cons.

Enasa, Rua Marechal Deodoro, 61, 69.005-000, Manaus, ✆ (92) 633 3280, ✉ (92) 633 3093. A 138-berth catamaran cruising from Belém to Manaus.

See also the information in the country chapters.

Cars and 4x4s can be hired in many of the larger cities. Details are given in the individual country chapters. If you plan to travel further than the environs of the local town, be sure to tell someone reliable where you are going, when you are leaving and when you intend to arrive at your destination. Do not consider using anything other than a 4x4, and preferably a Land Rover or a Toyota Land Cruiser, as anything else (particularly US pick-ups and Jeeps) probably won't be up to the job if the going gets tough. Take plenty of spare water and petrol, a couple of spare tyres, a sturdy shovel, a blanket and food. The Amazon is still a very wild place, roads frequently get washed out, and on the Trans Amazonas in Brazil or other 'major' roads, you may not see another vehicle for days.

If you get stuck DO NOT wander away from your vehicle: stay with it and wait for help.

Bus networks exist in all of the Amazon countries and, outside the core Amazon in Brazil, are the most popular form of travel for most locals. Roads frequently get washed out in the wet season, and it is easy to get stranded. Buses range in comfort from luxurious air-con with videos (not always a blessing) to old US school buses. For full details *see* the country chapters.

By Taxi

You can find taxis of every sort in Amazonia; many of them are metered. Where they aren't, always agree on a price before getting in. Drivers do not expect a tip, but will of course appreciate anything offered. Motorcyclists may offer pillion rides; in Iquitos in Peru there are nifty three-wheeled motorcycle rickshaws or *motocarros*. At many airports you can find aerotaxis. These are expensive, and occasionally poorly maintained and dangerous, but they will able to take you directly to some of the most out-of-the-way hinterlands, sometimes landing on one of the rivers themselves. For full details see the country chapters.

Hitch-hiking

Hitching may be risky, but many travellers do it and find it one of the most rewarding ways of getting round. In the bigger towns head for a gas station or police checkpoint; in smaller towns your chances of getting a lift are higher. It is also possible to hitch a ride on a riverboat.

Specialist Tour Operators

The South American special-interest tour ranges from rugged (white-water rafting, jungle survival etc.), to luxury (riverboat cruises) to natural history (birding, wildlife photography, lepidoptery, botany). For information on companies specialising in ecotourism, contact:

The Ecotourism Society, PO Box 755, North Bennington, VY 05259, USA, ✆ (803) 447 2121, ✉ (802) 447 2122, *ecomail@ecotourism.org, www.ecotourism.org.*

Green Globe, PO Box 396, Linton, Cambridge CB1 6UL, UK, ✆ (01223) 890 250, ✉ (01223) 890 258, *greenglobe@compuserve.com, www.wttc.org.*

Tour Operators in the UK

Austral Tours, 20 Upper Tachbrook Street, London SW1V 1SH, ✆ (020) 7233 5385, *www.latinamerica.co.uk.*

Cox & Kings, 10 Greencoat Place, London SW1 1PH, ✆ (020) 7 873 5000, ✉ (020) 7630 6038, *cox.kings@coxkings.sprint.com. .*

Dragoman, Camp Green, Debenham, Suffolk IP14 6LA, ✆ (01728) 861 133, *www.dragoman.co.uk.* Overland expeditions in converted army trucks.

Encounter Overland, 267 Old Brompton Road, London SW5 9JA, ✆ (020) 7370 6845. Organizes a 21-day expedition by truck and riverboat through Bolivia and Brazil. Also offer a 19-day trip by motorised long boats through the Ecuadorian Amazon basin.

Explore Worldwide, 1 Frederick Street, Aldershot, Hants GU11 1LG, ✆ (01252) 760 000, *www.explore.co.uk.* Three-week tour of Amazonia and the Galapagos, including a three-day jungle cruise from Iquitos to Leticia; alligator-spotting at night.

Geodyssey, 29 Harberton Road, London N19 3J5, ✆ (020) 7281 7788, ✉ (020) 7281 7878, *www.geodyssey.co.uk.* Venezuela specialists: riverboats to Angel Falls, expeditions to the rainforests of the Upper Orinoco and wildlife spotting in the Llanos.

Hayes and Jarvis, 152 King Street, London W6 0QU, ✆ (020) 8222 7844. The top end of the market; a little too comfortable to allow for really getting off the beaten track.

Interchange, 27 Stafford Road, Croydon, Surrey CR4 4NG, ✆ (020) 8681 3612, ✉ (020) 8760 0031, *interchange@interchange.uk.com.* Venezuela specialists.

Journey Latin America, 12–13 Heathfield Terrace, Chiswick, London W4 4JE, ✆ (020) 8747 3108 (flights) or ✆ (020) 8747 8315 (tours), ✉ (020) 8742 1312; and Suites 28–30, Barton Arcade, Deansgate, Manchester M3 2BH, ✆ (0161) 832 1441, ✉ (0161) 832 1551.

Last Frontiers, Swan House, High Street, Long Crendon, Bucks HP18 9AF, ✆ (01844) 208 405, ✉ (01844) 201 400, *www.lastfrontiers.co.uk.* Specializing in tailor-made itineraries, also bush plane adventures in the Venezuelan Amazon.

Overland Latin America, 13 Dormer Place, Leamington Spa, Warks CV32 5AA, ✆ (01926) 311 332, ✉ (01926) 435 567, *worldlspa@aol.com.* Small group expeditions, treks and overland travel through the Amazon.

Reef & Rainforest, Prospect House, Jubilee Road, Totnes, Devon TQ9 5BP, ✆ (01803) 866 965, ✉ (01803) 865 916, *reefrain@btinternet.com.*Tailor-made itineraries with an emphasis on natural history to Ecuador, Peru and Venezuela. Highly recommended.

Tribes Travel, 7 The Business Centre, Earl Soham, Woodbridge, Suffolk IP13 7SA, ✆ (01728) 685 971, ✉ (01728) 685 973, *www.tribes.co.uk.* Highly recommended: visit the Ecuadorian rainforest as guests of the Siecoya, Huaorani and Achuar tribes.

Veolos Tours, 33 Warple Way, London W3 0RG, *www.veloso.com.* Tailor-made itineraries and rainforest expeditions for discerning travellers.

Worldwide Journeys, 8 Comeragh Road, London W14 9HP, ✆ (020) 7381 8638, ✉ (020) 7381 0836, *www@wjournex.demon.co.uk.* Tailor-made itineraries throughout South America, in particular the jungles of Ecuador, Peru and Brazil.

Overland and Adventure Specialists

Several other agencies specialize in overland or adventure trips to South America which focus on one country and may involve travelling across the Amazon Basin by boat. They include:

The Imaginative Traveller, 14 Barley Mow Passage, Chiswick, London W4 4PH, ✆ (020) 8742 8612, ✉ (020) 8742 3045, *www.imaginative-traveller.com.*

Bukima Expeditions, 55 Huddlestone Road, London NW2 5DL, ✆ (020) 8930 6702, ✉ (020) 8830 1889, *bukima@compuserve.com.*

Kumuka, 40 Earls Court Road, London W8 6EJ, ✆ (020) 7937 8855, ✉ (020) 7937 6664, *sales@kumuka.co.uk.*

Tour Operators in the USA

Brazil Nuts, 1150 Post Road, Fairfield, CT 06430, ✆ (0800) 553 9959. Escorted trips to the Amazon Basin and the Pantanal.

Eco Expeditions/Zegrahm, 1414 Dexter Avenue North, #327, Seattle, WA 98109, ✆ (206) 285 4000, ✆ 0800 628 8747, ✉ (206) 285 5037, *www.zeco.com.*

Luxurious cruises and stays in rainforest lodges throughout the Amazon.

Explorers Travel Group, 1 Main Street, Suite 304, Eatontown, NJ 07724, ✆ 0800 631 5650. Customised tours around the Amazon Basin.

International Expeditions, ✆ (205) 428 1700, @ (205) 428 1714, *www.ietravel.com*. Expeditions on board classic riverboats to the headwaters of the Amazon, based from Iquitos where there are stays in rainforest lodges and an excursion to the ACEER Canopy Walkway.

Latin America Reservation Center Inc., PO Box 1435, Dundee, FL 33838, ✆ (941) 439 1486, ✆ 800 327 3573, @ (941) 439 2118, *LARC1@worldnet.att.net*. Travel and accommodation database and resource centre for the Latin American continent.

Nature Encounters, 9065 Nemo Street West, Hollywood, CA 90069, ✆ (310) 247 454, ✆ 0800 529 9927, @ (310) 247 4543, *www.phrantic.com/nature*. General rainforest tours for groups and individuals.

Nature Expeditions International, 6400 East El Dorado Circle, Suite 210, Tucson, AZ 85715, ✆ (520) 721 6712, ✆ 0800 869 0639, @ (520) 721 6719, *www.naturexp.com*.

Ocean Connection, 211 East Parkwood, Suite 108 Friendswood, TX 77546, ✆ (281) 996 7800, ✆ 0800 365 6232, @ (281) 996 1556, *adventure@oceanconnection.com*.

Natural History and Birding Tour Operators

In the UK

Animal Watch, Granville House, London Road, Sevenoaks, Kent TN13 1DL, ✆ (01732) 741 612, @ (01732) 455 441, *mail@animalwatch.co.uk*.

The EarthWatch Institute, 57 Woodstock Road, Oxford OX2 6HJ, ✆ (01865) 311 600, @ (01865) 311 383, *www.earthwatch.org*. Working holidays and scientific research placements all over Latin America, with a few Amazon options.

Ornitholidays, 29 Staight Mile, Romsey, Hampshire SO51 9BB, ✆ (01794) 519 445, @ (01794) 523 544. Highly recommended. Land-based and ship-orientated natural history and birdwatching holidays across South America and the Amazon region.

Wildlife Worldwide, 170 Selsdon Road, South Croydon, Surrey, ✆ (020) 8667 9158, @ (020) 8667 1960, *www.wildlife-ww.co.uk*.

World Expeditions, 3 Northfields Prospect, Putney Bridge Road, London SW18 1PE, ✆ (020) 8870 2600, *www.worldexpeditions.co.uk*. Dugout canoe trips accompanied by naturalist guides in the Peruvian Amazon Basin, also taking in Machu Picchu, Cusco and Lake Titicaca.

In the USA and Canada

The Smithsonian Institution, The Smithsonian Associates, Dept 0049, Washington DC 20073-0049, ✆ (877) 338 8687 (*lines open Mon–Fri 9am–5pm*), *smithsonianstudytours.si.edu/*.Natural history trips and occasional tours.

Earthwatch, PO Box 9014, Watertown, MA 62272, ✆ (617) 926 8200, ✆ (0800) 776 0188, @ (617) 926 8532, *info@earthwatch.org*. Working holidays and scientific research placements all over Latin America, with a few Amazon options.

Earth River Expeditions, 180 Towpath Road, Accord, CA 12404, ✆ (914) 626 2665, ✆ 0800 643 2784, ✉ (914) 626 4423, *earthriv@envirolink.org*. White-water rafting expeditions, principally in Ecuador.

Flights of Fancy Adventures, 901 Mountain Road, Bloomfield, CT, 06002, ✆ (860) 243 2569, *magesfried@aol.com*. Highly recommended. Offer low-cost, high-quality general natural history and birding tours for small groups to a variety of locations.

Suggested Itineraries

With a week in **Peru**: Take a helicopter trip to Machu Picchu and fly in and out of Manu National Park.

With two weeks: Walk the Inca Trail and bus in and fly out of Manu National Park.

With three weeks: Add the ACEER canopy walkway near Iquitos.

With four weeks: Walk the Inca trail, raft the Tambopata River and visit Manu National Park.

With ten days in **Bolivia**: Fly to Noel Kempff Mercado National Park from Santa Cruz and divide your time between the Lodges of Los Fierros and Flor de Oro. Visit El Encanto waterfall, the La Florida community, the savannah, the oxbow lakes off the Itenez, and the meseta.

With two weeks: Add another two days onto your time in Noel Kempff and trek to Arco Iris waterfall (if you're fit). Take a two-day trip to the Amboró National Park or the Jesuit missions.

With three weeks: Add a trip to Chalalam Lodge or a river-boat journey on the Mamoré River.

With four weeks: Add a trek in the Yungas and unwind in Coroico.

With a week in **Brazil and Colombia**: Visit the *fazendas* of the Southern Pantanal or the Amacayacu National Park and Sacambu Lodge in Leticia.

With two weeks: Visit the Ticuna Indians for a week and unwind in Amacayacu National Park and Sacambu Lodge in Leticia, or visit the Rio Cristalino and the Northern Pantanal.

With three weeks: Add a visit to the Ilha do Marajó, Alta Floresta and the Northern Pantanal.

With four weeks: Add the little towns of Santarém, Bonito or the Morro da Seis Lagos.

With a week in **Ecuador**: Visit Quito and Sacha or Kapawi Lodge.

With two weeks: Add Tiputini or a visit to the Huaorani.

With three weeks: Add a visit to the Galapagos Islands.

With a week in **Venezuela**: Visit the Angel Falls and Gran Sabana.

With two weeks: Add the Rio Cauca or a trip from Puerto Ayacucho.

With three weeks: Add a climb up Mount Roraima or Auyan Tepui.

With a week in **the Guianas**: Visit the Kaieteur falls and Karanambu Lodge.

With two weeks: Add Dadanawa Lodge, Iwokrama Forest Reserve or the city of Paramaribo.

With three weeks: Take Wilderness Explorers' Wai Wai expedition, visit Kaieteur Falls and Karanambu Lodge or one of the turtle nesting beaches in Suriname or Guyane.

With four weeks: The Wai Wai expedition, Kaieteur Falls and/or Karanambu Lodge, overland to Paramaribo and a stay at the turtle nesting beach of Les Hattes (in nesting season).

Practical A–Z

The Amazon Basin has distinct rainy and dry seasons, but as it is divided by the Equator these are different for the northern and the southern extremities (the Guianas, Venezuela, Colombia and Ecuador in the north and Bolivia, southern Peru and the Brazilian Pantanal in the south).

In the north most rain falls between May and December. In the south most rain falls between December and April. You can nonetheless expect rain in the dry season, and sunny, clear days in the wet. The central Amazon from Iquitos to Belém is unpredictable—a month can be the wettest on record one year, and the driest the next. But generally this region follows the southern pattern. More important are the annual rising and falling of the rivers. The river floods annually from December, rising by as much as 12.5 metres at its peak in April or May. In the low water season (July–February) the river will clog and some regions will become completely inaccessible: this is the best time for spotting wildlife, especially on the broad sandy river beaches that are exposed at this time.

The high water season (March–June), swells all the tributaries of the Amazon, opening up the forest to a series of creeks and flooded areas called in Brazil *igarapés* and *igapós*. This seasonally flooded forest is called varzea forest, and the forest that lines its sides, gallery forest. Fish with huge molars fill the varzea forest during the high water season. The water reaches the canopy, giving them access to seeds and fruits for these few months each year. Caiman and otters follow them, and other animals retreat into the gallery forests and terra firme forests that lie behind them. This makes wildlife generally harder to spot. But, as much of the forest fruits at this time, it is a good season for birds (particularly parrots and macaws) and primates.

Average Temperatures

Belém °C

	Jan	Feb	Mar	Apr	May	Jun	Jul	Aug	Sept	Oct	Nov	Dec
max	31	30	30	31	31	32	32	32	32	32	32	32
min	23	23	23	23	23	23	22	22	22	22	22	22

Manaus °C

	Jan	Feb	Mar	Apr	May	Jun	Jul	Aug	Sept	Oct	Nov	Dec
max	30	30	30	30	31	31	32	33	33	33	32	31
min	23	23	23	23	24	23	23	24	24	24	24	24

Average Wet Days Per Month

Belém

Jan	Feb	Mar	Apr	May	Jun	Jul	Aug	Sept	Oct	Nov	Dec
24	26	25	22	24	15	14	15	13	10	11	14

Manaus

Jan	Feb	Mar	Apr	May	Jun	Jul	Aug	Sept	Oct	Nov	Dec
20	18	21	20	18	12	12	5	7	4	12	16

Children

Taking the kids is no problem, especially if you're travelling on a private riverboat or staying one of the well-run forest lodges (*see* Where to Stay). Parties of schoolchildren regularly visit rainforest lodges in Tambopata and Iquitos (in Peru), Ecuador and the softer, more luxurious lodges around Manaus (Brazil).

Disabled Travellers

Even at international airports and luxury hotels, accommodation for the disabled is poor to say the least. For advice and information before you go contact:

UK

Holiday Care Service, 2nd floor, Imperial Buildings, Victoria Road, Horley, Surrey RH6 9HW, ✆ (01293) 774 535. Travel information and information packs on long-haul holidays.

RADAR (Royal Association for Disability and Rehabilitation), 12 City Forum, 250 City Road, London EC1V 8AF, ✆ (020) 7250 3222.

Tripscope, Alexandra House, Albany Road, Brentford, Middlesex TW8 0NE, ✆ 0345 585 641. Limited practical advice and information on every aspect of travel and transport for elderly and disabled travellers. Information can be provided by letter or tape.

USA and Canada

Mobility International USA, PO Box 3551, Eugene, OR 97403, ✆ (541) 343 1284, ✆ (541) 343 6812, *info@niusa.org*. $35 membership fee.

SATH (Society for the Advancement of Travel for the Handicapped), 347 5th Avenue, Suite 610, NY 10016, ✆ (212) 725 8253. Advice on all aspects of travel for the disabled, on an ad hoc basis for a $3 charge, or unlimited to members ($45, concessions $25).

Electricity

Peru: 220 volts, 60 cycles (except in Arequipa which has 50 cycles).

Bolivia: 220 volts, 50 cycles (except La Paz, which has 110 volts at 50 cycles).

Brazil: 127 volts in Manaus (110 or 220 volts elsewhere in the country).

Colombia: 120 volts.

Ecuador: 110/120 volts.

Venezuela: 110 volts, 60 cycles.

Guyana: 100 volts in Georgetown; 220 volts in most other places.

Suriname 1:10/127 volts, 60 cycles.

Embassies and Consulates

Embassies and consulates are listed under '**Tourist Information and Useful Addresses**' at the beginning of sections describing major towns and cities. If you want to gather some information before you go, try the following (overleaf).

Embassies and Consulates in the UK, USA and Canada

Bolivia   UK, 106 Eaton Square, London SW1W 9AD, ✆ (020) 7235 4248.

USA, 3014 Massachusetts Avenue NW, Washington DC.

Brazil   UK, 32 Green Street, London W1Y 4AT, ✆ (020) 7499 0877.

USA, 630 5th Avenue, 27th Floor, New York NY 10111, ✆ (212) 757 3080.

Canada, 2000 Mansfield, Suite 1700, Montreal H3A 3AS.

Colombia   UK, 3 Hans Crescent, London SW1X 0LR, ✆ (020) 7589 9177.

USA, 2118 Leroy Place, NW Washington DC 20008, ✆ (202) 387 8338.

Canada, 380 Albert Street, Suite 1130, Ottawa, Ontario K1R 7X7.

Ecuador   UK, Flat 3B, Hans Crescent, London SW1X 0LS, ✆ (020) 7584 1367.

USA, 2535 15th Street NW, Washington DC 20009, ✆ (202) 234 4744.

Peru   UK, 52 Sloane Street, London S1X 9SP, ✆ (020) 7235 1917.

USA, 1700 Massachusetts Ave, NW, Washington DC 200036, ✆ (202) 833 9860.

Suriname   USA, Van Nex Center, 4301 Connecticut, NW Suite 108, Washington DC 20008, ✆ (202) 244 7590.

Venezuela   UK, 56 Grafton Way, London W1P 5LB, ✆ (020) 7387 6726.

Food and Drink

Food in the Amazon Basin is generally pretty bland: a rustic mixture of *feijao* and manioc flour or cake, spiced up with delicious river fish and a wealth of incredible tropical fruit. Most of the 2–3,000 different species of river fish can be eaten, and as they have different names not only in the various countries, but in the various regions within those countries, we cannot list them here. Vegetarian fish tend to be the tastiest, with rich white flesh and subtle, delicate flavours. The larger catfish are almost as delicious, and carnivorous fish like piranha, though offered on most tourist trips for curiosity's sake, are a little oily and bony.

Amazon Fruit, Juices, Energy Drinks and Tonics

Amazon fruits are astonishing in their diversity. Many have entirely unique tastes. Juice bars throughout Amazon Brazil often offer as many as 150 different fruit juices to choose from, and raw fruit is available in markets throughout the Amazon. The more unusual are as follows: **Cupuaçú** is a relative of the cacao, with acrid, yellow flesh surrounding heavy woody seeds. Although horrible on first taste, it is utterly delicious thereafter. Cupuaçú beans are used to make cupuaçú chocolate, and the flesh is used as cream in wonderful cakes (try these in Manaus). Cupuaçú juice is one of the most refreshing. The seeds of the **cacao** fruit which are used to make chocolate are milky and deliciously refreshing as a juice, **camu-camu** has light yellow flesh, with a mild taste. The juice is very thirst-quenching and has recently been discovered to have the highest vitamin C content of all fruit. The **nispero** is a dark brown fruit that looks like a potato. The flesh is gloriously sweet and tastes like dates; it is known in Asia as a *chicu*. **Tapereba** is an acrid fruit which makes a refreshing drink when plenty of sugar is added; **acerola** are sub-tropical cherries (originally brought to the Amazon from Madeira by the Portuguese) which are very refreshing and are packed with vitamin C. **Cajú** is the apple-like fruit of the cashew tree—the famous nuts grow off the end of the fruit like bizarre probosces. The fruit has a delicious, peachy flesh, whose flavour is unique, indescribable and very much an acquired taste. The **açai** is a blackurrant-coloured palm-fruit that produces an oily, thick juice rich in nutrients; the **ingá** is a pulpy fruit surrounding large seeds in what looks like a giant bean pod. It grows around flooded forest and is delicious but useless for juice. The **uva da mata** is a palm fruit that looks and tastes almost exactly like a grape. The **tomate de arbol** is a sweet, oval tree tomato with a more delicate flavour than its temperate cousin. It is very good in juices. There are some popular **Amazon energy drinks and tonics**; among them is **Guaraná**, an Amazon seed renowned for keeping you alert and awake, without the mugginess of caffeine; **mastruz** (**com leite**) is an Amazon tonic. It tastes unpleasant but is reputed to make you feel full of vigour. Even less appetising is **masata**, manioc froth as thick as beef soup, and fermented with saliva. It is full of nutritious goodness though, and if you are invited to have some by *caboclos* or Indians, it is very, very bad manners to refuse.

Avoiding Eating Endangered Species

Most Amazon game is tasty, and in places readily available, but eating it often encourages the killing of endangered species. If you can't resist then try paca (a large rodent), which are pretty common so you are unlikely to be causing much damage eating them. A few fish regularly dished up are endangered species, mentioned on the CITES list. Brazilians in Manaus flout their country's ban on fishing pirarucu (called 'arapaima' in Guyana), and the fish, which has to surface for air, is in real danger of extinction. The larger river turtles are also offered on many menus. Once they were farmed by the Omagua people, but today they are highly endangered. Currasows and guans are among the first birds to disappear when humans invade the rainforest. You are likely to see them only in Indian villages or isolated areas—their flesh is notoriously tasty, and only the indigenous peoples kill them sustainably.

Food and Etiquette in Indian and *Caboclo* Villages

Food is generally scarce in Indian villages in Brazil. Be sure to bring some of your own, and offer it to your hosts too. This discourages the over-exploitation of fish and game stocks for tourists, and respects Indian etiquette: eating is a community affair. Avoid sweets and junk food—the nearest dentist tends to be a long way away. Try and bring familiar, local produce like *feijao* beans, manioc flour, rice and potatoes. If you want to be really popular, offer to buy a couple of live chickens. Be sure to dispose of all wrappers: most indigenous and poor people in the Amazon are not aware that plastics etc. are not biodegradable. Other popular gifts include pens and paper, petrol for motor boats, work tools like chisels and machetes, and if they don't have one, a football (a round one—oval balls will be regarded as mutant). Even thoughtful gifts can be a double-edged sword. Avoid giving money, and try to be sure your gift is given in exchange for services rendered, or something you have already received—like assistance or accommodation. Otherwise, your hosts will feel obliged to hand you one of their favourite possessions—like a bow and arrow that have been in the family for generations.

Health and Insurance

It is vital to take out comprehensive insurance which will cover emergency medical treatment as well as emergency medical evacuation. Many travel agents will offer some kind of travel insurance, or else can recommend a reputable agent. **Journey Latin America**, ✆ (020) 8747 8315, or Manchester ✆ (0161) 832 1441, offer complete cover, and an annual multi-trip policy from £89 for up to 10 weeks' cover.

You will need vaccination against yellow fever, anti-malarial tablets, 15–30 SPF suncream and insect repellent containing DET. Vaccinations for typhoid and hepatitis are also recommended. Essential items for your medical kit might include: a mosquito net, contraceptives, tampons, painkillers, water-purifying tablets, foot powder, rehydration salts, anti-diarrhoea treatments and antibiotics, first aid kit and contact lens solution. Drink bottled mineral or filtered water only. For more information, *see* pp.77–80.

Holidays

Bolivia
Jan 1, Carnival (week before Lent), Easter Sunday, Corpus Christi, Aug 6 (Independence Day), Oct 12 (Columbus Day), Nov 2 (Day of the Dead), Dec 25.

Brazil
Jan 1, Carnaval (three days up to and including Ash Wednesday) Good Friday, April 21 (Tiradentes), May 1 (Labour Day), Corpus Christi (early June), Sept 7 (Independence Day), Oct 12 (Nossa Senhora Aparecida), Nov 2 (Dia dos Finados, Day of the Dead), Nov 15 (Day of the Republic), Dec 24, Dec 25.

Columbia
Jan 1 (Circumcision of Our Lord), Jan 6 (Epiphany) Mar 19 (St Joseph), Easter, May 1, Corpus Christi (early June), July 20 (Independence Day), Aug 7 (Battle of Boyacá), Aug 15 (Assumption), 12 Oct (Columbus Day) Dec 8 (Immaculate Conception), Dec 25.

Ecuador
Jan 1, Jan 6 (Three Kings' Day, Reyes Magos y Día de los Inocentes), Feb 12 (Anniversary of the Discovery of the Amazon River), Feb 27 (Patriotism Day), Carnival (three days before Ash Wednesday), Holy Week, May 1, May 24 (Battle of Pichincha), Corpus Christi (early June), July 24 (Simón Bolívar Day), Aug 10 (Independence Day), Oct 12 (Columbus Day), Nov 1 (All Saints' Day), Nov 2 (Day of the Dead), Dec 24, Dec 25.

Guyane (French Guiana)
Jan 1, Easter Sunday, May 1, July 14, Aug 15, Nov 1, 2 and 11, Dec 25.

Guyana
Jan 1, Feb 23 (Republic Day), Easter Sunday, May 1, May 26 (Independence Day), Caricom Day (first Mon in July), Freedom Day (first Mon in Aug), Dec 25, Dec 26.

Peru
Jan 1, June 24 and 29, Jul 28 and 29, Aug 30, Oct 8, Nov 1, Dec 8, Dec 25.

Suriname
Jan 1, Holi Phagwa (March), Easter Sunday, May 1, July 1, Nov 25, Dec 25.

Venezuela
Carnival (Mon and Tues before Ash Wednesday), Easter Sunday, April 19, June 24 (Feast Day of San Juan Bautista) July 5, July 24, Oct 12, Dec 25.

Internet

Some useful websites:

www.latinworld.com: Directory of internet resources on Latin America.

www.spanishconnection.com: Search engine for Latin American subjects.

www.runningmanonline.com: Interactive tribal journeys: follow a team of explorers online as they trek through the Suriname jungle searching for a cure for cancer. Photographic, video and sound clips, plus the world's only witchdoctor school.

www.planeta.com: Ecotravel in Latin America.

www.samexplo.org: South American Explorers' Club.

www.peruembassy-uk.com and *www.peruonline.net*: Tourist information on Peru.

www.ecuador.org: Basic travel information on Ecuador.

www.bolivian.com: Information on Bolivia.

www.socioambic.utal.org: Information on Brazilian Amazon and indigenous peoples.

Languages

Bolivia	Spanish (60%), Quechua, the language of the Incas (25%), Aymara, the language of the Altiplano, spoken before the Incas (15%).
Brazil	Portuguese, and over 200 indigenous dialects within the Carib, Arawak and Tupi-Guarani linguistic groups, including Tucano and Ticuna, which has its own language group and sounds oriental in its pronunciation and complexity of tones.
Colombia	Spanish (and over 180 indigenous dialects and languages).
Ecuador	Spanish (Quichua is spoken by most tribes, also Cofan, Siona, Shuar and Huaorani).
French Guiana	French (and other dialects).
Guyana	English (and Hindi and other dialects).
Peru	Spanish, Quechua, and over 300 other dialects and languages including Shipibo and Huitoto.
Suriname	Dutch, also English, Sarnami, Indonesian, Lao and Taki-Taki (a Creole dialect).
Venezuela	Spanish and indigenous dialects including Yanomamo.

Maps

The maps in this guide are for orientation only.

Good map suppliers in London include Stanfords, 12–14 Long Acre, London WC2 9LP, ✆ (020) 7836 1321, and The Travel Bookshop, 13 Blenheim Crescent, London W11 2EE, ✆ (020) 7229 5260. In the USA and Canada, try The Complete Traveler, 199 Madison Avenue, New York, NY 10016, ✆ (212) 685 9007, or International Travel Maps, ITM Publishing, PO Box 2290, Vancouver BC V6B 3W5, ✆ (604) 687 3320. Maps of Ecuador are hard to get outside the country: for 1:100,000 or 1:50,000 scale maps try the Instituto

Geográfico Militar, Calle Paz and Miño, Quito, ☏ (00 593 2) 522 066. Most South American capitals have a Military Geographical Institute or a National Parks Office which can supply you with more accurate maps and charts than those available in Europe or North America.

More detailed maps can be obtained within the countries in question. Ask South American Explorers or the Tourist Offices for details.

Money and Banks

Take dollars: preferably pristine bills in a mixture of denominations. Large bills ($50 and above) will give a better exchange rate, and small denominations are good for small purchases if you run out of local currency. Buy local currency on arrival. Traveller's cheques make a good back-up, but will be hard to change in smaller towns and villages. In larger towns, credit cards are widely accepted in the more expensive hotels, restaurants and shops and ATM and cash machines are widely available. Bolivia, Ecuador, Brazil, Guyana, Suriname and Peru are among the cheaper destinations—travellers on a budget can get by on as little as $30–$40 a day. Colombia and Venezuela are about half as much again, and French Guiana is as expensive as rural France. These costs can change overnight.

National Currencies

Brazil	*real* (R$) of 100 centavos.
Bolivia	*boliviano* (Ns) of 100 centavos.
Colombia	*peso* of 100 centavos. You will get a slightly better rate using *pesos* rather than dollars.
Ecuador	*sucre* (S/) of 100 centavos. Ecuador is considered one of the cheapest destinations for travellers on a budget.
Guyane (French Guiana)	French *franc* (F) of 100 centimes. Use Visa machines: there is one in the airport, or bring French franc/Euro or sterling traveller's cheques. The dollar is virtually useless here.
Guyana	Guyana *dollar* ($) of 100 cents.
Peru	*nuevo sol* (S/) of 100 cents.
Suriname	*suriname guilder* (Sf) of 100 cents.
Venezuela	*bolívar* (Bs) of 100 céntimos.

ATM Machine Locations

The following websites have information on credit cards and ATM machine locations.

Visa	*www.visalatam.com.*
Mastercard	*www.mastercard.com.*
American Express	*www.americanexpress.com.*
Western Union	*www.westernunion.com* .

Packing

Take a rucksack (backpack). Pack the following essentials: light cotton trousers; long-sleeved cotton shirt; T-shirts and shorts; light fleece; light raincoat or poncho; tough Goretex walking boots (Karrimor KSBs are about the best; Timberland and other designer labels are useless);

swimming gear; underwear and socks (including one thick pair); sheet sleeping bag; torch (flashlight) we recommend a maglite; sun cream; insect repellent; string; padlock; gaffer (duct) tape (very useful for patching up holes in mosquito nets); Swiss army knife or Leatherman; camera; tripod or high ASA film as the forest can be dark; binoculars (an essential); a daypack. Buy a hammock and flip-flops and warm clothes for the Andes when you arrive.

Travelling Light, 35 Dover Street, Piccadilly, London W1, ✆ (01931) 71448. Specializes in 'smart but practical' tropical rainforest clothing and accessories.

Post

Postcards to the USA or Europe take roughly a week (Colombia, Bolivia, French Guiana, Brazil, Venezuela), or even three weeks (Ecuador). In Peru post is ridiculously expensive, and in Guyana especially letters are liable to go astray: for important communications you should use a private courier. Parcels are expensive to send unless you use surface mail (around three months to Europe, one to North America). If you plan to use a poste restante make sure any letters you receive are labelled as clearly as possible using only your surname and initial. For urgent messages home sending a fax may be easier: fax machines are available in many post offices, shops and hotels.

Safety

You are unlikely to encounter any difficulties in Latin America. Though robbery is fairly common in the large capital cities, particularly Rio de Janeiro, the Amazon tends to be quieter and safer. Border towns can be a little rougher (especially between Ecuador and Colombia through Coca and Puerto Quijarro), and care should be taken on the Santa Cruz–Puerto Quijarro train. Travel with people on this route and watch your luggage like a hawk. Use common sense on the streets of Manaus and Belém, Lima and Quito after dark. If you are away from the crowds, catch a cab rather than walk. Do not wander into indigenous territories without an indigenous guide or a friend of the indigenous people. You will not be welcome. Women travelling to remote areas, or on long river boat journeys should try and find a travelling companion for the journey. You are unlikely to have any problems beyond irritating grins, winks and whistles but it is best to be as safe as you can. Where there are any special areas of concern, we have indicated so in the body of the country chapters.

Telephones

Phoning home from one of the main centres is easy. Most countries have international direct dialing, and it's best to buy pre-paid phone cards from a newsstand, post office, pharmacy or other concession. In remoter areas like São Gabriel da Cahoeira it is an impossibility.

Country codes: **Bolivia** 591; **Brazil** 55; **Colombia** 57; **Ecuador** 593; **Guyane** (French Guiana) 594; **Guyana** 592; **Peru** 51; **Suriname** 597; **Venezuela** 58.

Time

The following times are given as hours behind GMT: **Bolivia** –4; **Brazil** –5 (–3 outside Amazonas state); **Colombia** –5; **Ecuador** –5; **Guyane** (French Guiana) –3; **Guyana** –4; **Peru** –5; **Suriname** –3; **Venezuela** –4.

Tourist Information

Peruvian tourist offices are generally helpful, particularly in Cusco. Staff speak English and have written information in several languages. The Guainas are similarly efficient, and Bolivia Ecuador and Venezuela are beginning to get their acts together too, though in these countries you will generally be better off visiting a private operator.

Brazil is a giant that lags behind its tiny neighbours. Its tourist offices are bureaucratic and generally oblivious to tourists' needs and concerns. In Belém, for instance, they are unable to provide any information about visiting the rainforest, and have no idea why tourists would want to go there unless it is to fish for peacock bass. Brazil's current plans are also indicative of their general ignorance of Amazon tourism. They plan to open up the Amazon to large-scale resorts on the Cancún model.

For details of the office addresses, *see* the country chapters.

Where to Stay

You will have no problem finding a place to stay throughout the Amazon, even if you turn up late at night and have to knock on a few doors. All the major cites and towns have comfortable, air-conditioned rooms with private bathrooms that are generally every bit as good as what you will find back home. They tend to be around 30–50% cheaper too.

The very cheapest rooms (under $25 a double) can be a bit shabby in Lima, Manaus and Belém, where they tend to double up as whorehouses. But other towns have clean, safe and often charming cheap options, and Cusco has some real delights in all price ranges.

Rainforest lodges are the real reason to come here, and range from rustic shacks in the heart of the wild, to luxurious cabins with en suite bathrooms and a swimming pool. These are never going to be as comfortable as home, for the obvious reason that you are out in the damp, sticky tropical wild.

For seeing wildlife, you should aim to stay in a lodge without generator driven electricity. If you are scared of spiders and insects, don't fret. There are plenty here, but you are unlikely to see anything huge and hairy unless you put in a special request. Most stick to the forest.

Amazon Wildlife .

Fauna of the Amazon *by Marianne van Vlaardingen and Miles Cohen*

The world's rainforests occupy about 8 per cent of the earth's surface and contain about 60 per cent of all animal species and one third of all flowering plant species. One might be forgiven for thinking, then, that life for these animals was easy, but nothing could be further from the truth. The once fertile Amazonian soils are leached and exhausted; the waters from ancient mountains run anaemic and the scales of life are finely balanced with wars being fought on many small fronts in the struggle for survival. The rainforests give nothing away; they can't afford to. The only thing a rainforest has to offer is wonderment and enlightenment that words can't begin to convey.

Insects (*Insectae/Neopterae*)

This class is vast and only a few of the families are mentioned here. In terms of biomass, the ants and termites alone represent about 66 per cent; in terms of species the coleoptera are by far the most abundant. If all the different species of animals and plants on earth were randomly lined up, every fifth one would be a beetle.

Arthropods (*Arthropodae*)

Arthropods with their jointed limbs, segmented bodies and hard jointed exoskeletons are one of the most successful groups of animal on this planet. They benefit from their small size and a well-developed ability to produce large numbers of offspring regularly and frequently, thereby greatly increasing the chances of their progeny adapting themselves to changing conditions. As a consequence, we can still only speculate about the number of species of arthropod in the Amazon rainforest. The number of insects alone runs into many millions.

Spiders (*Arachnidae*)

There are few dangerous Amazonian spiders; even the bite of the giant tarantulas such as the 25cm males of *Theraposa lablondi* pose little threat. They prefer nesting places high up in trees where they poach frogs, toads, lizards and small birds. It is rare to meet these big hairy spiders in undisturbed forest and even rarer to get bitten by one and the venom to cause more than a mild discomfort.

Man-made trails, streams and other insect highways are ideal places to find and observe spiders both day and night. Many trail dwellers belong to the family of **spiny orb weavers** (*Araneidae, Asteracanthinae*) and can be recognized by their colourful and often thorned abdomens. On trail margins one finds the small and friendly looking **jumping spiders** (*Salticidae*) while, on the the banks of streams and in the trunks of trees, **funnel web spiders** (*Agelenidae*), their peculiar webs hidden in the darkness, patiently await unsuspecting prey.

At night time, the bluish eye-shine of nocturnal spiders such as the lightning fast **wolf spiders** (*Lycosadae*) and the **bolas spiders** (*Mastophorae*) is readily visible with a torch. Bolas spiders spin a hanging line with a sticky round globule (*bola*) at the tip and, in the case of the **podadora** (*Mastophora gasteracanthoides*), this globule contains a volatile substance that mimics the sex pheromones of nocturnal **owlet moths** (*Spodoptera sp.*), its favourite prey. Most spiders are solitary but sociability occurs at a primitive level in about 1 per cent of the worlds' 3,500 spiders and colonies are frequently encountered along trails. The tiny **mallos spiders** share the same web structure and food but there is no division of labour or caste structure, although adults may share in the caring of young.

Termites (*Isopterae*)

Termites are soft bodied insects which, by weight, make up about a third of the animal bio-mass in the rainforest. The most common, the **nasute termites** (*Termitidae*), build big nests (1–2m diameter) of chewed wood and faecal cement, resulting in a cardboard-like substance usually well above ground level. Termites are insects with a complex social behaviour, similar to that of ants, social bees and wasps. Their success and importance derives from a unique symbiotic relationship with a flagellate protozoa and bacteria which enables them to break down and utilize the cellulose in dead wood. Termites recycle huge quantities of nutrients back into the system, circumventing the natural decay process and facilitating the demise of weak individuals. Like other ruminant animals, they also produce large quantities of greenhouse gases such as methane: definitely no smoking, please! Many species of birds make their mounds inside the termite nests, and **caiman** (*Paleosochus trigonatus*) and the **Amazonian tortoise** (*Geochelone deticulata*) find termite ground nests convenient incubators for their eggs.

True Bugs (*Hemipterae*)

True bugs have their mouth parts formed into a proboscis, to suck fluids, such as plant saps, nectar, and insect or vertebrate blood. Members include the **cicadas** (*Cicadidae*), **planthoppers** (*Fulgoroidae*), the foul-smelling **stink bugs** (*Pentatomidae*) and the gory **assassin bugs** (*Triatomae*) that vacuum their victims dry.

Cicadas are large bugs (20–50mm) with bulging green or blue eyes. They are commonly heard and seen both in the adult and nymphal stages. The males produce characteristic sounds ranging from clicks to a loud throbbing wail in order to attract females. After mating, the eggs are deposited in a tree and, on hatching, the nymph drops to the ground where it burrows deeply and may remain for many years feeding on sap from roots. The nymphs of *Fidicina chlorogena* cicadas construct tall (20–30cm) hollow mud chimneys on the forest floor in which to pass their final days before becoming adults. The final stage occurs above ground and the cycle is complete. Adults only live a few weeks or months.

Planthoppers are sap-sucking and the species most often depicted is the large (7cm) **dragon-headed bug**. Its enormous head mimics the up-turned head of a medium-sized, arboreal reptile like **plica, anolis** and other small lizards. Locals bitten by this insect will know that they must sleep with their girlfriends within 24 hours or die.

Butterflies and Moths (*Lepidopterae*)

Butterflies and moths are normally good indicators of bio-diversity and the condition of an ecosystem because both their larvae and adults are highly dependent on key elements at the bottom of the trophic pyramid (food chain). Amazonia probably boasts in excess of 2,000 butterfly species and at least twice this number of moths. Butterflies use their proboscis to ingest sugar concentrates and they also seek moisture and nutrients from wet sand, bird droppings, dung and carrion, rotting fruits and fungi, perspiration and the eye liquid of turtles and caiman. It is only the males who do this. For the little yellow male **phoebis butterflies** (often seen on the banks of lakes and rivers), their mineral reserves are a measure of their virility.

Many butterflies are toxic, using bright colours to advertise to birds of prey and other creatures that they should not be eaten. An example is the narrow-winged red, black and yellow **passion vine butterfly** (*Heliconius sp.*), abundant in lower and middle parts of the forest. The caterpillars of these butterflies gorge themselves on the leaves of passion vines (*Passiflorae*) which contain toxic glucogenic cyanides. These toxins are retained during development so that the adult butterfly remains inedible. As part of the ongoing warfare between plants and the animals that eat them, some *Passiflorae* have now evolved little raised yellow patches on their leaves which fool the female passion vine butterflies into thinking that the plant is already occupied. What will the butterflies do next? Many other butterfly species take advantage of the passion vine butterfly toxicity by mimicking its coloration.

Morphos butterfly

Night-flying moths may be toxic as well. In the dark, however, bright colours warning predators of their toxicity, serve no purpose. The **tiger moths** (*Arctiinae*) use clicks to warn feeding bats about their toxicity. In some species of moth, the high frequency click may 'jam' the echolocation of bats and deter other predators, such as monkeys, birds and toads, as well. The majority of rainforest butterflies are extremely small and are never seen. **Morphos** butterflies (*Morphinae*), however, have resplendent metallic blue wings which serve either to startle and confuse attackers or are perhaps used for sexual recognition. To natives, this beautiful butterfly is just another manifestation of the Chullachaqui, an evil forest spirit who leads its victims deeper and deeper into the jungle never to be seen again.

Beetles (*Colopterae*)

This is a huge group with many species that are easy to find and identify by their characteristic shape and structure. Beetles are found in all shapes and at all levels of the trophic pyramid.

Scarab beetles (*Scarabaeidae*) are usually small to medium in size, but also include some of the largest insects. Characteristically, they have short, straight antennae, ending in a club of 3–9 flat plates that may be spread apart. The **dung scarabs** (*Scarabaeinae*) are compactly built almost spherical beetles, well armoured, and many are brightly coloured in metallic green, blue or copper hues. Dung scarabs have highly developed dung-rolling techniques, with male and female beetles cooperating to shift faeces many times larger than themselves. **Horned scarabs** (*Dynastinae*), which may weigh up to 40g, are fist-sized and renowned for their strength and tenacity; the male **Hercules beetle** (*Dynastes hercules*), for example, has two enormous curved horns with which it can fork-lift weights of nearly 2kg.

Click beetles (*Elateridae*) are dull blue or green with elongated bodies up to 5cm in length. Their characteristic sound is generated when they catapult themselves into the air. This predator-escape mechanism is a popular amusement for the children of the Amazon Indians. The **headlight beetles** (*Pyrophorus sp.*) produce an intense glow from two round luminescent organs on the pro-thorax. This luminescence is designed to signal their presence to the wingless females normally just after dusk. The larvae of the **palm weevil**, found in decaying logs, is an Indian delicacy called *suri*, eaten raw or lightly fried.

Ants, Bees and Wasps (*Hymenopterae*)

This group always exhibits some degree of sociability although many, particularly the **predatory wasps** (*Sphecidae*), are solitary for most of their adult lives. The *hymenoptera* are important herbivores, carnivores and pollinators, with many dependents and dependees in the rainforest ecosystem, and are usually endowed with stingers.

Fig wasps (*Chalcidoidae, Agaonidae*) are important species that have co-evolved together with the New World **figs** (*Ficus sp.*) in a complex tale of dependency. The story begins with a female wasp entering the fig fruit via a small opening that closes once she is inside. The fig tree fruit has female and male flowers mixed and scattered on the internal surface and invisible from the outside. There are two types of female flowers: the gall type with short styles and the reproductive type with long styles. Development of the male flowers is retarded by carbon dioxide levels, which build up once the wasp is inside. The female fig wasp uses her long ovipositor to bore through the styles of female flowers and deposit her eggs among the immature ovules. She can only reach the ovules of the short-styled flowers; long-styled flowers are left untouched to form galls, which feed her progeny once they hatch. In the process she conveniently fertilizes both types of flowers with pollen from her body but only the long-styled flowers develop into seeds. Wingless male wasps develop first and seek out mature female pupae, which they fertilize. These impregnated females emerge to find the males boring an exit hole in the fruit and the male flowers developing as the carbon dioxide levels decline. As the females leave the fruit, they pick up pollen and the process repeats itself. The males die.

Ants (*Formicidae*) are enormously successful thanks to their small size, social habits and adaptability. Ants are found in partnership with a range of plants and with other insects such as **mealy bugs** (*Pseudococcidae*). They are singly responsible for harvesting in excess of 15 per cent of green plant material and directly or indirectly support a range of birds and higher mammals. Ants vary greatly in size: the largest, the **dinoponera** (*Ponerinae*), has a body length of over 3cm and is usually found on tree trunks and lianas. The females are shiny black while the males are brown and smaller. Dinoponeras are primitive hunting ants which live in small colonies of a hundred or so at the base of trees. The slightly smaller reddish brown **paraponas** are frequently confused with dinoponeras; paraponas are the more aggressive of the two and may inflict a painful paralyzing sting.

Army ants (*Ecitoninae*) have highly evolved social systems with several different-sized workers and soldiers. Their nests are formed by the interlocking bodies and limbs of the workers coiled around the queen and brood. Army ants are carnivores, and the workers blanket vast areas of the forest floor in search of insects and small vertebrates. Local Indians use the enormous jaws of the soldiers to suture flesh wounds; they pinch the edges of the injury together and hold the ant close so that it bites across the cut. They then wrench off the body, leaving the head intact and jaws fixed like sutures. An army of bird species feed off the insects disturbed by these migrating ants.

Leaf-cutter ants (*Attae, Acromyrmex sp.*) are easy to find; the surface of a single nest may be 40–50 square metres in size, with many craters of soil fragments and other debris. Long trails of workers carrying oval fragments of leaves over their heads lead up to the entrances. Inside, the ants chew off the leaves' waxy layer, graft it with a specific fungus and fertilize it with a droplet of their faeces to make a 'garden'. The ants tend this garden, removing foreign fungi and bacterial growth until the fungal hyphae are ready to eat. This is an effective strategy for dealing with indigestible plant material.

Fire ants (*Solenopsis sp.*) are most notorious for their stinging behaviour. They respond rapidly and aggressively to any disturbance of the colony or a food source. A single fire ant can sting and will continue to sting even after its venom sac has been depleted. Initially, the sting(s) result in a localized intense burning sensation (hence their name); the long-term effect is hypertensive but rarely serious.

Cockroaches (*Blattodae*)

Cockroaches are a successful group of insects little altered since the Carboniferous period 250 million years ago. With over 1,000 indigenous species and several domestic species imported from the Old World over the last four centuries, the cockroach's success lies in intracellular bacteria, which aid its digestion. This means it can virtually eat anything. **Giant cockroaches** (*Blaberidae*) may grow up to 8 or even 10cm whilst the smallest are minute **Attiphila cockroaches**, which live in symbiosis with the Atta leaf cutter ants.

Flies (*Diptera*)

Flies (*Diptera*), with halters instead of a second pair of wings, are tenacious insects whose members include the mosquitoes (*Culex sp. Anopholes sp.*), the large **horse flies** (*Tabanus sp.*), the frustrating **sand flies** (*Phlebotomus sp.*) among many others. Flies are effective vectors for a variety of diseases including malaria, yellow fever, dengue fever and leishmaniasis, which pass into the body in the insect's saliva as it bites.

Amphibians and Reptiles (*Amphibiae and Reptiliae*)

Amphibians and reptiles are usually medium-sized, cold-blooded animals, that do not have to expend energy keeping their body temperature at a constantly high level. This means that their activity levels are highly dependent on the ambient temperature- in the tropics this is seldom a problem.

Amphibians (*Amphibia*)

Amphibians have moist skin allowing the exchange of both gases and body fluids with the environment. They are still water-dependent, at least at certain stages in their development.

Salamanders (*Gymnophionae*) and Caecilians (*Caudatae*)

Salamanders and **caecilians** (strange, worm-like amphibians with no legs) are not well represented in Amazonia. They are more dependent on water, and lack many of the physical characteristics that have made the frogs, for example, so successful. They live underground or are aquatic. It is very rare to encounter either of these animals in the Amazon.

Frogs (*Anurae*) and Toads (*Bufonidae*)

Nowhere else in the world are frogs as diverse as in the neotropical rainforest. In the Cocha Cashu Biological Station of Manu National Park in Peru, around 80 different species have been found, as many as in the United States and Canada together. Frogs avoid predation by jumping, and possess many physical characteristics, such as effective vocalization and hearing, and well-developed 3D vision that have made them successful. Nearly all neotropical frogs also secrete cocktails of piperidine alkaloids, which deter predators by depolarizing nerve and muscle cell membranes. This natural defence is particularly well developed in the **poison dart frogs** of the genera *Dendrobates* and *Phyllobates*; *Phyllobates terriblis* being fatal to the touch. All these frogs and their mimics are typically small and, like butterflies, advertise their toxicity with vibrantly bright colours. Other frogs such as *Chiasmodeis ventriculata* exploit their toxicity to gain entrance and further protection from large tarantula burrows. The dry and **warty-skinned toad** (*Bufo marinus*), weighs more than 1kg and grows to a massive 20cm, also produces complex parotid gland toxins that interrupt the heartbeat.

Some of the most beautiful and easily visible frogs belong to the family *Hylidae*, and are only mildly toxic. Adults are predominately arboreal, normally descending only to breed, using suction pads on the feet to secure themselves to leaves and branches. The *Hylidae* are typically leaf green and brightly coloured along the flanks to startle predators as they jump.

Many frog species have evolved efficient strategies for increasing the survival rates of their offspring. Typically, they expend less energy and lay fewer eggs away from large bodies of water and conventional predators, to give the offspring a better chance of survival. They may also exhibit a degree of parental care. **Glass frogs** (*Centrolenellae*), for example, are small, green tree frogs with transparent bellies. The female of this species attaches her eggs to leaves hanging over water, into which the larvae immediately drop after hatching. She may guard her eggs day and night, her transparent form closely blending with the gelatinous egg mass. *Eleutherodactylus* frogs also deposit eggs away from water. The hatching tadpoles then wriggle onto the back of the attending adult who carries them safely to the nearest stream. In some poison dart frog species, the female removes her eggs to the bromeliads high up in the canopy. The 20 or so eggs she lays are distributed one per bromeliad, thereby reducing the chance of losing all her offspring in one kill. Afterwards she returns to provide each developing tadpole with unfertilized eggs as a source of food.

The fertilized eggs of the aquatic **Surinam toad** (*Pipa pipa*) and the **marsupial frogs** (*Gastrothecae*) actually develop on the back of the female. The skin on her back swells up and the eggs embed and develop, leaving in some species as tadpoles; in others as fully developed froglets.

Reptiles (*Reptiliae*)

Reptiles are cold-blooded and, having evolved from the amphibians, are a step further away from life in the water. Their skin is dry, and usually covered with scales, so they don't lose body fluids as readily and can sit in the sun and warm up without drying up. Their eggs have a leather-like skin that need not be directly in the water; some lizards and turtles have calcified eggs, that need no humidity at all. **Anacondas**, **boa constrictors** and most **pit vipers** brood their eggs inside their bodies and deliver live young.

Lizards (*Sauriae*)

The biggest lizard of the Amazon is the terrestrial black and yellow **Tegu** (*Tupinambis teguixin*), which can measure more than 1.25m from nose to tail and eats everything it finds. At the smaller end of the scale are the common **anolis lizards** (*Anolis sp. and Norops sp.*)

which grow up to 20cm and are arboreal. Their colour varies from brown to bright green and can change in some species with their mood. Males have a brightly coloured dewlap, which serves to signal to other males in territorial or mating disputes.

Geckos of the *Geckonidae* family can be found all over the world. They are small, usually nocturnal, and can scale vertical surfaces with ease using little suckered feet. Geckos, like the **turnip-tailed gecko** (*Thecadactylus rapicaudus*), are cute insectivores valued for their domestic cleaning abilities in the neotropics.

Snakes (*Serpentes*)

Contrary to popular belief, most snakes are seldom seen in undisturbed forest; they are non-aggressive and few are poisonous. In all of the vast Amazon Basin, there are only 23 species of poisonous snake, of which just a handful may be fatal. Two of these are **pit vipers** (*Crotalidae*) which have broad, almost triangular heads, heat-sensing pits between the eyes and nose and retractable fangs through which they inject venom deep into their victim. Their venom is a haemo-toxin, that destroys tissues and cells, making their bites extremely painful. The most dangerous pit-vipers are the **fer-de-lance** (*Bothrops atrox*) which grows to two metres and the **bushmaster** (*Lachesis muta*) which can grow to four metres. The former is common and accounts for most bites inflicted on humans, though few are fatal. The latter is more seldom seen, but may attack unprovoked if disturbed, injecting an extremely toxic and fatal venom. Both pit vipers are terrestrial and nocturnal, passing the daylight hours between the buttresses of large trees and blending perfectly with the forest substrate.

Coral snakes (*Elapidae*) are small, and beautifully ringed with black, red, white and yellow. They possess a powerful venom, a neuro-toxin, that causes heart and respiratory failure. Unlike the pit vipers the corals have small mouths, and lack both retractable fangs and a dislocatable jaw. Their bites are therefore superficial and rarely fatal for humans.

The last group, the *Colubridae*, are a diverse family with a number of mildly venomous individuals. The *Colubridae* include the false corals (*Lampropeltis sp.*) or coral snake mimics.

Boas, such as the 4m **boa constrictor** (*Boa constrictor*), are primitive snakes with vestigial hind legs and a pelvic cradle still present. Boas kill by asphyxiation, then swallow their prey whole, head first. They are ovoviviparous, meaning the eggs hatch internally and the female gives birth to life-young. The **tree boa** (*Corallus enydris*) and **emerald tree boa** (*Corallus caninus*) also have heat sensors on their upper jaws, to locate and attack warm-blooded prey. They are excellent climbers, frequently feeding upon roosting bats and small birds high up in the canopy. The

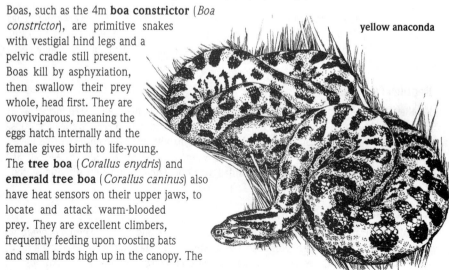

yellow anaconda

anaconda (*Eunectes murinus*), measuring up to 10m in length and 30–40cm in diameter weighs over 225kg. Anacondas spend most of their time in water and only come out on to land to bask in the sun or eat prey. The largest anacondas can asphyxiate and swallow a small child, but this is rare.

Tortoises and Turtles (*Cheloniae*)

The Amazon rainforest's only tortoise is the vegetarian **yellow-footed tortoise** (*Geochelone denticulata*). It has been an easy target for migrants to the Amazon, and is now endangered throughout its range. Males will fight aggressively over the females at mating times.

Turtles have undergone little change in over 300 million years. The biggest freshwater turtle is the **arrau** (*Podocnemis expansa*). Its shell can reach 90cm. These animals were once so common in the Amazon Basin that entire sections of a river could be blackened by their presence. Unfortunately for them, their eggs are considered a delicacy. Now only a few nesting beaches are left along just two rivers in the region. The **side-neck turtles** or **taricayas** (*Podocnemis unifilis*), spend most of their time feeding on aquatic vegetation and basking to maintain their body temperature. They are so called because their heads retract side ways, rather than directly backwards.

Caiman (*Crocodylia*)

The caiman are unsophisticated eating machines unaltered in nearly 150m years. Despite this they date in the fossil record to the ancestors of birds and are probably what remains of a terrestrial reptile that returned to the water rather than an aquatic one that evolved away from it. The South American caiman is related to the North American alligator, with only superficial differences in body armouring. Unlike their relatives the crocodiles, the caiman are generally not aggressive towards humans and show varying degrees of parental care. The **white** or **common spectacled caiman** (*Caiman crocodilus*) is the most common of the South American caiman. It eats fish, crustacea, birds and small mammals, can grow up to about 4m and is found close to almost all bodies of water. *Caiman crocodilus* lays its eggs in nests or incubators of decaying organic matter that maintain a steady temperature of between 28 and 35 degrees Celsius. The female guards the eggs until they hatch and the young remain in her protection for a few months afterwards. The **black caiman** (*Melanosuchus niger*) is the biggest of the South American caiman, reaching nearly 7m and is found principally around large open spaces of water. It preys on big mammals, such as capybaras and peccaries, pulling them into the water when they come to drink and drowning them. The female also prepares a nest on land to deposit her eggs and the young hatch roughly three months later. Once they were abundant in the whole of the Amazon but, owing to their conversion into handbags, purses and shoes, they are now almost extinct and are only to be found in remote areas such as Manu National Park.

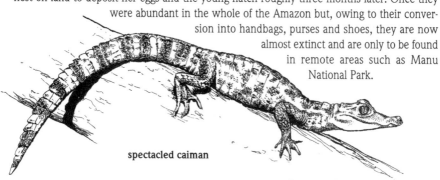

spectacled caiman

Amazonian mammals are an interesting mixture of very old and evolved forms. The old forms already existed when the American continent was isolated from the original continent of Gondwana 70 million years ago. The *Xenarthrae* or *Edentatae* (sloth, anteaters and armadillos), typical Amazon mammals, are the descendants of these first placental mammals that lived more or less unopposed, until the influx of more active modern placental mammals via the Central American land bridge took place around 4 million years ago. The fossil record shows, however, that the primates and some rodents were present in the late Oligocene as long as 25 million years ago. Mounting evidence suggests that these individuals somehow arrived from Africa, perhaps by island hopping—but nobody really knows.

Sloths, Anteaters and Armadillos (*Xenarthra, Edentatae*)

Sloths (*Bradypodidae, Megalonychidae*) are medium-sized mammals that spend most of their lives upside down in trees. Their feet have no toes, but two or three long curved claws that form a hook, from which the sloth can hang passively, without spending energy, from a branch. They have short bodies, long limbs and stumpy tails. There are two different genera, the **three-toed sloth** (*Bradypus sp.*), with both fore- and hind-feet with three claws, and the **two-toed sloth** (*Choloepus sp.*), whose forefeet have only two claws. Despite their awkwardness, sloths are probably an example of a species pushed to the brink and are thus adapted perfectly for their lifestyle. To avoid predation, they are slow moving and well camouflaged and as a result, are virtually impossible to spot. Their long algae- and beetle-infested coat and lack of muscle make them hardly worth the effort anyway. Due to their low metabolic rate, sloth can tolerate long periods without food and can digest, over a period of weeks, almost anything green. Seldom encountering members of the same species, a female can stagger the development of fertilized embryos from a single mating. Sloths seldom venture down from trees as they are poor walkers and vulnerable on the ground but they may swim long distances. However, the two-toed sloth routinely descends to defecate and thereby fertilize its favourite tree.

Anteaters (*Myrmecophagidae*) have small eyes and ears and tube-like snouts with no teeth. They have, instead, a very long, thin sticky tongue that can be greatly extended to reach into inaccessible crevices and extract insects. They feed on social insects (ants, termites and bees), always leaving nest reconstruction possible and a stable food supply intact. Four different species of anteater are found in Amazonia. The largest is the terrestrial **giant anteater** (*Myrmecophaga tridactyla*) with a body length excluding tail of about 1.5m. It has formidable muscled forelegs, armed with strong curved claws, which it will use to defend itself effectively even against jaguar. The other three are the smaller **southern tamandua** and **northern tamandua** (*Tamandua tetradactyla, Tamandua mexicana*) and the tiny **silky** or **pygmy anteater** (*Cyclopes didactylus*), which is only 15 to 20cm long. All are arboreal and have prehensile tails.

Armadillos (*Dasypodidae*) can be easily recognized by the bony shield that covers the head, back and sides, and sometimes even the legs and tail. The mid-portion of the body armour is arranged into bands separated by soft skin to allow the animal to bend its body. Armadillos are incredibly shy nocturnal individuals and little is known about them. The **giant armadillo** (*Priodontes maximus*) is between 75cm and 1m in length and weighs about 30kg. Its carapace appears several sizes too small, and does not cover its sides or legs. *Priodontes maximus* also lives off ants and termites, digging tunnels beneath the brood chambers of large colonies.

Opossums (*Marsupialiae*)

The marsupial opossum family successfully survived the influx of modern mammals, and there are now about 70 different species in Central and South America. The opossums are small to medium-sized, densely furred mammals with pointed snouts. The first toe of their hind feet is widely separated from the other digits to form an opposable 'thumb'. They use this while climbing. Most of them are nocturnal and arboreal with excellent night vision. The tails of most species are strongly prehensile and can tightly grip an object as thin as a wire with many times the force needed to support the weight of the body.

Primates (*Primates*)

The primates of the New World belong to the group of Platyrrhini monkeys with short muzzles and flat, naked faces. All are primarily arboreal, and most have long tails. In all the bigger and most of the medium-sized monkeys, these tails are extremely prehensile. Colour patterns of these monkeys vary considerably with geographical range. The group is divided into three different families: the marmosets and tamarins, the Goeldi's monkey and the true monkeys.

Marmosets and Tamarins (*Callitrichidae*) and Goeldi's Monkey (*Callimiconidae*)

These are small animals (between 100–600g), un-monkey-like to most observers. They have claws instead of nails on their toes, except for the nail on the big toe. Their tails are long, usually longer than the body, but not prehensile. They not only have many striking colour patterns, like the grey body, white moustache and orange tail of the **emperor tamarin** (*Saguinus emperator*), but also other adornments, such as ear tufts, tassels, ruffs, manes, moustaches and mantles of long hair. These adornments probably exist to impress the opposite sex. Marmosets and tamarins have a varied diet but are fundamentally frugivores, surviving on small fruits, sap and berries. They have probably reduced in size to fill a niche unoccupied by larger monkeys. Tamarin and marmoset groups are typically polyandrous with one reproductive female and a number of attendant reproductive males.

True Monkeys (*Cebidae*)

The *Cebidae* have nails on all digits and are typically monkey-like. They are all arboreal and the biggest have prehensile tails. **Night monkey** (*Aotus sp.*), with their big round eyes, is the only nocturnal monkey on our planet. They are monogamous, with the father contributing towards the raising of offspring. They have a very characteristic call, especially audible on moonlit nights, which has given them one of their local names: '*musmuqui*'. Going nocturnal has been the *musmuquis*' answer to food scarcity in the dry season; they simply eat when the bigger monkeys are asleep.

Dusky titi monkeys (*Callicebus moloch*) are brown, primarily leaf-eaters and are commonly found near bamboo thickets whose leaves they relish. These monkeys are very territorial, producing a combination of rapid whoops and high screams, usually early in the morning. However, generally they are quiet and secretive and very difficult to spot.

Squirrel monkeys (*Saimiri sp.*) travel and roost in big groups of up to a hundred individuals, providing safety in numbers and enabling them to intimidate larger monkeys vying for the same sources of food. Squirrel monkeys are skilled at locating food and are often accompanied by groups of opportunistic brown capuchins.

Capuchin monkeys (*Cebus sp.*) possess a highly technical intelligence, which enables them to unlock food sources, such as nuts that other monkeys do not have techniques for. They do this with their strong jaws, or by banging the bigger nuts against branches. They are also adept at manipulating inedible fruits, seeds and twigs, to remove juicy larvae.

Saki monkeys (*Pithecia sp.*), the **bearded saki monkeys** (*Chiropotes sp.*) and **uakari monkeys** (*Cacajao sp.*) are rare in Amazonia, having been heavily hunted near human settlements for their meat, strange appearance and decorative bushy tails. The sakis (also known as **flying monkeys**) feed on ripe and unripe seeds in the forest middle layers; the uakaris on leaves and flowers.

Howler monkeys (*Alouatta sp.*) are large monkeys and, like the Old World gorilla, are entirely herbivorous. The males and females alert other groups to their presence by a throaty growl that carries for miles through the forest. Howlers consume vast quantities of upper canopy leaves and, because many leaves contain toxins, they have vast home-ranges, giving them a good chance of finding sufficient quanitites of non-toxic leaves.

The **spider monkeys** (*Ateles sp.*) and **woolly monkeys** (*Lagothrix sp.*) are the New World's largest monkeys, with long prehensile tails and absent or reduced thumbs. The spider monkey is easily recognizable by its long arms and legs, which it uses to run or swing through the trees. Groups of both genera can be noisy and vocally aggressive towards humans. Woolly monkeys are known to hurl sticks and other objects.

Bats (*Chiroptera*)

There are about 220 different species of bats representing 25 per cent of all mammal species in Amazonia. Bats are normally omnivorous and are one of nature's most important seed dispersing mammals, with around 130 genera of plants specifically adapted to make use of bats in the mid to lower canopy. Such plants usually have large, whitish flowers with pungent odours that the bats can easily detect at night. In addition, many trees, such as the cannon ball tree (*Couroupita guianensis*), may exhibit cauliflory where the flowers and fruits grow directly out of the tree trunk instead of from lofty branches.

Amazonian bats also exploit less expected food sources; the **greater bulldog bats** (*Noctilio leporinus*) have enormous feet with which they grab fish, after locating it on the water surface using echolocation. **Round-eared bats** (*Tonatia bidens*) are reported to feed intensively on small birds, and the common **fringe-lipped bat** (*Trachops cirrhosus*), specializes in frogs by homing in on their calls.

Last but not least are the common **vampire bats** (*Desmodus rotundus*). These are stealthy individuals that stalk their prey by using both thumbs and feet to walk, hop or climb quadrupedally along the ground or on branches. *Desmodus rotundus* feeds on blood from mammals, including man, but other vampire bats specialize on birds, etc. Vampire bats never suck blood from their prey, but lick up the drops flowing from a small scoop they bite in the skin using long, razor-sharp, forward-pointing upper incisor teeth, and large, blade like canines. These teeth make a quick and painless wound, and their saliva has an anticoagulant that keeps the blood from clotting.

One of the most commonly seen bats is the **long-nosed bat** (*Rhynchonycteris naso*), belonging to the family of sheath-tailed bats. These roost in large groups on tree trunks over or near water, hanging in a characteristic straight line. Their grizzled furs blend with the tree bark, making them almost impossible to spot, unless one knows where to look.

Rodents (*Rodentiae*)

capybara

Rodents all have a single pair of large, ever-growing incisors in the front of each jaw. These serve many purposes; they can cut, slice, gouge, dig, stab, pry open or hold like a pair of tweezers; they can cut grass, open nuts, kill animal prey, dig tunnels and fell large trees. Rodents are generally omnivorous, adaptable in their behaviour and produce large numbers of offspring on a regular basis—unbeatable credentials in the struggle for survival.

Amazonian rodents range in size from the smallest of the **pygmy rice rats** (*Oligoryzomys sp.*) weighing 9g, to the **capybara** (*Hydrochaeris hydrochaeris*), which can weigh up to 65kg. The **paca** (*Agouti paca*) is a similar shape to the capybara but has reddish brown fur with white lateral strips and lines of dots. There are arboreal species like the **climbing rats** (*Rhipidomys sp.*), terrestrial species like the **rice rats** (*Oryzomys sp.*), semi-aquatic species like the **water rats** (*Nectomys sp.*), vegetarians like the capybara (its name means 'lord of the grasses'), fruit and/or seed eaters like the **squirrels** (*Sciurus sp.*), insectivores like the **spiny mice** (*Neacomys sp.*), crab-eating species like the **water- and crab-eating rats** (*Ichtyomys sp.*) and still several new species are found each year. Despite this they are seldom seen, as most are nocturnal and solitary or live in pairs. The one most often heard is the **Amazon bamboo rat** (*Dactylomys dactylinus*), which calls at dusk in bursts of eery laughter.

Porcupines (*Erethizontidae*) arrived in South America before the other rodents and developed thick heavy bodies, short legs and strong spines with barbed tips. Their spines

paca

are an excellent defence mechanism, detaching when touched and anchoring themselves in to the victim by the barbs. The feet and tail of porcupines are highly adapted to arboreal life, having a broad, naked pad going sideways where the first digit would be and toes with long curved claws that flex in a tight pincer-like grip over this pad. Their tails are also very strong and prehensile.

Carnivores (*Carnivora*)

Carnivores are often admired for their intelligence, strength, speed and health. They have developed these characteristics in the intense competition for survival. All five carnivore families have found their way to the Amazon, though with varying degrees of success.

Bears (*Ursidae*) are only represented by one species, the **Andean bear** (*Tremarctos ornatus*). Its local name, *oso anteojo*, means '**spectacled bear**' from the white circles around its eyes. The rest of the body is black. Spectacled bears stands about 2m tall and roam solitary in search of their mostly vegetarian diet in forested habitats between 1,800 and 3,300m. Only when food is scarce do they descend to lowland forest. They were common once, but, after many years of hunting and habitat destruction, this bear, like so many large mammals, is now endangered.

The **short-eared dog** (*Atelocynus microtis*) which is solitary, and the **bush dog** (*Speothos venaticus*) that lives in small groups, are both rare throughout their range in the Amazon. Both look more like foxes than dogs, with short legs and long bodies. The first is blackish, with a long tail, and the second is reddish-brown with a short tail. They are shy and elusive individuals and little is known about their natural behaviour.

coati

Raccoons (*Procyonidae*) have mobile hands, with which they are able to dig and rummage for prey or hold and manipulate food items. The **South American coati** (*Nasua nasua*) is reddish brown with a long pointed snout and a very long yellow and black ringed tail. Like most of the others in this family they are omnivorous. The coati is day-active and forages both on the ground and high in the canopy. The larger males are often solitary, the females and young travel together in conspicuous groups. There are two nocturnal raccoons, the solitary **olingo** (*Bassaricyon sp.*) and the social **kinkajou** (*Potos flavus*), confused both with each other and with the night monkey, particularly as they often feed in the same trees. Only the kinkajou has a prehensile tail.

kinkajou

Weasels (*Mustelidae*) can be recognized by their plantigrade feet and humped backs when the animals are standing. Most weasels have a large anal gland that produces a strong-smelling musk. The nocturnal **grison** (*Galictis vittata*) looks like two creatures put together: one was black and gave the muzzle, eyes, chin, chest and fore- and hind-feet, and the second one was grizzled pale grey and contributed the back of the head, back, belly and tail. Its cousin, the **tayra** (*Eira barbara*), is more common around human settlements and can sometimes be seen on the enormous branches of mature kapok trees (*Ceiba pentarana*), walking as casually as if it were on the ground.

There are two species of otter among the Amazon weasels, the **neotropical or river otter** (*Lontra longicaudis*), with a combined head and body length of 53–81cm, and the **giant otter** (*Pteronura brasiliensis*), which can reach up to 2m. The former is little studied as it is solitary and frequents rivers. The giant otter, however, has been both relatively well studied and hunted, although not necessarily in that order; less than 2,000 remain in the wild. Giant otters are sociable animals that live in extended family groups where the male and

giant otter

adolescents help to raise the young. Females give birth to quadruplets, but rarely more than two survive. Giant otters are susceptible to habitat destruction and are now confined to small enclaves in southern Peru and the Guianas.

Cats (*Felidae*) prey on anything they encounter which is not too large, even large insects. There are six species in the neotropical rainforest and all are primarily nocturnal. Three are small and spotted: the **ocelot** (*Leopardus pardalis*), the **margay** (*Leopardus wiedii*) and the **oncilla** (*Felis tiogrina*), while a fourth, the **jaguarundi** (*Herpailurus yaguarondi*), is also small, although grey to black without spots. All are common around human settlements, from where they often poach poultry and other livestock.

puma

The **puma** (*Puma concolor*), a larger cat without spots, is found in boreal and tropical climates, and from desert to dense rainforest. It can be common without ever been seen.

The **jaguar** (*Panthera onca*), on the other hand, originally lived in many different habitats, but has now been driven away from all but the most

jaguar

dense and undisturbed forests. It is the biggest of the South American cats and has been extensively hunted for its pelt and for sport. To the Indians this cat is the most spiritual animal in the forest and master of the *curandero* (shaman). The jaguar is the top predator in the rainforest, taking big mammals such as capybara, peccary, and deer. Turtles, which smaller cats can't manage, also make up a large proportion of its diet.

Hoofed Animals (*Perissodactylae and Artiodactylae*)

Tapirs (*Tapiridae*) have fore-feet with four toes and hind-feet with three toes. They are herbivores and use their small prehensile trunks to reach out and sweep food into their mouths. The **Brazilian tapir** (*Tapirus terrestris*) is the largest land mammal of the Amazon, weighing up to 250kg with a body length of up to 2m. It is the only native survivor in the New World of the **odd-toed ungulates** (*Perissodactyla*) order, which also includes horses and rhinoceroses. It can usually be found in or near water, where it deposits enormous piles of dung. When alarmed, tapirs run unstoppably, crashing through the undergrowth, for the protection of water.

The **even-toed ungulates** (*Artiodactylae*) are represented in the Amazon by **peccaries** (*Tayassuidae*) and **deer** (*Cervidae*). Peccaries look like pigs, which are also their closest relatives. The **collared peccary** (*Tayassu tayacu*) is a social animal, living in groups of up to 20 individuals. They release a strong odour, like decaying animal dung, especially when alarmed. They are common in the forest and are frequent visitors to salt licks. The **white-lipped peccaries** (*Tayassu pecari*) leads a completely different life from their cousins. They can be found in groups of 300 or more.

They travel long distances, periodically visiting each area for a few hours or a day or two and then moving on. They also have a strong, peculiar odour and the rumbling of the herd's hooves and the clicking sounds of their teeth while feeding can be heard from far away. They are reputedly very aggressive but, generally they are wary of humans.

Brazilian tapir

Amazon deer look very much like European deer. Their ability to make a rapid escape depends on their reduced size in the dense rainforest, so the forest deer are small, have low forequarters and simple antlers to be able to slip through dense vegetation.

Waterlife

The Amazon is not the longest river in the world, but a quarter of all the world's fresh water meanders along it to the sea. It is a slow moving, brown suspension of fine clay particles for most of its length, neither enriched by the poor Amazonian soils, nor the ancient mountains at its source. In the absence of light and minerals, the algae content of the water is low and yet many invertebrates, more than 2,500 species of fish and a number of mammals, call it home. This is thanks to the forest through which food enters the river system; the forest itself benefits because the animals in the river prevent valuable resources being washed away into the oceans, and fish are also major seed dispersers for many species of trees and plants.

Aquatic Mammals

There are two groups of mammals in the aquatic waters of the Amazon basin, the **dolphins** and the **manatees**. Both groups have descended from the original saltwater forms.

Dolphins (*Delphinidae*) are small-toothed whales that breathe through a blowhole on top of their heads. Like the bats, they can detect prey by echolocation. The dolphins have large developed fore brains, with the related complex social behaviour.

The biggest dolphin is the **pink dolphin** or **boto** (*Inia geoffrensis*), which weighs about 160kg, and really is pink. It belongs to the same group of river dolphins (*Platanistidae*) as the freshwater dolphins of China (Yangtze) and India (Ganges); this means that that it is likely that the ancestors of the pink dolphin had already adapted to freshwater before Gondwana split up. They are thought to be less social than their saltwater relatives, and are usually found alone, or, rarely, in groups of two to four. River dolphins use their sonar for catching fish, turtles and crabs scooped from the river bed.

The smaller **grey dolphin**, or **tucuxi** (*Sotalia fluvitialis*), about 1.5m long and weighing in at about 53kg, is closely related to dolphins along the east coast of South America. It must have become adapted to freshwater much later than the pink dolphin and can still tolerate coastal waters. The grey dolphin seems to be more sociable, living in small groups of between two and nine and conforms much more closely to the dolphin stereotype. The grey dolphin has specialized in hunting fast-swimming fish found close to the surface. In this way, the two dolphin species have avoided competing for the same sources of food. Many myths exist about the dolphins, illustrating their importance to the Indians and the Indians' recognition of its social intelligence. Dolphins are frequently perceived as incarnations of humans that can revert to their original forms and mingle unnoticed amongst communities.

The **Amazonian manatee** (*Trichechus inunguis*) is a colossal 2.7m long, 350–500kg, cigar-shaped vegetarian. Manatees (*Sireniae*) are often described as ugly, unwieldy animals, but they are also the origin of the mermaid figure, supposedly a beautiful creature that lured handsome young men into the river forever. It eats floating vegetation, such as grasses, water hyacinth and water lettuce and can eat up to 40kg per day—which is 8 per cent of its body weight. Since vegetation is hard to digest, manatees produce big balls of macerated fibres that float to the surface. This is the only way one might be alerted to their presence since, even when breathing, only their nostrils break the water surface. Manatees, having been hunted for meat, oil and hide, are now on the verge of extinction.

Fish (*Pisces*)

Compared to the Old World, the balance of fish species In the New World is very different. Both continents had common ancestors but the *caracidae* grew to dominate the New World, the *cichlids* in the old. The reason for this probably lies in the nature of Amazonia itself; its formation from an inland sea; the continual flooding in its very flat basin; the range of habitats created by the meandering rivers and, finally, the murky, nutrient-poor waters. In short, the toothed *caracidae*, with their sound-detecting Weberian apparatus (the set of structures which connect the air-bladder with the ear), were much better poised to exploit the new set of conditions presented in South America than the cichlids. The South American fish are divided as follows; 40 per cent belong to the characins, 40 per cent the catfish, 5 per cent are cichlids and the remainder are made up of archaic fishes, toothcarps, swamp eels and marine fishes.

Characins (*Caracidae*) include many of the common aquarium fish such as **tetras** (*Hemigrammus and Hyphesobryon sp. etc*), **penguin fish** (*Thayeria sp.*), **hatchetfish** (*Gasteropelecus sp.*) and the **piranhas** (*Serrasalmus or Pygocentrus sp.*). In total there are probably only about three species of true piranha, of which the most common is *Pygocentrus nattereri*, the **red-bellied piranha**. It is a small fish with sharp teeth, strong jaws and excellent sight and hearing, that normally preys on small fish and mammals or scavenges dead or dying larger animals. Despite its reputation it rarely attacks larger animals except in extreme food shortage conditions; during droughts, for example, thousands of piranhas can get stranded in a small area, or when the piranha population increases uncontrolled because a top predator such as the caiman is removed. A recent scientific study investigating human deaths attributed in the press to piranhas concluded that, in every case, the individuals concerned were probably either dead or dying before they even fell into the water. There are about 12 other species of piranha which consume a mixture of fish, fins, scales, and vegetation. Most members of the family are in fact docile vegetarians, feeding on fruits, seeds and leaves that have fallen into the water. The **pacu** (*Myelus pacu*) and **tambaqui** (*Colossoma macropomus*) for example, are excellent food fish, and can reach a length of about 1m and a weight of about 30kg. They eat fruit and seeds and have replaced their incisors with crunching molars of which, there are two rows on the upper jaw. An offshoot of the *Caracidae* are the *Gymnotoidae* which possess specialized electric sensing and generation organs. The largest of these is the well-known **electric eel** (*Electrophorus electricus*), whose 800-volt discharge can prove fatal.

Catfish (*Siluridae*) can be distinguished from other fish by the long barbs around their mouths and bony plates. They range in size from the **zungaro** (*Zungaro lutkeni*) which can grow to 2m and weigh 110kg and is an important food fish for the Indians, to the **candhiru** (*Vandellia cirrhosa*), just a few centimetres long. Many catfish are carnivores or scavengers, but *Vandellia cirrhosa* is a parasite. It swims into the gills of bigger fish and attaches itself in order to suck blood. Once satisfied, it lets go and swims out through the mouth, using the spines at the end of its tiny body to prevent it from slipping or moving backwards. The candhiru is attracted by salts and has been drawn urine, faeces or blood from a wound. Should this individual swim into a human body orifice, surgical removal is normally required due to its spines.

Cichlids and Others

The Cichlids include such aquarium fish as the **oscars** (*Astronotus sp.*), **angel fish** (*Pterophyllum sp.*) and the **dwarf cichlids** (*Apistogramma sp.*). They are spiny-finned fishes lacking teeth and Weberian apparatus. When the Andes pushed up sufficiently for an inland saltwater lake to form, a number of species were trapped and adapted to freshwater as the salt was diluted by precipitation. These comprise a group which we can collectively call the **marine fishes**, today represented by more than 50 species spread over 14 families. They include **rays** (*Batoidei*), **sharks** (*Selachii*), **puffers** (*Tetradontidae*), **sleepers** (*Eleotridae*), **herring** (*Clupeidae*) and **anchovies** (*Engraulidae*). **Stingrays** (*Dasyatidae*), found throughout the basin, are warily respected for their huge poisonous tail-spine. The **toothcarps** (*Cyprinodontiforms*) include egg-layers such as the **killifish** (*Lucania sp.*) and the live-bearers such as the **guppies** (*Poecilia sp.*) and **mollies** (*Mollienesia sp.*). Last but not least, the **swamp eels** (*Synbranchidae*) are are widely distributed spiny-finned fishes found throughout the world in fresh and brackish waters. They are air breathers, often living in burrows.

Archaic Fishes: Bony Tongues, Lungfish, Leaf-fish

These fishes, not necessarily primitive, are relics of ancient times, with teeth only in the upper jaw and a bony tongue to crush food. Bony-tongue fish include the **old world elephant** (*Mormyrus sp.*) and **butterfly fishes** (*Pantadon sp.*). The world's second biggest freshwater fish the **arapaima** or **pirarucu** (*Arapaima gigas*), which reaches 4m and weighs 100kg is also a **boney tongue fish** and, like its cousin the **lungfish** (*Lepidosiren paradoxa*), has a swimbladder that doubles as a lung. This fish has a flat bony head and elongated body and looks very much like a duck billed platypus. Despite its size the arapaima is known to leap out of the water and grab small birds from the overhanging trees. Once common, this carnivorous creature is now scarce due to over fishing. Native people use the dry scales of the fish as sandpaper and the tongue as a grater.

pirarucu

The **arowana** (*Osteoglossum sp.*) is a smaller fish, approximately 1m in length, found extensively in flooded forest. It feeds on insects, frogs and small birds, which it catches by launching itself vertically out of the water. It can spot prey and attain sufficient velocity to jump even from shallow water, thanks to eyes on the top of its head and a powerful eel-like body .

About the Authors

Marianne van Vlaardingen was born and educated in the Netherlands. Trained as a biologist, her real appreciation and understanding of nature came while researching monkeys in the rainforest of the Manu National Park in Peru. Although she feels she is always learning, she aims to pass on the knowledge she gained in the rainforest, which she considers is invaluable for the Earth's survival, to visitors to the Amazon. She and her husband, who is originally from the rainforest, run an ecotourism company in Cusco, Peru, called Pantiacolla Tours. It has recently received a Peruvian government award for the best ecotourism company.

Miles Cohen is a UK-born post-graduate physicist turned naturalist who has published a number of articles in magazines and journals based on studies carried out in the Peruvian Amazon. He currently lives and works in Cusco, Peru.

Reptiles

Anaconda (*Eunectes murinus*) ☐
Arrau turtle (*Podocnemis expansa*) ☐
Black caiman (*Melansuchus niger)* ☐
Spectacled caiman (*Caiman crocodilus*) ☐
Boa constrictor (*Boa constrictor*) ☐

Mammals

Monkeys and Sloths

Black spider monkey (*Ateles paniscus*) ☐
Night monkey (*Aotus sp.*) ☐
Pygmy marmoset (*Cebuella pygmaea*) ☐
Red howler monkey (*Alouatta seniculus*) ☐
Squirrel monkey (*Saimiri scicureus*) ☐
Woolly monkey (*Lagothrix sp.*) ☐
Three-toed sloth (*Bradypus sp.*) ☐

Herbivores

Amazonian manatee (*Trichechus inunguis*) ☐
Brazilian tapir (*Tapirus terrestrisis*) ☐
Capybara (*Hydrochaeris hydrochaeris*) ☐
Giant anteater (*Myrmecophaga tridylacta*) ☐
Giant armadillo (*Priodontes maximus*) ☐
Paca (*Agouti paca*) ☐
Peccary (*Tayasudiae sp.*) ☐

Carnivores

American coatimundi (coati) (*Nasua nasua*) ☐
Giant otter (*Pternura brasiliensis*) ☐
Jaguar (*Panthera onca*) ☐
Puma (*Felis concolor)* ☐
Ocelot (*Felis pardalis*) ☐
Spectacled bear (*Tremarctos ornatus*) ☐
Red river dolphin (boto) (*Inia geoffrensis*) ☐

Birds

Waterfowl

White-faced whistling duck
(*Dendrocygna viduata*) ☐
Black-bellied whistling duck
(*Dendrocygna autumnalis*) ☐
Purple gallinule (*Porphyrula fmartinica*) ☐
Black crowned night heron
(*Nycticorax nycticorax*) ☐

Capped heron (*Pilherodius pileatus*) ☐
Cocoi heron (*Ardea cocoi*) ☐
Green ibis (*Mesembrinibis cayennensis*) ☐
Wood ibis (*Mycteria americana*) ☐
Southern lapwing (*Vanellus resplendens*) ☐
Limpkin (*Aramus guarauna*) ☐
Horned screamer (*Anhima cornuta*) ☐
Jabiru stork (*Jabiru mycteria*) ☐

Raptors

Harpy eagle (*Harpia harpyja*) ☐
Black-collared hawk (*Busarellus nigricollis*) ☐
Black-faced hawk (*Leucopternis melanops*) ☐
King vulture (*Sarcoramphus papa*) ☐
Snail kite (*Rostrhamus sociabilis*) ☐
Great horned owl (*Bubo virginianus*) ☐
Amazonian pygmy-owl (*Glaucidium hardy*) ☐
Greater rhea (*Rhea americana*) ☐
Blue and yellow macaw (*Ara ararauna*) ☐

Parrots and Toucans

Chestnut-fronted macaw (*Ara severa*) ☐
Hyacinth macaw
(*Anodorhynchus hyacinthus*) ☐
Red and green macaw (*Ara chloroptera*) ☐
Scarlet macaw (*Ara macao*) ☐
Blue-headed parrot (*Pionus menstruus*) ☐
Toco toucan (*Ramphastos toco*) ☐

Others

Andean cock-of-the-rock
(*Rupicola peruviana*) ☐
Purple-breasted cotinga (*Cotinga cotinga*) ☐
Razor-billed currasow (*Crax mitu*) ☐
Blue-throated piping guan (*Aburria pipile*) ☐
Undulated tinamou (*Crypturellus undulatus*) ☐
Hoatzin (*Opisthocomus hoazin*) ☐
Giant hummingbird (*Patagonia gigas*) ☐
Great potoo (*Nyctibius grandis*) ☐
Silver-beaked tanager (*Ramphocelus carbo*) ☐
White-tailed trogon (*Trogon viridis*) ☐
Blue-crowned trogon (*Trogon curcui*) ☐
Umbrellabird (*Cephalopterus ornatus*) ☐

The Pantanal of Western Brazil is the largest freshwater wetland in the world. It is also an important cattle-ranching area, with many flowering trees and patches of remnant forest creating a diverse and attractive landscape. Water levels are highest between November and March, although the end of the dry season (around September) is a wonderful time to visit as the waterbirds are most concentrated. It is also the breeding season for most species. Most visitors drive south from Cuiabá along the Transpantaneira, a road that terminates at Porto Jofre. The road is 132km long, officially beginning just south of Poconé, 109km south of Cuiabá. Since it is possible to see 100 species in a day in the Pantanal, the family accounts below describe only the most common and conspicuous species. Many species overlap with the Amazon region, but here we concentrate on the Pantanal specialities. Keen observers should make frequent stops in different habitats, carry a good pair of binoculars, and use a field-guide such as the *Collins' Birds of Southern South America*, by de la Peña and Rumboll (1998).

Rhea

The **greater rhea** (*Rhea americana*) is South America's answer to the ostrich of Africa or emu of Australia. The male reaches 1.5m in height and weighs up to 25kg, while the female is slightly smaller. They mostly eat seeds, but will also tackle grasshoppers and small mammals. Being flightless, they need to be constantly on the lookout for danger, although, once adult, their only enemy is man. Though not abundant in the Pantanal, they can be seen grazing among cattle. Rheas are prolific egg-layers: up to 80 eggs have been found in a single nest, contributed by various females, for the long-suffering male to incubate.

greater rhea

Herons, Storks and Ibises

Many species of waterbirds congregate around pools as fish become trapped at the end of the dry season. Mixed flocks of herons, storks and ibises make a spectacular sight: herons fly with their long necks bent back in a squashed S-shape, while storks fly with the neck fully extended, and (unlike herons) often soar to great heights. Ibises have long, slender, curved bills like a curlew.

The tall, grey heron that resembles the familiar European species is the **white-necked or cocoi heron** (*Ardea cocoi*). Its stands well over a metre tall, and its white neck is smartly capped by a black crown (with two long plumes in the breeding season). The **whistling heron** (*Syrigma sibilatrix*) is a tall, slender heron of dry pastures. It eats grasshoppers, snakes and frogs. The **black-crowned night heron** (*Nycticorax nycticorax*) is more active at dawn, dusk and night than by day. Adults are grey above and white below, with black back and crown. They are most often seen standing motionless in a tree or by the water's edge.

Egrets are white herons: three species are a common sight in the Pantanal. Most abundant are **cattle egrets** (*Bubulcus ibis*) which are to be found wherever there are cattle, as they mainly feed on insects disturbed by the grazing animals. Their snowflake flocks, flying to and from roosts at dusk and dawn, are a familiar sight. The other two egrets are fish-eaters: the **snowy** (*Egretta thula*) and the **great** (*Ardea alba*), both found throughout the Amazon.

In addition to the **wood stork** (*Mycteria americana*) of the Amazon, the Pantanal has two other species of stork: the larger is the **jabiru** (*Jabiru mycteria*), a huge white creature with a thick, black neck and a grotesquely large black bill. They build huge nests of sticks in the tops of trees; typically, two or three young will hatch in August. The **maguari stork** (*Ciconia maguari*) resembles the European white stork, and is the least common of the three.

Of the four ibis species in this area, three are readily seen in open habitats: the **bare-faced ibis** (*Phimosus infuscatus*), the **plumbeous ibis** (*Theristicus caerulescens*) and the **buff-necked ibis** (*Theristicus caudatus*). The **bare-faced ibis**, often called **whispering ibis**, are entirely bronzy black, and is found in groups probing in damp pastures. They are easily the smallest of these ibises. The **plumbeous ibis** is all grey, ('plumbeous' means lead-coloured), with orange legs, a bushy crest and a white flash on the forehead. The noisy **buff-necked ibis** has striking white wings, a black belly and red legs. Their honking calls at dawn are sure to act as alarm-clocks. Farmers protect them as they eat harmful insects. The shy **green ibis** (*Mesembrinibis cayennensis*) is here too, but also well distributed throughout the Amazon region.

Screamers and Duck

Screamers, found only in South America, are heavy goose-like birds that walk over floating, marshy vegetation with unwebbed feet. Most commonly seen is the **southern screamer** (*Chauna torquata*), which hoots loudly rather than screams. Hunting and the draining of wetlands have dramatically reduced their numbers.

The Pantanal is a paradise for duck of various species: of which the best known is the **muscovy duck** (*Cairina moschata*). Domesticated varieties are more white than black; but wild birds are all black, except for a white patch on the wings. They nest in tree-hollows or cavities, from which the downy young jump when first hatched. They tend to be shy, since they are popular targets for hunters. Other tree-nesting ducks are the **black-bellied whistling-duck** (*Dendrocygna autumnalis*) and the **white-faced whistling-duck** (*Dendrocygna viduata*). Both these species are very gregarious, forming tight flocks on the water or in the air. The former has striking black and white wings, and an orange bill; the latter has a conspicuous white face, contrasting with dark bill and black nape. Also common is the **Brazilian duck** (*Amazonetta brasiliensis*), a small species with bright orange legs, pale cheeks, and a beautiful green and white wing pattern.

Birds of Prey

Vultures and Caracaras

This section comprises the scavengers, as opposed to the hunters. Brazilian skies are often full of **black vultures** (*Coragyps atratus*) and **turkey vulture**s (*Cathartes aura*), soaring for hours, on the lookout for the next meal. But here we also have the lesser yellow-headed vulture (*Cathartes burrovianus*), which feeds on smaller prey and carrion than its cousin, the very similar but red-headed **turkey vulture**.

Caracaras are a group of scavenging raptors related to the falcons. Most often seen is the **crested caracara** (*Polyborus plancus*), a handsome black bird with black cap and crest, a bare red face, white cheeks and neck. It is much attracted to toasted prey at grass fires, road-kills and other carrion.

Hawks, Kites and Falcons

These are the raptors that hunt their own food by day (for owls, *see* p.53). In addition to common species like the **roadside hawk** (*Buteo magnirostris*) and the fish-eating **black-collared hawk** (*Busarellus nigricollis*) which we have come across in the Amazon region, look out for the **savanna hawk** (*Buteogallus meridionalis*), a long-legged raptor often seen on fence-posts in open country. It is of similar colouring to the black-collared hawk, but without the pale head and black collar.

The **white-tailed kite** (*Elanus leucurus*) is a small, pale grey raptor sometimes seen hovering over open country. It has distinctive black shoulder patches. The **snail kite** (*Rostrhamus sociabilis*) hunts over water, a specialist feeding on apple-snails.

The commonest falcon is the **American kestrel** (*Falco sparverius*), only 25cm long, which is often seen perched on wires, or hovering over open country. It has a rufous back and tail, and two black streaks on the face. Twice the size is the **laughing falcon** (*Herpetotheres cachinnans*), a boldly marked black and white predator with pirate-like black mask on its white head, like a giant panda. Its food is mostly snakes and lizards.

Gamebirds: Chachalacas and Curassows

The **chaco chachalaca** (*Ortalis canicollis*) is a long-tailed, grey-brown fruit-eating bird weighing half a kilo. Groups clamber in trees and call their name loudly ('cha-cha-la-CA!') at dawn and dusk. Much larger and rarer is the **bare-faced curassow** (*Crax fasciolata*), weighing 2.7kg. Males are all black, while females have buff underparts and finely barred plumage. They feed on fruits that have fallen to the ground. The familiar story of habitat loss and hunting has reduced the numbers of this beautiful bird.

razor-billed curassow

Shorebirds and Terns

Many species of **plovers** and **sandpipers** visit the Pantanal, some staying to nest, but others only passing through on migration. The most abundant resident is the **southern lapwing** (*Vanellus chilensis*), most often seen in pairs, standing in pastures. The black and white wing pattern and loud scolding calls make this a conspicuous species. Smaller and more strikingly marked is the **pied lapwing** (*Vanellus cayanus*), which feeds on sandy and muddy margins. Among the migrants, most often seen are the **solitary sandpiper** (*Tringa solitaria*), 19cm, and **greater yellowlegs** (*Tringa melanoleuca*), 33cm, which both migrate from North America to wintering grounds along lakes and rivers.

Large-billed terns (*Phaetusa simplex*) are a common sight here, as in the Amazon. The **black skimmer** (*Rhynchops nigra*) is black above, white below, with an unusual bill: the lower mandible is far longer than the upper. Flocks fly low over the water with bills open, allowing the lower mandible to collect small fish or crustaceans.

Other Waterbirds

Where there are rafts of floating vegetation, look out for **wattled jacana** (*Jacana jacana*), or 'lily-trotter'. The **limpkin** (*Aramus guarauna*) looks like a brown ibis with white spots on the neck, but in fact is more closely related to the cranes. The **American purple gallinule** (*Porphyrio martinica*) is slightly smaller, and has brilliant purple underparts with a bronzy green back. A lucky or alert observer may glimpse a secretive **sunbittern** (*Eurypyga helias*) walking like a slender heron along a riverbank.

Pigeons and Parrots

blue-headed parrot

The common large pigeon of the region is the **picazuro pigeon** (*Columba picazuro*), a thickset, grey-brown bird with a scaly neck. Far smaller is the **ruddy ground-dove** (*Columbina talpacoti*), only 16cm long. The male is orange with a grey crown. Another tiny dove is picui dove (*Columbina picui*), pale grey with black and white wings. Two more tiny doves have long tails: the **scaled dove** (*Scardafella squammata*) with scaly plumage all over; and the **long-tailed ground-dove** (*Uropelia campestris*) which has unmarked underparts.

Parrots, parakeets and macaws are commonly seen in the Pantanal. The **bue-fronted Amazon** (*Amazona aestiva*) is a large, green, short-tailed parrot with a yellow face. The blue forehead that gives the bird its name is not a conspicuous field-mark. **Monk parakeets** (*Myiopsitta monachus*) build communal stick nests in trees and fly around in noisy flocks. The **nanday** or **black-hooded parakeet** (*Nandayus nenday*) is all green, with a long tail and a black head. The **peach-fronted parakeet** (*Aratinga aurea*) is a little smaller, also all green with a peachy forehead. The **yellow-chevroned parakeet** (*Brotogeris chiriri*) is a short-tailed green parakeet with a yellow wing-patch.

Finally, the trio of macaws: the **yellow-collared macaw** (*Propyrrhura auricollis*) is by far the smallest of the three, about 40cm long and weighing 250g. It is only found at the very centre of the continent. The **red-and-green macaw** (*Ara chloroptera*) is 90cm long and weighs up to 1.7kg. Pairs of these magnificent scarlet birds flying slowly and noisily over their nesting forests and savannas are an unforgettable sight. Perhaps the most famous bird of the Pantanal, however, is the globally threatened **hyacinth macaw** (*Anodorhynchus hyacinthinus*), a deep cobalt-blue all over, becoming more violet on the wings. During the 1980s, an estimated 10,000 birds were taken from the wild for the cage-bird trade, leaving only 3,000 flying free. Since then, various conservation initiatives, some involving ecotourism in the Pantanal, have stabilized numbers.

hyacinth macaw

Cuckoos and Owls

The **guira cuckoo** (*Guira guira*) is a large, long-tailed cuckoo that travels in noisy groups, with untidy orange crests raised. The **smooth-billed ani** (*Crotophaga ani*) is all black, and often seen around cattle. They live in family groups, eating grasshoppers with their unusually thick, curved bills. Unlike European cuckoos, these species build their own nests.

Look out for **barn owls** (*Tyto alba*) appearing as a white shape in the headlights when driving at night. Other owls include the tiny rust-coloured **pygmy owl** (*Glaucidium brasilianum*), whose repeated whistle can be heard during the day, and the **burrowing owl** (*Athene cunicularia*), a small, long-legged owl sometimes seen on fence-posts at dawn and dusk.

Kingfishers, Toucans and Woodpeckers

All the kingfisher species of the Amazon area are well distributed in the Pantanal too. The **toco toucan** (*Ramphastos toco*) is well known from the old Guinness advertisements: it is black and white with a huge yellow bill.

The **field flicker** (*Colaptes campestris*) is unusual among woodpeckers in feeding mostly on the ground. It is almost entirely dark, but has a yellow throat and a conspicuous white rump as it flies away. The **pale-crested woodpecker** (*Celeus lugubris*), with a lemon-yellow head, is often associated with palms.

Flycatchers and Swallows

There are over 100 species of flycatchers in Brazil: here are only a few of the most conspicuous. The **black-backed water-tyrant** (*Fluvicola albiventer*) is a sparrow-sized flycatcher, black above and white below. This and the **white-headed marsh-tyrant** (*Arundinicola leucocephala*) are always found by lakes and rivers. The marsh-tyrant is a little smaller than the water-tyrant, and the male is all black but for its white head and throat. **Vermilion flycatchers** (*Pyrocephalus rubinus*) are often seen on posts and wires in cattle country. The **fork-tailed flycatcher** (*Tyrannus savana*) is grey and white, with black cap and a hugely long, forked tail. **Tropical kingbirds** (*Tyrannus melancholicus*) and **great kiskadees** (*Pitangus sulphuratus*) are as abundant in this area as in open parts of the Amazon basin.

The **white-winged swallow** (*Tachycineta albiventer*) is often seen flying low over water. It is a small swallow, with a glossy blue-green back. Much larger (19cm) is the **grey-breasted martin** (*Progne chalybea*), which often nests under the eaves of buildings.

Icterids, Tanagers and Finches

The **icterids** are a diverse family of American birds including the blackbirds and orioles, which, confusingly, are not related to European blackbirds and orioles. Several conspicuous species live in the Pantanal, such as the **bay-winged** (*Molothrus badius*) and **shiny** (*Molothrus bonariensis*) **cowbirds**, which are common in pastures and villages. They are both starling-sized; the male **shiny** is all black, and the **bay-winged** is dull brown with chestnut wings. The **crested oropendola** (*Psarocolius decumanus*) draws attention to itself by its size (40cm), black plumage with yellow tail, and its colonies of huge hanging nests like stockings. The swizzling song is also memorable. The **troupial** (*Icterus icterus*) is a brilliant orange and black oriole, with a cheerful, musical song, seen in pairs in forest edge. The **scarlet-headed blackbird** (*Amblyramphus holosericeus*) is all black except for a brilliant scarlet hood; it is found in pairs in reedbeds.

Tanagers are mostly brightly coloured fruit-eating birds; the **sayaca tanager** (*Thraupis sayaca*) is the most abundant in our area. It is 16cm, blue-grey all over, with brighter blue wings. The **silver-beaked tanager** (*Ramphocelus carbo*) is a velvety maroon colour, with a large silver bill. Pairs are often found along watercourses and roadsides.

The **greyish saltator** (*Saltator coerulescens*) is one of the largest of the Brazilian finches, being 21cm. It is grey, with a white eye-stripe and a black moustachial stripe. Two Cardinal species, **red-crested** (*Paroaria coronata*) and **yellow-billed** (*Paroaria capitata*), are common, especially near water. So called because of their scarlet heads, they are otherwise dark above and white below. The **yellow-billed** has a rounded head, while the **red-crested** has a long, peaked crest. The **rusty-collared seedeater** (*Sporophila collaris*) is 12cm long, and has a complex pattern of black, white and orange. It is found in marshes. The **saffron finch** (*Sicalis flaveola*) behaves like a yellow sparrow, often feeding on the ground. Males are a brighter yellow than females.

Garden Birds

Here are a few miscellaneous species likely to be found in Pantanal gardens. The commonest among many hummingbird species is the **glittering-bellied emerald** (*Chlorostilbon aureoventris*), a tiny green species (9cm) with a red bill. It weighs 4g, and feeds at a wide variety of flowers. The **rufous hornero** (*Furnarius rufus*) is the national bird of Argentina. It struts confidently around on the ground, often near houses and along roads, and builds football-sized mud nests on fence-posts and in trees. The **common thornbird** (*Phacellodomus rufifrons*) is a dull, brown bird, remarkable for its huge nests built of sticks: they can be 2m long, and are often taken over by other birds. Almost the only member of the crow family is the **purplish jay** (*Cyanocorax cyanomelas*), which travels in noisy flocks. They are 37cm long, and a drab purplish-brown all over. The **house wren** (*Troglodytes aedon*) is a close relative of the familiar wren in Europe. These small brown birds with loud songs are much attracted to houses and gardens. The **chalk-browed mockingbird** (*Mimus saturninus*) are grey, long-tailed birds with imitative songs. Both **rufous-bellied** (*Turdus rufiventris*) and **pale-breasted** (*Turdus leucomelas*) **thrushes** are well-known in the area, though the latter is more often found in woodland than garden. Lastly, the **house sparrow** (*Passer domesticus*) has been introduced from Europe, and has adapted well to life in Brazilian towns and gardens.

About the Author

Simon Boyes became a tour guide in 1977, and has now guided over 200 bird-watching tours for the English company **Ornitholidays**. *Twenty of these have been to South America. When not abroad, he lives with his family on a smallholding on the Welsh border near Shrewsbury.*

Birds and Birdwatching in the Western Amazon *by Barry Walker*

The Western Amazon Basin, which shares its birds with the Republics of Colombia, Ecuador, Peru, Brazil and Bolivia, is the most diverse area on the planet for birds, and indeed, most species of living organism. When the great southern continent Gondwanaland broke up during the Cretaceous period, the land mass that is now South America broke off from present-day Africa and drifted northwest until it came to rest against modern Panama and Costa Rica and formed a permanent land bridge. Before this land bridge to North America was formed, South America was an island continent of low relief for about 100 million years. As South America separated from Africa, it must have carried some primitive passerines (perching birds). Modern descendants of this primitive stock include the **manakins** (*Pipridae*), the **tyrant-flycatchers** (*Tyrranidae*), the **cotingas** (*Cotingidae*), the **ovenbirds** and **woodcreepers** (*Funariidae*), the **tapaculos** (*Rhinocryptidae*) and the **antbirds** (*Thamnophilidae*). The other passerine families that exist in South America are almost certainly of northern origin that spread south into south America when the Central American land bridge was formed. The colonist families of northern origin belong to the oscines or 'true songbirds', the southern group of Gondwanaland origin; the suboscines are deemed to be more primitive. Classification is controversial and in constant flux.

Two major theories are offered as explanations of why there are so many birds in the Western Amazon. The first suggests that during the last Ice Age, continuous rainforests broke up into separated patches (refuges), isolated from each other by large stretches of grasslands or savannah in which birds evolved over time. When the ice retreated and rainfall increased, the rainforest once again flourished and refuges were reconnected, but species which had evolved from the same common ancestors no longer recognized each other. They had evolved in isolation and become distinct species, thus producing a high number of different bird species. According to the second theory, the incredible variety of different ecosystems, habitat zones and micro-habitats in the region has allowed birds to find a narrow niche in which to evolve and has resulted in the great avian diversity of the Western Amazon.

Birdwatching Tools in the Amazon

Binoculars with good light-gathering capabilities and close focusing in the 8x to 10x range are recommended. A spotting scope with a 25x–50x fixed wide-angle lens can be useful for more lethargic species such as **trogons** and **puffbirds**, and a great asset if you have access to the rainforest canopy in the form of canopy walkways or static tree platforms. A **telescope** is a great help for scanning the distant tree crowns for **cotingas** or observing feeding aggregations of birds at a distant fruiting tree. A **recorder** of some kind and a **shotgun microphone** can be a useful tool for enticing difficult species out of their tangled abodes, though experience and care is needed with this kind of equipment. There are still comparatively few field guides in South America, although several projects are underway. There is an excellent *Field Guide for Colombia* by Hilty and Brown, and an imminent *Field Guide for Ecuador* by Ridgely and Greenfield. *Birds of Peru* is scheduled to be published in 2004 and Bolivian and Brazilian guides are in the pipeline. At the time of writing, however, birders must use a combination of books for the Amazon and carry a fairly comprehensive library. **Recommended literature** includes: *A Guide to the Birds of Colombia* (Princeton University Press, 1986) by Hilty and

Brown; *Birds of South America* Vols 1&2 (University of Texas Press 1989 and 1994) by Ridgely and Tudor; *South American Birds: A Photogrpahic Aid to Identification* (Harrowood Books, 1987) by John Dunning; *An Annotated List of the Birds of Mainland Ecuador* (G. Editorial Vouluntad, 1987) by Ridgely, Greenfield and Guerrero; *Annotated Checklist of Peruvian Birds* (Butei Books, 1982) by Parker, Parker and Plenge. Many travelling birdwatchers compile their own customized field guides by scanning or colour-photocopying existing plates, including relevant paintings from the excellent *Handbook of the Birds of the World* series (Lynx Editions, Barcelona) by del Hoyo, Elliot and Sargatal and other bird family monographs that are increasing available.

Whichever aids to birdwatching you carry, remember that the rainforest is always humid and that equipment must be **waterproofed** or be tried and tested in humid conditions. Equipment failure whilst on a birdwatching trip can be a very frustrating experience.

How to Look For and Watch Birds in the Amazon

The Amazon is perhaps one of the world's greatest challenges for a birdwatcher. Ornithologists and birdwatchers who have lived and worked in the Amazon for long periods still see new species that have eluded them for many years, often in an area they have walked countless times before. Every excursion in the Amazon is a learning experience. Some birds only sing for a few weeks out of the year and even then many are very, very hard to see, for example the **antpittas** (*Formicaniidae*) and the **rails** and **crakes** (*Rallidae*). Patience is needed for many species and on a first trip to the Amazon, some small **flycatchers** (*Tyrannidae*) and **antwrens** (*Thamnophilidae*) will initially go unidentified. There are birds everywhere you go; it is possible to watch birds on an Amazon river cruise, a three-day visit to a rainforest lodge or even in the gardens of hotels in large towns or cities. If a trip is being planned specifically for birdwatching, then a rainforest lodge is the obvious choice as a base; over 500 species is the norm at most Western Amazonian localities. Around the lodge clearings, over the rivers and along lake edges, many of the more prominent species such as **herons** (*Ardeidae*), **parrots** (*Psittacidae*), **large flycatchers** (*Tyrannidae*) and **oropendolas** (*Icteridae*) will be seen, but it is in the forest interior that the more enticing and mysterious birds such as **antbirds** (*Thamnophilidae*), **ovenbirds** (*Funariidae*) and **manakins** (*Pipridae*) will be found. When choosing a lodge, some factors should be taken into account: is the area protected and are the large indicator species such as **guans** (*cracidae*), **currasows** (*cracidae*) and **trumpeters** (*psophiiae*) still there?. Does the lodge have access to an oxbow lake and canoes on the lake? Does it have access to the rainforest canopy in the form of canopy towers or walkways? Are there stands of bamboo that trails pass through and are there plenty of trails traversing different forest types? Is there a nearby macaw lick? If the answer to all these questions is yes, then you have a good birding lodge. There are several lodges in the Western Amazon that meet this criteria but some of the better-known include **Cristalino River Lodge** (*see* p.228) in Brazil, the **La Selva**, **Sacha and Kapawi Lodges** (*see* pp.186 and 190) in Ecuador, **Amazonia Lodge**, **Exlornapo Lodge**, **Manu Wildlife Centre** and **Tambopata Research Centre** (*see* pp.135, 141, 128 and 132) in Peru. Wherever you go, explore all the habitats at your disposal and make sure you walk through different parts of the forest on different trails. Try and visit seasonally flooded, terra firme and transitional floodplain forests, bamboo patches, oxbow lakes, river margins and use any tree towers available. Birds in the Amazon are most active from dawn until about 10am, so start early. Take a siesta during the heat of the day and follow it with some late afternoon birding. Walk slowly and be alert for bird sounds; learn to recognize the **distinctive sounds** of an approaching canopy or under-story flock (*see* below) and the special calls made by **antbirds** at an army ant swarm.

Canopy Flocks and Understory Flocks

le-crowned trogon

Many different species in the Amazon join together in mixed feeding flocks that roam through the forest together. There are two main types: **canopy flocks** and **under-story flocks**. They defend a communal territory against neighbouring rival flocks and, when the two kinds of flock joins together, there can be as many as 80 species of birds together, usually a pair of each species. Each flock has a leader, always of the same species; in the Western Amazon, canopy flocks are led by **fulvous shrike-tanagers** (*Lanio fulva*) in the north and **white-winged shrike tanagers** (*Lanio versicolour*) in the south. Under-story flocks are led by **cinereous antshrikes** (*Thamnomanes caesius*) in the north and **bluish-slate antshrikes** (*Thamnomanes schistogynus*) in the south. The advantage of being part of a flock is that there are more pairs of eyes to look for predators such as **forest-falcons** (*micrastur sp.*); all species in the flock have distinctive alarm calls that other flock members recognize as warning signals. There is little competition for food as each species is looking for prey in a different place; **antwrens** (*Thamnophilidae*) investigate leaves, **woodcreepers** (*dendrocolaptidae*) probe bark, **foliage-gleaners** (*Furnariidae*) rummage in dead palm leaves, **tanagers** (*Tanigridae*) search for small fruits, **trogons** (*Trogonidae*) for large anthropods and **flycatchers** (*Tyrannidae*) fly-catch in the shady under-story and so on. Learning to recognize the calls of the flock leaders will help greatly to locate these species-rich flocks—in the Amazon, birds of a feather don't necessarily flock together.

Some of the Birds

Manakins (*Pipridae*)

Some of the most enigmatic and interesting species in the world live in the Amazon; perhaps the most enigmatic of all the Amazonian species are the **manakins** (*pipridae*), similar to **tits** (*Paridae*) or **chickadees** (*Paridae*), compact, stocky and energetic. They can be difficult to see unless you find a display area. Most hover-glean for small fruits and many have modified flight feathers that make whirring and snapping sounds. They live mainly in the forest interior, sometimes coming to the forest edge for fruits. They have elaborate courtship displays that vary from species to species, where two or more brightly coloured males display at courtship arenas known as leks. Females are shades of olive. Manakin leks can be found scattered around the forest and several gaudy species can be encountered, including **red-headed** (*Pipra rubrocapilla*), **round-tailed** (*Pipra chloromeros*), **wire-tailed** (*Pipra filicauda*), **blue-crowned** (*Pipra pipra*), **band-tailed** (*Pipra fasciicauda*), **golden-headed** (*Pipra erythrocephala*) and **fiery-capped manakins** (*Machaeropterus pyrocephalus*).

Cotingas (*Cotingidae*)

Another brilliantly plumaged family that, like the **manakins** (*Pipridae*), is strictly American, is the **cotinga** family (*Cotingidae*). Mainly found in the immense Amazonian rainforests, many species are showy, with deep reds and shades of mauve, purple or blue, for example, the lustrous **blue cotingas** (*Cotinga sp.*). In the foothills of the Andes, variations on green are more common and in the **bellbirds** (*Procnia sp.*), almost totally white plumage occurs in two of the species. **Cotingas** (*Cotingidae*) eat fruit and mainly live high in the rainforest canopy; they include the **dazzling blue** (*Cotinga nattererii*), **spangled** (*Cotinga cayana*), **plum-throated** (*Cotinga maynana*) and **purple-breasted cotingas** (*Cotinga cotinga*); the **fruiteaters** (*Pipreola sp.*) of the

cock-of-the-rock

foothills including the gaudy **fiery-throated** (*Pipreola chlorolepidota*) and **scarlet-breasted** (*Pipreola frontalis*); the strange-looking **Amazonian umbrellabird** (*Cephalopterus ornatus*) with its crown of feathers and long bare wattle, the striking Andean **cock-of-the-rock** (*Rupicola peruviana*) of the hill country that croaks and dances daily in a raucous display at favourite dancing grounds and the jay-like **black-necked red cotinga** (*Phoenicircus nigricollis*). These are real prizes, and many can be seen with ease if you have access to a tree tower.

Toucans, Aracaris and Toucanets (*Ramphastidae*)

Toucans and their allies, the **aracaris** and **toucanets** (*Ramphastidae*) are often found feeding in the same fruiting trees that **cotingas** (*Cotingidae*) attend. They are South American counterparts to the **hornbills** (*Tockus sp.*) of the Old World and are readily recognized by their large colourful bills and the astounding ability to lay their tail flat over their backs. Raucous and brightly coloured, this family is a conspicuous member of the rainforest bird community. They nest in holes in trees and roam the forest in groups searching for fruit. Their diet is supplemented with insects and they are not beyond raiding nests of other birds for nestlings and eggs. **Aracaris** (*Pteroglossus*), the smaller members of the toucan family, include **chestnut-eared** (*Pteroglossus castanotis*) perhaps the most familiar, **ivory-billed** (*Pteroglossus flavirostris*), **curl-crested** (*pteroglossus beauharnaesii*), with its curiously curled, plastic-like crown feathers, **many-banded** (*Pteroglossus pluricinctus*) and **lettered** (*Pteroglossus inscriptus*), named for the strange scribble-like markings along the cutting edge of its bill. Among the **toucanets** (*Aulacortyachus sp.*) is the **emerald** (*Aulacortyachus prassinus*) and the **croaking golden-collared** (*Selenidera reinwardtii*). The large toucans of the Amazon whose characteristic cries echo in the late afternoons and evenings include the **yellow-ridged** (*Ramphastos culminatus*) and **Cuvier's toucans** (*Ramphastos cuvieri*) which yelp in unison as the sun sets over the rainforest canopy.

Tanagers (*Tanigridae*) and Hummingbirds (*Trochilidae*)

The treetops are also the home of another typically American family, the **tanagers** (*Tanigridae*), who are important distributors of seeds of rainforest trees, shrubs and vines. Tanagers have perhaps reached their greatest diversity and gaudiness in the misty cloud forests and foothills of the Andes, but they are well represented in the Amazon. They have distinct foraging calls as they move through the rainforest canopy, often accompanying **toucans** (*Ramphastidae*), **aracaris** (*Pteroglossus sp.*) and **cotingas** (*Cotingida sp.*) in mixed canopy feeding flocks or feeding aggregations at fruiting trees. The **honeycreepers** (*Cyanerpes sp.*) and **dacnis** (*Dacnis sp.*) are specialized tanagers that are designed to extract nectar from flowers; their bills are thinner and longer than those of true tanagers. They are brightly coloured little birds, the males being strikingly black and purple, deep blue, turquoise, green and bright yellow, although the females are duller.

Often the **honeycreepers** (*Cyanerpes sp.*) and **dacnis** (*Dacnis sp.*) will be found in the same flowering trees as **hummingbirds** (*Trochilidae*). Brightly coloured hummingbirds tend to be found in the canopy and can be difficult to see, whereas the under-story is dominated by the drab **hermit hummingbirds** (*Phaethornis sp.*). **Euphonias** (*Euphonia sp.*), brightly coloured and musical small tanagers, and true tanagers pluck berries and supplement their diet with insects whilst perched. At a fruiting or flowering tree in the rainforests of the Manu Biosphere Reserve, the following might be seen in the same tree at the same time: **green and gold tanager** (*Tangara schrankii*), **masked tanager** (*Tangara nigrocincta*), **red-billed pied tanager** (*Lamprospiza melanoleuca*), **guira tanager** (*Hemithraupis guira*), **turquoise tanager** (*Tangara mexicana*), **masked crimson-tanager** (*Ramphocelus nigrogularis*), **white-winged shrike tanager** (*Lanio versicolor*), **yellow-crested tanager** (*Tachyphonus rifiventer*), **white-shouldered tanager** (*Tachyphonus luctosus*), **yellow-backed tanager** (*Hemithraupis flavicolis*), **green** (*Chlorophanes spiza*) **and purple honeycreepers** (*Cyanerpes caeruleus*), **blue** (*Dacnis cayana*), **black-faced** (*Dacnis lineata*) and **yellow-bellied dacnis** (*Dacnis flaviventer*), **orange-bellied** (*Euphonia xanthogaster*), **thick-billed** (*Euphonia laniirostris*), **white-vented** (*Euphonia minuta*) and **rufous-bellied euphonies** (*Euphonia rufiventris*), a vision to whet anyone's appetite for Amazonian birding.

Under-story Birds: Tinamous, Trumpeters and Ovenbirds

The more sombrely coloured bird families find their home in the shady under-story and close to the trunks of the giant rainforest trees, where fallen fruits or insects and grubs hidden amongst the leaf-litter provide food. Foraging is a risky business because of predators and most under-story species are extremely wary; dedication and stealth from the bird-watcher are required here. Often **currasows** and **guans** (*Cracidae*) will venture onto the ground from their leafy sub-canopy to take advantage of fallen fruits and can startle you as they flush noisily into the cover of trees. The **tinamous** (*Tinamiidae*) are more often heard than seen; the haunting call of the **great** (*Tinamuis major*) or **bartletts tinamou** (*Crypturellus bartletti*) on a moonlit night is one of the most beautiful sounds on earth. **Undulated** (*Crypturellus undulates*) and **cinereous tinamous** (*Crypturellus cinereus*) often give their whistled calls on the hottest of tropical afternoons. **Tinamous** (*Tinamiidae*) are sought after by many experienced Amazonian bird-watchers and there is no easy way to find them; although their calls betray their presence, sightings are all too few. If you are lucky, a flushed tinamou may reveal a nest of brightly coloured porcelain textured eggs. The tinamous (*Tinamiidae*) share the forest floor with **wood-quails** (*Phasianidae*), whose even-song rings through the forest at dusk and after dark, and the strange **trumpeters** (*Psophiidae*). Trumpeters are shy and one of the first birds to disappear if there is too much human impact. They are related to cranes and rails and have a well developed social behaviour, patrolling their territory in family groups, keeping in contact with low purring and whooping calls which escalate into the full song of guttural humming notes if they sense danger. They sing at full moon also, and eat insects, fallen fruits, lizards and snakes. Many Amazonian tribes keep trumpeters as pets in their villages as they are good watchdogs, raising the alarm if an intruder or snake is in the vicinity.

The **ovenbirds** (*Furnariidae*) are denizens of the shady forest as well, seldom coming out into full view. They are shades of brown and chestnut and can present identification problems until their songs and behaviour are learned. The **foliage-gleaners** (*Automolus and Philydor*) and **leaf-tossers** (*Sclerurus*) are common members of mixed feeding flocks; the automolus foliage-gleaners keep low in thick undergrowth, while the philydor group are more conspicuous and forage higher. They specialize in rummaging in dead leaf clusters and investigating palm leaves or throwing aside leaf litter in search of insects. Some are bamboo specialists, always found within large bamboo stands, such as the **Peruvian recurvebill** (*Simoxenops ucayalae*), with its strangely upturned bill used for cracking off pieces of bamboo to search for grubs and its nanny-goat like call, and the inconspicuous brown-rumped **foliage-gleaner** (*Automolus melanopezus*). Unless you look for these birds in bamboo you will not see them; this is a good illustration of how important it is to examine the available literature rather than just looking at a picture. Other **ovenbirds** (*furnariidae*) include the spinetails, woodhaunters and the ***horneros*** who build mud oven-like nests on exposed branches along the oxbow lakes (*horno* is Spanish for oven).

One of the largest and more complicated groups, now placed in the ovenbird family, is the **woodcreeper** (*dendrocolpatidae*) sub-family. **Woodcreepers** (*Dendrocolapatinae*) climb trunks and large tree limbs in the manner of a **woodpecker** (*Picidae*) (no relation). They are drab brown and olive with varying amounts of streaks and spotting, and identification is difficult. Even learning their songs and calls is difficult as many species imitate each other's calls and each species gives a variety of calls, dawn songs, dusk songs, etc. The common **buff-throated woodcreeper** (*Xiphorhynchus guttatus*) gives a bewildering variety of calls and it is worthwhile learning this bird's call well in order to be able to compare all other woodcreeper species to it. Some **woodcreepers** (*Dendrocolapatinae*) are most easily encountered at army ant swarms, for example the **plain-brown** (*dendrocincla fulginosa*), **strong-billed** (*Xiphocolaptes promeropirhynchus*), **barred** (*Dendrocolaptes certhia*) and **bar-bellied woodcreeepers** (*Hylexetastes stresemanni*). The **white-chinned woodcreeper** (*Dendrocincla merula*), is an obligate army ant follower (*see* below) and is always found at ant swarms.

Army Ant Followers

Obligate army ant followers are birds that, as part of their survival strategy in the forest, are always present at army ant swarms. They don't eat the carnivorous ants, which are full of formic acid and unpalatable, but prey on the fleeing grasshoppers, spiders, other insects and even frogs, that are trying to escape the marauding hoards of ants that carpet the forest floor. This is one of the great wildlife experiences of the Amazon and to watch an ant swarm in full swing with attendant birds is a wonderful bird-watching spectacle. Spiders and grasshoppers run and jump in panic trying to escape the ants only to be snapped up by a waiting attendant bird. Many of the species that attend the swarm are of the **antbird** (*Thamnophillidae*) family, which, although consisting mostly of non ant-following species, derives its name from a few species of professional army ant followers, like the **white-throated** (*Gymnopithys salvini*) and **lunulated antbirds** (*Gymnopithys lunulata*) and the **bare-eyes** (*Phlegopsis sp.*)—spectacular members of the antbird family and a real prize.

Antbirds, Antpittas, Antwrens, Antshrikes, Gnateaters, and Anthrushes

Some species are not obligate army ant followers but attend periodically at swarms; these include the **hairy-crested** (*Rhegmathorina melanosticta*), **sooty** (*Mymeciza fortis*), **plumbeous** (*Myrmeciza hyperythra*) and **white-browed antbirds** (*Myrmoborus leucophys*). The majority of the **antbird** (*Thamnophiliidae*) family are to be found occupying various niches in the forest away from ant swarms. They are usually small to medium sized birds and 30 or 40 species may be found at the same locality in the Amazon. They consist of several groups: antshrikes, antbirds, antwrens, gnateaters, anthrushes and antpittas. The latter two are terrestrial and sometimes considered a separate family—the **ground-antbirds** (*Formicariidae*). They are inconspicuous and shy and often only betray their presence with far carrying calls and songs. **Antpittas** (*Formicariidae*) are the stuff of legend and their names often reflect that—for example, the **elusive antpitta** (*Grallaria eludens*). The antwrens, antshrikes and antbirds (*Thamnophilidae*) are more easily seen and occupy many habitats and levels in the forest, often accompanying mixed species flocks. Most show great sexual dimorphism, with males being shades of grey and black and females exhibiting shades of brown, buff and rufous. They feed by gleaning foliage for insects at all levels from the ground to the sub-canopy. Some are restricted to bamboo, such as the **ornate** (*Myrmotherula ornata*) and **Ihrings antwrens** (*Myrmotherula iheringi*), some to lake edges and swamps such as the **Amazonian streaked antwren** (*Myrmotherula surinamensis*), the **band-tailed antbird** (*Hypocnemoides maculicauda*) and the **silvered antbird** (*Sclateria naevia*). Some never descend from the canopy, like the **chestnut-winged** (*Terenura humeralis*) and **sclaters antwrens** (*Myrmotherula sclateri*), and some prefer mid-levels and are much more likely to be seen, such as the **white-browed** (*Myrmoborus leucophrys*) and **black-faced antbirds** (*Myrmoborus myotherinus*), the **dusky-throated antshrike** (*Thamnomanes ardesiaca*) and the **white-flanked** (*Myrmotherula axillaris*) and **long-winged antwrens** (*Myrmotherula longipennis*).

Predators: Falcons, Kites and Eagles

Antbirds (*Thamnophiliidae*) have to deal with predators in the form of **forest-falcons** (*Micrastur sp.*) that lurk in vine tangles following mixed feeding flocks, waiting for a chance to snatch an unwary bird. Birds of prey have occupied virtually every rainforest niche. **Plumbeous** (*Ictinia plumbea*) and **swallow-tailed kites** (*Elanoides forficatus*) hawk above the rainforest canopy for large flying insects, sharing this aerial environment with a variety of swifts (*Apodidae sp.*). **Double-toothed kites** (*Harpagus bidentatus*) follow monkeys, snatching large insects flushed out as the primates move through the forest. Accipiters like **bicolored** (*Accipiter biculur*) and **tiny hawks** (*Accipiter superciliosus*) dash through undergrowth also after smaller birds. **Snail kites** (*Rostrhamus sociabilis*) and **black-collared hawks** (*Busarellus nigricolis*) specialize in lake edge habitats. **Ornate** (*Spizaetus ornatus*), **black** (*Spizaetus tyrranus*) and **black and white** (*Spizastur melanoleucus*) hawk eagles share the canopy with **short-tailed** (*buteo brachyurus*) and **slate-coloured hawks** (*Leucopternis schistacea*). The most powerful eagle in the world lives here: the magnificent **harpy eagle** (*Harpia harpyja*), over-shadowing the closely related **crested eagle** (*Morphnus guianensis*) by only a centimetre or two. These eagles reach up to 40 inches in length and feed on large arboreal mammals such as monkeys and sloths. Despite their size, they are difficult to see as they seldom soar and usually keep within the tree crowns, only showing themselves when crossing rivers or clearings.

Nocturnal Predators

common potoo

At dusk there is a changeover. As diurnal mammals go to sleep and nocturnal mammals awake, so do the predators that have evolved to feed on them; **hawks**, **eagles** and **falcons** (*Accipitridae*) are replaced by **owls** (*Strigidae*), and the nocturnal insect population is preyed upon by **nighthawks**, **nightjars** (*Caprimulgidae*) and the strange **potoos** (*Nyctibiidae*). **Spectacled owls** (*Pulsatrix perspicillata*) give their long reverberating calls; **screech-owls** (*Otus sp.*) hoot around clearings; the magnificent **crested owl** (*Lophostrix cristata*) replaces the eagles hunting in the sub-canopy; and the tiny **Amazonian pygmy owl** (*Glaucidium hardyi*) trills in the canopy between insect-hunting bouts. The **nightjars** and **nighthawks** (*Caprimulgidae*) occupy various niches, searching for insects in the canopy, along rivers and in the under-story. **Potoos** (*Nyctibiidae*), South America's answer to the **frogmouths** (*Batrachostomus sp.*), sit motionless all day mimicking dead tree limbs; they become active at dusk, giving haunting cries as the sun sets or at full moon, and silently float through the forest catching moths during the night.

Along the Rivers and Lakes

Not all Amazonian birds inhabit the forest; many are found along tropical Amazonian rivers and oxbow lakes. As the mighty rivers drop in level during the dry season between June and September, many birds take advantage of the exposed sandy beaches to raise their young. On little-disturbed rivers (unfortunately harder and harder to find), **orinoco geese** (*Neochen jubata*), **muscovy ducks** (*Cairina moschata*), **pied lapwings** (*Vanellus cayanus*), **collared plovers** (*Charadrius collaris*) and **sand-coloured nighthawks** (*Chordeiles rupestris*) nest. Two freshwater terns, the dainty yellow-billed (*Sterna superciliaris*) and the more powerful **large-billed terns** (*Phaetusa simplex*), share the fish according to size and take advantage of the beaches for breeding along with the **black skimmers** (*Rynchops niger*). oxbow lakes, formed as the rivers meander and finally cut through the narrow neck of an exaggerated loop, create a distinct habitat that is used by the **river-nesting terns** (*Laridae*) and **ducks** (*Anatidae*). **Herons** (*Ardeidae*) are a great

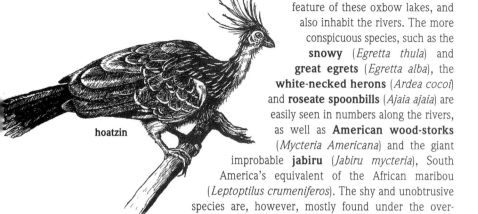

feature of these oxbow lakes, and also inhabit the rivers. The more conspicuous species, such as the **snowy** (*Egretta thula*) and **great egrets** (*Egretta alba*), the **white-necked herons** (*Ardea cocoi*) and **roseate spoonbills** (*Ajaia ajaia*) are easily seen in numbers along the rivers, as well as **American wood-storks** (*Mycteria Americana*) and the giant improbable **jabiru** (*Jabiru mycteria*), South America's equivalent of the African maribou (*Leptoptilus crumeniferos*). The shy and unobtrusive species are, however, mostly found under the overhanging vegetation. The sought-after **agami heron** (*Agamia agami*) is here, along with **striated** (*Butorides striatus*) and **boat-billed herons** (*Cochlaerius cochlaerius*). If you are lucky you may see a **pinnated** (*Botaurus pinnatus*) or **stripe-backed bittern** (*Ixobrychus involucris*). **Green ibis** (*Mesembrinibis cayennensis*) and **anhingas** (*Anhinga anhinga*) also find a home here, the latter often swimming with just its elongated neck showing above the water and the body submerged, giving rise to one of its other names—'snake-bird'. One strange oxbow lake inhabitant is the **hoatzin** (*Opisthocomus hoazin*), a prehistoric-looking turkey-like bird that grunts and hisses in the lakeside vegetation. The **hoatzin** (*Opisthocomus hoatzin*) is a member of the cuckoo family and nests on flimsy stick platforms in bushes above the water. The nestlings have a strange evolutionary development, a hook on the bend of the wing; this enables young birds to clamber back to the nest after ejecting into the water to escape the attentions of a predator—a neat defence mechanism and a good survival strategy.

Flycatchers

Also here on these tranquil lakes and rivers are conspicuous flycatchers, among them tropical **kingbirds** (*Tyrannus melancholicus*), **social** (*Myiozetetes similes*) and **gray-capped** (*Myuozetetes granadensis*) **flycatchers**, **great** (*Pitangus sulphuratus*) and **lesser kiskadees** (*Pitangus lictor*) are fairly common. The **tyrant-flycatcher** (*Yyrannidae*) group is an enormous family, which ranges from small **tody-tyrants** (*Todirostrum*) and **tody-flycatchers** (*Hemmitriccus*), **canopy elaenias** (*Elaenia* and *Myiopagis sp.*) and **tyrannulets** to the large noisy **attilas** (*Attila sp.*) and **mourners**. Not all are found along the lakes and rivers; indeed, the vast majority are to be found in the forest interior, inhabiting all niches and habitats from the canopy to the ground. Many specialize in bamboo thickets, such as the **dusky-tailed** (*Ramphotrigon fuscicauda*) and **large-headed flatbills** (*Ramphotrigon megacephala*), the **white-cheeked tody-flycatcher** (*Poecilotriccus albifacies*) and the **flammulated bamboo-tyrant** (*Hemmitriccus flammulatus*). Others, like the **sulphury flycatcher** (*Tyrannopsis sulphurea*) and **citron-bellied attila** (*Attila citriniventris*), are found in stands of palms. Many are canopy-dwellers and, until their calls and songs are learned, they can be almost impossible to see and identify.

Parrot Family: Parrots, Parakeets, Parrotlets and Macaws

The **parrots**, **parakeets**, **parrotlets** and particularly the **macaws** (*Psittacidae*) are as much a part of the Amazon as are giant otters and Brazil nut trees. Noisy, gregarious and gaudy, they are everywhere, and include the tiny **dusky-billed** (*Forpus sclateri*), **Amazonian** (*Nanopsittaca d'achilli*) and **scarlet-shouldered parrotlets** (*Touit huetti*), the great flocks of **white-eyed** (*Aratinga leucopthalmus*), **dusky-headed** (*Aratinga weddelli*), **cobalt-winged** (*Brotogeris cyanoptera*) and **tui** (*Brotogeris sanctithomae*) parakeets flying over the rivers in the evening, the big Amazon parrots such as **mealy** (*Amazonas farinose*), **yellow-headed** (*Amazonas ochrocephala*) and **orange-winged parrots** (*Amazonas amazonica*) to the smaller **short-tailed parrots** (*Graydidascalus brachyurus*), **blue-headed** (*Pionus menstuus*) and **orange-cheeked parrots** (*Pionopsitta barrabandi*) and the great, noisy and colourful **scarlet** (*Ara macao*), **red and green** (*Ara chloroptera*) and **blue and yellow** (*Ara ararauna*) **macaws**. The big macaws, and their smaller relatives—**chestnut-fronted macaws** (*Ara severa*) and **red-bellied macaws** (*Ara manilata*) in the palm swamps—are an integral part of the makeup of the Amazon and no trip to the Amazon rainforest would be complete without a visit to one of the great wildlife spectacles: a macaw lick. There are several macaw licks close to lodges in the Western Amazon: macaws, parakeets and parrots all attend these clay river banks. Great numbers gather at these traditional sites to eat clay, which is essential to their digestion, acting as a neutralising agent for the mild poisons that exist in the limited variety of fruits they are obliged to eat during the dry season from July to September. It's rather like a human taking kaolin for an upset stomach. Just after dawn, great numbers of **blue-headed** (*Pionis menstruus*), **mealy** (*Amazonas farinose*) and **yellow-headed** (*Amazonas ochrocephala*) parrots, with a sprinkling of the gaudy **orange-cheeked parrots** (*Pionopsitta barrabandi*), gather at the lick. Often **dusky-cheeked** (*Aratinga weddelli*) and **cobalt-winged parakeets** (*Brotogeris cyanoptera*) are present too, adding to the astonishing clamour. After they have had their fill, as if to an invisible signal, they fly off the lick in a crescendo of noise and colour, circling briefly before heading into the forest, leaving an eerie silence in their wake. It is now time for the macaws to gather. In pairs and family groups of three and four, the gaudy macaws fly in, calling in a subdued manner, and begin to gather in the trees above the lick. As the numbers grow they seem to gain in confidence and drop lower and lower until they are just above the lick. Suddenly, one brave soul drops onto the clay bank, signalling for all and sundry to join the party. For perhaps an hour the great colourful macaws caw and squabble on the bank as they get their bi-daily intake of clay. Suddenly, as with the parrots that preceded them, they leave the lick in a swirling multicoloured mass and break up into family groups and pairs to get on with their daily routine in the forest. The lick is then deserted and silent until the next day. A sight to see indeed.

About the Author

Barry Walker has extensive birding experience in Ecuador, Colombia and particularly Peru and Bolivia. He has participated in several ornithological expeditions and contributed to manyscientific and general publications, and is currently compiling a major field guide. He has been leading bird tours for private groups and well known bird tour companies for the last 10 years. He has seen more than 1,500 species in Peru alone, and is well known for his field craft when leading tours. He is married with a young daughter. He and his wife own Manu Expeditions (see p.128) at a pioneer eco-tour operator in Manu National Park.

As one flies over the Amazon rainforest one might be forgiven for thinking that it is rather uniform in its composition. However, exactly the opposite is true; the diversity of species and types of vegetation that can be encountered within the Amazon Basin is quite remarkable and is one of the main attractions for the visitor to Amazonia. There are many causes of variation within Amazonia: soil type, the amount and seasonality of the rainfall, the topography, the altitude, the flooding regime and also the climatic history of the region. The great German explorer Baron Alexander von Humboldt (1769–1859) travelled extensively in Venezuela and Colombia and was the first scientist to make detailed descriptions of how the vegetation altered with altitude on tropical mountains. One of the most obvious causes of difference is whether an area is seasonally flooded by the rise in river level in the rainy season or whether it remains above the flood level. In Brazil the forest that does not flood is usually referred to as forest on terra firme or just terra firme. Since many visitors experience the Amazon largely by ship or boat on the rivers, we will begin with the description of the vegetation along the rivers.

heliconia

Riverside Vegetation

There are two main types of riverside forest; **varzea** and **igapó** in Brazil. The **varzea forest** (called Tahuampa in Peru) grows in the floodplain of the muddy white water rivers and **igapó** occurs along the black- and clear-water rivers. The vegetation is different because of the properties of the water: the white water is full of sediment and is only slightly acidic, while the black water has little sediment but much dissolved tannin and so is very acidic (pH 4–4.5). The white water deposits alluvial matter on the flooded area which enriches the soil annually, whereas the nutrient-poor black water does not enrich the soil. As a consequence the varzea vegetation is much more luxuriant than the igapó. The varzea has been much disturbed because it is quite suitable for agriculture by growing crops when crops are grown during the low water season. Because of the difference in water the varzea forests usually have higher river banks (natural levees) while the black water and clear water rivers usually have gradually sloping sandy beaches. In the Amazon delta the varzea forest floods twice daily because of tidal movements. In the rest of Amazonia the flooding is annual. The plants of tidal and seasonal varzea are similar, but there is a greater abundance of palms in tidal varzea.

Some Easily Recognized Varzea Plants

Kapok or Silk-cotton tree (*Ceiba pentandra*)

One of the largest trees of the varzea with a characteristic umbrella-like crown emerging above the rest of the vegetation. If you see one in flower, watch it at night to see the pollinating bats visiting the flowers. The light cotton around the seeds enables the wind to disperse them and is also the source of kapok wool, used for stuffing mattresses, life vests and in insulation. The trunks of young trees are covered with spines.

Calabash (*Crescentia cujete*)

This small tree is much cultivated along the rivers for the gourd-like fruit that is used for bowls, water pots, and canoe balers, etc. The flowers are pollinated by bats and the young developing fruit are protected by ants that drink the nectar secreted on the outside of the fruit. The seeds, like those of many riverside plants, are dispersed by characin fish (*see* p.46).

Amazon Cannon-ball Tree (*Couroupita subsessilis*)

A common tree on the upper Amazon which can be easily recognized by the large round fruit borne on the trunk and larger branches. On the upland forest you may come across *Couroupita guianensis,* the other species of cannon-ball with larger red flowers. The flowers of the Amazon cannon-ball are yellow. The pulp around the seeds is used as chicken and pig food by local people and the seeds are dispersed by wild pigs.

Munguba Tree (*Pseudobombax munguba*)

This large, thick-trunked tree grows in more open disturbed areas. The large red fruit look rather like Christmas-tree decorations hanging down from the bare branches. It is a member of the same family as the silk-cotton tree and the seeds are also surrounded by a kapok-like fibre which is used by Indians to make flights for their blowgun darts.

Buriti Palm (*Mauritia flexuosa*)

This is the commonest and largest of the fan-leaved palms of wet areas and is sometimes found in pure stands. The fruits are rich in provitamin A and are used for desserts and ice cream. A fibre from the leaf is used to make hammocks and mats in Eastern Amazonia. In Peru this palm is called Aguaje. On the black water rivers another related species grows with finer leaves, *Mauritiella aculeata.*

Açai Palm (*Euterpe oleracea*)

This elegant multi-stemmed palm with up to 25 stems per clump has finely divided leaves. It is the principal source of heart-of-palm in the state of Pará, Brazil, and the fruits yield a purple juice which is used to flavour ice cream. The related *Euterpe precatoria* is a single-stemmed palm that replaces *Euterpe oleracea* in western Amazonia and is called **Huasai** in Peru.

Aninga (*Montrichardia arborescens*)

This is an aquatic member of the arum lily family with large soft woody stems growing in water along the edges of varzea or more rarely in igapó. The leaves are heart-shaped, like many elephant-ear plants in the same family. The flower consists of a cream-coloured spathe surrounding a white spadix. The spongy trunk has been used for rafts by Indians and also to extract a fibre to make cord.

Mulato tree (*Calycophyllum spruceanum*)

This tall tree, characteristic of Amazon river banks, is well-named because of the shiny smooth brown bark of the trunk. It is distributed from the upper Amazon in Peru to the delta region. It is often cut for its timber and is a member of the coffee family.

Some Common Igapó Plants:

Monkey Gourd (*Eschweilera tenuifolia*)

This is a common tree along the Rio Negro, found with its trunk in the water during the flood season. It is recognized by the cup-shaped lower part of the fruit, which remains attached to the tree after the lid and seeds have been released into the water. The yellow flowers are pollinated by large bees that lift up the hood that covers the top in order to obtain nectar.

Arapari (*Macrolobium acaciaefolium*)

This elegant tree with its fine mimosa-like leaves is most common along black and clear water rivers, but is not confined to them. The small round flattened fruit help to identify this species and are said to be a favourite food of river turtles. The white flowers with purple stamens give this a distinctive aspect during flowering.

Jará Palm (*Leopoldinia pulchra*)

This small palm is easily recognized by the persistent leaf sheaths that surround its trunk. It is most characteristic of the sandy beaches of the Rio Negro. A related species, the **piassaba palm** (*Leopoldinia piassaba*), grows in the upper Rio Negro region in Brazil, Colombia and Venezuela. The trunk is covered with pendulous brown fibres used for broom-making.

Muruci (*Byrsonima amazonica*)

This large shrub bears spikes of yellow flowers. Underneath the clawed petals are paired glands that secrete an oil that is gathered by the pollinating bees. The small round pea-sized fruit are very popular with local children. The genus *Byrsonima* is large with many species throughout the region, including *Byrsonima verbascifolia* which occurs in most savannahs.

The Moon-flower Cactus (*Selenicereus wittii*)

You will only find this extraordinary cactus if you travel up the Rio Negro. The stems are flattened against tree trunks. It is called moon-flower since each flower opens for one night only. The long tube bearing white petals at the end is characteristic of moth pollinated plants. Commoner epiphytic cacti with similar flowers are the species of the genus *Epiphyllum.*

In addition to the two main forest types varzea and igapó of the floodplain, you will also find many other types of vegetation beside the rivers and lakes of Amazonia.

Canarana Grassland

In the lower Amazon behind the varzea forest there are often large natural grass meadows on lower ground that is flooded for longer. These grasslands also border many of the lakes. The dominant species of grass is **canarana** (*Panicum spectabile*) which grows rapidly as flood level recedes. The flooding often washes away large floating islands of grass, sometimes towed into land by farmers for use as forage for their cattle. Another grass in this formation is *Paspalum repens* (called **creeping canarana** by locals). Various trees and shrubs may grow amongst the canarana grass. Here and on muddy open river banks you can see the Amazon willow tree, *Salix martiana.* This species is called **oierana** and occurs mainly on the muddy beaches that are in the process of deposition. Another look-alike species in the spurge family, *Alchornea castaneaefolia*, is also called **oierana** by locals, which grows in the same habitat. The latter has a white latex in the bark which the willow does not. *Alchornea* also has a large green fruit that is eaten and dispersed by fish whereas the willow has a light wind-dispersal seed.

The Flora of Lakes

Beyond the grass there is often a fascinating variety of truly aquatic plants. The most spectacular is the **royal water lily**, (*Victoria amazonica*). The pads, with their upturned margins, can be up to two metres in diameter. The flowers open at dusk and are coloured white. At that time the flower temperature is 6–11°C warmer than ambient and a strong fruity smell is emitted. Large scarab beetles of the genus *Cyclocephala* are attracted to the flowers. The flowers then close and entrap the beetles inside. The flowers gradually change colour from white to a reddish-purple and reopen the next evening. At that time pollen is released and so, as the beetles emerge, they are dusted with pollen and carry it to another first-day flower. *Victoria amazonica* is confined to the Amazon Basin of Peru and Brazil and a related species, **Victoria cruziana**, is native to the Paraguay and Plate river systems. The magnificent hybrid between the two species is often grown in botanic gardens such as Longwood in the USA and Kew and Edinburgh in the UK. Several other water lilies in the genus *Nymphaea* occur in the Amazon and Pantanal area. The night-flowering ones are also beetle-pollinated. The day-flowering **Nymphaea ampla** is bee-pollinated.

There are several aquatic species of **ferns** on Amazon lakes: *Azolla microphylla* and *Salvinia auriculata* often cover large areas of lakes. **Marsilea polycarpa** has distinctive divided fronds that look like large clover-leaves. The **water lettuce** (*Pistia stratiotes*) can often be seen floating in lakes, streams and rivers. It is an unusual member of the arum lily family and its floating rosettes of pale green leaves are easily recognized. The **water hyacinth** (*Eichhornia crassipes*) is an infamous Amazonian floating aquatic that has become a troublesome weed. The blue flowers have a central nectar guide on the upper petal to attract pollinators. The water hyacinth is interesting because it exhibits the phenomenon of heterostyly, where there are three different forms or morphs of the flowers. Individual plants have either long, short or intermediate length styles. For seeds to be set pollen must be transferred between different morphs. A similar system occurs in the European primrose (*Primula vulgaris*). There are many other species of the water hyacinth family, *Pontederiaceae* in Amazonia and the Pantanal in the genera *Reussia* and *Pontederia*. An interesting aquatic plant is *Neptunia oleracea*. This is a relative of the sensitive plant mimosa, and its leaves fold up when touched in the same way. This is an effective defence against predators.

Mangrove Forest

Mangrove forest occurs in coastal areas around the tropics; it is flooded twice daily by salt water because of tidal movements. In South America it is distributed around the coasts of both the Pacific and Atlantic Oceans. The Amazon mangrove is a narrow littoral belt on the coast of the Guianas and Brazil. The most common species are the three species of the **red mangrove**, (*Rhizophora*). These have characteristic arching prop roots arising from the stem and branches. This anchors the tree much better in the tidal area where it grows. The red mangrove seeds germinate while still on the tree. After a long radicle has been produced, the seedlings drop from the tree and are dispersed by currents until stranded on the coastline. The other mangrove species in Amazon mangrove are the **white mangrove** (*Avicennia nitida*), *Laguncularia racemosa* and the **buttonwood**, *Conocarpus erectus*. Many mangrove species have aerial breathing roots or pneumatophores emerging from the ground in order to oxygenate the roots.

This is the most abundant forest type in Amazonia, covering just over fifty percent of the Amazon Basin. It has a greater biomass than any other forest type and has a rather clear understory so that you can generally walk through the forest without the aid of a machete. In this forest there are frequent **woody vines** or **lianas**. It is interesting to understand how they reach the tops of the trees. Some vines climb straight up looking like normal trees initially and only begin to entwine when they reach the canopy. Some species of ***Strychnos***, the vine that provides one of the ingredients of curare arrow poison, have this form of growth. Some members of the ***Araceae*** and ***Bignoniaceae*** when young are slender climbers with flat leaves pressing firmly against tree trunks. When they reach a certain height, the leaves and stem change completely into a vine or an epiphyte so that an uninitiated person would never associate the two such different-looking growth forms together.

The terra firme rainforest is divided into different strata or levels and most species of trees are specialists that occur at one level. The canopy of Amazon rainforest is usually at a height of between 20 and 40 metres. Some species, called **emergents**, grow up above the canopy. The largest tree in the Amazon forest is *Dinizia excelsa* which reaches up to 60m and often has a trunk diameter greater than three metres. Another emergent tree is the **Brazil nut** (*Bertholletia excelsa*) which also can grow to 60m tall and have a trunk diameter of 4m. Other species of tree grow at a lower level underneath the canopy and never reach the top of the forest. These species are adapted to grow under the low light intensity there. At ground level there is a layer of shrubs and herbs that is not very dense.

The most striking feature of the terra firme forest is the amazing diversity of species. As you stand in the forest you will often see that no two tree trunks look alike. Recent inventories have shown that in western Amazonia there can be as many as 300 species of trees of 10cm diameter or more on a single hectare of forest. Inventories throughout the region have varied from 81 to 300 species per hectare depending on the rainfall, the length of the dry season and the soil. In any hectare analysed some trees are more frequent than others but, unlike forests of the temperate region, no one species dominates.

Although the forest looks luxuriant, the soil on which it grows is generally very poor. The prolific growth is maintained by efficient recycling of all the nutrients rather than by rich soil. As a result the trees mostly have shallow roots, and instead are supported by buttressed trunks. Look for a fine mass of roots among the leaf litter. These are directly reabsorbing the nutrients in the rotting leaves. It is also common to find roots of living trees growing into the trunks and stumps of dead trees. Nothing is lost in this efficient recycling system. Because of the poor soil much of the region is unsuitable for agriculture and this explains why so many projects that have attempted to turn the forest land to other uses such as cattle pasture, have failed.

Some Common Terra Firme Forest Plants

Pequi (*Caryocar species*)

There are several species of the pequi, *Caryocar*, in the forest. Two, *Caryocar glabrum* with red flowers and *Caryocar villosum* with yellow flowers, are emergents. If you find a carpet of flowers on the forest floor with a ring of petals and long filamentous stamens, it is probably a *Caryocar*. The locals often build hides near a flowering pequi to hunt the nocturnal rodent the paca. All species of *Caryocar* are bat-pollinated. After the flowers have been open for one night they fall, hence the red or yellow carpet under the tree in the flowering season. The fruit of the pequi is also considered a delicacy and is cooked with rice, but don't try it raw because of the vicious spines on the inner seed case.

Visgueiro (*Parkia pendula*) and other Bat-Pollinated Trees

The legume *Parkia* is truly one of the most striking trees of the terra firme with its broad, spreading, very flat crown. The flowers are borne in pom-pom like clusters on long stalks that hang down below the crown. They have an unpleasant smell but are readily accessible to bat-pollinators. Several other Amazon species make their flowers accessible to bats in this way, which is termed flagelliflory. In the forests of Guyana another member of the legume family, the **wallaba**, has pendulous flowers. This species of *Eperua* so dominates some areas of forest on white sand that the whole formation is known as Wallaba forest. Around Manaus the **chicken nut** (*Couepia longipendula*) is a common tree. After flowering the egg-like fruit that gives it its local name (*Castanha de galinha*) hang down on the long stalks. These fruit are used locally to extract an oil for cooking.

The Brazil Nut (*Bertholletia excelsa*)

Brazil nuts are borne in large round fruit a bit larger than a cricket ball at the top of one of the largest trees of the Amazon forest. The trees flower in October and November and the fruit take 14 months to mature and fall from the trees in January and February. Don't walk under a tree then, it could be dangerous! The fruit are gathered and split open to extract the nuts which are arranged inside rather like the segments of an orange. The fruits that are not gathered by nut collectors are gnawed open by agoutis who extract the seeds and bury them in caches away from the tree and thereby disperse them. Brazil nuts are still mainly harvested from wild trees in Bolivia, Peru and Brazil.

Monkey Ladder Vine (*Bauhinia species*)

This liana has a remarkable growth form where the stem curves alternately in different directions and gives it a ladder-like appearance. It is a common vine throughout the Amazon that you can't mistake.

Ant Plants

There are many species of trees and shrubs that have evolved a symbiotic relationship with ants. The plant houses and often feeds the ants and the ants protect the plant from predators. Some species of shrub have pockets at the base of their leaves where the ants live: for example, species of **Tococa** (*Melastomataceae*), **Duroia** (*Rubiaceae*) and **Hirtella** (*Chrysobalanaceae*). These plants usually are covered with bristly hairs which help to protect the ants. Other arboreal ant plants are inhabited by ants within the trunks, with **Cecropia**, a common plant of secondary forests, and the **tachi** trees (*Tachigalia* and *Triplaris*) which are inhabited by vicious fire ants (*see* p.34).

Palms

There are many different palm trees in the terra firme forests. The definitive book, *The Palms of the Amazon,* by Andrew Henderson (Oxford, 1995) describes 151 species in 34 genera. Only four of the most frequently encountered can be mentioned here.

Bacaba (*Oenocarpus bacaba*)

A medium to large tree 7–22m tall, common in central and northeastern Amazonia in Colombia, Venezuela and Brazil. The deep purple fruits are used to make a drink.

Pataua (*Oenocarpus bataua*)

A large tree which can grow to 25m tall. The fruits provide a drink and the kernels an oil that is similar to olive oil. This palm occurs both in terra firme and varzea forest.

Inajá (*Maxmilliana regia*)

This magnificent palm often occurs in clusters, especially on disturbed areas. It is distributed throughout northern South America, east of the Andes. The leaves are a favourite material for thatching, the fruits are edible and the outer part of the leaf stalk is used to make blowgun darts.

Babaçu (*Attalea speciosa*)

This is the most abundant palm along the southern fringes of Amazonia, but also occurs in Guyana, Suriname and Bolivia. It is often in large one-species stands in the transition forests between Amazonia and the cerrado region of central Brazil. The oil from the seed is an important local industry in Maranhão State of Brazil.

Transition Forests

Between the dense Amazon rainforest on terra firme and the drier savannah and caatinga formations of northeast and central Brazil, there are various types of transition forests. The principal transition vegetation formations are:

Babaçu forest dominated by the **babaçu palm,** *see* above. This occurs around the eastern fringes of Amazonia principally in Maranhão and Pará.

Liana forest, which is an open type of forest with an exceptional abundance of lianas. The largest area of liana forest occurs between the Xingu and Tapajós rivers in Pará State, Brazil. Liana forest occurs mainly on geologically ancient terrain with a somewhat elevated altitude with rich mineral deposits such as iron, aluminium, manganese and nickel. It is abundant near the Carajás iron mines. The trees in this forest are species that also occur in the terra firme rainforests, such as the **Brazil nut**, the **copal** or **jutaí** and the **tatajuba**.

Bamboo forest is an open transition forest which occurs in large areas in Amazonian Peru, Acre State, Brazil and Bolivia. Species of bamboo in the genus *Bambusa* and *Merostachys* are abundant in the under-story and even up to the canopy where they spread over the crowns of the trees. Some of the bamboos have large thorns that make this forest hard to penetrate.

Dry forest occurs mainly in southeast Amazonia where there is a long dry season and consequently the trees are semi-deciduous.

Vegetation on White Sand

With the Amazon region there are various areas where the soil is a bleached white quartz sand (podzols). This is commonest north of the Amazon river especially in Venezuela, the Guianas and the basin of the Rio Negro in Brazil. This nutrient-deficient soil supports a distinctive vegetation which varies from areas of open savannah to a low closed forest. In contrast to forest on clay soils there are fewer species and a tendency towards dominance of one or a few species. In some areas there are endemic species. In the Guianas, white sand forests are dominated by *Eperua falcata* and is known as Wallaba forest. In western Amazonian Brazil, white sand forest is known locally as *caatinga*. This is a somewhat confusing terminology since the semi-desert region of northeast Brazil, which is a completely different type of vegetation, is also called *caatinga*. A better term for the Amazonia white sand forest is **campina forest**. The largest area of this formation occurs in the region between the Rio Negro and the Rio Branco of northern Brazil. Many small patches of campina occur elsewhere where former river beaches have become elevated. The campinas of the lower Rio Negro around Manaus are dominated by **mucucú** (*Aldina heterophylla*), a legume, or by **umirí** (*Humiria balsamifera*) or **casa doce** (which means 'sweet bark') (*Glycoxylon inophyllum*). The trees are gnarled and twisted and loaded with large numbers of **epiphytic orchids**, Araceae, gesneriads, ferns and Peperomias. In the lower Rio Negro the campina is lower and poorer in species and open areas may occur. Many of the open areas contain pottery shards and beads in the soil indicating that they were cleared by former indigenous inhabitants. These remnants have been dated to 1200 AD to the Guarito culture. The understory vegetation of the campina forest of the upper Rio Negro is extremely rich and contains many endemic species in such families as the ***Bromeliaceae*** (pineapple family), ***Marantaceae*** (the prayer-plant family) and ***Rapateaceae*** (rapatea family).

orchid of the Cattleya genus

Montane Formations

Montane forests, as the name indicates, are the forest formations that occur on higher ground, generally at altitudes above 700m. The lowland Amazon basin is surrounded to the north, west and south by higher ground which forms a C around it. The montane vegetation can either be forest or more open formations. Humidity increases with altitude and at higher levels there is much mist and cloud, so mountain forests have a large number of mosses, lichens, and ferns which form carpets over rocks and cover the trunks and branches of the trees. There is a great variety of vegetation around the periphery of Amazonia and some of the main ones are given below.

The Tepuis

Tepui is the Venezuelan term for the sandstone table mountains that dominate the Guayana Highland region. The easternmost tepui is Tafelberg in Suriname; they extend through Guyana and Venezuela into Amazonian Colombia. Two occur further south in Brazil, Araca and Tepequem, and two are on the Venezuela-Brazil border: Mount Roraima and, the highest of all, Pico do Neblina (3,014m). The lower slopes of the tepuis are forested and the summits are either forested or open scrubland, depending on height and rock formations. On Neblina the tree line is at about 2,600m altitude; above that it is open vegetation. The tepuis are of special interest botanically because of their long isolation from each other which has enabled the evolution of many endemic species. There are several genera of plants with a different species on each tepui where they occur. An example is the **South American pitcher plant** genus

Heliamphora where the five species of this carnivorous plant occur on different tepuis. One genus, named Tepuianthus after its habitat, is so distinct that it is classed in a separate family and, again, several of the species are confined to a single or only a few of these table mountains. One of the most interesting of all Guayana endemics must be *Saccifolium bandeirae* which only occurs on the summit of Pico de Neblina and has folded-over pouch-like leaves.

Inselbergs

This term is given to high granite outcrops that occur in scattered locations throughout the Guianas and Amazonia. Since the different outcrops are widely separated geographically they too have many endemic species. As a rock outcrop can be a very dry place many of the plants have adaptations to withstand drought. Cacti and orchids such as *Cyrtopodium anderson* with large pseudobulbs to store water, are common on inselbergs. Depressions in the rocks form pools in the rainy season: these contain many ephemeral plants that reproduce rapidly during the rains and lie dormant as seeds during the drought. Many members of the **pipewort** family (*Eriocaulaceae*), and the **carnivorous bladderworts** (*Utricularia*) exhibit this form of growth.

The Andes

Where the natural vegetation remains as you progress from the lowlands up the Andes, there is a gradual transition from **lower montane forest**, at between 700 and 1,000m, to **upper montane forest**, which is often called **cloud forest** because of the extreme humidity. The tree line is at 3,200 to 3,500m on the Andean slopes. Above this more open grassland occurs. In the northern Andes in Venezuela and Colombia this is called *páramo* and is dominated by the spectacular **frailejon**, the genus *Espeletia* in the daisy family. Further south in Peru, beyond the range of *Espeletia*, the alpine formation is called **puna**. It is there that the largest of all bromeliads occurs, *Puya raimondii*. The flowering stalks extend to 10m tall, but they are only produced after the plant is 80–150 years old. It flowers once, producing about 8,000 flowers on branches which act as perches for the pollinating birds, and then it dies. These plants are often grubbed up by spectacled bears (*see* p.42) who feed on the soft tissue at the leaf bases.

The montane forests have a quite different floristic composition from the lowland ones. Plant families that are rarely represented in the lowlands include the **heathers** (*Ericaceae*), *Cunoniaceae*, *Cyrillaceae*, *Winteraceae* and the cone-bearing *Podocarpaceae*.

Amazonian Savannahs

Not all of the Amazon region is closed forest. Several large tracts and many small patches of open grassland savannah occur. There are both flooded and terra firme savannahs. The principal flooded savannahs occur on the eastern half of Marajó Island and in the Brazilian state of Amapá. These savannahs are dominated by **sedges** (*Cyperaceae*) rather than grasses.

The three largest areas of upland grass-dominated savannah are the llanos of Colombia and Venezuela, the Roraima-Rupunami savannah covering the frontier area between Brazil and Guyana and the cerrado of the plateau of central Brazil to the south of Amazonia.

Savannahs differ from forest in that they are fire-adapted ecosystems where regular fires help to maintain rather than destroy the vegetation. In the cerrado and the savannahs of Venezuela there are many plants with large subterranean trunks or xylopodia. Only the tips of the branches shoot above ground and produce flowers and fruit. When fire burns them off the rest of the plant survives underground to resprout. Many savannah trees have thick corky bark which protects them from fire. Some plant species are restricted to one savannah, others are widespread throughout South American tropical savannahhs.

Some Common Savannah Species

Caimbé (*Curatella americana*)

This is called the sandpaper tree because the leaves are full of sand grains and are much used to scour pots. This gnarled, thick-barked tree is found in almost all savannahs.

Murici (*Byrsonima crassifolia*)

This tree has yellow flowers and small round fruit that are often used in local ice creams. It is also cultivated as an ornamental plant.

Mangabeira (*Hancornia speciosa*)

A member of the dogbane family (*Apocynaceae*) and the fruits are also used in jams and ice creams. The bark is the source of mangabeira rubber.

Secondary Forest

Unfortunately, because of deforestation of the original forest, secondary forest has become a much more common type of vegetation throughout Amazonia. Left to its own devices, an area that has been cleared will soon begin to regenerate with fast-growing, short-lived species that were originally adapted to colonize natural clearings following tree falls, landslides and storm damage. The most characteristic genus of secondary forest, whether on terra firme or beside rivers, is **Cecropia**. The various species of *Cecropia* have large deeply divided palmate leaves which are often pale-coloured beneath. The trunk and branches are usually light-coloured and are hollow. They are inhabited by Azteca ants which feed on food bodies produced on pads at the base of the leaf stalk. These food bodies are rich in glycogen. The ants protect the plant from other leaf-eaters and also from the growth of vines, the tips of which they nip off. One large animal, the sloth, is impervious to the ants and uses cecropia leaves as its principal source of food. Another common genus of secondary forest is *Vismia*, the sealing-wax plant. The trunk contains a red latex that resembles sealing-wax. The petals of Vismia are covered with small glandular dots.

Ducamilla (*Trema micrantha*)

This member of the elm family turns up in most secondary forests. It is used as a source of bark cloth in Mexico. The seeds of all three of these secondary forest genera are small and are carried by bats or birds that eat the fruit and excrete the seeds as they fly over open areas. Rapid and efficient seed dispersal is an essential property for colonizer species to survive.

The Pantanal

To the southeast of the Amazon on the borders between Brazil, Bolivia and Paraguay, lies the largest tropical wetland in the world, **the Pantanal** (Pântano means a swamp or marsh in

Portuguese). The Pantanal covers an area of approximately 100,000 square kilometres in the basin of the Paraguay River. The area is flat and undulating and most of it lies at only 100m above sea level. Although some areas are permanently waterlogged, much of the Pantanal is flooded only during the crest of the Paraguay River. Because this drains out only slowly there is a prolonged flood season. A plan to straighten out the river and join it to the Amazon river system to make the so-called Hidrovia, is a real threat to the existence of the Pantanal ecosystem. There is also much high ground on terra firme within the Pantanal region.

The Pantanal consists of sedimentary deposits of relatively recent origin and as a result the vegetation incorporates elements of each of the major nearby vegetation types. The vegetation has been classified as a mosaic because it is a mixture of elements from the Amazon region (mainly in the riverside forests and the aquatic habitats), the cerrado of Central Brazil and the dry Chacó vegetation of Argentina and Paraguay. As a result of its recent origin the Pantanal does not have many endemic species of plants. There are four principal types of vegetation within the Pantanal ecosystem.

Cerrado

Many areas of typical cerrado occur especially in the eastern part of the Pantanal. The Pantanal cerrado is dominated by species such as the legume *Bowdichia virgiloides*, the **cerrado pequi** (*Caryocar brasiliense*), the **sand-paper tree** (*Curatella americana*) and *Qualea parviflora* in the Vochysiaceae family. Cerrado occurs mainly on the non-flooded upland, but in some areas it may be inundated for short periods at the height of the flood season. Within this wetter cerrado there are numerous islands of cerradão, or dense savannah forest, on any area that is slightly elevated above the flood level. Some of these areas have been raised up by the activity of termites.

Semi-deciduous Forest

This taller and denser forest occurs on higher ground, especially on slopes and also in elevated non-flooded forest islands within the cerrado areas. The species composition is a mixture of elements from the Chaco and the Amazonian transition region. For example: from Amazonia, the **jutaí** (*Hymenaea courbaril*), the source of copal resin; from the Chaco the **monkey-ear plant** (*Enterolobium contortisiliquam*). The latter tree is easily recognized by its well-named curled seed pods. One of the commonest trees in this forest type is another legume *Acosmium cardenasii Irwin* and *Arroyo*. Two members of the **sumac** family are common; the **aroeira** (*Astronium fraxinifolium*), an important source of timber, and the **yellow mombin** (*Spondias lutea*) with a popular edible fruit.

Swamp

The swampland of the Pantanal varies from woody varzea-like riverine forest to open lakes with floating aquatics in the permanently water-logged areas. Different areas of the swamp are dominated by different species of plants. There are large areas dominated by the papyrus-like **sedge** (*Cyperus giganteus*) and others dominated by *Thalia geniculata* in the Marantaceae family. Other areas are dominated by the **reed mace** (*Typha dominguensis*). Floating aquatics include the **water hyacinth** (*Eichhornia crassipes*) and its relative *Pontederia cordata*, the **water fern** (*Salvinia auriculata*, and *Ceratopteris pteridoides*), and a member of the **willow-herb** family (*Ludwigia sedoides*).

Xeric (dry) vegetation

On the terra firme within the Pantanal there are patches of very dry areas dominated by plants from the Chaco such as the **cacti** *Cereus peruvianus*, *Opuntia stenarthra* and *Pereskia saccharosa*. A most distinctive tree is the **pot-bellied chorisia** in the Bombacaceae or kapok family. The swollen trunk, like that of the African baobab, serves to store water during the season of drought.

Some Common Pantanal Trees

Cambará (*Vochysia divergens*)

This yellow-flowered tree is characteristic of lightly flooded areas and often grows in large clusters called cambarazals. The flowers have nectar spurs. This is also an Amazonian species.

Paratudo (*Tabebuia aurea*)

This member of the trumpet creeper family Bignoniaceae flowers in a leafless condition and gives a beautiful display of yellow. It is also a cerrado plant. It is so popular in folk-medicine that its local names translates as 'for-everything'.

Canjiqueira (*Byrsonima orbignyana*)

This member of the genus *Byrsonima* is a small tree of up to 5m with yellow flowers. It frequently dominates flooded areas to make a formation locally called a *canjiqueirae*. The ranchers hate this species because it invades cattle-pasture.

Caranda (*Copernicia alba*)

An attractive fan-leaved palm that is characteristic of lightly flooded areas and also is common in the Chaco region. It is a close relative of the carnauba wax palm of northeastern Brazil.

Acuri (*Attalea phalerata*)

This is a common palm of the terra firme and lightly flooded areas of the Pantanal. It often forms pure stands (acurizals). The hard woody fruit is the main food of the rare hyacinth macaw and is also an important food for peccaries and agoutis.

Bocaiúva (*Acrocomia aculeata*)

This palm differs from those above by its very spiny trunk leaves and spathe. It is common in non-flooded areas. This is a widely distributed species also occurring in Colombia, Venezuela and eastern Brazil, but rare in Amazonia. The fruit is also an important food for macaws.

About the Author

Professor Sir Ghillean Prance FRS, VMH was Director of the Royal Botanic Gardens, Kew from 1988 to 1999. He is currently Scientific Director of the Eden Project in Cornwall and a Visiting Professor at the University of Reading. He has conducted numerous botanical expeditions and tours to the Amazon region and the Pantanal and has collected over 350 new species of plants. He is the author of 17 books and over 400 scientific and general articles, mostly about the Amazon region and its flora. In 1993 he was awarded the International Cosmos Prize for his work on Amazon conservation.

Health in the Amazon

by Jane Wilson-Howarth

Preparations

Visit a travel clinic or family doctor for your immunizations at least six weeks before travel (in Britain, call ✆ 01276 685040 for the nearest British Airways travel clinic). Recommended vaccines for all visitors to the Amazon region are presently **yellow fever, tetanus, typhoid** and **hepatitis A**. Immunization against diphtheria, TB, hepatitis B, rabies and meningitis are also often suggested, especially for those going to remote locations. Yellow fever is making a comeback in parts of Bolivia near Amboro and also in Roraima, Brazil and it is sensible to be immunized against this very serious and untreatable viral infection. Brazilian authorities won't let you in overland unless you have a valid **vaccination certificate**. Many travel clinics as well as Nomad stores for travellers (✆ 020 8889 7014) sell repellents, bednets, etc.

Once you are properly immunized, realise that it is **accidents that are most likely to harm**; play safe and remember that few people experience significant medical problems abroad and of these few, a tiny minority succumb to tropical infections or creatures. This chapter rather over-emphasises exotic infections and scary animals, because it is these low-risk topics that seem to interest many travellers.

Malaria (*Plasmodium vivax* and *Plasmodium falciparum*) is a problem in much of the region but recommended prophylactics vary according to the exact destination; seek up-to-date advice on the best tablets to take. For recorded information in the UK on prophylaxis, call ✆ 0891 600 350. If mefloquine (*Lariam*) is recommended (this probably provides the best protection) start taking it 2–3 weeks before departure to check that it suits you. It is always wise to protect yourself from insect and tick bites by wearing long loose clothes and applying a DEET-based insect repellent to exposed skin. Those not staying in screened air-conditioned rooms should sleep under a permethrin-impregnated bednet or hammock with inherent mosquito-net, which are available at most medium-sized ports.

Sun protection is also important. The incidence of skin cancer is rocketing amongst Caucasians because more people are exposing their skins to strong sunlight radiation. Don't allow yourself to get sunburned. Finally, the Amazon can get quite **cold** when winds blow off the Andes and a speed-boat journey in the rain gets very cold so take a waterproof.

Diarrhoea

A common health problem in the region is gastro-intestinal unease, and the chances of a bout of travellers' diarrhoea are probably greatest while you are in centres of population. International city hotels can be the source of Montezuma's Revenge and, if your digestive system is prone to upsets, it is best to stick to the **'peel it, boil it, cook it or forget it'** rule. Most travellers' diarrhoea comes from food being handled unhygienically, rather than from unsafe water. If struck by gastroenteritis, it is dehydration that makes you feel really bad; wise travellers pack oral rehydration sachets (such as Electrolade), and take two large glasses of this (or any clear, non-alcoholic fluid) each time the bowels are moved. Keep drinking and you should come to no harm, whatever the cause of the diarrhoea. Signs implying you need medical help (or reference to a medical guide) are fever, blood in the stools or severe abdominal pain that is not relieved by opening the bowels or passing wind.

There is a good range of unpleasant arthropod-borne diseases in Amazonia, and it is therefore sensible to prevent bites in the first place. Wear long, loose clothes, apply an effective insect repellent to exposed skin, sleep in a mosquito-free environment (a tent with a built-in net sprayed with insecticide, or in an air-conditioned room or under an impregnated bednet). **Malaria**-carrying mosquitoes are mostly active from dusk until dawn. The mosquitoes that spread **dengue** and **yellow fevers** are day-active and bite from dawn until dusk, so that at dusk both the night- and the day-shifts are on duty and they're hungry. **Dengue fever** is a big problem; it is a serious infection with no real cure so bite prevention is all-important. Another biter, the sandfly, is most active at twilight but bites throughout the night. Small enough to penetrate mosquito nets, they will not get through a permethrin-impregnated bednet. They can spread a nasty disease called **leishmania** (*espundia*) that starts as a painless ulcer that won't heal and, if left untreated, can lead to a leprosy-like condition. It is treatable but best avoided. **Chagas' disease** is a parasitic infection that is talked about a great deal, but the chances of a traveller catching it are small. It has been almost completely eradicated from Brazil, but continues to be a problem of extreme poverty in Venezuela, Peru and Bolivia. It is transmitted by large cone-nosed bugs that also go under the name of **assassin** or **kissing bugs**. They live in the roofs and walls of adobe huts. Bites are painful but are avoided by sleeping off the ground, tucked into an impregnated bednet or enclosed hammock. The **macaw** or **warble-fly** (*Dermatobia humanis*) lay eggs on mosquitoes so that when she takes her blood meal, the fly larva can penetrate the victim's skin via the bite-hole. The larva then grows over 2–3 months until it measures 2cm, when its host can feel it moving about. They can be removed surgically.

Skin infections are common in hot humid environments; so even slight scratches or insect bites should be cleaned and kept covered. Skin goes rotten very fast and fungal infections are common so shower frequently and wear 100% cotton clothes. Itchiness, flaking or soreness in the groin or between the toes should respond to an antifungal cream such as Canesten (*clotri-mazole*), or Whitfield's Ointment (compound benzoic acid ointment) or crystal violet. A fine pimply rash on the trunk is likely to be heat rash; cool showers, dabbing (not rubbing) dry and talc will help. Slowing down, wearing only loose 100% cotton clothes and sleeping naked under a fan or in an air-conditioned room reduce the problem.

There are a few Amazonian skin-specials. G**eography worm** (*cutaneous larva migrans*) is acquired if your skin comes in contact with a ground contaminated with doggie doo. The infestation is harmless but the flaky, intensely itchy track that slowly moves under your skin is something you'll want to be rid of. Doctors can freeze the head of the dog hookworm (decide which is the leading end) with some wart treatments, or you can apply thiabendazole cream or crush thiabendazole tablets, mix with aqueous cream and apply under a waterproof dressing. Thiabendazole cream is widely available in Brazil but may be hard to find in other Amazonian countries; it is far safer that the alternative of albendazole tablets. **Chigger mites** (*chivacoa*) also cause intense itching; they climb aboard if you go pushing through vegetation. Protect yourself from these and also from **ticks** (*garrapatas*) by wearing long loose clothes, trousers tucked into socks and repellent on any exposed skin. Ticks (but not jiggers) carry a range of nasty infections including **Rocky Mountain spotted fever**, so if you discover a tick (and they often settle down to dine on the scrotum, armpit or wherever clothes become tight) pull it off promptly by grasping the tick between finger and thumb as close as possible to your skin, pinch and pull away at right angles to the skin without jerking or twisting. This hurts because the tick has cemented its mouth parts to you, but the whole animal should come away intact. The wound should be doused in spirit alcohol (*pisco*, whisky, etc.) and dressed. See the doctor if an illness with fever or an area of redness spreading around the bite-site follows. **Jiggers** (*niguas*, *bicho de pe*) are fleas, collected by wandering barefoot on contaminated ground. These grow to a sore pea-sized swelling often on a toe or under a nail and are best picked out by a local expert.

Animal Hazards on Land

Most people fear snakes yet the venomous creatures that kill most people worldwide are the **wasps** and **bees**, through allergic reactions to stings. If you are allergic to wasp, bee or fire ant stings, be sure to travel with injectable adrenaline (*epinephrine*) or an Epipen.

Spiders

Cold compresses or applying ice is sufficient treatment for most spider bites. The very few spiders that are dangerous either dispense (by biting) nerve poisons (*Lactrodectus, Phoneutria*) or toxins that kill an area of skin (*Loxosceles, Lycosa*). Some of the large hairy spiders flick off their body hairs; these cause itching and are particularly unpleasant if they go into the eyes. **Brown recluses** or **fiddle spiders** (*Loxosceles*) are long-legged, brownish and have a violin-like mark on the back of many species. Bites cause localized death of skin tissue and underlying structures. There are occasional fatalities. Men have been bitten on the genitals while sitting on outdoor toilets: check before you sit. Antivenom is made in Peru, Brazil and Argentina. **Wolf spider** (*Lycosa rartoria* and *L. pampeana*) bites can result in a scar up to 20cm long. There is antivenom in Brazil. **Widows** (*Lactrodectus*), small black or blackish-brown spiders with a red hour-glass shaped design on their backs, have a bad reputation although deaths are unusual. Bites cause pain at the bite site that spreads up the limb, then to muscles which suffer cramps and spasms. Hot baths help the pain if antivenom can't be found. Deaths are rare but occur occasionally in small children, the elderly or those with long-standing heart or lung disease. Antivenom is made in the USA and South America. [Huntsman wandering] or **banana spiders** (*Phoneutria*) are large, with 4cm bodies and 13cm leg-spans. Their bites cause intense pain, sweating and cramps, but recovery is usually complete in 12 hours. Deaths are unusual and occur in children and weak adults. Antivenom is made in Brazil. Most **scorpion** stings will be painful for a few hours, but there are dangerous species locally: *Tityus trinitatis* in Venezula; *Tityus bahiensis* in Brazil. Treat them with respect and wear proper shoes if wandering about in the forest after dark (scorpions are nocturnal). Antivenom is manufactured in Brazil.

Snakes

In South America about 2,000 deaths a year are blamed on snakes and the pit viper *Bothops atrox* is responsible for about one third of these; this is known as the *barba amerilla* (yellow beard) or *mapanare* or, erroneously, as the *fer-de-lance* (the true fer-de-lance is restricted to the island of Martinique). It is a common snake, well-camouflaged, and grows to a length of about 2m (6ft 6in). The remainder of the death toll is due to other *Bothops* species, a **rattlesnake** (*Crotalus durissus*) and **coral snakes** (*Micrurus*). Although highly venomous, coral snakes have such small mouths that it is most unusual for them to manage to bite people (unless offered an ear lobe or a finger-web). The **bushmaster**, *Lachesis muta*, a pit viper with a fearsome reputation that can grow over 3m (10ft) long, is rarely seen; it is known as *mapapire ananas* (pineapple snake) because of its rough scales. Deaths following snakebites tend to be amongst people—mostly locals—who are bitten far from medical help; antivenoms are available and effective. **First aid after a snake bite** is to stay calm and immobile and apply a crêpe bandage (not a tourniquet) to the bitten limb. Then evacuate to a hospital where medical experts can administer antivenom (*suero antiofidico*). Suction devices and cutting into the bite does more harm than good. Protect yourself from bites by wearing long loose clothes, stout shoes, and trousers tucked into socks. And retiring under a bednet keeps out more than mosquitoes.

Vampire Bats

Beware of sleeping out: you might get bitten, and bat bites carry a significant risk of rabies. After any bite by a mammal (be it vampire or village dog), scrub with soap under running water for five minutes and then flood the wound with spirit (*pisco*, gin, etc.), and then seek medical help for anti-rabies and tetanus injections.

Hazards in the Water

The biggest risk from swimming or bathing in open waters is from drowning, although there are some exotic hazards to keep in mind. Wearing old plimsolls, sneakers or jellies on the beach or riverside will help protect from **geography worm, hookworm, jiggers,** from cuts and from smaller noxious animals. **River stingrays** lash out with their venom-laced tail. Treatment, as for any fish envenoming, is to immerse the affected limb in hot water until the pain subsides, then seek medical attention. **Piranhas** are not a real hazard unless you happen to plunge into a river just downstream of an abattoir and find yourself in the centre of a feeding frenzy. The **candiru** catfish *Vandella cirrhosa* undoubtedly exists, but there is a dearth of properly documented cases of them parasitizing people: I would place them in the category of travellers' tales to scare the naïve. **Electric eel**-like fish (*Electrophorus electricus*) of Brazil, Colombia and Peru are fairly common, shallow freshwater fish. This is probably the only electric fish worldwide capable of killing a man on contact (although they rarely do), and reportedly horses attempting to cross streams have been knocked unconscious at a distance of 7m. They are not aggressive and do not attack, but will shock and stun you if approached. Take advice on where to swim; locals will know where they are a danger. People pull **caiman** out of rivers for fun and the animal—not unreasonably—protests. Crocodilians don't brush their teeth so bites go septic. Animal bites of all kinds require vigorous first aid (*see* above under vampires) and proper medical treatment. There are a few areas of freshwater in north-eastern Brazil, the Guianas and Venezuela that harbour **bilharzia**, *Schistosoma mansoni*. The parasites need at least 10 minutes to get in through your skin, causing **swimmer's itch**. They usually settle down to cause a feverish illness that should take you to the doctor.

Post-trip medical screening is of little value in travellers who feel well, unless there is a chance of bilharzia infection. If travellers have exposed themselves to this parasite, there is a blood test that should be done more than six weeks after last possible exposure. Those who have a skin-sore that refuses to heal over a period of a month or more could have **leishmaniasis** and should consult a doctor. Anyone who has symptoms of anything after a trip should also consult their doctor.

About the Author

*Dr Jane Wilson-Howarth is a zoologist and medical practitioner who has spent 11 years working on health projects in the tropics. She is author of Cadogan's **Bugs, Bites and Bowels** the definitive guide to travel health that even covers do-it-yourself remedies for evicting flesh maggots.*

History and People of the Amazon Basin

Long ago there was a great war between our ancestors in which many thousands were killed. The great Father God appeared to the losers and asked them to leave their homeland. 'There is a paradise waiting for you', He promised them, 'a land empty of people, where you will have to work little, where the water is clean and fresh and fruit and animals are abundant. It is My country, and you will look after it for Me whilst I am not walking there.' So these chosen people left their homeland and journeyed far until they reached a great forest, full of rivers and trees laden with fruit. 'This is Father God's land,' they said. 'This is the land we were promised. We will live here and look after it for Him whilst He is not here.

As told to the authors by Tucano Indians in São Domingo do Alto Tiquié

The story of the early Amazon is inextricably connected with the pre-Columbian history of the Americas, whose mystery seems only to be deepening with time. Indian artefacts are made from perishable materials like palm and reed, and only a few isolated fragments—spear- and arrowheads, charcoal and fossilized footprints—remain to archaeologists working to transpose the Amazon's clues into a historical story.

The Clovis People: Chasing Elephants Across the Prairie

Until the last few years, opinion had changed little since 1949 when Willard Libby and his associates invented radiocarbon dating. It seemed that none of the sites found in the Americas contained artefacts that dated back further than 11,200 years and archaeologists were of the opinion that these were left behind by Siberian nomads who came to be known as the Clovis, after the distinctively bi-facially worked flint spear and arrow heads first found near Clovis, New Mexico. Archaeological remains showed that the Clovis people were hunter-gatherers who followed the migrations of herds of giant woolly elephants (mammoths and mastodons), horses and camels over North America from the Yukon to Panama. The Clovis gradually settled and spread to the Pacific coast and north to the Arctic, becoming the ancestors of the North American indians and the Inuit. They also came to be considered the donor culture for South America.

The Clovis model tied in nicely with evidence from other sciences. Geologists had long known that Northern Canada was covered in a great ice sheet 100,000 years ago that began to melt in about 11,000 BC, exposing a land bridge at the Bering Straits between the Asian and American continents. The model was widely accepted until the early 1980s, when fresh anthropological, genetic and linguistic analyses suggested that the Beringia migration had occurred in three stages. The first wave of Siberian migrants, who crossed about 11,200 years ago, entering the Yukon and migrating south through the great plains east of the Rockies, became the Clovis. (The second and third waves crossed many thousands of years later: the first group, who migrated southwest of the Rockies and settled on the North American Pacific coast, were ancestors of the Pacific Coast Indians, while the second populated the Arctic, making the Inuit the most recently arrived native Americans.)

Controversy from Brazil

In the 1990s, Brazilian and North American anthropologists working in the Amazon began seriously to question the accepted Clovis model. Walter Neves at the University of São Paulo noted that American Indians have far too great a degree of physiological diversity to be descended only from the Clovis. In 1992, a Brazilian team led by Anna Roosevelt, granddaughter of Teddy, unearthed evidence for a sedentary Amazon civilization, based in caves at Monte Alegre, near Santarém in Brazil. These 'Pedra Pintada' Indians had been living off the rainforest about 11,000 years ago, making them roughly contemporary with the North American Clovis. But the Pedra Pintada were very different; even at this early stage, they lived more like the Indians who met the first conquistadors, foraging in the forest, making use of a wide variety of plants and animals, manufacturing rock tools and crafting triangular, and distinctly un-Clovis spear points. Fastidious carbon-dating has shown that they were also the first artists in the western hemisphere (the Pedra Pintada caves are called so because of their painted walls). In 1997, the year when Roosevelt's results were published, discoveries at Monte Verde, a peat bog in southern Chile, presented further problems for the Clovis model. Chunks of mastodon meat, fossilized footprints, charcoal and bits of llama bone dated back more than 12,500 years— 1,300 years before the Clovis were meant to have arrived in the New World. Findings at 30 sites in Ecuador and Peru in 1999 were equally surprising, suggesting that these coastal communities were trading with Central America, cultivating gourds, squash and maize, and fishing off-shore at a time contemporary with Clovis.

The polite world of paleoarchaeology split into two camps: the traditionalists, who dismissed the dates as the products of poor analysis; and the new guard, who bridled at suggestions that their scrupulous research was unscientific. A bloody battle began in Santa Fe in late 1999. The new guard were spurred on by surprise reinforcements: suppressed researchers spoke quite openly of 40,000-year-old flakes of mammoth bone, of ignored flints from a pre-Clovis age and even of articles and requests for research grants rejected by 'the Clovis mafia'.

Since the conference, our understanding of the first Americans has continued to broaden, and a picture is emerging of a sophisticated and varied group who made the Americas a genetic melting pot long before the founding of Rio de Janeiro or São Paulo. These were skilled artisans and navigators who arrived from several directions: across Beringia and other Pacific land bridges and by boat, perhaps across both oceans. It has even been suggested that the Clovis were influenced by the Spanish Solutrean culture: Iberia and not Siberia.

The Incas were from the Amazon

> *Charcoal is believed to underlie three quarters of the Amazon. Some scientists believe that this is the product of man...the implications are astonishing. Not only might much of the Amazon rainforest, patch by garden patch, have been burnt down by the Indians who live there, but those Indians appear to have preserved, possibly even enhanced, the natural systems' diversity.'*

George Monbiot, *Amazon Watershed*

Theories about the various South American civilizations before the arrival of the conquistadors are only a little less controversial than those about the first Americans. Before the 1970s, it was presumed that the Amazon peoples were primitive Stone Age communities, lost in a cultural backwater when compared to their illustrious Andean cousins. Only the findings of Erland Nordenskiöld, a Swedish anthropologist working in the 1930s, suggested otherwise. Nordenskiöld had spent a considerable time with the Shipibo-Konibo peoples of the Amazon in the first two decades of the century, painstakingly studying their cultural history and ceramics, and concluded that the Amazon civilizations were not only older than the Andean, but had given rise to them. But Hiram Bingham's sensational discovery of Machu Picchu in 1911, and the publication of his book *Machu Picchu, a Citadel of the Incas* in 1930, biased opinion against Nordenskiöld. His claims that the glorious Incas were descended from an unstudied tribe were not taken seriously.

In the 1960s, the American archaeologist Donald W. Lathrap came across some botanical studies that made him look again at Nordenskiöld. The botanical findings suggested that many if not all of the earliest cultivated plants to appear on the coast of Peru were first domesticated on the eastern side of the Andes within the Amazon Basin. Like his Swedish predecessor, Lathrap began work in the Shipibo lands of the Upper Ucayali river, near the eastern slopes of the Andes, finding evidence to suggest that sedentary communities producing sophisticated pottery were at least as old as they were in the central Andes, a fact that could be verified using carbon dating, invented since Nordenskiöld's time. Lathrap also demonstrated that most of the major migrations impinging on the Upper Amazon moved upstream out of the Central Amazon Basin between 2000 and 3000 BC, from a stretch of the river between Santarém and Manaus in modern Brazil.

Though he had faded somewhat from favour, Roosevelt's 1992 findings have given further credibility to Lathrap, though at a date far earlier than anything even he could have imagined. A sterile layer on the floor of the Pedra Pintada cave floor suggested that the caves had been left vacant for a period after the very earliest occupation, but ceramics found above this layer were dated by Roosevelt's team to between 7,580 and 6,625 years ago, and shards found in a shell midden near Santar, 90km to the south west, were 1,000 years older, making them the oldest so far discovered in the Americas. Earlier digs by Roosevelt and her Brazilian team have shown that the Amazon at Marajó and near Monte Alegre fostered a dynamic civilization over thousands of years. Roosevelt found burial chambers where mummified Indian bodies were surrounded by carved images, suggesting a stratified society led by venerated rulers. Analysis of their skeletons suggests that they had access to cultivated manioc, maize and grasses, presumably using agricultural techniques that all but the modern rainforest Indians like the Brazilian Kayapó and the Mexican Lacandon have to this date failed to master.

Europe Discovers the Amazon and is Given It by the Pope

> *They would make fine servants… With fifty men we could subjugate them all and make them do whatever we want*

> Christopher Columbus

The Amazon was discovered in January 1500 by a Spaniard, Vicente Yáñez Pinzón, a few months before Pero Alvares Cabral discovered Brazil and claimed it for Portugal. Both voyages presaged what was to come for the peoples of the Amazon. Pinzón, who sailed for some 100 miles up the Amazon, naming it Santa María de la Mar Dulce (St Mary of the Freshwater Sea), was the first Iberian to battle with Brazilian Indians. Cabral brought the first colonists: convicts under sentence of death who had been taken from Portugal in 1500, with the intention of leaving them somewhere to intermarry with the natives. When Cabral's fleet left, the convicts began to weep. But the Indians comforted them, displaying the trust that, together with the Portuguese and Spanish colonists' brutality and their own intertribal vendettas, was to prove their downfall.

Once discovered, the river and its people were left relatively undisturbed for nearly a century. The Portuguese were occupied elsewhere, playing various groups of feuding Indians off against each other and harvesting the Caesalpinia echinata tree, whose wood yielded a red dye known as *brasile* after the Latin word for 'red', which was later to give Brazil its name. The Spanish had been given the right to claim and occupy all heathen lands to the east of the line of Tordesillas—a swathe that included the Amazon—by Pope Alexander VI, who considered them the property of God, and therefore of Christian peoples. But, like the Portuguese, they were too busy elsewhere, fighting the Aztecs and Incas and settling the Caribbean and Panama. The only Europeans to venture along the Amazon either ended up there by accident or were driven there by an obsessive desire for gold. All were mercilessly cruel to the Indians; Ambrosio de Alfinger, a Velser merchant from the German colony of Coro in Venezuela, who travelled up the Magdalena in 1528 was typically though not exceptionally harsh. His Indians were chained together with iron halters round their necks to prevent their escape. When they tired, he beheaded them rather than wasting time breaking them free.

Orellana Stumbles on the World's Greatest River

The most historically significant of these adventurers was Francisco de Orellana who, quite by accident, became the first westerner to journey the entire length of the Amazon in 1542. Captain Orellana was recruited by Gonzalo Pizarro, the brother of the conqueror of Peru, to explore the upper reaches of the Amazon in search of gold and cinammon. Pizarro was determined to have his slice of the colonial cake, and had heard 'many reports from prominent and very aged chiefs…to the effect that the province of La Canela and Lake El Dorado were a very populous and rich land.'

Gonzalo marched out of Quito at the head of his 4,000-strong army of Spaniards and Indians. After nearly a year of random wandering, finding nothing but trees and water, most of his party were dead. But whilst his minions were literally reduced to cooking their boots, Pizarro clung on to his dream of a mountain of gold. He made camp on the bank at modern-day Coca, and determined to build a brigantine and sail downstream along the Napo. The boat-building rendered most of his remaining men so weak that they were in no fit state to continue, so Pizzaro dispatched Orellana downstream in the brigantine, together with sixty men and all of the firearms, to search for food. Orellana never returned. He was to claim that the crudely built brigantine could not sail against the current. Pizarro was not convinced, reporting that Orellana 'displayed the greatest cruelty that ever faithless men have shown'.

Whatever the truth was, Orellana and his men were seized with a desire to explore the great river, and were almost certainly glad to be rid of the cruel and tyrannical Pizarro. They were reasonably sure that by drifting down the Napo they would reach the Atlantic; the Spanish had a fair idea of the shape of South America by this time, if they had no idea of its breadth. Their only problem was food. After a week, seven of the crew had died of starvation and the rest were mad with hunger. It was at this point that they met their first Indians, a tribe of startled

Irimarai (probably modern Ticuna) who, after intitial panic, embraced the gaunt Spaniards with open arms, fed them, clothed them, helped build new boats, and unwittingly annexed their lands to Spain. In February 1542, a year after they had first left Quito, Orellana's men left the Napo and entered the main stream of the Amazon, just downstream of modern Iquitos. Encounters with other Indians were uneventful until the boat entered Machiparo territory in modern Brazil: the Indians attacked after the hungry Spanish ran amok, and the Spanish were lucky to escape with only two dead. Downstream lay the Curicarai tribe, who seem to have been part of an advanced lowland civilization. Roads radiated out from their villages, and storehouses were abundantly stocked. The Curicarai made fine glazed pottery and candelabra that the Spaniards declared to be superior to any found in Spain: 'thin and smooth, glazed and with colours shading off into one another in the style of that made in China'. Beyond were the territories of the hostile Paguana, whose larger villages stretched for about ten kilometres (six miles) along the banks of the river. On the second of June, the Spanish passed the mouth of a black river, which they called the Rio Negro, and whose name survives to this day. Further downstream they met with a tribe who had erected two giant jaguar totems in homage to their rulers: a tribe of warrior women whom the Spanish later referred to as Amazons, after the classical legend of the Amazons of Asia Minor. But news of the strangers was spreading faster than the Spaniards' boat, subsequent encounters were hostile and villages well-prepared.

Somewhere near modern Monte Alegre, perhaps close to the Caverna da Pedra Pintada, the Spanish passed beautifully constructed villages which they were sure lay in the land of the women warriors they referred to as the Amazons. Once again they were mercilessly attacked. Carvajal, the expedition's chronicler, writes of 'ten or twelve of these women, fighting there in front of all the Indian men as women captains. They fought so courageously that the Indian men did not dare turn their back. They killed anyone who did turn back, with their clubs, right there in front of us...these women are very white and tall, with very long hair braided and wound about their heads. They are very robust, and go naked with their private parts covered, and their bows and arrows in their hands, doing as much fighting as ten Indian men.'

The Spaniards battled their way through the lower Amazon, and finally emerged into the Atlantic on the 26th of August 1542, reaching the coast of Venezuela in September 1542. In 1546 Orellana returned to the Amazon to formally claim the area for himself, and for Spain, and to find and conquer El Dorado. But he found only his death.

The Bloodthirsty Mania of Lope de Aguirre

In 1549, the citizens of Chachapoyas in modern Peru were amazed at the arrival of hundreds of Tupi Indians from coastal Brazil who had fled the brutality of the Portuguese. They were taken to meet the Viceroy of Peru to whom they recounted stories of the great wealth of the Omagua tribe, seemingly confirming the El Dorado legend that had been the downfall of Gonzalo Pizarro. The Viceroy was sufficiently inspired to organize a massive war party under Don Pedro de Ursua, who set off with his mistress, Doña Inés de Atienza, myriad Inca slaves, Tupi Indian guides from the band fleeing the Portuguese and an unsavoury group of Spanish marauders in 1560. The worst of these was Lope de Aguirre, murderous even by conquistador standards and as cunning and patient as a wild animal. After a public flogging, he bore a long-standing grudge against the colonial system and was determined to replace it with a tyranny led by himself. He saw his opportunity to stage a coup using Ursua's army, enlisted and bided his time.

Even without Aguirre, the expedition would have been doomed; Ursua spent far more time dallying with Inés than he did disciplining his men. Eventually the soldiers decided to mutiny but, determined to do it correctly in the eyes of God, they appointed Fernando de Guzmán, the only member of the war party who had any pretensions to noble blood, as their leader. Aguirre was the real power behind Guzmán; he persuaded the nobleman to murder Ursua and Inés. Guzmán himself was dispatched soon afterwards, and Aguirre assumed formal command and declared himself the King of Amazonia. Anyone who disagreed was cut up and fed to the caiman.

Aguirre was determined to get back to Peru to conquer the country with Ursua's army and claim the throne. After getting lost on the Rio Negro, the party somehow arrived on Margarita Island, Venezuela, in July 1561 at a bay still known as 'The Tyrant's Port'. The island was immediately claimed as Aguirre's imperial headquarters, and a letter was dispatched to the King of Spain announcing the new ruler's intention to march on Peru. But a royalist force quickly put paid to his renegade army and Aguirre was killed.

Throughout the 1560s, conquistadors continued to tumble over the Andes in search of mythical treasure. But they got no closer to El Dorado and the supposed gold of the Omaguas, and most of them found only death for their trouble. The Amazon therefore remained undisturbed until well into the seventeenth century.

The First Colonies

> *They do nothing without deliberation, but weigh something in their judgement before giving an opinion on it. They remain quiet and reflective and are not precipitate in speaking...*
>
> 17th-century French account of Amazon Indians

> *They kill Indians as if they were animals, sparing neither age nor sex. They (kill) babies because they impede their mother's march, and old men and women for the same inconvenience of being unable to march or be useful workers. They kill them by hitting them on the head with clubs. They also kill chiefs or braves, because these inspire the rest to return to their homes.'*
>
> 17th-century description of a raid by Portuguese *bandeirantes*

Ireland, dominated and misunderstood by the English, never had the opportunity to become a European imperial power in an age when even Belgium was helping to carve up the un-Christian corners of the world. But she nearly had her chance on the Amazon. By the second decade of the 17th century, the Irish had established a fort on the northern bank of the lower Amazon and a settlement, in conjunction with the English, on the modern-day Ilha dos Porcos. Other Europeans, notably the Dutch, were settling in too, and the French were even treating the Indians humanely, as equals, inviting them to share a croissant with Louis XIII in the Louvre, giving them French brides, and writing dissertations on the noble savage that were later to inspire Rousseau.

The Portuguese colonists, who had concentrated their efforts further south, were appalled. They saw the Indians only as 'Red Gold'; and had long been sending *bandeira* slaving expeditions to the interior of Brazil to reap a cargo of human treasure. When they learned of the human riches to be found on the Amazon, they quickly dispatched an army to attack the other European strongholds. By 1615 they had conquered the French fort of St Louis and the various other settlements and established their own further upstream at Belém do Para. Their success was a disaster, particularly for the Tupinamba tribe who had been under the protectorate of the French. Even though many villages switched allegiance from France to Portugal, all were slaughtered or enslaved. Many were the children of other Tupinamba from the Brazilian coast, who had fled Portuguese slaving a century before.

The Slave Trade and the Jesuit Reductions

It is a strange irony that, whilst the Indians have been accused of laziness since the arrival of the first Portuguese colonists, those who accuse them of this laziness have long enslaved them to make them do their work. This slavery, first on the colonial plantations and later in the rubber-tapping forests, has depopulated the tribes of the Amazon more than any other single cause but disease.

Cristóbal de Acuña, a Jesuit who criss-crossed the Amazon in the 1620s, describes an incredible density of villages along the river's length. The largest tribe, the Omagua, he wrote, lived an easy life of happy abundance: farming turtles, harvesting manioc and maize, sweet potatoes and gourds, baking bread and weaving cotton into fine, intricately patterned cloth. Over the following three centuries the Omagua and all of the other tribes on the river, and those that lived on the Amazon's other tributaries, were killed, enslaved or forced to flee by Portuguese slave traders.

Since Bartolomé de las Casas had so vocally complained about the ill-treatment of Indians by the conquistadors in the 1580s, slavery had been illegal in the Iberian colonies. Several popes and all the Iberian kings had outlawed it in bulls and edicts that expounded the virtues of the Indians in glowing terms. But Europe was a long way from the colonies, and her laws were not taken seriously; nor did the European leaders completely expect them to be. When the colonists complained vociferously that the empire needed workers, the regal conscience was easily persuaded that 'just enslavement' would solve the problem. In 1611 a new law was passed stating that slaves could be taken only if they were prisoners of war. What constituted war was left to the colonists to decide.

The first settlers quickly decided that all of the tribes in the area were declaring war on them, and by the late 1620s the two forts of São Luis and Belém do Para had grown into full-scale plantation settlements, populated by the spoils of these wars. The once populous lower Amazon soon began to run out of Indians; the droves brought in to farm the plantations were kept in appalling conditions and were dying almost as quickly as they were captured. Belem and São Luis began to look for fresh human pastures, and headed further and further upstream. As the tribes of the middle Amazon were sucked into the bottomless hole of the Portuguese slave trade, the Omagua culture and others were decimated. The turtle they once farmed so lovingly is today an endangered species.

The only colonial powers that sought to abate this human traffic were the Jesuits. The society had long successfully defended Guarani and Moxo Indians against *bandeirante* raids in the Brazilian Pantanal and Bolivian Amazon by persuading thousands to leave their villages and settle in 'reductions'. These were settlements organized on European lines, where the Indians were converted, clothed, and given paid work by Jesuit priests. In the late 1650s, Antonio Vieira, still considered to be the greatest Portuguese writer since Camoes, was appointed head of the Jesuit missions on the Amazon. He hoped to rescue Indians from the Maranhao and Belém slavers as his colleagues had rescued the Pantanal Indians from the *bandeirantes*.

Vieira was appalled by what he saw, and wrote eloquently of the Indians' plight in a series of letters to King Joao IV: '...when people who are not our subjects do not wish to leave their lands this is called rebellion here. And this crime is considered worthy of punishment by war and enslavement.' His protests fell on deaf ears in Belém, but he was more successful in São Luis do Maranhão. 'What is a human soul worth to Satan?', he asked the citizens of São Luis, 'There is no market on earth where the devil can get them more cheaply than right here in our own land... What a cheap market! An Indian for a soul... Christians, nobles, people of Maranhao,' he begged, 'break the chains of injustice and free those whom you hold captive and oppressed!' He eventually persuaded Maranhão to part with her slaves and send them to Jesuit reductions, known as *aldeias* after the Portuguese word for village. In return, the Indians would be lent to the people of Maranhão for six months a year to work on the plantations.

Yet, although enlightened by the standards of their contemporaries, the Jesuits were as responsible for the loss of Indian life on the Amazon as the slavers. Their *aldeias* were breeding grounds for European disease. And, as in the plantations, the thousands that died were replaced with fresh recruits. They never became as successful as the reductions further south and were always forced to compromise with the Portuguese colonists. In 1661 Vieira's work came to an abrupt end when an infuriated mob ransacked the Jesuit college in Belém and succeeded in having the priests expelled from both Pará and Maranhão. Though they were later to return, the Jesuits would never again have the same influence in South America. The powerful reductions in Bolivia, the Pantanal and Paraguay were to go the same way less than a hundred years later. The governor of Portugal, the Marquis de Pombal, began a campaign that eventually led to them being expelled from Portuguese Brazil in 1757, and all the Iberian colonies ten years later.

After this, legislation was introduced by Pombal and his half-brother, the Maranhao governor Mendonça Furtado, proclaiming the Indians free and slavery illegal. But the directorate system that replaced the Jesuit *aldeias* was the administrative equivalent of putting a fox in charge of a hen coop. Soon there were so few Indians left to enslave on the Amazon that the Portuguese had to find a new continent to terrorize, and began to ship in Africans from Guinea Bissau. When this fresh batch of African Red Gold intermarried with the underclass of Portuguese Indian mixed-bloods (who were more often than not the children of rape) they began to form the *caboclo* people who populate the Amazon today (*see* p.230).

The Early Scientists: La Condamine and Humboldt

It wasn't until the age of enlightenment in the late 18th century that Europeans began to come the Amazon to study rather than ravage. Among the first was the Frenchman Charles-Marie de la Condamine, who came to Andean Equator in the mid-1700s to test Newton's theory that the Earth was shaped like a squashed orange. But colonial Ecuador was still a long way from the Age of Reason; the colonial population refused to believe that anyone would travel halfway round the world to measure its shape and suspected the party were in reality after gold. An angry mob attacked the scientists, murdered La Condamine's colleague Senièrgues and stoned the rest of the party in the streets of Cuenca. La Condamine decided to return to France, this time via the forest and Cayenne. He was enchanted by the Amazon and wrote detailed descriptions of the terrain, produced the first accurate map and was shown a tree by Oamagua Indians that secreted milky resin that hardened and darkened in contact with air. He took some of the resin back to Europe where it became known as rubber.

La Condamine's writings inspired other scientists to follow him. The first to do so was Baron Alexander von Humboldt, who is today best known for the Humboldt Current, which he did not discover, and the Humboldt River, which he never saw. His contemporaries, however, referred to him as 'the greatest man in the world'. He was a master of all branches of science, a polylinguist, mountaineer, explorer and humanitarian, who spent five difficult and hazardous years on the Orinoco and Upper Rio Negro from 1799. He was as indestructible as Captain Scarlet and as German as Kant. He ate everything from rubber sap to *curare* (the poison the Indians use to tip their arrows), received 300-volt shocks from electric eels whilst calmly taking notes, captured and dissected 20-foot-long caiman, and was the first European to describe and bathe with piranhas. He confirmed the existence of the Casiquiare canal, produced the region's first accurate maps, and brought back some 12,000 plant and animal specimens, establishing the region once and for all as the pre-eminent area in the world for the study of the natural sciences. It is entirely thanks to Humboldt that the great British naturalists Darwin and Wallace came to South America, whose forests were to inspire them to conceive the idea of evolution by natural selection.

Naturalists on the Amazon

I'd be an Indian here, and live content
To fish and hunt, and paddle my canoe,
And see my children grow, like wild young fawns,
In health of body and peace of mind,
Rich without wealth, and happy without gold!

Alfred Russell Wallace

The early decades of the 19th century saw Spanish South America struggling to break free of Europe. Brazil became quietly independent when the imperial Portuguese court ran away from Napoleon and set up home in Rio, but the *caboclo* rebellions (*see* p.230) that followed made the Amazon unsafe for foreigners until the 1840s. After then, the region was soon crawling with British and German scientists, eager to follow in Humboldt's footsteps. News of the Amazon's natural wonders reached the heart of what was then the most powerful empire in the world. Quinine, first extracted in 1810 from the bark of the cinchona tree, was soon supplying the far corners of the British Empire, together with other pharmacologically inert tonics like sarsaparilla and angostura bitters, after being taken from the forest by Richard Spruce. Exotic plants, birds and beasts were pouring into London, filling up Kew and inspiring countless lectures at the Royal Society. Henry Bates collected an astonishing 14,712 species, of which 8,000 were new to science; Spruce brought back 7,000 plants; and the Germans Spix and Martius amassed so vast a quantity of animal corpses that it took a full generation for them to be properly catalogued. In the 1840s, two Anglo-German brothers, Richard and Robert Schomburk, discovered the crowning glory: a giant water lily with leaves two metres across, which they christened *Victoria regia*, in homage to the British queen. Many of the naturalists wrote memoirs of their adventures, of which Waterton's wanderings are the most amusing: boasting of his bare-back ride on a giant caiman, he wrote, 'Should it be asked how I managed to keep my seat, I would answer, I hunted some years with Lord Darlington's fox hounds.' But it was Alfred Russel Wallace who was the finest writer, and the most perceptive observer of Amazon life. His contribution to modernity was also the greatest: the Amazon's forests and their plants and animals inspired him to postulate a theory that has changed the way we think about the world; evolution by natural selection, just as Brazil's Atlantic forests had inspired another British naturalist, Charles Darwin, ten years previously.

Wallace, Darwin and the Story of the Theory of Evolution

Wallace was introduced to the wonders of the natural world by Henry Bates. They used to spend lazy English afternoons together collecting beetles and dissecting caddis fly. But British insects could not satisfy their curiosity for long, and in 1848 they sailed for arthropod paradise on the Amazon. The young friends separated at Manaus, and Wallace set off up the Rio Negro. Of all the 19th-century Europeans to visit South America, Wallace was perhaps the most humane. Whilst most of his contemporaries (including Darwin) were frightened or shocked by their first encounters with native Americans, Wallace was delighted and exhibited a rare sympathy with Indian culture.

The seemingly infinite variety of plants and animals soon had him musing: how had all this variety come about, so alike in design yet so changeable in detail? 'Places not more than fifty or a hundred miles apart have species of insects and birds at the one, which are not found at the other. There must be some boundary which determines the range of each species; some external peculiarity to mark the line which each one does not pass.' What Wallace did not know was that Charles Darwin had hit on the explanation for this divergence of species two years after he returned to England from South America and his voyage in the *Beagle*. The South American forests near Rio de Janeiro, and Ecuador's Galapagos Islands had had the same effect on Darwin as they had on Wallace. But it was Thomas Malthus's essay on population that provided him with the final insight. In his essay, the economist argued that the realization of a happy society will always be hindered by its tendencies to expand more quickly than its means of subsistence. If this were true also of animals, thought Darwin, then they must compete to survive, and Nature must act as a selective force, killing off the weak. Aware of the enormity of this thought, Darwin did not even commit fully to paper until 1844, six years later, after which he deposited his draft with some money and instructions to his wife to publish it after his death.

Wallace was younger and not so timid. In 1858, he was in a high fever on the small volcanic island of Ternate in Indonesia. He too recalled the book by Malthus and the same thought that had struck Darwin flashed into his own mind: 'Then I at once saw, that the ever-present variability of all living things would furnish the material from which, by the mere weeding out of those less adapted to the actual conditions, the fittest alone would survive the race.' Wallace knew Darwin was interested in the subject and wrote to him of his new theory, asking for his advice. Darwin's hand was forced and, after papers written by both scientists were read in the Linnean Society, Darwin wrote the *Origin of Species*.

The Rubber Boom

*From the Omaguas the Portuguese of Pará learned the method of
forming syringes of the same matter (rubber), and pumps which need
no sucker. These syringes are made in the shape of a pear... This when
full being suddenly pressed, the contained fluid is expelled with the
same effect as from a syringe.*

La Condamine

Rubber had been known to Europeans since the conquest of Mexico by Cortés but it was not
until La Condamine's river journeys in the 1700s that the tree that produced the finest latex,
Hevea brasiliensis, was properly identified. In 1823 Charles Macintosh developed a technique
for coating fabric with rubber to make it waterproof, and soon after Charles Goodyear discover-
ered how to harden rubber latex by vulcanisation. By the turn of the century, rubber was being
used for everything from electrical insulation to false teeth. With the invention of the bicycle
came the invention of the tyre, and in 1885 Gottlieb Daimler invented the internal combustion
engine. By 1910, over 200,000 cars were being produced in the United States, all with rubber
tyres. Production on the Brazilian Amazon rose to 44,300 tons.

All of these inventions had a dramatic effect on the cities of the Amazon Basin. Belém and
Iquitos grew in size and finery, and the muddy settlement of Barra at the confluence of the
Amazon and Río Negro became the re-christened metropolis of Manaus with its own stock
exchange, street lighting, trams and an opera house. The prosperity only made life for the
Indians even harsher. Tribes such as the Bora, Andoke and Huitoto were rounded up by militia
hired by rubber barons like Julio Aranha, and forcibly settled in labour camps. On the Putamayo
all but 8,000 of the 50,000 Indians that once lived in the region were killed; each ton of rubber
cost seven human lives. The peasants of the region fared little better. They were trapped by
their masters under the *hacienda* system of debt peonage; the *seringuero*, as the rubber-tappers
were called, was given accommodation, clothes, a gun and rubber-tapping materials by his
padrão. This was charged to his account, together with all his food and produce, which he was
required as a condition of work to buy from the company store. This debt was designed to be
just large enough to require an impossibly high daily yield to pay it off. Thus he and his family
were trapped in a slavery of debt from which they could never escape. Debts were passed on
through generations. For the indigenous and poor it was perhaps a blessing when the rubber
bubble burst. In the late 1870s Henry Wickham had smuggled seeds out of Pará to Kew
Gardens in London and, by 1914, commercial plantations of fully grown *Hevea brasiliensis* in
Sri Lanka and Malaya were yielding as much as South American wild rubber at a lower price.
The *padrões* themselves fell into debt and the rubber boom was over. In 1892 Brazil accounted
for 61per cent of the world's rubber trade; and by 1910 it represented nearly half of the
country's total export earnings. Now Brazil cannot produce even enough for its own requirements. Rubber harvesting has died in Latin America, but much of our supermarket coffee, fruit
and beans is still harvested under debt peonage.

20th Century: Environmental Issues and Human Rights for the Indians

The advent of the industrial age in the Amazon brought a whole host of new problems.
Indigenous people were usually caught in the middle; almost as many died in the 20th century
as died in all the centuries before them. Their lands often held seams of gold or oil, or stood in

the way of roads and, therefore, progress. Concern for their welfare rarely extended beyond rhetoric. And although before she had seemed invincible, the mighty Amazon herself and her forests also begun to suffer. Her rivers were filled with mercury and run-off from the oil industry, and her trees were chopped down in greater numbers than ever before. The United States and Europe were as much to blame as the Latin Americans themselves: projects to open up the interior were approved and funded by the World Bank or IMF, and blinkered multinationals wreaked havoc on the forests and her peoples.

Brazil: *Integrar para não Entregar*, Opening up the Amazon

Activity on the Amazon quietened down during the first half of the 20th century. The struggle for political power within the various South American countries was dominated by the United States, who, rightly or wrongly, were determined to prevent another Cuba, and used this as an excuse firmly to establish trade dominance. Nationalization was prevented using economic pressure (cutting credits and refusing to negotiate foreign debt) and covert financing of grassroots right-wing organizations. When US interests were threatened by a left-wing government and peasants clamoured for land reform, the US backed a military coup.

Little changed for the peasant or the Indian; the rural landowners clung on to power and, but for a brief rubber resurgence in the Second World War, the Amazon was left alone. This began to change in 1954 under President Juscelino Kubitschek; he built a new capital, Brasilia, in the middle of nowhere, and linked it to Belém with the first Amazon road. This marked the beginnings of expansion into the vast Brazilian interior. The US-installed military dictatorship that came to power via a coup in 1964 continued the process. The military planned massive relocations of the population, mostly the rural poor, to secure what they referred to as empty areas and to ease the mounting pressure for land reform. The politic rhetoric was one of progress and the protection of Brazil's national security and borders and, inspired by the slogan '*Integrar para não entregar*' (integrate to avoid annexation), landless peasants were encouraged to re-locate to the new states of Roraima and Rondônia and carve out their own property from the forests. 'The people without land' would be transferred to 'the land without people'.

In 1972, the military decided to link the Pacific and Atlantic oceans with a trans-Amazon highway with a network of filter roads off it, linking the interior with São Paulo and Minas Gerais. *Agrovilas*, purpose-built settlements, were strung out along these new roads and families were airlifted in from the north east and south of the country. A network of over a hundred hydroelectric dams was planned to provide energy. Another ambitious project, Greater Carajás, followed in 1980, when an 18 billion-ton iron-ore mountain was discovered in the Eastern Amazon, and in the early 1990s the military announced plans to build 'Calha Norte', a road cutting across the northern Amazon, through the heart of the largest untouched section of virgin rainforest in South America.

The Yanomami and Parakaná Massacres

The 'opening of the Amazon' was of little benefit to Brazil's peasants, Indians, the forest and the economic prosperity of the country as a whole. The Amazon soils they had planned to farm turned out to be so nutrient-poor that they would only sustain crops or cattle for a year or two at most before turning to desert. Farmers and ranchers ate into the forest near the new roads at a terrifying rate. Soon they had encroached on indigenous territories, inciting conflict in which the Indians invariably came off worse, or spreading western disease to which the tribes had no immunity. Not since the days of the Portuguese had the Amazon's Indians suffered so badly.

In 1990, after the discovery of gold in western Roraima, peasant farmers unable to survive on their new Amazon barren lands flooded into the territory of the largest remaining isolated tribe in the Americas, the Yanomami. Many were supported by local businessmen, who saw them as the vanguard of a new colonization and were eager for a slice of the gold-rich territory. Indian 'hunts' were common; in 1990s Boa Vista it is said that taxi drivers offered Indian safaris to visitors: bring a gun and shoot a wild Indian. Since then, at least 2,000 Yanomami have died. Many more have been deprived of their land, either through annexation by gold miners or the pollution of their rivers. Other tribes fared equally badly. The Parakanã were deliberately infected with smallpox, influenza, tuberculosis and measles by FUNAI, the government's indigenous peoples' agency, ostensibly set up to protect them. Hundreds died. Then they were forcibly moved to make way for the Transamazon highway, and then again for the Tucuruí dam. The Xavantes lost their territory to the Italian company Liquigas; the Waimiri Atroari saw part of their reserve flooded by the Balbina dam; the Nabiquara were displaced first by a dam and then the Santarém–Cuiabá road; and the Uru-Weu-Wau-Wau and the Zorro were in the way of the World Bank-funded Polonoroeste road and development project. Ticuna, Guarani and many others were murdered by loggers, gold prospectors or settlers.

Chico Mendes and the *Caboclo* Rubber Tappers

The forest's *caboclo* people suffered too. Although the forests were no longer producing rubber in the quantities they once had, rubber tappers still lived and worked in Acre, Amapa, Rondônia and Roraima, and when the cattle ranchers and their vanguard of displaced (mostly north-eastern) peasants began to invade their territories and destroy their livelihood, they set-up a resistance movement, organized by unions. A series of *empates*, or passive stand-offs in the tradition of Gandhi and Martin Luther King led by charismatic locals like Francisco 'Chico' Alves Mendes, brought the plight of the rubber tappers to the attention of the world. It did little to pacify the ranchers, who murdered rubber tappers, supported by the local police. As he had predicted, Chico Mendes himself was shot dead in 1988.

The Amazon Suffers and Brazil Goes Broke

Opening up the Amazon did little to help Brazil's economy: the new roads cost billions and many are now impassable. Many of the dams were built in valleys that were insufficiently deep and narrow for the rapid water flow required to produce cheap electricity. The Balbina dam north of Manaus, which was the personal project of President Figueiredo, the last of the military rulers of Brazil, produces electricity four times more expensive than that available on the world market. The Greater Carajás project, which the then finance minister Delfim Neto claimed would provide enough iron ore to pay off the foreign debt, in fact doubled it, and the surrounding forest was cleared for his cattle-ranching friends. Brazil's economy and the Amazon have suffered deeply through the *Integrar para não Entregar* project. Together with the rising cost of oil, opening up the Amazon has made Brazil the Third World's largest foreign debtor.

The Hispanic Republics and the Amazon in the Late 20th Century

After the collapse of the rubber boom, most of the Andean republics had the sense to leave the Amazon to its own devices, at least until the late 1960s. Then oil was discovered under the forest, bringing a host of new disasters, which hit the long-suffering Indians the hardest.

Ecuador was the worst offender, with Peru and Colombia not far behind. Bolivia's Amazon was left largely intact, except around Santa Cruz, where logging and soya plantations were eating into the forest at the fastest rate on the continent at the turn of the millennium.

Apart from the first two decades of the century, and periods of military dictatorship, Ecuador's 20th-century governments came and went with the wind; there were ministers who lasted for hours, presidents who lasted for days and dictators who lasted for weeks. The banana boom brought some prosperity in the 1950s, but the governments didn't improve. All this had little effect on the Amazon until the late 1960s, when the oil was discovered. The North American company Texaco was swift to establish a 20-year contract with the government; during the course of this they allowed an estimated 16.8 million gallons of crude oil to spill from pipelines, abandoned 1,000 uncovered oil-waste ponds and discarded 20 billion gallons of toxic waste into the environment. The construction of 300 miles of roads opened up remote regions to landless peasants and the urban poor, leading directly to two million acres of forest being cleared. Huaorani, Siona and Secoya Indian populations declined from 20,000 in each group in the 1960s to somewhere between 700 and 1,200 today. The Cofane, in whose territory the main Texaco refinery was built, diminished from 3,000 to 300, and the Tetete people, whose village at Lago Agrio was the site of the very first well, are now extinct.

The U'wa people of the Sierra Nevada de Cocuy, in the Colombian Amazon, have faced similar problems at the hands of the US oil company Occidental. Occidental's Caño Limón pipeline, which runs north of the U'wa's territory, has spilled an estimated 1.7 million barrels of crude oil into nearby rivers, and lakes since it was completed in 1986. A study of these lakes has found pollution levels equivalent to the dumping of 5.5 barrels of crude oil per day. In addition to pollution, the oil projects have led to deforestation, through clearance for oil exploration and production and road building projects which have attracted settlers.

Looking to the 21st Century

Brazil after the Yanomami Atrocities

Two events from the end of the last century forced a temporary change in Brazilian attitudes towards the Amazon: the massacre of the Yanomami and the murder of Chico Mendes. Both cost Brazil's reputation dear. They were denounced to the United Nations and the Organization of American States for genocide in the 1990s, and NGOs and campaign groups continued to draw attention to their appalling indigenous rights record and abuses of power.

Brazil got frightened and ashamed. When they hosted the 1992 Earth Summit, they showed off a new infrastructure of specialized agencies for protecting the environment. Constitutional and legislative changes promised indigenous land demarcation and explicitly declared that private land titles on lands traditionally occupied by Indians were null and void. Environmental impact reports would be required before new development or industrial projects could go ahead. The world rejoiced, and Brazil obtained $290 million in grants for forest and Indian land protection. But all hopes were in vain; Brazil gratefully received the money yet none ever reached the Indians. Where it went is not hard to guess. And the powerful and corrupt landowning oligarchy who rule the country displayed their true colours only four years later, when they forced President Fernando Henrique Cardoso to pass decree 1775, which revoked the law granting protection of indigenous lands, opening them up to loggers, miners and ranchers.

Then the abuses began afresh. The following year, an area the size of Rhode Island was cut from Macuxi indigenous territory in Roraima and handed over to 14 cattle ranchers from the National Institute for Colonization and Agrarian Reform (INCRA). Further enclaves were created in the heart of the reserve for gold miners. Over the past decade, corrupt officials in the government's own environmental protection agency have been shown to have forged documents on a grand scale to allow the passage of illegally cut mahogany from Indian Reserves and National Parks into Europe and the USA, and attempts continue in Congress to open up indigenous areas to mining and reduce the size of the Yanomami territories.

In 1999 Jose Sarney junior, son of a former president, one of the wealthiest and most powerful of the landowners, was appointed as Minister for the Environment. Sarney immediately declared himself a passionate defender of the forest and the indigenous peoples. One of his first actions in power was to help draft a Bill of Congress, demanding, amongst other things, a reduction of the legal rainforest reserves in the Amazon from 80 to 50 per cent, the replacement of other protected areas with eucalyptus and complete amnesty for miners and illegal loggers who extract timber from protected areas. Following intense international pressure the bill was revoked. Brazil's plans to build a navigable waterway through the Pantanal were scuppered in August 1999, after UNESCO declared the area a world heritage site.

The Andean Republics

The only positive results of Texaco's shameful legacy in Ecuador has been to bring more global awareness to the problems of oil production in other parts of the Amazon. Nonetheless, oil production continues to threaten the Ecuadorean Amazon (with further concessions granted to the state oil company even in the heart of the country's largest national park), as well as parts of Peru. The worst problems have been in Colombia.

The Plight of the U'wa people

> We are seeking an explanation for this 'progress' that goes against life. We are demanding that this kind of progress stop, that oil exploitation in the heart of the Earth is halted, that the deliberate bleeding of the Earth stop.

> Statement of the U'wa People, August 8, 1998

Occidental's oil exploration in the late 1990s led them to estimate that a region within U'wa territory in Colombia, known to the oil industry as the Samoré Block, contained approximately 1.5 billion barrels of oil, the amount used by the USA in three months. Shell, Occidental's partner in a project to extract the oil, pulled out because of protests by the Uw'a. But Occidental pressed on and were given permission to commence drilling in September 2000 by the Colombian government, despite threats of mass suicide by the U'wa, who feared further pollution and violent attacks by guerrillas and paramilitaries. Their fears were well grounded. Tribal leaders have been repeatedly intimidated, beaten up and told that they will be killed if they do not keep quiet and authorize the drilling. In previous protests in 1997, the tribe's leader, Roberto Cobaría, had been pulled from his bed in the middle of the night and beaten up by hooded men, who threatened to kill him if he did not sign the authorization form. Three American activists and supporters of the U'wa were murdered in March 2000. As this book went to press, Occidental had no plans to halt drilling in the Sierra de Cocuy.

(*See* also 'History of Inca', p.110)

Indigenous Peoples of the Amazon: Past, Present & Future

by Marcus Colchester, Director of the Forest Peoples Programme

The Indians of the Latin America have always played a powerful role in the imagination of European travellers. Christopher Columbus portrayed them as trusting and guileless inhabitants of an earthly paradise who could be easily enslaved and their riches conquered for the Spanish crown. Fantasies about gold and silver, gems and precious woods may have been the main attractions which lured later *conquistadores* south into the heart of South America and down the forested coastlines, but it was a European fascination with the newly discovered forest-dwellers that best sold the many travel books about the new continent. Fascinating though these early accounts are, they tell us more about Europeans' views of themselves than the reality of Indian life.

In these early travelogues the Indians appear to us as contradictory beings; generous, well-bodied, honest, naked and open, but given over to demonic worship, cannibalism, war and excess. Indeed it was no accident that in these books Indians conformed to a European view of Nature. The Indians were perceived as wild beings, inhabitants of wilderness, subject to no laws but the laws of nature, where untamed, devilish and female forces held sway. They thus represented a perfect foil to the male-dominated, cultured world of Europe where feelings, beliefs and actions were subordinated to the demands of God and King.

When Sir Walter Raleigh travelled to the Guyana coast in search of El Dorado, the fabled king of the golden city on Manoa on the banks of Lake Parima, the interior was already peopled in the European imagination with the weird, wild beings of classical antiquity that personified uncontrolled nature. The maps of the era confidently placed dog-headed men, unipods and naked Amazons in the forests beyond the explorers' ken. The Indians were seen as quintessential 'salvages' (from the Latin for forest-dwellers, from which we get our English word 'savages' today), forest peoples subject to natural law.

For the general public the Indians satisfied a curiosity about themselves and about how they, as civilized beings, were able to control wild urges that the Indians gave way to without shame. For the French philosophers at the dawn of the 'Age of Enlightenment' these natural beings— *sans dieu, sans roi et sans loi* (without god, king or law)—were also important elements in their social critique of civilization's excesses and abuses of power. Here, in the jungles of the Amazon, were untainted examples of what humans could be without the trappings of high office and the crushing weight of tradition: Noble Savages, nearer to the ideal first people in the garden of Eden, who put in question all the received wisdom of western civilization.

And today? Are we any more enlightened about these peoples, the real inhabitants of the Amazon? The selective images we get to see in glossy coffee-table books and Hollywood movies still show them as noble and natural beings, no longer wild perhaps, but certainly closer to nature than we are. Indeed, today the favourite role for Indians in western newspapers is as plumed and naked defenders of nature who offer us a critique of the environmental excesses of our civilization. For cultural historians, their views shaped unconsciously by evolutionary biology, the Indians' ways of life are seen as backward, evidence of how we ourselves used to live in more primitive eras—'our contemporary ancestors' as one celebrated anthropologist once put it. Our vision of the Indians has not changed greatly in four centuries, although our prejudices are now dressed in the modern idioms of environmentalism and science.

For the new South Americans on the forest frontiers, who compete with Indians for land and to gain access to minerals, timber, oil and gas, these whimsical and romantic views provide little interest or gain. For them the Indians are still seen as 'obstacles to progress', as one Governor of the Brazilian State of Roraima expressed it, primitive people who use too much land but provide no economic return to the nation. In Venezuela, the frontier *criollo* (creoles), describe themselves as 'racionales'—rational beings to whom the pejorative word *indio* (Indian) is synonymous with irrationality.

On the frontier, the raw edge of our world is still as relentless as it was in the time of the *conquistadores*. The unilateral takeover of Indian territories to make way for development continues unabated despite some rightly celebrated campaign victories to stop or slow the most thoughtless interventions. Mining concessions handed over to Canadian, US, European and South African companies now cover over 10 per cent of the surface area of Guyana. Contracts change hands in the capital, Georgetown, without the Indians who make up the majority of the population in the interior even being informed, let alone given a say in their future. Since the 1990s, the Amazon is being opened up as a new frontier for transnational, mainly Asian, timber companies which, having logged out the forests of South East Asia, and flush with inter-national capital from floating their companies on the regional stock exchanges, now seek to repeat the bonanza in South America. Vast logging concessions the size of large principalities are granted to foreign enterprises without any consideration of the likely impact on the Indians.

Globalization, the creation of truly world markets in goods and services, is only intensifying a trend set in motion by the merchant empires of the 15th century, which underpinned Columbus' first voyages of discovery. The forests on Indian's lands in central Brazil are now being cleared at a ferocious pace to plant soya, demanded as feed by European livestock agribusinesses. To service the industrial development of southeast Venezuela and northern Brazil and to stabilize territorial rivalry, the Brazilian and Venezuelan states have signed a treaty to trade electricity across the frontier. Giant pylons are being erected on Pemon Indians' land to lead high tension cables from the Guri dam on the Caroni River, where Raleigh's maps locate the golden city of Manoa, past the actual gold fields on the Cuyuni and on down to Brazil. The cables will stalk across the face of the Canaima National Park, an international heritage site, made world-famous by the high sandstone mesas which rise over the savannahs and forests. Indian protests that their lands should be first secured have been met with empty promises, intimidation, threats, tear gas and bullets.

In the western Amazon, oil exploration has emerged as one of the major threats to the Indians' future. In Ecuador, where the exploitation of oil mainly by US companies has been going on for decades, Indian lands and the rivers which flow through them have been repeatedly poisoned by oil spills. The road network, established to service the oil wells and web of pipelines, has ushered in a wave of dispossessed farmers from the Andes who have invaded Indian lands with impunity. Oil exploration in western Brazil, Peru and Colombia now poses the same threats. Oil and gas pipelines, financed by the international development banks, now criss-cross the frontier between Bolivia and Brazil, bringing in hunters and land speculators in their wake.

Ironically, even the western model of nature conservation poses real threats to the Indians. A western notion that conservation is best achieved by locking up certain areas of 'wilderness' as protected areas, vacated of human residents, has resulted in many Indians being denied rights to their ancestral lands. Overnight, traditional hunting becomes illegal 'poaching'. By clearing forest for their farms the Indians become 'encroachers' and by remaining in their settlements they become 'squatters'. Even ecotourists are a problem; servicing their lifestyle demands for flush toilets, showers, insect-proof housing and processed foods obliges eco-tourism operators to depend on outside investors. Local control is lost to richer partners. In places, lands have been taken over for camps and huts without compensation or even a recognition of the rights of the Indian residents.

Happily the Indians are not unwitting victims of this careless process of development, driven though it is by consumer demand and capital transfers far from their lands and livelihoods. Resistance started with the first invasions and though most soon learned the futility of armed opposition to these intruders on their lands, non-violent opposition and protests have been sustained all over the Amazon. In the last half century, in particular, Indians have learned how to use the media, the law and new forms of organization to defend themselves. In Brazil, Kayapo Indians have repeatedly carried out high-profile media campaigns to successfully halt roads and dams planned for their territories. They have sued in the courts for millions of dollars in compensation to recover lost lands and re-establish themselves in areas from which they were removed.

In the 1960s, Shuar Indians in Ecuador set up a new organization to represent them in their struggle to halt the giveaway of their lands to outsiders. Since then the Shuar have been able to piece back together a substantial part of their ancestral lands and have set up clinics, radio networks, legal services and schools providing bilingual education. The Shuar's lead has been followed almost everywhere by other Amazonian peoples. Organizations representing river valleys or different tribes have joined together into regional federations and national confederations to ensure their voice is heard in the corridors of power. When confronted by intransigent national governments, reluctant to cede power and control over land and natural resources back to the original owners, the Indians have taken their complaints abroad.

Just as they have used the courts in their home countries, they have appealed to international human rights forums for redress. Banding together with other national Indian organizations and indigenous peoples organizations from Asia and Africa, they have spoken out at the United Nations and challenged major institutions like the World Bank to revise their development programmes. This concerted mobilization, backed by a handful of small support organizations in the USA and Europe, has obliged the international community to recognize the legitimacy of the Indians' demands for justice, respect for their human rights and recognition of their right to govern themselves and control what goes on in their territories. Human rights covenants have been re-interpreted by inter-governmental expert committees to recognize their immemorial rights to own and control their lands. New international laws and agreements have been passed to formally recognize these rights and procedures have been designed to put them into effect.

In the last decade, the laws and constitutions of the majority of Amazonian countries have been rewritten to incorporate these newly acknowledged principles. Most South American states now, with some sorry exceptions such as Suriname, recognize their multiethnic basis, accept the legitimacy of Indian languages, and recognize the Indians' rights to own their lands and govern themselves through their own institutions. The challenge, today, is to put these new principles into practice: to register Indian-owned lands in national cadasters; establish mechanisms to defend such lands in the courts; provide training and resources to promote new community development under local control. Surprising many observers, who had assumed the Indians were vulnerable and conservative societies doomed to extinction, Indian communities have emerged as vigorous proponents of innovation and change. Proud of their traditions and customs of hospitality, equality, respect for the spirits of the forest and self-reliance, they also seek the better things from Western civilization—health care, new communications systems, literacy and appropriate technologies for farming and stewardship of their environment.

In our own work with Indian peoples in Venezuela and Guyana, we have helped them learn to use Global Positioning Systems to survey their territories, re-label maps with their own names and knowledge, and fill them with information about their own systems of land use and history of occupation. Providing Indian organizations with computers, GIS software and printers has allowed them to actually print, update and have full control of these maps, which they then use to press for land titles and to develop management plans for their rivers and forests.

This explosion of local organizing has been based on the commitment of new Indian leaders and the determination of these peoples to take control of their own destinies. Much of the funding, however, has come from charitable organizations and the overseas aid budgets of northern countries. Intriguingly, more of this money has come from budget lines aimed at protecting the environment than those for community development and the defence of human rights.

A just future for the 'Indians' of the 'Amazon', will only come about when we learn to set aside our prejudices and recognize them as modern peoples endowed with histories, rights and philosophies just as valid as our own. They are not 'victims' to be 'saved' and 'protected' by paternalistic interventions but viable societies, with their own visions of where they are going. They have their own ideas of what is important and what is to be changed. They have their own models of what we call 'development' and 'conservation'. Moral and financial support for their initiatives will be crucial for many years to come but a more fundamental challenge for us is to find new means to restrain the excesses of the markets and companies which supply our needs and satisfy our whims at their expense.

About the Author

Marcus Colchester is Director of the Forest Peoples Programme (FPP) and author of numerous books on the political ecology of tropical forest destruction, including Guyana: Fragile Frontier—Loggers, Miners and Forest Peoples.

For more information about the FPP's activities and publications, contact 1c Fosseway Business Centre, Moreton-in-Marsh, GL56 9NQ, England, © + 44 (0)1608 652893, ☏ + 44 (0)1608 652878, info@fppwrm.gn.apc.org.

Amazon Spirituality: Rainforest Shamanism

The spirituality of the Amazon peoples, like that of their cousins throughout the Americas, is based firmly in shamanism, a religion that underlies all our belief systems and is found all over the world. Like Inca or Maya shamanism, Amazon shamanism has its roots in Siberia, the homeplace of America's ancestors. In the rainforest, it has long since developed into its own, complex form. Above all, shamanism is a way of life; a journey of spiritual evolution in which the shaman is teacher and guide. Although the ultimate goal is spiritual realization, few Indians opt for the long, almost monastic path that takes them there. Shamanism is more often concerned with the correct ordering of day-to-day life events and the marking out of ritual and symbolic space. Everything from a hunt to the positioning of a building has to mimic the higher, divine world. The use of symbols, as in the Catholic church, is more than merely representative: symbols are the means by which the material world is attuned to the spiritual. Shamans, who train aspiring shamans and oversee all the tribe's spiritual activities, are therefore priests and spiritual professors. Some have attained spiritual realization, whether through intense deprivation and suffering or the long process of shamanistic education; others are the holders of tradition that has been passed on to them.

Spiritual Realization

For the shaman, spiritual realization involves complete, instinctual understanding of the oneness of the physical and spiritual worlds. The shamanistic universe comprises two worlds which co-exist. The visible material world is the realm of the senses and is governed by the quest for food. But underlying this is a spiritual, invisible world that we share with all objects and beings in the Universe. This is the realm of pure being, archetype and spirit, and is where we apprehend and even meet the cosmic and divine powers. Whilst westerners tend to regard only the visible as real, Indians traditionally see the opposite as being true: *mári ariri kéro dohpá inyarí*, 'our existence dream-like appears'. All actions in the visible world must be evaluated in terms of the invisible world, for this is ultimately where they derive their form and meaning: what we do belongs to the material world; what we are, to the spiritual. When a shaman reaches the point of realization, he is like the enlightened of Buddhism or Hinduism: the scales fall from the eyes, the two realms are perceived as one and 'what-he-realises-himself-to-be' completely informs what he does. Such spiritual realization is accomplished through a journey of direct experience, but in shamanism, it is guided by symbol, tradition and psychotropic pharmacy. The Tucanoan concept of mind–brain relationships are an indication of this.

Tucanoan Mind–Brain Symbolism

The Tucanos equate the invisible world with the left cerebral hemisphere, and the visible with the right. The left hemisphere is that of the mature, enlightened adult, the 'older brother'. It is the seat of intuition, moral authority, order, intellectual and spiritual endeavours, music, dreams and abstract thought. Its name, *ëmëkóri mahsá turí*, means 'Sun-people-dimension'. The sun is the manifestation of the power of the creator of the Universe, the 'Sun-Father'. It is also the home of the gahí turí, the other dimension/house/world, where we apprehend and interact with the archetypes and forms of the invisible world. And it is the instrument for interpreting the bogári, energy fields and 'transmissions' that emanate from Nature. The right hemisphere is called *mahsá turí*, or 'human dimension'. It is subservient and is associated with the younger brother. Here lies practical knowledge and skill; tradition; customary rules and rituals; and everything pertaining to the physical. The fissure between the two hemispheres has a very complex symbolism associated with it. Simply speaking, it can be seen as an anaconda-river, with the dark patterns on the snake's back as stepping stones. The shamanic student learns to navigate the river, stepping on the stones to move from right-hemisphere-orientated life to enlightened, spiritual, left-hemisphere-orientated life. Just in front of the anaconda's head is a rock crystal symbolising the seat of cosmic (solar) illumination. For the Tucanoan Indians, the rock crystal is a model of the Universe. As rock crystals are hexagonal, the hexagon is regarded as a holy shape which infuses the rhythm of daily life.

Mind-altering tonics like ayahuasca are used to shift perception from right to left hemisphere, or from visible to invisible world orientation. Such remedies collapse the ego; and are said to completely silence the mental voice and to shift the perception away from our tendency to regard ourselves a separate to the external world. Shamans use ayahuasca and other such remedies very carefully, and with pharmaceutical precision. All tribal members imbibe them at one time or another, usually to mark key life events.

Shamans are informed not only by intuition but by age-old tradition. If intuition is shamanic prayer, then tradition is the text of shamanic life. It comes in the form of myriad taboos and rituals passed down through generations, and a giant cosmological map, in which positions and movements are imbued with Biblical significance. This map is comprised of the stars above and the forest around, and their harmonic movements. It is used to plot and interpret everything, from the timing of different harvesting seasons to the construction of buildings. For the Tucanoan Indians of the Upper Río Negro, Orion is the single most important feature on this map. This constellation is a macrocosmic model of the primal or cosmic human being, the Master of Animals, a figure who is to the Indians as Adam before the Fall might be to a Christian: the archetypal man whose correct relationship with the spiritual world ensures harmony within the Garden of Eden. In his path across the night sky the Master of Animals drags his catch behind him over a forest trail, the Milky Way. The constellations along his path announce different harvesting and hunting seasons, ordering the physical world to the spiritual. The six stars within Orion are linked in a holy hexagon. Another links the stars that surround this constellation. These astronomical clusters are the macrocosmic representation of the rock crystal, which Tucanoans regard as sacred. They serve as the basic architectural models for the construction of the communal longhouse, the *maloca*. Six points of reference mark the positions of the strongest house posts, one at each corner of the hexagon, and correspond to the stars surrounding Orion. Six further posts delimit a central hexagon in the heart of the *maloca*, corresponding to Orion itself. An imaginary line bisects the *maloca* through both hexagons, representing both the Equator and the Belt of Orion. The Indians perform ritual dances within this inner hexagon, whose movements are also symbolically related to the pattern of Orion. Two groups of dancers, one male and one female, move back and forth over the imaginary dividing line in triangular formations, tracing the hourglass-shaped outline of Orion. Like a dancing, living Yin and Yang, they represent the relationship between feminine and masculine archetypes: light and darkness, sun and moon, fertility and restraint. As Orion is the macrocosmic model of the human being, the *maloca* represents Man within the Universe, and the dances the eternal play that occurs within the soul.

Music and the Amazon

There are few great Amazon bands or singers, but the area has helped to produce many styles. The reed flutes and pipes that make Andean music so distinctive probably came from here. Tucano Indian music is as driven by pan-pipes and reed flutes as anything from the mountains. The sounds of the forest permeate Brazil's music, and have inspired numerous uniquely Brazilian percussion instruments. The *cuica* is a box with a sheet of skin on the top, perforated by a small stick. When the stick is moved in and out of the box, the *cuica* produces a cry like a human voice. *Cuicas* imitating the call of a jaguar have been developed in Santarém. The *berimbau* is a bow whose string, made of wire, is tapped with a stick and a stone to produce a distinctive twangy percussive. It provides the rhythm for *capoeira*, an Afro-Brazilian martial art dance of dazzling virtuosity from Bahia. Capoeira was born in the *quilombos*, communities of escaped African slaves that were established in the Amazon rainforests in the 17th and 18th centuries. Capoeira is an Indian word, and the fighting style incorporates Indian techniques. Its movements, brought to Los Angeles by Brazilians, form the basis of US black street dancing.

Aside from salsa and merengue, which are from the Caribbean and Latin New York, much of the music you will hear in South America has roots in the Amazon. Music is one of the delights of travel here, especially in Brazil. Here is a foretaste of the main styles and artists.

Brazilian Music

Samba and Bossa Nova

The harmonies and progressions of bossa nova and samba are as rich as almost any jazz. In fact, the traditions have inspired one another: jazz harmonies added to slow samba rhythms by Tom Jobim and João Gilberto in the late 1950s produced mellow, sophisticated bossa nova, made famous by songs like *A Garota da Ipanem*a ('The Girl from Ipanema'). Bossa inspired US musicians like Stan Getz, Joe Henderson, Herbie Hancock, Wayne Shorter and Larry Coryell, all of whom have recorded Brazilian music with Brazilian musicians. The worst US bossa/jazz sounds uncomfortably like cocktail-bar muzak. The home-grown stuff is far better.

The following is an introduction to the greatest proponents of both traditions. You'll find a few of these on David Byrne's *Luaka Bop* compilations.

Samba

Baden Powell: The Django Reinhardt of Brazil, one of the most innovative and technically proficient of the old school of samba guitarists. Any live recording is worth buying. Powell, who is now over 60, still tours and you may be lucky enough to see him live.

João Bosco: Bosco reinvented the samba in the 1970s, fusing it with new jazz-informed harmonies and politically and socially conscious lyrics. His early tunes tend to be melodic, very dancy and incredibly well played: his guitar technique is legendary. Later CDs are subtler and more mellow. *A Onda que Balança* is a fine recent album.

Papete: A master *berimbau* player who mixes classic samba rhythms with rainforest sounds and traditional Brazilian folk songs. *Berimbau e Percussão* is a good album.

Also look out for: **Paulinho da Violão** (guitar samba); any of the **Rio schools** of samba (Rio carnaval samba); **Clara Nunes** (the leading female samba vocalist).

Bossa Nova

Tom Jobim: Jobim and João Gilberto invented bossa nova in Rio's bars and clubs in the 1950s; both are now legendary in Brazil. *Familia Jobim* is one of his finest CDs. Many songs like *O Boto* ('The River Dolphin') and *Correnteza* ('The Current') are poems to Brazil's natural beauty. His 1970s US recordings are more wishy-washy.

João Gilberto: Gilberto introduced jazz harmonies to Brazilian guitar music. He and his wife Astrud introduced bossa to the world with 'The Girl from Ipanema'. *Live in Montreux* is one of his finest albums.

Elis Regina: Brazil's most famous and highly respected female bossa singer, with a beautiful, sensual and alluring voice. The wonderful CD *Elis e Tom* was recorded with Jobim.

Marcio Faraco: The fresh young face of bossa nova. Faraco had to leave Brazil for France to find renown. His debut, *Ciranda*, is a rich and varied collection of songs.

Also look out for: **Luiz Bonfá** (who wrote *A Manha do Carnaval*); **Leila Pinheiro** (modern bossa nova interpretations); **Nara Leão** (one of the first female bossa nova vocalists); **Edu Lobo** (his first CD, *Sergio Mendes presents Edu Lobo*, is a classic).

Brazilian Jazz/Percussion

Egberto Gismonti: Gismonti, a classically trained pianist, constantly reinvents his sound and explores the boundaries of Brazilian music. He records on ECM and, within Brazil, on his own label, Carmo. The Carmo recordings tend to be softer and more lyrical. *Circense* and *Árvore* are two of the finest. The latter is inspired by Brazil's forests.

Delia Fischer: A recent signing to the Carmo label. Fischer is a classically trained pianist in the Gismonti vein. Her compositions and playing mix sensitivity and emotiveness with virtuoso technique. *Antonio*, dedicated to her son, is wonderful.

Airto Moreira and **Flora Purim**: Two of Brazil's most highly respected musical ambassadors. Airto is a polyrhythmic percussionist, his wife Flora a singer with an astonishing six-octave range. *500 Miles* recorded live at Montreux captures both at their best.

Hermeto Pascoal: An eccentric multiinstrumentalist. Any Pascoal CD is worth exploring.

Nana Vasconcelos: One of Brazil's most influential and internationally famous percussionists; has recorded with David Byrne, Evelyn Glennie, Pat Metheny and Jan Garbarek. His solo work is orchestral. *Saudades* and *Storytelling* are among his strongest CDs.

Also look out for: **Eumir Deodato** (Brazilian jazz-funk); **Victor Assis** (wonderful bossa nova/jazz saxophonist).

Música Popular Brasileira (MPB) and Tropicalia

MPB is a broad term for any uniquely Brazilian popular music. *Tropicalia* is a type of MPB forged in the late 1960s in Brazil's northeast, particularly Bahia. It was a key instrument of political protest in the early 1970s, and many of its stars lived in political exile.

Gilberto Gil: A founder of Tropicalia, a light, sophisticated guitarist/singer with a vast, patchy catalogue. Very exciting live. *Parabolicamará* and *Quanta* are great when not cheesy.

Caetano Veloso: The wimpy side of Brazilian MPB; immensely popular both at home and abroad, partly because his music is so soft and accessible. *Estrangeiro* is representative.

Gal Costa: The voice of female *Tropicalia*, a rich, effortless and unforgettable singer. *Tropical* is her most highly respected album.

Chico Buarque: The Bob Dylan of Brazil. Chico's lyrics are his strong point; you must understand Portuguese to appreciate him fully. *Vida* is one of his most consistent albums.

Marisa Monte: Light, tight and with a voice of mellifluous sensuality, Monte is flavour of the month with Brazil's young urban sophisticates. *Barulinho Bom* captures her live, with her wonderful band at its best. Her lyrics are complete nonsense.

Karnak: Theatrical, experimental funky MPB, with a dog credited (and pictured) as a member of the band. Their first eponymous album is a must in any MPB collection.

Milton Nascimento: A very intelligent composer and lyricist, with an incredible voice. Milton's music is plaintive, melancholy and thought-provoking. One of Brazil's very best. *Clube da Esquina*, recorded with Lô Borges, is an excellent early recording.

Djavan: Wonderful melodic shifts and jazzy phrasing are incorporated into irresistible melodies. Stevie Wonder, a big fan, guests on *Luz*, but *Flor de Lis* is a better album.

Dorival Caymmi: The most sophisticated and plaintive of Bahia's musicians. Any recording by him or his son Dori is worth a listen. Dori's *Brazilian Serenata* is particularly good.

Also look out for: **Tom Zé** (quirky social protest); **Itamar Assumpção** (the Zappa of Brazil); **Osvaldo Montenegro** (good guitarist in the Chico Buarque vein).

Bahian Carnaval Music

Bahia is the capital of Brazilian carnaval music. Styles range from the drum orchestra to tight, frenetic dance music.

Olodum and **Ile Aye**: The 40-piece drum orchestra Olodum were discovered by Paul Simon and emasculated on his *Rhythm of the Saints*. They are best live; *Sol e Mar* captures them at Montreux. Ile Aye are in a similar vein and have a good eponymous CD.

Banda Beijo: The most exciting proponents of Bahian Axé, the frenetic dance music made popular by singers like Daniela Mercury. Beijo are far better. Catch them on *Ao Vivo*.

Carlinhos Brown: The prince of Bahian music. Original, funky and sophisticated Bahian MPB with some wonderful percussion. *Alphagamabetizado* is his best.

Also look out for: **Margareth Menezes** (great voice); **Daniela Mercury** (superficial Bahian pop but a great performer).

Forró

Brazil's most exciting dance style has its roots in the northeast countryside, but is immensely popular in the Amazon. Voice, accordion, guitar, triangle and the zabumba drum produce an infectious rhythm. The lyrics champion folk heroes like the 19th-century northeast rebel Lampião—a sort of Brazilian Robin Hood. *Forró* is best appreciated live at the **Boi Bumba** festival in Parintins, or in clubs in the Amazon towns. Ask a taxi driver or a university student to recommend one: *forró* breaks the class divide. Good *forró* is hard to find outside Brazil.

Mel com Terra: One of the tightest electric *forró* bands. *Amor que Fica* is a great CD.

Gonzaguinha: Son of the father of *forró*, Luiz Gonzaga. Catch him on *Luizinho de Gonzaga*.

Elba Ramalho: Brazil's biggest first-generation *forró* star. Her live material is her best.

Music from the Brazilian Amazon

Raices Caboclos: Folk songs from the river, including songs in Tucano. *Trem de Rio* is good.

Caprichoso: Regular performers at the Boi Bumba festival. One of their tunes was made into a revolting Euro-hit, 'Tic, Tic, Tac'. *A Festa do Boi Bumba* is enjoyable.

Lenine: Brazilian rock from Maranhão. Good live, dull on CD. Lenine is a great guitarist.

The Music of the Rainforest (Smithsonian Folkways) contains field recordings of, amongst others, **Shipibos** from the Peruvian Amazon and Surinamese **Maroons**.

The Ticuna museum in Benjamin Constant has a wonderful tape of traditional Ticuna ceremonial chants. It is a private recording, but perhaps you can persuade them to record it for you.

Classical

Brazil's most celebrated composer **Heitor Villa Lobos** (1887–1959), who has a huge recording catalogue available in Brazil, wrote a series of pieces inspired by the Amazon. These are available within Brazil on a recording made by singer **Ney Matogrosso** and others. The recording includes the exquisite *Melodia Sentimental*, which João Bosco recorded on his *Da Liçenca Meu Senhor*. Villa Lobos's wonderful guitar pieces, including his concerti, are best played by Brazilian guitarists, who accurately capture the rhythms of the *choro* style which influenced the composer. The contemporary guitarist **Heitor TP** is one of the best.

O Guaraní is a 19th-century Brazilian opera, the love story of a Guaraní Indian from the Pantanal and a Portuguese woman. If you're lucky you might see it in the Manaus Opera.

Andean Music

Andean music is best live, at a *peña* in La Paz or a Peruvian mountain town. Peñas are spit and sawdust pubs, full of dancing locals, and are wonderful fun. Cusco used to have a fine selection and was the capital of Andean folk music in the early 1990s when young westerners with their thirst for pounding rhythms put paid to them. Traditional bands still play at tamer venues like Chez Maggy on Calle Plateros. New *peñas* may be opening; listen out.

You may see local musician **Leandro Apaza** making his way down Avenida Tullumayo in Cusco, harp in hand, to busk on Calle Hatun Rumiyoq. **Benjamin Clara** sometimes accompanies him on mandolin. Both are blind, and Benjamin is lame. They are among Peru's poorest and most talented musicians. They sing mournful songs to happy rhythms in Quechua, the Inca language. Ask them to play *Wakcha Urpi*, an anthem to 'orphaned love'. Their music is about as close to the traditional music of the Incas that you are likely to get. Little has been recorded; some is on *Mountain Music of Peru* (Smithsonian Folkways), *Flutes and Strings of the Andes* (Music of the World) and *Bolivia—Calendar Music of the Central Valley* (Chant du Monde).

The leading Andean band, wonderful live, is Bolivia's **Kjarkas**, whose *Llorando se Fue* was the root for a lambada song that was impossible to escape in the early 1990s. Their CD *Canto a la Mujer de mi Pueblo* includes their best songs, including the original of *Llorando se Fue*. Other recordings with their cheesy romantic laments can get a bit trying. **Inti Illimani**, **Uakti** and **El Grupo Expresión** are similar to Kjarkas. **Rumillajta** are a group of superb musicians; their *Hoja de Coca* CD has some wonderful flute and pan-pipe playing. Bolivian **Emma Junaro** is more cerebral and folksy, and is reminiscent of Argentina's Mercedes Sosa. Her voice replaces Sosa's power with mournful delicacy.

Peru

Peru's very landscape begs you to believe in vanished mystical civilizations and lost cities deep within the forest. It is hard to imagine more inspiring and humbling sights than the Río Urubamba winding tortuously between the near-vertical forest-clad mountains of the Vilcabamba range, or the foothills of the Andes at dawn stretching away to the vast Amazon plains. The landscape may inspire the imagination, but archaeologists have learnt that they dismiss Peru's old legends at their peril. Only ten years ago, the largest pre-Columbian city in the western hemisphere was chanced upon by a US adventurer; within its tombs, archaeologists found tall, blond mummies. This find brought Peru's legends to life: since the time of the conquistadors, Indians had told of an advanced civilization of blue-eyed warriors who traded with the Incas. Machu Picchu itself, Peru's most famous lost city, was thought to be no more than a fantasy until Hiram Bingham discovered it in 1911.

On the map, Peru looks small and tame next to the vastness of Brazil, yet it is over five times the size of Britain. Geographically, it divides neatly into three strips, running north to south. The coast is dry, barren and foggy, with valleys of smoking volcanoes and precipitous canyons and gorges. The capital, Lima, lies here, an unwelcoming introduction to one of the world's most beautiful and welcoming countries, and the only city with an international airport. The Incas chose to establish the headquarters of their empire at Cusco in the mountainous central strip of the country. Cusco is one of the most interesting towns in the Americas; together with Iquitos in the north, it is the country's principal gateway to the Amazon. The forests begin east of Cusco, on the lush, verdant eastern slopes of the Andes, creating Peru's third strip. Here lie the Inca ruins of Machu Picchu, hidden in the cloud forest of the Vilcabamba range. Their beauty is best appreciated by arriving, tired and on foot, via the Inca trail.

Two of the Amazon's most magical protected areas, and the best places to see wildlife in the country, lie deeper within Peru's Amazon territory. The Tambopata-Candamo Reserve Zone has the highest recorded biodiversity on earth, and Manu Biosphere Reserve is one of the continent's most pristine areas of tropical forest. Iquitos has long been the most popular base for visiting the Peruvian Amazon, but it is still possible to visit remote and little-explored areas of the forest such as Pacaya-Samiria, Peru's largest and least explored protected area.

Peru	Highlights
Official language: Spanish, Quechua	1. The second and third days of the Inca trail.
Capital city: Lima (*see* p.298)	2. Descent from the Andes to the Amazon on the first day at Manu Biosphere Reserve.
Amazon gateway city: Iquitos (*see* p.136), Cusco (*see* p.110)	3. The Tambopata Research Centre and a dawn visit to the macaw clay lick.
Currency: *nuevo sol* of 100 *cents*	

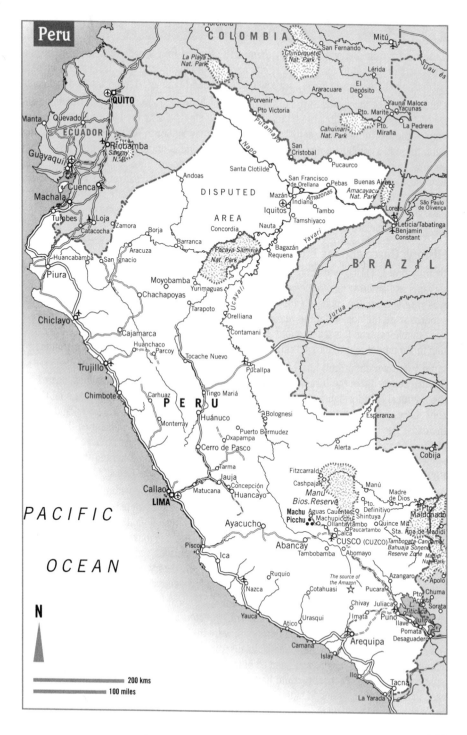

Peru

COLOMBIA
Florencia
Chiribiquete Nat. Park
San Fernando
Mitú
La Playa Nat. Park
Lérida
Uau ês
QUITO
Araracuare
El Depósito
Yauna Maloca
Yacunas
Manta
Quevado
Porvenir
Pto Victoria
Pto. Marite
Pto. Miraña
La Pedrera
ECUADOR
Riobamba
Sangay N.R.
Putumayo
Cahuinari Nat. Park
São Paulo de Olivença
Guayaquil
Cuenca
Andoas
Santa Clotilde
Napo
San Cristobal
Pucaurco
San Francisco de Orellana
Pebas
Buenas Aires
Amacayacu Nat. Park
Machala
DISPUTED
Mazán
Amazonas
Indiana
Loreto
Turubes
Loja
Zamora
AREA
Iquitos
Tambo
Leticia/Tabatinga
Benjamin Constant
Catacocha
Concordia
Nauta
Tamshiyaco
Borja
Barranca
Bagazán
Yavari
Huancabamba
San Ignacio
Aracuza
Pacaya Samiria Nat. Park
Requena
BRAZIL
Piura
Moyobamba
Yurimaguas
Chachapoyas
Ucayali
Tarapoto
Chiclayo
Orelliana
Jurua
Cajamarca
Contamani
Huanchaco
Parcoy
Trujillo
Tocache Nuevo
Pucallpa
Chimbote
Carhuaz
Tingo Mariá
PERU
Huánuco
Bolognesi
Esperanza
Monterray
Puerto Bermudez
Oxapampa
Cerro de Pasco
Alerta
Cobija
Tarma
Fitzcarrald
Jauja
Cashpajan
Manú
Madre de Dios
Callao
Matucana
Concepción
Huancayo
Manu Bios. Reserve
Pto. Definitivo
Shintuya
Pto. Maldonado
LIMA
Machu Picchu
Aguas Cauentes
Machupicchu
Quince Mil
Sta. Ana de Madidi
Ayacucho
Ollantaytambo
Paucartambo
Calca
PACIFIC
Pisco
Ica
Abancay
Tambobamba
CUSCO (CUZCO)
Abomayo
Tambopata-Candamo
Bahuaja Sonene Reserve Zone
Madidi Nat. Park
Ruquio
The source of the Amazon
Azangaro
Apolo
OCEAN
Nazca
Cotahuasi
Pucara
Chuma
Pto. Acosta
N
Urasqui
Chivay
Juliaca
Titicaca
Sorata
Yauca
Atico
Imata
Puno
Ilave
Julli
Pomata
Camana
Islay
Arequipa
Desaguadero
Ilo
Tacna
La Yarada

200 kms
100 miles

109

Cusco is far from being an Amazon town: it is situated in a broad Andean valley at over 3,000m, surrounded by terraced Inca fields and 6,000m-high mountains. Despite this, it is the best place to base yourself for visits to Machu Picchu and Manu and Tambopata National Parks.

Cusco was once the capital of the Inca empire, which stretched north as far as Colombia and south beyond the Atacama desert in Chile. At its height, it was the largest unbroken land empire the world had ever seen. The Spanish conquest of South America was consolidated here, through a combination of treachery, ruthlessness and cunning. The city became an architectural hybrid: the Spanish dismantled the magnificent Inca capital and built an Extremadura-style town on top of it. Now, elegant, carved Moorish balconies stand over cyclopean masonry slotted together like a three-dimensional jigsaw puzzle, orientated to the passage of the sun, and the streets are filled with traders and touts, begging or proffering in a babble of European and Native American tongues.

History: Cusco and the Inca Empire

In Inca times, Cusco was more a giant palace than a city. Only *karakas* (nobility), their servants and ambassadors to the court lived here. The centre of the city (now the main plaza) was reserved for the highest *karakas*, known as *hanan*. The lower part of town and the suburbs were the domain of the *hurin* (lower nobility). The total population would not have been much less than it is today, about 200,000, but, as there were only about 40,000 Incas all told in Tahuantinsuyu (their empire), the Inca tribe was itself an ethnic minority even here.

Little is known about how the empire functioned, and what role the nobility played. The Spanish believed that the Incas were a single dynasty of rulers. The first great Inca (apart from the mythical founder figure, Manco Capac) was Pachacuti, who established imperial Cusco after successfully defending the erstwhile undistinguished capital against invaders, and against the odds. The Spanish believed that Pachacuti himself had designed and planned the building of Cusco, to reflect the new-found glory of the Incas. The city was said to have been further embellished by Tupa Inca (Tupac Yupanqui), Pachacuti's son, who inherited the power after Pachacuti retired in 1471. He, in turn, handed it to his son, Huayna Capac.

Recent investigation, concentrating on Inca lore, suggests that there were no individual rulers at all. There are now two theories about how Cusco and the Inca empire were run. The least likely posits that the Inca court was a diarchy: one *karaka* (noble) would have ruled the upper *hurin* section of the town and community, and another the *hanan*, with the two co-operating over important decisions. Figures such as Pachacuti and Huayna Capac may have been senior and junior co-rulers rather than father and son. But if this theory were true, the Inca dynasty would be truncated, and would have lasted for just a few generations.

The Inca empire was probably more like 'Ewing Oil': a giant family company passed down through generations, with a board of all-powerful directors and no single president. The names the Spanish gave to Inca rulers, like Pachacuti, were the names of imperial offices operating at the same time and held by ten dynastic clans known as *panaqa*. These *panaqa* were split across the *hanan* and *hurin* classes and all of them resided in Cusco, administering the empire from there. Though Pachacuti could have been a single individual, it is more likely that he was, in fact, a whole series of individuals from one clan. Indeed, Inca lore suggests that the city was built and planned in the imperial corporate boardroom after the Inca had consolidated

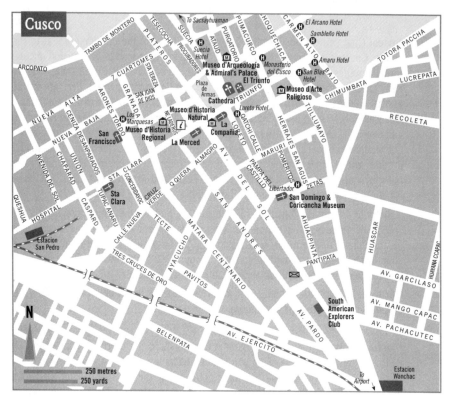

their homeland and expanded their empire. This makes sense—the Inca homeland did not have a tradition of fine stonework before the establishment of Tahuantinsuyu. The Incas may have been great corporate emperors, but the skilled craftsmanship must have been brought in from elsewhere, probably after conquests in the Lake Titicaca region.

All this may end up turning current theories about the duration of the Inca empire on their head. If the important events of the empire didn't take place over dynastic generations but over periods of office, then the empire may have lasted a good deal longer than previously supposed. And, just as Rome was most certainly not built in a day, it seems unrealistic to suppose that a city as grand as Cusco was built in just a few generations.

Cusco (© 084–)

Getting There and Around

by air

Thrice-weekly Lloyd Air Bolivian services to La Paz. Tickets can be booked with travel agents on the Av. del Sol. The airport departure tax is about $20.

At the time of writing, Aero Peru had gone bust; check with the tourist office for the latest details. Aero Continente (office at northern corner of Plaza de Armas) and Tans (Av. del Sol just before the post office) have reliable daily services to Lima and Puerto Maldonado and plan to recommence flights to Arequipa. Numerous travel agents tout tickets along Av. del Sol. Try to book yours a few days in advance. HeliCusco, Triunfo 379, run return trips to Machu Picchu from Cusco.

Buses: Cusco's new bus terminal is on the outskirts of the city; take a taxi to the centre. Cusco is well served by buses and though journeys tend to be long and uncomfortable, routes are usually spectacular. The only buses for the Peruvian Amazon leave daily for Quillabamba (9 hrs). The following other destinations within Peru are served at least once daily. The list is not exhaustive and times vary with weather conditions: Abancay (5 hrs); Arequipa (12 hrs); Ayacucho, with onward connections to Huancayo and beyond (21hrs); Juliaca (9 hrs); Lima (26 hrs); Nazca (20 hrs); Puno, with onward connections to Copacabana and La Paz in Bolivia (10 hrs). Buses for destinations in and around the Sacred Valley (Pisac, Calca, Yucay, Chinchero, Urubamba and Ollantaytambo) leave from a bus stop on Av. Tullumayo, which is one block east of the Av. del Sol. There are plans to move these services to the main bus station.

Trucks to Puerto Maldonado in the Amazon are only for the very brave; it's a long, spectacular journey through montane forest to the Amazon lowlands. The truck stop is on the Plaza Tupac Amaru, southeast of the city centre. Bring food and at least a couple of litres of water and a plastic bag for your rucksack. Onward connections from Puerto Maldonado to Porto Velho and the Pantanal, in Brazil.

Car hire: Localisa, Av. del Sol 1089, ✆ 242285. Expect to pay between $30–$70 per day, depending on the car you choose, with petrol on top.

by train

Machu Picchu: A daily train leaving at around six in the morning, runs from San Pedro Station in Cusco through the Urubamba valley, stopping at Ollantaytambo, Qoriwayrachina (Km 88—the beginning of the classic Inca trail) and Aguas Calientes (for buses up the ridge to Machu Picchu). Though there is track all the way to Quillabamba, services had been suspended beyond Aguas Calientes at the time of writing this book. The journey to Aguas Calientes takes between 3 and 4 hours. Buy your tickets the day before departure at the train station.

Arequipa and Titicaca: Trains to Puno (for Bolivia) and Arequipa (on the way to Nasca and the coast) leave four times a week from Cusco's other train station, Wanhac, at the southern end of Av. del Sol. The bus is quicker and cheaper.

Cusco (✆ 084–)   **Tourist Information and Useful Addresses**

Tourist office: Portal Mantas 188, with very helpful English-speaking staff.

Changing money: There are *casas de cambio* all around the Plaza des Armes, several banks with Visa or MasterCard cash points, and touts on Av. del Sol.

Internet: There are terminals at Telser, Medio 117, where you can also make international phone calls. Planeta Sur on Plateros, off the northwestern corner of the plaza, has a few terminals and great coffee, made with an old Italian espresso machine.

Medical services: Avoid the Hospital Regional. Call Tourist Medical Assistance (24 hours) on ✆ 222622/621838. They speak English.

Visitors ticket: The cheapest and most convenient way to visit the mounuments in Cusco and the Sacred Valley is with a Cusco visitors ticket, available from Instituto Nacional de Cultura, Garcilaso at Plaza Recocijo. It costs around $15.

South American Explorers (SAE): office at Av. del Sol 930, postal address: apartado 500, Cusco ✆/🖷 223102, *saec@amauta.rcp.net.pe*. SAE provide unbiased information, trip reports and advice on destinations throughout South America. They have other offices in Lima, Quito and in Ithaca, New York.

INRENA: A. Micaela Bastidas No.310, Wanchaq, ✆ 234179. Issue permits for the national parks and reserves.

Tour Operators: *see* p.127 and p.132.

Festivals

Cusco's biggest annual festival is the re-creation of the Inca Inti Raymi celebrations, on the winter solstice (June 21). Thousands dress up as Incas, and there are parades in Sacsayhuaman. Other important festivals include Mardi Gras and Semana Santa (Shrove Tuesday and Holy Week), with parades of life-size plaster saints and incense burning, and Peruvian Independence Day (28–29 July), with its military pomp.

The Sights

Cusco is a small city and all the important sights and monuments are most easily reached on foot. Taxis are cheap, safe and numerous.

Inca Cusco

When the Spanish first rode through the outskirts of Cusco in 1533, the buildings of mud and straw on a base of stone, some covered with plaster, looked not unlike those of a European city. It was only when they arrived in the centre of the city that they realized that Cusco, in the words of a chronicler, was 'the greatest and finest [city] ever seen in this country or elsewhere in the Indies. We can assure your Majesty that it is so beautiful and has such fine buildings that it would be remarkable even in Spain'. Cusco was built in the Pachacuti era (the mid- to late 1400s), in a broad mountain valley at the convergence of the Huantanay and Tullamayo Rivers. It was planned in the shape of a giant puma seen from the side, known as the 'Hatun Puma'. The head lay in the hills to the north west, the tail reaching a point where the two rivers met. The body of the cat was largely made-up of blocks of *wasis* and *canchas*: complexes of buildings typical of Inca architectural organization, found all over Tahuantinsuyu, and still used by Quechua and Aymara speakers today. *Wasis* were small one-room houses with thatched roofs attached to pegs, often linked together (like semi-detached houses), and organized around courtyards where all the work was done. *Canchas* were the enclosures that surrounded *wasis*. Both had single trapezoidal doors. Few remain amongst the colonial buildings of contemporary Cusco, but you'll see many in Machu Picchu and in the ruins along the Inca trail.

Also within the body of the Hatun Puma were *kallanas*: vast assembly halls with thatched or wooden roofs. Their bases can still be seen in the modern city centre, particularly on Loreto. In Inca times, the most important of these were built over a spit at the convergence of the two rivers, whose fast, clear water was diverted to run in wide gulleys down the centres of the streets and squares, carrying all the city's waste away.

The Plaza and City Centre: The Río Huatanay ran across the middle of a great central square, where the Spanish first set up their tents when they arrived in the city. The original square was twice the size of the modern plaza. The western side was a public area where rowdy festivals were celebrated, and the eastern, called the Aucaypata, was surrounded on three sides by the huge walls of four imperial palaces. These were the residences of living and dead Incas, surrounded by high, thick walls of the finest masonry in the empire. You can still see some on Calles Loreto and Hatunrumyioc (a much photographed 12-sided stone is perfectly fitted into the middle of a wall on the latter street). Spacious courtyards and buildings built on the *wasicancha* model lay inside the palaces, together with huge *kallanas*. During important festivals, mummies from inside, each of the corpse of a ruler, were offered food and drink by their living subjects and paraded around the square, surrounded by their furnishings and effigies of gold. None of the treasure of the Inca tombs survives today—grave robbing is a national pastime and is even celebrated on All Saints Day. Francisco Pizarro himself took the grandest building of all, the Palace of Pachacuti, lodging in a *kallana* as vast as a European cathedral. This was later converted into a colonial arcade, the **Portal de Panes**, now home to travel agencies and shops. Fragments of the original wall can be seen in the Roma restaurant on the western side of the plaza. The palace commandeered by Hernando, Pizarro's brother, was later converted into the Jesuit **church of La Compañía**. The Catholic Church was given a palace and hall standing on a platform looking over the square; these became the two **churches of El Triunfo**, and **Jesús María** and the **cathedral** that can be seen today on the plaza. Tupac Amaru, the last Inca ruler of the breakaway state of Vilcabamba, was executed here.

Inca Sacred Buildings: As state and religion were inter-connected for the Incas, it is no surprise that the headquarters of the empire was also a sacred place. In fact, Cusco was the centre of Tahuantinsuyu both terrestrially and cosmically. For the Incas, as for many Shamanic cultures, these two worlds were inseparable. Two points in the plaza, one a pillar, known as the *usnu*, the other a building, the *Sunturwasi*, were used as sighting points for a network of shrines or *huacas* on the horizons around Cusco. These *huacas*, together with the surrounding mountains, were used to track the movement of heavenly bodies, especially the Milky Way and the moon. The Incas erected distant pillars of stone to monitor the motion of the sun, to whom daily offerings were made. These pillars were also used to predict planting and harvesting times at different sites within the empire. These times varied tremendously: Tahuantinsuyu was a vertical empire, and altitude as much as season determined them. No matter where in Tahuantinsuyu, planting and harvesting could only begin after a special ceremony in Cusco. A runner was then sent to give the go-ahead. Runners would leave in one of four directions—the Inca empire was an empire of four quarters, the literal meaning of Tahuantinsuyu. The boundary lines of these four quarters radiated out of the main plaza along roads plotted to match the intercardinal axes of the Milky Way, which the Inca called *Mayu*.

The most important ceremonial and ritual building lay outside the plaza: the **Coricancha** (*open Mon–Sat 8–5, Sun 2–4*), a *cancha* enclosing six *wasis*. This was a giant 'sun, star and moon dial' used for tracking the movements of astronomical bodies and for connecting celestial and terrestrial events. It was the spiritual heart of the empire. Forty-one sighting lines, called *ceques*, grouped according to the four quarters of the Inca empire and orientated to the motion of heavenly bodies, stretched to the horizon from points within the temple. The two principal *wasis* were dedicated to the sun and the moon. Until it was stripped to pay off Atahualpa's ransom to the Spanish, the sun *wasi* was entirely clad in gold. The moon *wasi* was equally sumptuous but clad in silver. Around these *wasis* was a garden full of trees and plants made of solid gold and silver. Today the Coricancha forms the base of the **church of Santo Domingo**. Only the magnificent stonework, a curved and perfectly fitted wall, and the shells of the original *wasis* remain. The last Inca, Tupac Amaru and Juan Pizarro, the great conquistador's third brother, lie inside.

The Coricancha lay at the tail-end of the puma-city of Cusco. Another, equally remarkable building formed the head: the fortress of **Sacsayhuaman** (*open daily 7–5.30*), in ruins since Manco Capac's revolt against the Spanish in 1536. It once looked out over the city from a series of zigzag terraces formed of interlocking blocks, each weighing 90 to 100 tons. It took a work-force of 30,000 men several generations to complete. Inside the walls were *wasi-cancha* complexes, temples and channels probably used for the ritual manipulation of water (like the sacred baths at Machu Picchu or Wiñay Wayna). Only the highest echelons of the ruling Inca families were permitted to enter Sacsayhuaman, which was regarded as the holy house of the sun. During the winter solstice (21 June), the sun strikes Sacsayhuaman immediately before illuminating the Coricancha, thus sanctifying the holiest parts of the empire at the beginning of the season of rebirth, when winter turns to summer.

Just outside the plaza, along modern Loreto lay another important building, whose fine walls are still preserved today. The **Acllahausi**, was a residence of *acclas*, holy women, drawn from all quarters of the empire and chosen because of their noble lineage or their exceptional beauty to play an important part in the empire's official sun religion.

Colonial Cusco

It took 100 years to convert the Inca palace into **Cusco Cathedral** (*open daily 2–5.30*). The adjoining church of El Triunfo was completed long before, in 1536, and is the oldest church in the city. Jesús María, connected to it to the north, was not completed until 1773. The cathedral itself has some fine art from the Cusqueño school, which mixes Indian and Spanish styles. The most notable is the *Last Supper* by Zapata, depicting Christ eating guinea pig. The sacristy is full of paintings of bishops, including Pizarro's friar, Vicente de Valverde, who sanctioned the conquest. The *Crucifixion* behind the altar is said to be by Van Dyck.

During Manco Capac's great rebellion against the Spanish in 1536, Pizarro and his men found themselves under siege in Cusco's central plaza, trapped in thatched huts and facing a barrage of flaming arrows. Much of Cusco was burning, yet the thatched roof of Pizarro's hut escaped fire, flaming for an instant and then going out. This was attributed to divine intervention and, after the battle was won, the **church of El Triunfo** (*open daily 2–5.30*) was built to commemorate the miraculous escape. The remains of the mixed-blood chronicler Garcilaso de la Vega, author of *Comentarios Reales*, lie inside the church.

Other Churches and Museums

La Compañía on the southern corner of the plaza, has a portrait of Martín García de Loyola (nephew to Ignatius Loyola, founder of the Jesuits), who hunted down Tupac Amaru, the last Inca, who ruled the independent state of Vilcabamba until 1572. **La Merced** (*open daily 7–9 and 5–7.30*), on Mantas between Sol and San Andrés, has a 4ft-high monstrance encrusted with diamonds and pearls. Gonzalo Pizarro and Diego de Almagro have their tombs here, and there's a small museum (*open daily 8–12 and 2–4*). The gloomy 16th-century church of **San Francisco** (*open daily 6.30–8 and 6–8*), Tordo at Plaza San Francisco, has a huge depiction of the genealogy of St Francis. **Santa Clara** (*open daily 6–7am for Mass*), one block west of the Plaza San Francisco, is covered in mirrors which beautifully reflect the candlelight.

The **Museo de Arqueología and Admiral's Palace**, Ataúd at Córdoba (*open Mon–Sat 9–6, Sun 9–12*) contains a well-displayed collection of artefacts, including some Inca gold and paintings. The **Museum of Religious Art**, Hatunrumiyoc at Herejes (*open Mon–Sat 9–12.30* *and 3–5.30*), has paintings of the Cusqueño school. There is a good model of pre-Spanish Cusco and other curiosities at the **Coricancha Museum**, in the grounds of the Coricancha (*open Mon–Sat 8–5, Sun 2–4*). The **Museum of Natural History**, next to La Compañía, (*open Mon–Fri 8–1 and 3–6*), has a bizarre collection of stuffed animals, including a two-headed alpaca and a six-legged goat. For an overview of Peruvian history, head to the **Museum of Regional History**, Garcilaso at Heladeros (*open daily 8–6*), which has a Nasca mummy and a series of paintings of the Cusqueño school, including St Michael with a musket.

Cusco (© 084–)   ***Shopping***

Cusco is one of the best places in South America to pick up souvenirs. The shops and markets to the west of the Plaza de Armas sell the cheaper stuff—knitwear, ceramics and replicas of the Cusqueño school oil paintings. There's also a fine selection of tourist kitsch. If you're after alpaca woollens, make sure you're getting the real thing. Alpaca is at least as soft as cashmere, and it is not cheap. Expect to pay about half to two thirds of what's originally demanded, or more if you want to. Bargaining is expected, but don't expect something for nothing. Higher-quality items can be found on Triunfo and its continuations, Hatunrumyioc and Cuesta San Blas. **Amarinke Artesanias**, on Triunfo 387, © 227778, sell beautiful multicoloured Shipibo stitched wall hangings. The Shipibo are an Amazon tribe who live near Pucallpa; you can buy their goods directly from them, in Iquitos, at a slightly cheaper price.

Cusco (© 084–)   ***Where to Stay***

Cusco has some wonderful hotels, for all budgets, many of them in colonial buildings, arranged around a small tiled courtyard, or in quiet little streets in the San Blas area, a short walk from the centre.

expensive

Monastério, Palacio 140, © 241777/8/9, two blocks east of the Plaza de Armas. The most delightful hotel in Cusco, in a converted Augustinian monastery with two covered cloisters, a modern wing, and an excellent restaurant. Even if you decide not to stay, visit the chapel, which has some some superb wall paintings.

Libertador, Pzta Santo Domingo 259, © 231961/238600, ◈ 233152. A larger, even more luxurious hotel housed in a colonial palace. The service here is better than at the Monastério, though it cannot compare when it comes to charm.

moderate

Marquesas, Garcilaso 256, © 232512. A colonial delight, with antique furniture, carved wooden doors and elegant balconies overlooking a central courtyard.

Loreto, Loreto 115, © 226352. Rooms with Inca walls—without them, its rooms would be over-priced and dull.

Amaru, Cuesta San Blas 541, © 225933. A colonial hotel with a book exchange and a public piano in the quiet, artisan area of San Blas.

San Blas, Cuesta San Blas 526, © 225781. Similar to the Amaru, but a little cheaper and only a few doors away.

cheap

El Arcano, Carmen Alto 288, © 232703. A tiny, spotless and charming cheapie in a colonial house in the San Blas area.

Sambleño, Carmen Alto 114, ✆ 221452; cheap, yet clean, with cable TV in the lobby.
Suecia, Uriel Garcia 332, ✆ 233282, in a colonial house just off the main plaza. The best rooms look over the street but the disco nearby can be a pain at weekends.

Cusco (✆ 084–)   **Eating Out**

Thanks to its tourist status, Cusco has some reasonable restaurants, including several options for vegetarians. The best by far is the **Monastério** (in the hotel of the same name—*see* above)with the finest menu and wine list in the city. Others include:

El Truco, Plaza Recocijo 261, ✆ 235295, is popular with tour groups and has a live show, and good traditional Cusqueño dishes (*moderate*).

Mesón de Espaderos, Espaderos 105, specializes in local dishes, including *cuy* (guinea pig), which is delicious roasted and tastes a bit like chicken (*inexpensive*).

Chez Maggy, Plateros 339, the best of the numerous pizzerias, with long wooden tables, peyote-inspired paintings and live Andean music in the evenings (*inexpensive*).

La Tertulia, Procuradores 50, does enormous cheap breakfasts, which include as much yoghurt, freshly baked bread, and eggs as you can eat. **Ukukus,** just up the street is similar, though the service is better and it's less crowded (*both cheap*).

There are several vegetarian places: **La Libertad,** San Juan de Dios, has nothing fancy, but it's the best in town, with a good, inexpensive set menu and breakfast. The soups are great. **Kaleydaskop,** Triunfo 393, has a variety of salads, soups and tasty but small main courses for sale in a New Age bookshop to the accompaniment of whale music. **Acuarium,** Cuesta de Almirante 211, is little more than somebody's kitchen; the food is erratic, though the fresh soups tend to be reliable, and service is very slow. **Govinda,** Espaderos 130, has good cakes and thick, tasty bread.

Around Cusco: The Sacred Valley

The Río Urubamba, which flows past Machu Picchu and on towards the Ucayali and the Amazon, runs into what is popularly referred to as the **Sacred Valley**, 15km from Cusco. There are two important Inca ruins here, Pisac and Ollantaytambo, together with some of the best terracing in the region and some wonderful mountain views. There are a number of hiking opportunities around the valley, as well as rafting on the river, horse-riding and mountain-biking. Accommodation can be found in some of the valley's villages (*see* p.118).

Getting There

Buses leave from Urubamba or Pisac to Chinchero. Ask to be dropped off at the beginning of the road to Maras (for Moray), a 3km walk away. The ruins are a further 6km from here. Locals will put you on the right track. Driving to Moray is rough, but not impossible. The tourist office in Cusco can help you with the route.

It is possible to walk from Moray to the Salinas (*see* below), about 5km further on. Ask at Moray for the right path. Otherwise, any Ollantaytambo-bound bus can drop you off at Tarabamba. When you arrive, cross over the river via the footbridge and turn right along the path leading to the graveyard. Turn left here, climbing up the valley to the salt pans.

There are regular buses from Cusco (from a stop on Av. Tullumayo, or the bus station). Pisac is less than an hour away, Urubamba village is about 2–2½. You must change here to visit Ollantaytambo, a further 50 mins away, which can also be reached directly via the Machu Picchu train from Cusco (about 2hrs), *see* p.112.

The extensive Inca ruins of **Pisac** look out from the brow of a steep hill over extensive terraces and the picturesque colonial town below. There's an Intihuatana (meaning 'hitching post of the sun') here, one of the few that survived the ravages of the Spanish. These are thought to have been used for observing the movements of the sun in relation to the other astronomical bodies, thus determining the precise time of key calendar events such as the equinoxes. The best times to visit Pisac are on market days (Tues, Thurs and Sun mornings), when you can pick up souvenirs including fine knitwear. If you don't make it then, visit the shop on the plaza which is owned by a weavers' collective—all the money goes to them rather than a middleman. Try and visit the local baker, who breaks bread in a huge clay oven, pulling it out with a giant wooden spatula. If you find Pisac a little touristy, take a bus to **Chinchero**, nearby, which has some fine paintings in the church, smaller Inca ruins and a more traditional market.

Urubamba is the largest population centre in the valley, though it is barely a village. Trails lead from here to the Inca site of **Moray** and the Salinas (Inca salt pans), near Tarabamba. They look like snow-encrusted Balinese fields cut out of the hillside and are still in use. Moray's terraced bowls look like two abutting amphitheatres, lost in the hills of the Sacred Valley. It is speculated that they were used for agricultural experiments: each terrace has a different microclimate, depending on its depth within the bowl.

Ollantaytambo

Ollantaytambo is the site of one of the Cusco region's most impressive ruins, a fortress perched on a high, steep ridge, surrounded by precipitous terraced fields. It is easy to see why this was the only Inca stronghold to resist Spanish assault during Manco Capac's ill fated 1536 rebellion. Hernando Pizarro approached from behind, along the narrow Río Yucay. Along the way, he had to negotiate six fords, all fortified and heavily defended against him. When he finally reached Ollantaytambo his tired soldiers were dismayed: the fortress, perched like an eyrie on its ridge and bristling with angry Inca warriors seemed impregnable. But his bravest warriors spurred him on: Amazon Indian archers, recruited from the forests of Manu, stood and fought even as they were struck with missiles and buckshot. For a while it looked like the Amazons would turn the tide in favour of the Spanish, but Manco Capac had reserved his masterstroke for the last moment. While the Spanish were struggling through the fords, his engineers had been instructed to divert the course of the Río Patacancha and, when his enemies were battling their way up the terraces, he ordered the Incas to break the dam. The river rushed through the specially cut channels and flooded the narrow valley below. Pizarro ordered a retreat and returned with the remnant of his humiliated army to Cusco. The village below the fort is one of the few modern examples of Inca town planning, built on traditional foundations and still preserving its *wasi-cancha* layout.

Sacred Valley (©084–) **Where to Stay**

Most of the accommodation in the Sacred Valley is simple but comfortable: besides our recommendations, there are a number of smaller places in the villages. Urubamba has the greatest choice.

La Posada del Inca Yucay, Plaza Manco II de Yucay 123, Urubamba, ✆ 201107/201347, ✆ 201245. Comfortable accommodation in an old colonial hacienda. The posada organize walks and treks around the valley, rafting on the Río Urubamba, horse-riding and mountain-biking. **El Albergue**, Ollantaytambo, ✆ 244014, a kilometre from the centre, is simple, with hot water and a sauna. Run by a couple from the USA.

There's plenty of cheap accommodation in Urubamba, including the **Hotel Urubamba**, two blocks from the plaza on Jirón Bolognesi at Los Girasoles, ✆ 201390, which has dorms, doubles and singles and a camping site. Ollantaytambo and Pisac have fewer options. In Ollantaytambo, **Orquídeas**, 12 de Octubre, ✆ 204032, is good value. The **Tambo**, Homo 96, ✆ 204003, is more upmarket. In Pisac, choices are limited to the **Parador Pisac** on the square or the **Residencial Beho** on the way to the ruins. Both have cold water only. Although there is food in all the villages, it is limited to cheap eateries. Pisac has only very basic cafés.

The Inca Trail and Machu Picchu

This four-day trek, over mountain passes, through cloud forest, ruined cities and spectacular river valleys, to Machu Picchu, is one of the highlights of any visit to Peru. Much of the walk is along original Inca trails and brings you to Machu Picchu at dawn on the last day, when you'll have the ruins pretty much all to yourself. If you have the time and the energy this is the best way to arrive there. And you can take the restful train, or even a helicopter, back. It used to be possible to walk the trek independently but now it is open to tour groups only. These can be organized from Cusco.

Getting There

For **trains** and **helicopter** services to Macchu Picchu from Cusco, *see* p.112. The pricey **bus** to Aguas Calientes leaves from outside the Machu Picchu Ruinas Hotel. There are plans to build a cable car between Aguas Calientes and Machu Picchu.

Tour Operators for the Inca Trail and Machu Picchu

Peruvian Andean Treks, Av. Pardo 705, ✆ 22701, ✆ 2891, *postmast@patsuco.com.pe*, **Manu Expeditions** or **Pantiacolla** (*see* pp.127–8) are the best options. They are more expensive than other companies ($100 upwards) but offer a more luxurious service together with good guides who know the biology of the area as well as the archaeology of the ruins. The best of the cheaper operators is **United Mice** ($30 upwards). Avoid the very cheapest operators: they abuse their staff (especially the porters) and their equipment is often shoddy.

The Inca Trail: A Typical Four-day Itinerary

Day one: (*4–9 hours depending on acclimatization and strength*). There are a number of different ways of reaching the Inca trail (*see* 'Variations on the Classic Inca Trail' p.122). The 'classic trail' as it has come to be known, begins at Qoriwayrachina, commonly known as Kilometre 88; a collection of ramshackle vending huts. The trailhead is at the bridge over the Río Urubamba, where there is a park warden's booth selling tickets for just under $20. Put yours in a safe, dry place (you'll need it when you get to Machu Picchu) and head over the river to a fork in the path. A right turn leads to a half-hour detour to the ruins of **Wayñaquente** ('Young Hummingbird'). There are three Inca *huacas* (shrines) here, together with two spring-water baths and some stonework as good as any in Machu Picchu. This suggests that Wayñaquente was a small pilgrimage centre. The extensive Inca terracing around it would have made it self-sufficient. The detour trail continues beyond to the less impressive Machuquente ruins.

Turning left at the fork leads to the Inca trail proper and **Llactapata** ('Hillside Town'), an intricate maze of small buildings probably reserved for *karakas* (minor nobility), surrounded by extensive terracing that drops in levels to the Río Cusichaca below. The ruins are slightly older than Wayñaquente and were probably built in the mid-15th century in the middle of the the first great Inca epoch, that of Pachacuti (*see* p.110). From here, the path crosses the Cusichaca via a small bridge, climbs along the course of the river through groves of eucalyptus, and arrives at the village of **Wayllabamba**, which is often used as a lunch stop.

After the village, the path climbs relentlessly up the left bank of the Río Llullucha towards the first pass, which you'll reach the following morning. After an hour or so, you'll reach a fork in the river. The left turn leads to the Tres Piedras campsite where many tour groups make their first stop; if you want a quiet second day, persuade your group to press on—the trail continues across the bridge and up into the cloud forest. After an hour or so, you'll see a peaceful campsite in a clearing off to your right, next to the river, where few people stop. If you want to go further the limit of day one is the Llullucha campsite, less than an hour away on open grassland. The views down the valley to the snow-capped crags beyond are terrific.

Day two: (*5–10 hours*). This is the toughest day, with two high passes and the longest section to walk. **Warmiwañusca** ('Dead Woman') is the first and the hardest of the passes, a long hard slog that is doubly difficult because of the altitude. This is the highest point on the trail (4,200m or 13,776 ft); from here you can see the next campsite, **Pacaymayu**, on the bank of the river of the same name, nearly a kilometre below you. Beyond that lie the real delights of the Inca trail. Tiredness will probably make Pacaymayu look like a good place for lunch or even to camp, but as it is another agency favourite you may want to try to get to Runkuraqay, a mere 40 minutes away, or the fourth campsite at the Sayacmarca ruins, about two hours over the second pass.

The climb out of Pacaymayu is steep. The steps hug the valley side, eventually leading to **Runkuraqay**, a circular rock eyrie which may have been a *tambo* (a traveller's resting place). A short climb past two small tarns leads to the top of the second pass, where the view is even more magnificent than that from the first. Behind is the Pacaymayu valley, Runkuraqay perched over it like a sentinel, paramo stretching down to tropical forest with a thread of river far below. In front, a perfectly preserved stretch of Inca road follows the course of another, lusher valley past a cobalt lake. In the distance lie the snow-covered ridges of the Vilcabamba range.

An hour's walk culminates at the most impressive ruins yet, **Sayacmarca**, contoured to the ridge they occupy, with a steep flight of over 200 stone steps. Make camp next to the river below and visit at dusk when the ruins are empty and the only sound is of running water. Sitting in the back of the city is like looking out from the cockpit of a giant stone ship, its prow extending towards the craggy horizon. The sun sets over these mountains, followed, on a few special occasions, by Venus and a sweep of stars passing right through the belt of Orion. Then the full moon rises and eerily lights the stone and the valley beyond. Like Machu Picchu and Cusco itself, Sayacmarca was an eminent religious and astronomical centre, built in the late 15th century. Its position and stellar orientation is enough to persuade anyone that the Incas were an advanced civilization, their architectural priorities reflecting their spiritual principles— a harmonious integration with the natural world they so venerated. The campsite next to the river is the best place to stop for the night if you want to explore the ruins. There's a larger campsite at Qonchamarca just under half an hour away and, if you are really energetic, the third pass is two hours from here, and it is possible to camp there. The sunrise is astounding.

Day three: (*4–9 hours from Sayacmarca*). If you stayed at Sayacmarca, day three begins with another climb, the gentlest yet, and the last uphill stretch on the trek. The road here is mostly original Inca and is perhaps the most beautiful on the trail, lined with ferns and trees dripping with moss, orchids and other epiphytic plants. It passes through a tunnel cut through a massive monolith: how the Incas achieved this without metal is anyone's guess. There are some faded carvings inside the tunnel. From here it is a short stretch to the third and final pass, where you'll have your finest view yet. The tiny Río Urubamba, shrunken by more than a mile's difference in altitude, winds below walls of rock covered in cloud forest. Behind these lie the jagged ridges of the Vilcabamba range, their highest peaks covered in snow and glacial ice-fields. Looking back, you'll see the huge holy Inca mountain of **Salcantay**.

Down a flight of steep, slippery Inca steps from the third pass, are the ruins of the poetically named **Phuyupatamarca** ('City above the Clouds'). These are organically sculpted into the hillside, surrounded by fields of bright yellow ladies' slippers and watered by a series of ceremonial baths. To the north are glimpses of the terraces of Wiñaywayna and Intipata on the sides of the promontory which conceals Machu Picchu. Phuyupatamarca, discovered by Bingham and named and excavated by Paul Fejos in 1941, was probably another ceremonial centre devoted to the ritual worship of water. The architectural style dates it to the end of the Pachacuti's era, or the onset of his successor's, at the end of the 15th century.

The walk to the final camp is a trip from the sublime to the hideous. The trail follows a series of steps to more Inca road bisected by occasional gulleys, built by the Incas to divert the course of springs. A right turn near an ugly pylon winds up at a squat hostel and campsite, the last base before Machu Picchu, swarming with other tour groups. If you carry on along the Inca trail instead of turning right at the pylon, you'll end up in the agricultural settlement of **Intipata**. There is an extensive system of terraces here, three of which are hollow and hide houses. The ruins are being allowed to return to forest as they are the breeding ground for a rare orchid. The only redeeming feature of the ugly hostel and campsite is their proximity to **Wiñaywayna**, the most classically beautiful ruins on the Inca trail. The city's tiny maze of buildings is perched on the end of a ridge lined with a steep procession of spring-water baths, tapering to a final triangular platform of Inca stone that falls almost sheer into the Urubamba valley far below. From every point of view but the aesthetic, this is an absurd place to build a city.

Day four: Try to get to Machu Picchu as early as you possibly can before the bus loads arrive and destroy its serene beauty. The ideal time to arrive is dawn which means walking for nearly three hours in the dark: two hours to get to Intipunku (the Gateway of the Sun), which marks the entrance to the city and affords your first, long-anticipated view, and an hour from there. At times the path is cut out of sheer rock, with terrifying drops off to the right.

No attempt to describe the view of Machu Picchu at dawn can even begin to capture the real thing: like dawn at the Taj Mahal or from the top of Mount Sinai, this is a sight that must be appreciated first hand. Our best advice, no matter what time of day you arrive at Machu Picchu, is (if your tour guide can be persuaded) to sneak to the 'porter's lodge' at the back of the site, avoiding officials, and hide your rucksacks inside. This way you can steal your first half hour or so for silent awe-inspired contemplation and avoid being asked to leave as soon as you arrive. Rucksacks are not allowed in the ruins and the officials show no mercy and give no time to take in the beauty you've walked three days to see. After your stolen half-hour you can leisurely stroll down to the main entrance, where you'll find a locker room off to the left next to a kiosk selling cheap food at expensive prices. This and the even more over-priced restaurant in front of the entrance are the only places that serve breakfast.

Variations on the Classic Inca Trail

If you want to miss the crowds, at least for part of the time, there are a number of less travelled trails around Cusco and Machu Picchu, which link up with the classic Inca trail. The best of these are the walk up the Silque valley (from Chilca or Kilometre 82) to Machu Picchu and the Mollepata trek. Both add an extra 1–2 days to the trail, and are hardly ever walked. The **Silque valley trek** takes 6–7 days past glaciers, waterfalls and the ruins of Inca Paucacancha on the old Anta to Machu Picchu road. There's a pass of nearly 5,000m. The trail joins up with the classic Inca trail at the village of Wayllabamba (*see* p.120). The **Mollepata trek** is even tougher, but the scenery is stunning: glaciers, beautiful copper green tarns and the watersheds of both the Urubamba and the Apurímac Rivers. This trail joins the Silque valley trek at Paucacancha, continuing on to Machu Picchu. More detailed information on these treks can be found in *The Inca Trail* by Richard Danbury (Trailblazer Publications).

Manu Expeditions (*see* p.128) offer an 'In Search of Machu Picchu' **horse-ride and trek**, which is basically a hybrid of the Silque and Mollepata treks. After a visit to Ollantaytambo, the trek begins at an old Inca bridge over the Río Urubamba, where you make your way up a winding trail into the Cordillera Vilcabamba on horses or on foot. A support crew of porters and cooks follow. The geometric patterns of Inca fields and terraces gradually shrink as you leave the valley below and ascend towards the Wawayoq Orquo Pass. Camp is made on the other side, at Chanqochuqu. The next morning is spent crossing a high ridge, lunching at Coralpata, where there's a magical view out towards the Veronica massif, and following an Inca trail into a gully below the icy walls of Mount Nevado Huayanay. There's an optional visit to a small herder's village down the valley the next morning, followed by a climb to the Puerto Huayanay Pass. Climbing a switchbacking trail, you follow an old stone paved Inca road to the ruins of Incarakay. Another steep climb to the Milpucasa Pass then leads downhill to the next camp. The following day begins with the Milupampa Pass and magnificent views of the glaciers and snow peaks of the 6km-high holy Inca mountain of Salcantay, the highest peak in the Vilcabamba. Camp is made next to an Inca canal at Pampacahuan. The next day is downhill all the way, soon reaching the treeline and relative warmth. Lunch is taken at Paucarkanca, which probably served as a *tambo*. From here, the trek descends to the beginning of the classic 'Inca trail'. Camp is made at Llactapata. From here, you have the option of continuing on the classic trail or taking the train to Kilometre 104 for the path to Wiñaywayna via the little-visited site of Chachabamba. If you're really tired, it's possible to go all the way to Aguas Calientes. The trek costs around $1,850 if you are met in Lima and less if you join in Cusco or Ollantaytambo.

Machu Picchu and Espíritu Pampa: Discovery and Mystery

Like all of the ruins on the Inca trail, Machu Picchu was never pillaged by the Spanish. What you see are the houses, *huacas*, temples and administrative buildings of a complete Inca city, seen by a foreigner for the first time when a Yale historian and adventurer, Hiram Bingham, chanced upon it in 1911. After partially clearing the site, Bingham thought he'd found the ruins of Vilcabamba, capital of the breakaway Inca empire of the same name. For over 50 years the archaeological community believed him. Then another American, Paul Fejos, an accomplished archaeologist, led the Werner Gren Scientific Expedition to Hispanic America, in 1940–1, and concluded that none of the towns in the region, including Machu Picchu, were built with strategic or military purpose and that there was no evidence that the Spanish had looted or occupied them. Even though Bingham was declaring confidently, as late as 1951 that Machu Picchu was the site of Vilcabamba, archaeologists began to look elsewhere. In July 1964, maverick archaeologist Gene Savoy partially cleared another set of ruins discovered by his predecessor on his first expedition in 1911. These were far deeper in the forest, on the banks of the San Miguel River, 60km from Machu Picchu. Bingham had dismissed Espíritu Pampa, as he called the site, as a minor ruin. He could not have been more wrong. Savoy discovered 50 or 60 buildings, 300 houses, a 70m-long temple, palaces and an extensive network of Inca roads. Espíritu Pampa was larger and more important than Bingham could ever have imagined. Significantly, it almost exactly matched Spanish descriptions of ancient Vilcabamba.

In stumbling across Machu Picchu, Bingham had chanced upon a mystery deeper than the whereabouts of Vilcabamba. What he had discovered was an enclave of Tahuantinsyu, the Inca empire, dating from the time of the first emperor, Pachacuti. How and why it remained hidden from outsiders for so long is only part of the mystery. Recently discovered Spanish documents suggest that the lower Urubamba valley was conquered by Pachacuti, so we can presume that it was he or his successor, Topac Yupanqui, who built the cities in the region, including those along the Inca Trail and Machu Picchu itself. Their architectural style would suggest this to be true. Beyond this we can only guess. The most likely explanation at present, based on the numbers of *huacas* and the orientation of Machu Picchu and the other cities along the route, is that this was a pilgrimage centre given to the Inca cult of the divine in nature. We know that the lower Urubamba valley was used for growing coca—as sacred to the Incas as it is to most tribal people of South America. Anthropologist Johan Reinhard has recently shown that Machu Picchu is the spoke for a whole series of *ceques*—the name given to the sighting lines which connected shrines. These were also sacred to the Incas.

Further studies have suggested that buildings in the city are orientated to astronomical phenomena known to be important to the Incas. For instance, the intricately carved and precisely aligned Intihuatana is thought to have been used for observing the movements of the Sun in relation to other astronomical bodies. At dawn on the winter solstice (21 June), the sun pierces the central window of the Sun Temple or Torréon, striking the rock in the centre of the building. And the Temple of the Moon is aligned with the Pleiades, which were also venerated by the Incas. As for the mystery of why Machu Picchu was abandoned, no one has any idea.

Wildlife and Birding on the Inca Trail and around Machu Picchu

It may only be a small area but there are seven different ecosystems on the Inca trail, ranging from subtropical alpine tundra and sub-alpine subtropical pàramo to subtropical montane rainforest and subtropical wet forest. These support a large variety of plants and animals.

Mammals: Apart from semi-domesticated llama and alpaca, you'll be lucky to see any large mammals even though the trail passes through their habitats—there are simply too many walkers and they have become accustomed to avoiding man. You are most likely to see white-tailed deer or the smaller *pudu* (pygmy deer). You may be very lucky and see Andean spectacled bear, puma and ocelot, especially if you walk off season. Of the smaller mammals you may not have seen before, the commonest are viscacha, which look like stoned rabbits with a long tail. Others include tayra, a large, fearsome weasel, the rare and elusive mountain cat, and the southern river otter. In the trees, keep a look-out for inquisitive squirrel monkeys and capuchins. Squirrel monkeys hang around in large troops and have a black snout, black upper head and white areas around the eyes. Capuchins are similar but larger. Their wide-eyed relative, the night monkey, which has a pale face with white eyebrows, and an orange underside is active after dark, calling like an owl to attract a mate.

Poisonous Snakes: Be wary of snakes unless you are sure you know what you are doing. Some of the world's largest vipers live in the environs of the trail. These include **bushmasters** which can grow up to 3.5m (12ft) long, have heads shaped like arrowheads and are camouflaged to look like dead leaves. Their bite is fatal, sometimes even if anti-venom is given. **Coral snakes**, which look like a brightly coloured red, black and yellow necklace, are better known. They are very poisonous too but not so aggressive. You are very unlikely to see either, let alone get bitten—bushmasters hunt at night and coral snakes are very shy.

Birds and Birding: Inca wren live along the trail, especially around bamboo thickets—there are some around the highest part of Machu Picchu. Green-and-white hummingbird, white-bellied woodstar and Andean cock-of-the-rock are sometimes seen in the cloud forests near and around the trail. Other hummingbirds seen here include the world's largest, the giant hummingbird, as well as the white-bellied and the speckled. Of the water fowl, the most spectacular is the highly endangered, fasciated tiger-heron and the torrent duck, which can be seen braving the Urubamba or in streams and ponds along the trail. In the mountain areas, you'd have to be lucky to see a condor, though they do live here. There are other birds of prey around too, like the black-chested buzzard eagle and the aplomado falcon. The endangered imperial snipe is widespread, and golden-collared tanagers and tit-like dacnis live on the slopes or in the high cloud forests, together with various trogons, quetzals and Andean guans. The bizarrely named bearded mountaineer is attracted to the tobacco trees that grow along the trail, particularly in the ravines. Manu Expeditions or Pantiacolla (*see* p.128–9) can arrange specialist birding trips to Machu Picchu and along the various Inca Trails. Contact them well in advance.

Beyond Machu Picchu: Espíritu Pampa (Vilcabamba), Vitcos, and Chuquipalta

It is possible to walk through the jungle to the capital of the breakaway Inca empire of **Vilcabamba**. It is more of a jungle expedition than a mountain trek and you'll need a guide.

Vilcabamba was set up by Manco Inca in 1537, after the Spanish took over Cusco, and was autonomous under Manco and Titu Cusi until 1572, when the Spanish finally invaded. The then emperor, Tupac Amaru, fled into what are now the forests of Manu Biosphere Reserve, where some say his followers established another city called Paititi. Tupac himself surrendered to the Spanish and was executed in Cusco. The ruins were rediscovered by American adventurer Hiram Bingham in 1911. Ironically he was searching for Vilcabamba and thought that he had found only a minor site here along the way, christening it Espíritu Pampa after the nearby river (see p.123). Bingham's mistake is easy to understand—Vilcabamba is no Machu Picchu and Bingham was no archaeologist. The forest here is thick and the ruins look far less grand. They've not even been properly explored, let alone excavated. The path there, if it can be called that, is two to three days of rough going, with many ascents and descents. Nonetheless, you are in a little visited and beautiful part of Peru where few foreigners ever stray.

The trek begins in Huancacalla village which is itself difficult to reach. First you must get to Quillabamba, the old end of the line for trains running along the Río Urubamba past Machu Picchu. There are currently no plans to restart these services, but check with the tourist office in Cusco. A bus leaves daily and takes about nine hours. From Quillabamba you can find a truck to take you to Huancacalla direct or, failing that, to Chaullay Puente, 20km away, from where there's regular transport to Huancacalla. At Huancacalla you can hire guides and mules to visit Vilcabamba. Bring enough packet food from Cusco to last a week and a water filter.

Huancacalla is close to another important Vilcabamba site, **Vitcos**, also discovered by Bingham, who called it Rosaspata. Vitcos was another Vilcabamba city and the centre of a *huaca* cult dedicated to the oracle of Chuquipalta, who appeared to the Incas on top of a huge block of granite, covered in carvings and enclosed in a Temple of the Sun, that would have looked like the Torreón in Machu Picchu. The final war between the Spanish and the Incas that resulted in the invasion of Vilcabamba was started, in part, because Spanish friars set fire to Chuquipalta and the surrounding temple. The huge white rock and the ruined temple still stand above the ruins of Vitcos, built on the tip of a spur above Huancacalla. Like Machu Picchu, it offers superb views of forested valleys and jagged mountain snowfields. But it's far smaller and less excavated. There are 14 rectangular houses on the plaza, arranged in a square with courtyards, and a long palace with 15 finely-worked doors.

Several agencies in Cusco offer trips to these ruins. The best of these is Manu Expeditions (for details see p.129). This company provides professional naturalist and birding guides and uses Bingham's expedition notes for the trek to Vilcabamba. It also offers nature walks to and around Machu Picchu and interesting variations on the Inca trail. You'll need to book in advance. Further details of the trek to Vilcabamba, together with detailed maps, are published in a book called *Sixpac Inca* by Vincent Lee, available in Cusco.

Machu Picchu and Aguas Calientas (©084–) **Where to Stay and Eating Out**

Machu Picchu

Machu Picchu Ruinas Hotel, opposite the main entrance, Carretera Bingham, Monumento Histórico Machu Picchu, Urubamba, ✆/✉ 211038; bookings ✆ 240742. Overpriced and incongruous, but the only place to stay or eat at the ruins (*expensive*).

Aguas Calientes (Machu Picchu Pueblo)

Ten years ago, Aguas Calientes, the nearest village to Machu Picchu, was little more than a dusty street with a couple of basic pensions. Now it's Ciudad Gringo and though it's still not beautiful there's a greater choice of hotels and restaurants, and even a few that don't have pizza-dominated menus. **Machu Picchu Pueblo Hotel**, ✆ 211122/3, ✉ 211124, is the best place here and in the whole valley. Individual heated bungalows are ensconced amongst the trees and gardens, there's a swimming pool, and an excellent restaurant (*expensive*). **Gringo Bill's**, Collaraymi 104, ✆ 211046, is the best budget hostal in town, with a range of imaginatively decorated rooms, a book exchange and a restaurant with a bar and grill (*cheap*). There is a handful of others including the clean **Machu Picchu**, next to the train station on Av. Imperio de los Incas 127, ✆ 211034, with a little patio overlooking the Urubamba.

There is a reasonable French-owned restaurant, **Indi Feliz**, on Yoque Yupanqui, hidden amongst the pizzerias and rave-music cafés. The best restaurant, however, is at the **Machu Picchu Pueblo Hotel** (*see* above). There's a Govinda veggie shed on Pachacutec, which runs off the northeastern corner of the plaza.

Manu Biosphere Reserve (National Park)

Legend has it that when the Inca followers of Tupac Amaru set light to and fled from the ruins of Vilcabamba, they headed into the forests beyond the Andes, where they founded their last great city, Paititi. These forests are now part of one of South America's most famous national parks, the Manu Biosphere Reserve, formed in May 1973 and declared a World Heritage Site in 1987. The Incas could not have chosen a more appropriate place to worship the divine in nature: the first view of Manu, mist evaporating off a forest that stretches out over the sharp ridges of the Andean foothills to the endless expanse of the Amazon plains, is unforgettable.

Manu is virgin rainforest. A trip along one of her rivers affirms this: the enormous buttresses and crowns of giant cedars spread uncut on the river banks, alongside tropical mahogany and shihuahuaco trees. Guans and currasows, the first birds to disappear when there is even light settlement, are abundant in Manu. There are even Indians deep within the park who have yet to make contact with the outside world. They have been seen only once, before disappearing back into forests larger than Switzerland.

It is not merely Manu's untouched state that makes it special; it is its habitats and the quantity and diversity of life they support. The protected area starts high up in the Andes going down from over 4,000m through elfin, cloud and other montane forests to the gallery forests of the lowlands 200m above sea level. The park holds world records for species diversity, with more than 15,000 plants, millions of insects, most of which are still unknown to science, and so many unclassified bird species that 860 have been identified so far at the Cocha Cashu Biological Research Station alone, a figure equivalent to 10 per cent of all the species on the planet. Manu is one of the best places to see mammals such as spectacled bear, jaguar, puma and tapir and the smallest primate in the world, the pygmy marmoset.

Protecting the park from the ravages of loggers, oil companies and drug traffickers is an ongoing concern and not just because of the plants and animals. Manu is home to a number of tribal peoples. Apart from the uncontacted groups, known as the Amahuaca people, there are Machiguenga, who have their own lodge within the cultural zone—staying there directly supports them, and there are Yaminahua, Piro, Amarakaeri, Huachipaire, Mascho-Piro and Nahua groups, together with 30 Quechua *campesino* (peasant farmer) communities. Other unknown groups have left their heritage at the Pusharo petroglyphs, and unexcavated Inca ruins prove that their presence here is not purely mythological.

The Lost Inca City of Paititi

Somewhere in the jungles of Peru lies the lost Inca city of Paititi. According to legend only one person has ever seen it and lived to tell the tale: an Indian who set out with two gold hunters a century ago. His two companions were struck blind and died deep in the forest. He stumbled back to Puerto Maldonado, half starved and half mad. The treasure, he said, was not gold but the secrets of the Incas: secrets that they themselves had learned from the Indians of the Amazon. They lie preserved in a city guarded by powerful shamans, which exists both in and out of space and time, in the real world, and in a mythic, eternal dimension.

Tour Operators for Manu Biosphere Reserve   *Cusco (℃ 084–)*

It is possible to visit the park on your own, but is more expensive and more time-consuming than going with a travel agency from Cusco, and you will struggle to get beyond the Cultural Zone (*see* below) without hiring an accredited guide and having a permit from INRENA in Cusco (*see* p.113), who are responsible for the park. These are rarely given to individuals.

All the travel agencies offering trips to Manu have offices in Cusco. But only some of those touting trips can take you into the Reserve Zone, a pristine, unsettled area open to controlled tourism and requiring a permit for entry. Others will take you into or the environs of the park or the Cultural Zone, where there is some small-scale development. Though these are both beautiful, visitors are not regulated, which means that the forest is less pristine and you have a smaller chance of seeing rare Amazon fauna.

Tours to Manu are expensive and are usually only available between April and November/December which is the dry season (though Manu Nature Tours offer trips all year round). Visiting in the wet is uncomfortable and your chances of seeing animals are greatly diminished. Expect to pay between $100 and $150 a day. All tours that can take you into the Reserve Zone offer basically the same trip (*see* p.129); this is because visits are limited to designated areas within the Reserve Zone, and there are only a few lodges available to all the companies. What varies is the amount of time spent camping in the forest, the quality of the service, the quality of the guides and the environmental responsibility of the company.

We list only companies offering trips to the Reserve Zone that we feel we can recommend. Of those below, only the first three are companies recommended by SAE (*see* p.113). The first two offer the best value for money, biological expertise and service.

Pantiacolla Tours, Plateros 360, ℃ 238323, @ 252696, *pantica@terra.com.pe, www.pantiacolla.com*. The company is run by highly professional, enthusiastic and environmentally conscientious Dutch biologist Marianne van Vlaardingen and her Peruvian husband, Gustavo Moscoso, who was born and brought up in the lowland forests near Manu. Marianne spent several years studying some of the world's smallest and most endearing primates, tamarins, in Manu and knows the area and the flora and fauna very well. This is reflected in the trips, which are carried out either by Marianne or Gustavo or local guides they have trained, and in a genuine love and respect for the area. Proceeds go towards protecting the park—so you know your money is helping to preserve it. Marianne's book, *Talking about Manu*, given as part of the tour, is written in English and includes basic species checklists for the park. Pantiacolla have two basic types of tour: camping trips in the jungle next to oxbow lakes and on river beaches, and lodge-based tours around the company's own Pantiacolla Lodge in the Cultural Zone and Blanquillo Lodge near the oxbow lake of the same name. Both these lodges are outside the Reserve Zone, but abut on to it and are in unspoiled forest. The lodge trip is more comfortable, but accommodation in a rainforest is almost always fairly rustic. The food on the trips is excellent and Pantiacolla can cater for vegetarians. They have guides who can speak Spanish and English (*see* wildlife essay, p.29.)

Manu Expeditions, PO. Box 606, Cusco, Av. Pardo 895, ✆ 226671/239974, ✉ 236706, *Adventure@ManuExpeditions.com*, *www.ManuExpeditions.com*. One of the best options for birders and wildlife enthusiasts interested in tours to any part of Peru or Bolivia. The company was set up by Barry Walker, the British owner of the Cross Keys pub on the plaza. Barry arranged Michael Palin's carefully rigged journey through Peru as part of the Pacific Rim series. Barry's guides are no less professional than he is—all have a background in ecology or field biology, as well as knowledge of traditional medicines and the Machiguenga and Piro Indian communities. Trips include camping and time at Manu Wildlife Centre, a lodge in a private rainforest reserve partly owned by Manu Expeditions, just outside the Reserve Zone and near the Blanquillo clay lick. Manu Expeditions have English-, German-, Spanish- and Quechua-speaking guides and can arrange food for vegetarians (*see* birding essay, p.55).

Manu Nature Tours, Av. Pardo 1046, ✆ 252721, ✉ 234793. This company is the costliest option and boasts two well-equipped, comfortable lodges: Manu Cloud Forest Lodge, near the cock-of-the-rock lek in the Andean foothills, and Manu Lodge, within the Reserve Zone itself. Both offer a jungle experience with slightly greater luxury than their competitors together with much the same quality of guide. However, the elevated price hardly justifies the modest increase in comfort and more choice on the menu.

Manu Ecological Adventures, Plateros 356, ✆ 225562. This company is the cheapest option. Though once much criticised for ecologically unsound practices, Manu Ecological Adventures seem to have got their act together of late. However, it is worth checking before booking with them: they should abide by the principles of Ecotur Manu, a confederation of operators (which includes all of the above) that promotes low-impact ecological tourism within Manu. The tourist office, SAE or INRENA (*see* pp.112–3) should be able to offer you advice. Manu Ecological Adventures cannot provide the same quality of specialist guides as the above companies but their basic services are not dissimilar. This makes them a good choice for those on a tight budget. Visitors are provided with a basic species checklist with English, Spanish and scientific names, and the trips mix camping with sleeping in the charming new Indian-run Machiguenga Lodge which helps support the local indigenous people. Guides speak Spanish and English.

There are other agencies operating within Manu, including the recently opened **International Cusco Adventures**, Suecia 339, ✆ 239669, ✉ 225098. Again, check with INRENA or SAE (p.113) before making your decision about these. Many operators have poor reputations.

Specialist Biology Field Trips and Birding in Manu Biosphere Reserve

Manu Expeditions and Pantiacolla Tours are the only companies in Manu that cater for serious bird-watchers and naturalists. The leaders for such trips, which should be prearranged, are experienced neotropical birders or field biologists with many years' experience and knowledge of where to find the more sought-after and difficult species. If you want to plan specialist trips such as these, it is best to let either company know as far in advance as possible. Both can send you details of specialist tours or discuss bespoke options. Some companies take **volunteer biologists** on their staff to help out as guides: write to them for details. You should have a good knowledge of Spanish and be of at least graduate level in one of the biological sciences.

Birding on the road to Manu: The road to Manu is a fine place for birders, traversing the eastern Andean slope and temperate and subtropical forests that support many species. To get there, you must hire a car in Cusco (*see* above). Then take the Cusco–Puno road, turning off at Huacarpay lakes towards Paucartambo. Turn right after 25km and begin birding. The puna and elfin forest here support paramo pipit, golden-collared tanager, moustached flower-piercer and other rarities. Once you reach temperate forest, look for marcapata spinetail and drab hemispingus. In the subtropical forest just beyond Pillihuarta you'll find Andean potoo and blue-banded toucanet. At the beginning of the tropical forest there's an Andean cock-of-the-rock lek and you may see Amazonian umbrella birds.

Manu Biosphere Reserve: A Typical Eight-Day Itinerary

Day one: Leave Cusco in a tourist bus around dawn, stopping in the colonial village of Paucartambo to visit some Inca *qollqas* (circular storehouses). The bus ascends steeply to a rarefied 3,500m, with the forested ridges of the Andes spread out endlessly beneath. Make camp in the forest where the scarlet and black Andean cock-of-the-rock cavorts for its drab wife, or lodge in a guesthouse in Pilcopata. A few agencies make it all the way to a Manu lodge.

Day two: Wake to the bizarre call of the russet-backed oropendola. After a walk, head to a canoe on the Río Alto Madre de Dios, which is quite turbulent, looking out for wildlife. Though jaguar have been spotted here, you'll mostly see montane forest birds—with luck an Amazon umbrella bird, so named because it appears to be wearing a sombrero. With a great deal of luck, you may spot a harpy eagle, or a king vulture. Turn up the sluggish Río Manu after passing through the small village of Boca Manu, making camp on one of the beaches.

Day three and four: The next two days are spent on and around the Río Manu; the best place for seeing larger animals—jaguar, the alligator-like black caiman, and its rarer and smaller relative the smooth-fronted caiman, the only caiman that hunts on land. Explore two beautiful oxbow lakes in the heart of the forest: Lake Salvador (by canoe or catamaran) and Lake Otorongo, which has a 4m-high observation platform. You may see giant otter and hoatzin, inelegant crested birds. There are 13 different species of monkey found in the trees around the lakes and a wealth of aquatic bird life, including agami heron, sungrebe and three species of kingfisher: Amazon, green and ringed. At night, explore the forest and lakes with a lamp to catch the red-eye shine of caiman, or the yellow-green eye-shine of a jaguar.

Day five: The morning will probably be spent on or around Lake Salvador—dawn and dusk are the best time for birds and animals. Then take a walk along a forest trail to learn about some medicinal plants. A journey along the Manu and Madre de Dios Rivers brings you to the Blanquillo Lodge, where you will spend the night after another nocturnal walk.

Day six: A dawn start ensures arrival at the *colpa* or clay lick in time for first light: hundreds of macaws, parrots and parrokeets converge here in raucous chorus to eat clay from the river bank, a detoxicant for chemicals from various rainforest seeds they ingest. You'll see scarlet, blue-and-yellow and red-and-green macaws and possibly military or blue-headed macaws together with mealy parrots and numerous parakeets. Return by the Río Madre de Dios.

Day seven: The reverse of day two: you'll camp near the airstrip (a mere gash in the forest).

Day eight: Fly out from Boca Manu airport over the rainforest and the Andes, or bus out from the port of Atalaya.

Other trips tend to be variations on the same theme. Pantiacolla Tours have a nine-day trip that includes treks in the Pantiacolla mountains where the Andes and lowland forests meet, with opportunities to see species from both ecosystems, including perhaps the rare spectacled bear. Manu Expeditions offer a nocturnal trip to another forest lick visited by Brazilian tapirs.

Puerto Maldonado

Puerto Maldonado is a scruffy but endearing Amazon town on the banks of the Río Madre de Dios. There is nothing special to see here and, though the local people are wonderfully friendly and it's a relaxing place to spend a few slow days, the only reason to make a special journey is if you want to visit the forest or take the difficult back road into the Brazilian state of Acre. The town was founded at the turn of the 20th century by the usual mixture of renegades, Indian slavers, drunks and criminals who flocked here in the rubber boom. Livelihoods have peaked and troughed since, fluctuating with demands for timber, gold and oil. Nowadays, locals indignant that the Tambopata-Candamo reserve is protected and they can no longer log there with indiscriminate ease, are now looking to ecotourism as a source of income. This is another reason to visit Maldonado.

Puerto Maldonado (✆084–)   ***Getting There***

Tans and Aero Continene **fly** (the only civilized option) daily between Cusco and Puerto Maldonado. Both cost about $60. Book in advance (*see* p.111). If you are up for adventure, **trucks** leave from the Mercado Modelo on Calle Rivero in Cusco. Take warm- and cold-weather clothing, water, and some food and be prepared to stand at least some of the way (at least two days journey).

To Bolivia and Brazil

The **Bolivian** border is at Puerto Pardo in Peru. Puerto Heath lies just across the river. The journey to Puerto Pardo takes half a day by launch (you can hire one for just under $100). From here, you can go downriver to Riberalta and from there back into Bolivia or on to Porto Velho in Brazil. This is best attempted in a group, as boat hire may be necessary—there are cargo boats but these are occasional. It is also possible to get to Brasiléia in Brazil, via Cobija in Bolivia.

Brazil is more readily accessible by road. The border is at Iñapari, six hours truck-ride away. The journey begins on the other side of the river from Puerto Maldonado. Pick-ups leave every day. The Brazilian town of Assis Brasil has onward connections to Rio Branco, via Brasiléia. Rio Branco is linked by road to the rest of the country. This route passes through some drug-trafficking areas.

Puerto Maldonado (✆084–)   ***Tourist Information and Useful Adresses***

Tourist office: On the plaza near the waterfront.

Conservation: Conservación Internacional, Acash 950, ✆ 571521, can provide you with up-to-the minute information on all the protected areas in the region.

Internet: Credihogar, Jr Tacna 127, ✆ 572122, has four terminals.

Changing money: There are two banks on the plaza which change traveller's cheques and have Visa withdrawal facilities. Better rates can be had at the *casas de cambio* on the 6th block of Puno.

Immigration: 2nd floor at Jr. Ica 727 (*open Mon–Fri 8–2*).

Puerto Maldonado (✆084–)

Where to Stay

moderate

Wasai Lodge, Plaza Grau 1, ✆/✉ 571355. The best place in town with restaurant, bar, pool and air-conditioned rooms.

inexpensive

Cabana Quinta, Jr Cusco 535 (between Moquegua and Rivero), ✆ 571864. Some rooms have air-conditioning and there's a restaurant.

Libertador, Jr Libertad 431, (further out of town than the two above), ✆ 572661. Cheaper, with a pool; some rooms have a fan, others have air-conditioning.

cheap

Iñapari Posada is far and away the best place in this category (*see* p.134). Other, less preferable, options include the **Rey Port**, León Velarde 617, between Dos de Mayo and Jirón Cusco, ✆ 571177.

Eating and Nightlife

There are a number of no-frills restaurants on and around the plaza; none of them vegetarian. The **Casa Nostra**, León Velarde 515, has great cakes and will make a bespoke veggie snack. The **Witite Nightclub**, León Velarde, Block one, is the most popular night haunt, and the locals will be curious to see a foreigner in there.

Tambopata-Candamo Reserve Zone & Bahuaja-Sonene National Park

Though Manu claims to have the greatest biodiversity in Peru, this accolade is actually reserved for the Tambopata-Candamo Reserve Zone and the contiguous Bahuaja-Sonene National Park. Together they form an even bigger area of protected and semi-protected forest than Manu, and the third biggest in the country, with as great a range of habitats and even more plant and animal species. No one has ever lived in the core areas of the reserved zone of the park—or if they have, they've left as yet undiscovered remains.

Tambopata-Candamo is linked with Manu by unbroken and semi-settled forest and, like Manu, it stretches from the Andes (beginning at a lower altitude) to lowland plain. According to SINANPE, the Peruvian government's environmental protection agency, 14 years of study show that the reserve has broken records for species diversity. It is particularly rich in insects, reptiles and amphibians—1,230 species of butterfly, 103 species of dragonfly, and, you'll be delighted to learn, 67 species of horsefly. Reptiles include 67 species of snake, 36 tortoise species and more than 60 amphibian species. The 575 different types of bird include some highly endangered species such as crested and harpy eagles, zigzag heron and orange-breasted falcon. Plant diversity per hectare is the richest in the world and there are eight species of mammals on the endangered-species list. The best way to explore the park, if you are fit and adventurous, has to be white-water rafting from the source of the Río Tambopata all the way through to the lowlands. This will take in all the habitats, get you into some of the remotest areas and afford some of the best opportunities to see animals. Head for one of the excellent lodges if you want more comfort, but ensure that a dawn visit to the *colpa* (clay lick) is on the agenda. Tambopata boasts the world's largest such lick; at any one time there can be more than 1,000 macaws, parrots andparakeets of 15 different species raucously congregating there.

Bahuaja-Sonene, declared a national park in 1996, is part of a vast tract of forest, chaco and seasonally flooded savannah continuous with Madidi and Rios Heath National Parks in Bolivia. Access is difficult, and only two agencies (both listed below) currently offer trips. Scientific studies have not been carried out in Bahuaja-Sonene but, together with Madidi, it includes a greater diversity of habitats than Manu and Tambopata put together. The Pampas de Heath savannahs harbour highly endangered species such as the giant armadillo, which looks like a VW Beetle on legs, and the incredibly rare and little-known South American maned wolf. Unfortunately its inability to survive when there is even a small human population nearby put it in danger of extinction. The park is one of its last remaining habitats.

Tour Operators in Tambopata-Candamo and Bahuaja-Sonene (©084-)

There are a number of operators offering stays in jungle lodges along the Tambopata and Madre de Dios Rivers. Some are based in Cusco, others have offices in Puerto Maldonado only (*see* p.130), the nearest town to Tambopata. All the lodges, with the possible exception of the rainforest expedition lodge furthest up the river, lie in areas where there has been some forest development. This is very small scale, but nonetheless, animals are shyer than they are in Manu. For really untouched forest, you'll have to take a rafting trip down the Río Alto Tambopata to Puerto Maldonado—one of Peru's finest rainforest experiences (*see* below.) Again, we only list those agencies that we feel we can recommend.

Rainforest Expeditions, Galeón 120, Lima 41, © 511 421 8347/511 221 4182, @ 511 421 8183, *rainforest@amauta.rcp.net.pe*, have two of the best lodges: the Tambopata Research Centre and Posada Amazons, both on the Río Tambopata.

Tambopata Research Centre (TRC), though an arduous 10–12 hours by boat from Puerto Maldonado, must be the top choice on the Río Tambopata for those in search of animals and pristine forest. Built in a remote location in the uninhabited core area of the Tambopata Candamo Reserve Zone, it is only 500m from the world's largest macaw clay lick. The centre was originally designed for visiting scientists and is pretty basic. The guides are all young, fit, English-speaking Peruvian biologists. Walks along the extensive system of trails around the camp are kept to a maximum of six tourists per guide, and groups are never in audible distance of each other. The emphasis here is on seeing wildlife, so staff try to keep everyone quiet and attentive—something other lodges along the river fail to do. There's a lot to take in here— seven distinct habitats with high concentrations of large mammals, including all of the Amazon's cats, many primates and over twenty-five macaw nesting sites. But the highlight is the macaw lick, the most diverse and bird-rich habitat so far recorded on earth, which attracts sought-after species such as red-bellied, blue-headed, chestnut-fronted and military macaws, white-bellied parrots, Amazonian parrotlets and cobalt-winged parakeets.

Posada Amazonas is located two hours up the Río Tambopata from Puerto Maldonado in Esse'eja indigenous territory next to the Tambopata-Candamo Reserve Zone. The site is part-

Protecting Bahuaja-Sonene and Madidi

Though Conservation International are doing sensitive and important work in Madidi, it is vital that these parks receive more international attention. At present they are parks on paper only. Peru and Bolivia are poor, and environmentally policing an area as large as a European country is no cheap task. They do a good job with the resources made available to them but need international help. Westerners, Latin Americans claim, bemoan the destruction of the forests and point out that they are of international heritage and importance. Yet in the same breath they demand huge percentages of GDP to pay off the foreign debts often encouraged and fomented by them in the first place. Latin Americans scream 'hypocrisy' and there are no resources left over to protect the forests. Manu was saved partly because a few Westerners attracted the attention of the world's media and NGOs and then more money came in. You can be part of doing the same for Bahuaja-Sonene. But first visit it to see if you think it's worth the trouble. We feel that the park's beauty will convert even the most cynical. Agencies that can take you there are listed below and if you want to help by giving a donation, contact one of the NGOs listed on pp.306–7.

owned and completely maintained and run by indigenous people. Though surrounded by forest, this is not pristine wilderness but managed tropical rainforest in a 10,000 hectare Indian reserve and, though there are plenty of rare species here, including giant otter and harpy eagle, the emphasis is as much on encountering, learning about and supporting indigenous people as it is on wildlife. The lodge is a complex of different sections, and building materials and techniques are the same as indigenous peoples throughout the Amazon have been using to build their homes for millennia. Tours are usually for four days and three nights: days one and four are taken up with arrival and departure; day two takes in a forest walk and a canoe trip on the oxbow Tres Chimbadas Lake, where there is a chance of seeing giant otters, and a visit to an Esse'eja farm to learn about rainforest agriculture. Day three is divided between a parrot and macaw clay lick. Through the lodge's trail network, you'll learn how the indigenous people use rainforest plants and animal forest resources and there is a 35m-high canopy observation tower. Guides are Esse'ja and English-speaking Peruvian naturalists, and the majority of the lodge's staff are also indigenous people. Expect to pay about $60–70 a night all-inclusive.

Buenaventura Baltimore Lodge, Jaime Troncoso 748, Puerto Maldonado, ✆ 572590, 🖂 571646. A new lodge which opened in 2000 and is run by Yerko Herrera Torres, a Peruvian who grew up in the forest near Puerto Maldonado and lived there alone for some five years. There are no guides on the river who know the forest, its medicinal plants and its animals better than Yerko—most are from Cusco or Lima. The lodge is in a beautiful setting, on the bend in the river near the community of Baltimore, three to four hours from Puerto Maldonado by launch. Trips include visits to the little-visited Mississipi oxbow lake in search of giant otters, walking 3km of trails near the lodge, and a dawn trip to a macaw clay lick. Yerko also knows of some locations in the forest unexplored by the other lodges or agencies. There's a 10 per cent discount for students, and those who wish to stay longer to study the forest pay 25 per cent. As it is, the lodge is one of the best value bases on the river at around $50 a night all-inclusive. Only Spanish is spoken.

Tambopata Jungle Lodge, Av. Pardo 705, PO Box 454, Cusco, ✆ 225701, 📠 238911. A charming, comfortable, smallish lodge on the river, 3–4 hours by boat from Puerto Maldonado. This is not virgin wilderness—there are a few communities near here and the animals are shy. Your best chance of seeing anything is on the trips to the oxbow lakes (Condenado and Sachavacayoc) or at night-time around the camp. Cats are frequent nocturnal visitors—venture out with a torch and look out for their yellow-green eye shine around the library and creek. The lodge has an intimate lay-out and there's a small five-a-side football (soccer) pitch behind the kitchen—you'll get dragged into a very sweaty, muddy and very enjoyable game if you show any interest. Guides are bilingual and, though most of them are not naturalists, they have a good working knowledge of the flora and fauna.

Iñapari Camping Lodge, Av. Aeropuerto Km 5.5, PO Box32, La Joya, Puerto Maldonado, ✆ 572575, 📠 572155. Rather than being a jungle lodge proper, Iñapari is a charming, family-run posada in secondary forest on the edge of Puerto Maldonado, in a peaceful location with the friendly and attentive service of Spaniard Joaquín and his Peruvian wife. Simple rooms with terraces look out on a lawn and gardens full of tropical orchids and heavily scented flowers. It's close to Puerto Maldonado's tiny airport, which makes it a convenient place to stay if you want an extra night before catching the morning plane. Nights are absurdly cheap at $6 including a breakfast of tropical fruit. Apart from this, Iñapari also offer excursions to all the major attractions on the Río Tambopata together with horse-riding trips and two of the most interesting and adventurous tours on offer in the region: the first is a five-day, four-night camping and rafting trip through rainforest and returning along the Rio de Las Piedras on a balsa raft made by you and the guides. The second is a six-day, five-night camping trip into the Pampas del Heath in the Bahuaja-Sonene National Park next to Tambopata-Candamo. This is one of the least spoilt and least visited areas of wilderness on the continent and Iñapari are one of the few operators that take people there. The diversity of flora and fauna probably exceeds even Tambopata or Manu. Though studies have yet to be carried out, there's a larger range of habitats in the park—from montane and cloud forest through gallery forest and lowland rain-forest to savannah. Some English is spoken.

Explorer's Inn: Plateros 136, Cusco, ✆ 235342; Puerto Maldonado office: Av. Fitzcarrald 136, ✆/📠 572078. This was once *the* place to stay on the Río Tambopata, with pioneering species counts carried out, but in recent years it has tended to rest on its laurels. Considering its basic facilities, the lodge is overpriced. Nonetheless if you are a birder, the Explorer's Inn and Tambopata Research Centre (*see* above) are the best places on the river to base yourself—the lodge boasts one of the largest bird lists in the world, with in excess of 590 species, 30km of trails and a canopy walkway, and the guides and staff are used to catering for birders. There is a banded-tail manakin lek along the swamp trail and a needle-billed hermit lek near the beginning of the high forest trail. Near the first bridge, on the La Torre trail and in a bamboo thicket across the Tambopata near Virgilio's Clearing, you may see bluish and white-throated jacamars and the bridge is also good for chestnut-winged hookbills. Orange-breasted falcons, white-cheeked tody flycatchers, striated antbirds and starred wood quail can be seen on the bamboo trail. On the main trail, passing a small swamp and leading to Cocacocha Lake, you'll see black antbird, zigzag heron, Bartlett's tinamou, hoatzin and pointed-tailed palm creeper. Bamboo antshrike occurs in the bamboo at the beginning of Katicocha trail and in the thicket beyond Virgilio's Clearing. English is spoken.

Wasai Tambopata Lodge and Wasai Maldonado Lodge, Plaza Grau riverfront, Puerto Maldonado, ℰ/✆ 571355; Cusco ℰ 221826. Both are new lodges. The former is situated on the Río Tambopata between the Tambopata Jungle Lodge and Buenaventura Baltimore, three or four hours from Maldonado. The latter is on the waterfront in Puerto Maldonado and is one of the most comfortable and convenient places to stay in town, with a swimming pool, private bar and mountain bikes for hire. Both are new, well-built and well-managed facilities. The Wasai Tambopata Lodge is in a beautiful location with a small waterfall across the river from the lodge. The surrounding forest is unspoilt but not pristine. A dawn visit to the macaw clay lick is featured on all the lodge's programmes. There are also options to visit the Río Heath on a seven-day expedition. English is spoken.

Eco-Amazonia Lodge, Portal de Panes 109, Oficina 6, Plaza de Armas, Cusco, ℰ 236159 ℰ/✆ 225068. This is the best lodge on the Río Madre de Dios, only two hours from Puerto Maldonado, situated in a beautiful private reserve backing onto forest that extends far into Brazil. There are some huge ceiba and brazil-nut trees and a shallow, forested lake with over 2km of walkway. A terrifying stairway built into the side of a towering ceiba tree next to the lake gives views out over the canopy. An island opposite the lodge is full of wild capybara and is home to a troop of semi-domesticated monkeys led by a tiny saddle-backed tamarin called Martin. The monkeys are usually accompanied by a very inquisitive and friendly coatimundi. There's plenty of wild wildlife here: the lake is full of huge black caiman and there are plenty of cat prints everywhere. The forest is particularly good for primates: red howler monkeys, black spider monkeys, pygmy marmosets, and occasionally Goeldi's monkeys are seen on or near the extensive network of trails. Night monkeys come into the camp nearly every night, though they are hard to spot even with a powerful torch. The only negative aspects of the lodge are its size—in high season there can be as many as 20 people in a group (the animals run scared), and the rather sad and angry clipped-winged macaws that squawk about mocking the lodge's name. It's best to check how many people are booked in before you make your reservation and, if you feel strongly, complain about the macaws to the management in Cusco, who are very approachable. The lodge is marginally cheaper than all its competitors bar Baltimore and Iñapari. Basic English is spoken.

Tambopata: A Typical Four-day Itinerary

The lodges are usually pretty flexible and the following is only a sketch to give you an idea what to expect. If you want to see something particular, or have specific birding, wildlife or botanical interests, most lodges will be able to cater for those. Try to let them know before you arrive. Birders should head to Tambopata Reserve Centre or the Explorer's Inn.

Day one: This will be spent getting there. You may see some wildlife along the river, although the traffic is quite heavy (by rainforest standards this means about one boat an hour). Then an introductory walk on one of trails and perhaps a slide show at night finish the day.

Day two: A long walk to an oxbow lake in the morning, coming back for a late lunch. The afternoon will be spent on one of the lodge trails, learning about the plants and their medicinal uses. After dinner you'll go out with a halogen lamp looking for caiman.

Day three: Up at dawn to see the riotous assembly of parrots and macaws at the clay lick or early to look for animals on the trails, with another trip to a different oxbow lake to follow. There's more caiman-spotting at night.

Day four: Another early rise and a boat ride to Puerto Maldonado to meet the morning plane.

Rafting Expeditions in the Tambopata-Candamo Reserve Zone

One of the most adventurous options for seeing Tambopata-Candamo is to raft from the source of the Río Tambopata near Puno to the Tambopata Research Centre. Expeditions take place roughly twice a month between May and mid-October with Instinct (Procuradores 50, Plaza de Armas, Cusco, ✆ 238366, ✉ 233451) and once a month between July and September with Amazon Explorer (PO Box 722, Cusco, ✆ 225284, ✉ 236826) and should be reserved well in advance. The expeditions have optional added extras, enabling people to visit Titicaca and Machu Picchu should they choose to, but you can do this independently at less expense. Few experiences can compare.

Day one: Arrival either in Lima or Cusco with optional tours to the tourist sights.

Day two: Journey to Titicaca with a visit to the floating islands of the Uros people who, in addition to weaving their islands, make boats and souvenirs which they sell to the busloads of tourists who come to see them.

Days three and four: Two-day journey in a private minibus across the altiplano, over a pass in the Carabaya Cordillera, culminating in a spectacular descent through cloud forest to the headwaters of the Río Tambopata.

Days five to ten: This is where the action really starts: negotiating white water and rapids and passing through some of the world's most beautiful and untouched forest. There is no one living in this part of Tambopata-Candamo and you will share this vast swathe of tropical wilderness only with wildlife. On the final day a motor boat will take you to the relative luxury of the Tambopata Research Centre.

Day eleven: A dawn visit to the clay lick (see p.132) and a hair-raising boat journey over fierce rapids to Puerto Maldonado, where you will stay overnight before heading for Cusco.

Iquitos

Like Manaus, downriver in Brazil, Iquitos got rich through the rubber boom. Elegant colonial houses, including one supposedly designed by Eiffel, were built in imitation of European cities a world away, or shipped out wholesale. The city's elegance has faded, and it's hard to imagine horse-drawn carriages clattering through streets now busy with a thousand mopeds, or ladies with parasols out on the river near the ramshackle suburb of Belén; but the waterfront still has hints of the old charm, and a walk along the promenade at dusk, the sun sinking in glorious colour over the Amazon, is a delight.

The city was founded in 1739, as a Jesuit mission settlement to the fierce and fiercely independent Yagua Indians. It grew twenty-fold as a result of the rubber boom during the mid-19th century (see p.92), but when the rubber bubble burst a few decades later, Iquitos, like Manaus, returned to obscurity. The barons left for richer pastures, the prostitutes followed them and epiphytic plants began to crack the stucco on the city's colonial façades. Iquitos survived on agriculture, logging and Brazil-nut harvesting until the 1960s when more black gold was discovered: this time it was oil. Within a decade, Iquitos quickly grew to its current size of about 400,000 inhabitants. Thankfully, the region has been spared some of the ravages of oil exploration that have caused so much damage in Ecuador. This is, in part, due to the concurrent emergence of ecotourism in Iquitos—this city was one of the first places to open to tourists in the Amazon. It is still an excellent place to begin exploration of the surrounding forests and remoter regions such as the Pacaya-Samiria National Park.

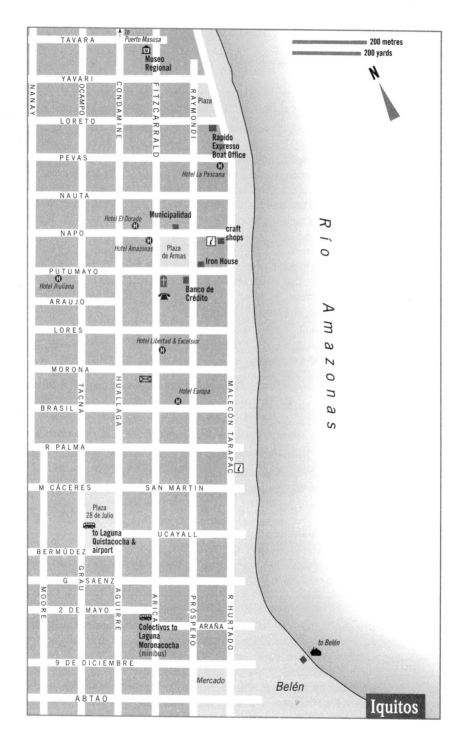

200 metres
200 yards

N

Iquitos

Río Amazonas

to
Puerto Masusa

TAVARA

Museo
Regional

YAVARI

NANAY

NANAY

OCAMPO

CONDAMINE

FITZCARRALD

RAYMONDI

Plaza

LORETO

Rapido
Expresso
Boat Office

PEVAS

Hotel La Pascana

NAUTA

Hotel El Dorado

Municipalidad

NAPO

craft
shops

Hotel Amazonas

Plaza
de Armas

Iron House

PUTUMAYO

Hotel Jhuliana

Banco de
Crédito

ARAUJO

LORES

Hotel Libertad & Excelsior

MORONA

TACNA

HUALLAGA

Hotel Europa

BRASIL

MALECÓN TARAPACÁ

R PALMA

M CÁCERES

SAN MARTIN

Plaza
28 de Julio

to Laguna
Quistacocha &
airport

UCAYALI

BERMÚDEZ

GRAU

G   SAENZ

MOORE

AGUIRRE

ARICA

PRÓSPERO

R HURTADO

2 DE MAYO

Colectivos to
Laguna
Moronacocha
(minibus)

ARAÑA

to Belén

9 DE DICIEMBRE

Mercado

Belén

ABTAO

There are no roads to Iquitos, so you must either fly or boat in.

by air

Flights from Lima or Pucallpa with Aero Continente (Jirón Próspero 232, ℗ 242995) or Tans (Jirón Próspero 215, ℗ 231071). The airport is 15 minutes from the centre by taxi or rickshaw.

by boat

Downstream—international: Brazil and Colombia are a day's fast boat, or two to three day's slow boat ride away. All dock in Tabatinga, the scruffy Brazilian side of the two-nation town of Leticia/Tabatinga. Ticket offices for the fast boats are on Calle Raymondi between Pevas and Loreto, two and a half blocks downstream of the plaza. Customs are at the point of departure, Puerto Masusa, on Av. Marina, about 3km from the plaza, downstream. Slow boats also leave from Puerto Masusa. Schedules vary, so check at the port or with the tourist office or your hotel. You'll need a hammock. The most luxurious way of getting there is with Amazon Tours and Cruises, who operate air-conditioned three-day voyages to Tabatinga and Leticia (*see* p.218). Whatever option you choose, your passport is exit-stamped in a sweaty shack in the Peruvian hamlet of Santa Rosa, 8 or 9 hours downstream.

Upstream—national: Pucallpa is 6–8 days upriver. Yurimaguas, linked by a rough road to the Andes and Lima, is 4–6. Boats for both leave once or twice a week. Again, departures are scheduled according to when boats show up; ask at the dock.

Tourist office: The old one burnt down in 1999, and the present one can be found at Ramirez Hurtado 912, ℗ 234609, an anonymous house in the fish market. By the time you read this, a new office should have opened near the plaza. Ask in your hotel.

Changing money: There are several banks with Visa or MasterCard withdrawal facilities and several money changers around the plaza. Jirón Próspero has the most.

Visas: Migraciones, for visa extensions, is in the Prefectura building at Malecón Tarapaca 368, along the waterfront, two blocks from the plaza.

Internet: Two minutes upstream of the plaza, on Jirón Próspero 273, ℗ 242148.

Festivals

Iquitos' main festival is spread over three days at the end of June, usually on the weekend nearest the 24th. It is said to be raucous.

The Sights

Belén: Touted as the 'Venice of Peru', a comparison valid only in the imagination of the tourist office, Belén is in fact a seasonally flooded shanty-town of thatch and reed. But it's still a fascinating place and well worth a visit. Between October and May, the river reaches nearly to the floor of Belén's stilted houses, shops, churches and community halls, covering football pitches in fields of floating water hyacinth and lilies. And like the river, trade here is seasonally tidal. For six months it's carried out on foot and for another six by dug-out. Belén will show you more of the reality of Amazon life than a thousand documentaries. In the market on the waterfront, manioc flour, rainforest medicines and piles of dried frogs and fish are hawked next to fundamentalists shouting out the word of God. They compete for an audience with distorted music from the community radio station blasting out through the public loud-speakers. Watch your wallet and camera closely, and make sure you are there to catch the wonderful evening light. Boatmen will take you around for a few dollars an hour. They'll find you at the riverfront near Belén market.

The promenade: Sunset views from here are wonderful and the light beautifully warms the faded plaster of the colonial houses upstream of the plaza. At weekends, there are stalls selling arts and crafts, crowds of young middle-class *Iquiteños* and lovers smooching like pairs of parrots. A good place to people watch and an interesting contrast to Belén.

The Iron House: One of Iquitos' houses is said to have been built by Eiffel and shipped out from France piece by piece. No one really knows which one it is, and each book you read suggests a different option. The most likely candidate is the meccano house on the Plaza that stands behind the supposed Rodin statue.

Laguna Quistacocha: The only reason for including the lagoon here is to advise you not to go. The dirty water is full of paddle-boats and next to it is a disgraceful zoo, with sad-looking animals displaying repetitive behaviour patterns. Steaks of the endangered *pirarucu* (*paiche*) fish are served at the bar. The management has been taken over by the Ministry of Fisheries, who are said to want to use the lake to breed *pirarucu*, so perhaps things will improve.

Iquitos (℅ 094–)   *Shopping*

The only good buys in Iquitos are the beautiful Shipibo Indian mats and knitted shawls, sold by very poor Indians that have journeyed all the way from Pucallpa, and the herbal medicines and tonics sold throughout the city (particularly in Belén). These tend to hang around the main plaza but are rarely tolerated by restaurant owners.

Iquitos (℅ 094–)   *Where to Stay and Eating Out*

Iquitos does not have a wide choice of good hotels; most of those in the upper and mid-price ranges are much the same. A new hotel, opening on the northwestern corner of the plaza in late 2000, will be the best in the city.

expensive–moderate

Victoria Regia, Ricardo Palma 252, ℅ 231011, ✉ 232203. Pool, small air-conditioned rooms and a good restaurant.

El Dorado, Napo 232, ℅ 237326, ✉ 232203. Much the same standard as the Victoria Regia, but with a pool open to non-guests.

Réal Hotel Iquitos, Malecón Tarapacá (on the waterfront). A dilapidated colonial mansion in a wonderful location. The air-conditioned rooms are nothing special, but the sunsets make it one of the best places to stay in Iquitos.

Jhuliana, Putumayo 521, ℅/✉ 233154. Air-conditioned rooms, a great pool and a good restaurant. Reasonably priced.

Europa, Jirón Brasil 222, ℅ 231123, ✉ 235483. Good service, and good air-conditioned rooms with TV, fridge and a bar.

Amazonas, Arica 108, on the main plaza, ☎ 232015, ✉ 242431. A dull, conveniently located modern building with spacious air-conditioned rooms with TV.

Safari, Napo 118, ☎ 233828. One of the best in Iquitos for this price range. Air-conditioning in every room, spick and span and well run.

Hotel La Pascana, Jirón Pevas 33, ☎ 231418. Bare and basic rooms around an orchid-filled courtyard. Despite this, it is the best of the cheap hotels in town.

Libertad, Arica 361, ☎ 235763. Similar to the Pascana but has air-conditioned rooms.

With one or two exceptions, Iquitos's **restaurants** are as exciting as its hotels.

La Casa de Jaime, Tarapaca 248. One of the best in town. The owner speaks very good English and German. Good steaks. Vegetarian food available.

El Mesón, Napo 116, half a block from the river. Air-conditioned, with a good menu (aside from some endangered species) and decent wine list. The river fish is delicious.

Don Giovanni, Plaza de Armas. Good *ceviche* and river fish, and reasonable pizza and pasta.

La Maloca, Tarapaca, on the waterfront. Local specialities in a wonderful location, on a floating restaurant in the river. The food is OK.

Ari's Burger, Plaza de Armas. Every gringo in town seems to have at least a breakfast here: fast food in slow surroundings. Simple fare. Good for watching the world go by.

Tour Operators and Lodges Around Iquitos
Iquitos (☎ 094–)

There are a bewildering number of agencies and private guides offering trips to the forest around Iquitos and the list below is far from exhaustive. This is because some companies are far better than others. The tourist office has a list of accredited guides. There are two types of operator in Iquitos—expensive companies like Explorama that offer all mod cons and a comfortable forest experience with guides who know the biology well, and cheaper, more adventurous operators that take you to remoter areas and demand more physically. These tend to give you a far better view of the forest from the point of view of those that live there.

Don't expect to see thousands of animals; rainforest wildlife is elusive. Backpackers wanting guarantees of seeing anaconda, sloths and so on, has led to cheaper companies trapping animals in hidden cages and then going off to 'find' them to show tourists. This is a very cruel practice and many of these animals die soon after being caught. Unfortunately it is all too common. If the company you choose does this then report them to the tourist office and WWF on Calle Pevas next to the waterfront.

Amazonia Expeditions, Arica 361, ☎ 243100, ☎/✉ 232974. A good budget option with one of the remotest lodges in the Loreto region near the Pacaya-Samiria Reserve. The lodge is on the Río Curahuayte, over 200km (140m) from Iquitos, and the surrounding forest is pristine. The camp is basic, but this is more than made up for by the cheap price (around $50 per day) and remote location. Activities include swimming with river dolphins, forest survival skills and the usual safari activities like piranha-fishing and caiman-spotting. Amazonia Expeditions are one of the few companies offering trips into Pacaya-Samiria (*see* p.142).

Amazon River House, Piura 162, ☎ 253082, ✉ 231111. This is the best operation for those looking for budget trips and/or for adventure and intimate contact with the forest. The company is run by Andrés Peña Guerra, a local who grew up in the forest near Iquitos and knows the area better than almost anyone in town. Trips are varied and good value, usually centering on one of their three lodges: the Amazon River House, 60km from Iquitos, Wilderness Camp, 185km away or Auca Tambo, 215km away. The **Amazon River House** is the last lodge on the Río Yanayaco, a black-water tributary of the Amazon. Both species of river dolphin can be seen here, with luck as you are dining and watching the sun set over the river. The surrounding forest is virgin and full of Brazil-nut trees. Andrés calls monkeys down from the trees—marmoset and tamarin mating calls are his speciality. The **Wilderness Camp**, on an oxbow lake near the Río Yarapa, is remoter and more basic. In summer it is one of the best places to see jaguars in the Iquitos area, together with large black caiman and timid forest birds like guans and currasows. The **Auca Tambo** is little more than a shack; there are no facilities at all. It is used on the company's remoter treks. Standard three-day, two-night tours operate from the Amazon River House, and include caiman spotting, basic jungle survival and tribal medicine, together with trips in a dug-out in the *igarapés* (creeks) and minor tributaries of the river. The longer trips are more interesting and include a 10–15 day trek around the Rivers Ucayali, Gálvez and Yaviri. After a journey up the Amazon and Ucayali, exploring the forest along the way, camp is made at Auca Tambo, where you spend a few days walking trails. Then five days are spent crossing virgin forest, to reach the Gàlvez. Two days' rafting from here takes you to the Yaviri, where you visit Matís Indians, who paint their faces to look like jaguars. A plane takes you back to Iquitos. Andrés also takes trips into Pacaya-Samiria (*see* p.142). Trips cost $40 per day all-inclusive, and $50–60 to the remoter locations. The considerable cost of the plane is extra (about $70). Groups are small and boats are covered against sun and rain.

Amazon Tours and Cruises, Requena 336, ✆ 233931, ✉ 231265. This company offers a variety of touristy but comfortable cruises along the Amazon itself, with side trips to explore the smaller tributaries. You won't see much in the way of wildlife, and the blow-gun demonstrations in the Huitoto villages are irritating and staged. The cruises are best considered as a light introduction to the forest and river or as a luxurious way of getting to or from Tabatinga/Leticia. Their seven-night 'Tacha Curaray' light aircraft trip up the Río Napa is far more interesting. The upper reaches of the Napo and Curaray are little visited and afford excellent birding opportunities. A naturalist guide conducts the trip. Expect to pay between $60 and $100 per day for the cruises (depending on the boat and the size of the group) and $100 for the 'Tacha Curaray' light-aircraft trip.

Explorama Lodges, Exploraciones Amazónicas S.A, PO Box 446, Iquitos, ✆ 252530, ✉ 252533. This North American-owned and -run company is one of the longest established anywhere in the Amazon and is by far your best upmarket choice in Iquitos. Countless important biological studies have been carried out at their various lodges and their work supports CONAPAC, a Peruvian NGO (charity) set-up to protect, study and preserve the forest. Guides, all of whom are local people are well-versed in rainforest biology and ecology. The company have three lodges: the **Explorama Inn** is the newest, most modern and most luxurious. Individual palm-thatched huts, with private bathrooms, fans and double beds, overlook the Amazon itself and there's a bar, restaurant and series of walkways. However, at only 40km from Iquitos, you are far from primary forest here and though there are trips to their Napo camp, three or four hours away, the **Explorama Lodge**, 80km from Iquitos, is a better choice for wildlife. Accommodation here is more rustic and there's an extensive system of trails. The jewel in Explorama's crown is the **Explornapo Camp**, 160km from Iquitos, in the privately owned Sucsari Nature Reserve. The camp consists of palm-thatched houses with private bathrooms, a restaurant and bar, and is situated close to the ACEER (Amazon Centre for Environmental Education and Research) canopy walkway, the real reason for coming here. This fenced walkway, 35m above the ground, extends for a third of a mile through the rainforest canopy, giving you the opportunity to get close to the biological action—this is where most of the forest's plants and animals actually live. It is the longest walkway in the world and is one of the best places to visit in the Peruvian Amazon. Next door is the Renuperu ethnobotanical medicinal plant garden, tended by a local 'shaman' and his family who explain the various uses for the plants. If you compare them to equivalent lodges in Tambopata-Candamo, Explorama are over-priced and a little impersonal—maybe they are resting on their laurels a bit. Expect to pay around $75 per night at the Inn, $80 at the Lodge and $120–$200 (depending on the size of the group) at the Camp.

Yacumama Lodge, Sargento Lores, ✆/✉ 21022. A model ecotourism project in first-growth forest 145km from Iquitos. All materials are recycled, sewage is treated, detergents used are all biodegradable and the lodge is entirely solar powered.

Pacaya-Samiria National Reserve

Pacaya-Samiria is the largest protected area in Peru, the second largest in the Amazon basin and the fourth largest in South America. And all of it is tropical forest, ranging from premontane to tropical lowland. Its remoteness means that it has been little explored, let alone visited by tourists. The reserve is managed with the co-operation of local people, who are encouraged to use it sustainably by SINANPE, the environmental department of the Peruvian government. To enter the reserve you need a permit from INRENA (Los Petirrojos 35, Urbanización El Palomar, ✆ 01 224 3298, ✉ 01 224 3218, *jtakahashi@inrena.org.pe*) in Lima. Two of the companies listed above have this permit and will take you there from Iquitos. It used to be possible to visit the park illegally from Lagunas, which was not a good idea as it was encouraging hunting. Rangers, paid for by contributions from the US government, have rightly been very strict about enforcing permits of late—so avoid Lagunas and help them protect the park. July to October are the best months to visit. Bring plenty of insect repellent, long trousers and long-sleeved shirts.

The list of species so far discovered is impressive, and it will no doubt expand greatly as further studies are undertaken. There are 130 species of mammals (most of them bats, rodents and monkeys, though all the lowland forest cats are present), 330 species of birds, of which 23 are migratory, and more than 150 species of reptiles and amphibians in 20 families. Despite this plethora, the park was set up primarily to protect aquatic fauna. As well as giant otter, there are abundant Amazonian manatee, giant Amazonian turtle, and *pirarucu*, one of the world's largest and most endangered freshwater fish. These can reach over two metres long and eat only fruit from flooded forest.

Bolivia

Land-locked Bolivia is associated more with high barren plateaux, smoking volcanoes and herds of alpaca than it is with tropical rainforest. But the altiplano accounts for less than half the country, ending abruptly north of La Paz. Here the 5km-high jags of the Andes rapidly descend into misty forest-clad ripples, and then into vast tracts of lowland rainforest and savannah interrupted only by the broad meanders of warm brown rivers and table-top mountains that rise sheer out of the flat plains. Hidden in these sparsely populated backlands are some of the Amazon's most magical Edens: the National Parks of Amboró, whose steep, convoluted valleys lie heavy with evaporating cloud and provide shelter for some of South America's rarest birds and animals; Noel Kempff Mercado, where waterfalls cascade from sheer sandstone cliffs into limitless rainforests; and in the remote Bolivian northeast, Ríos Blanco y Negro; Isiboro Sécure; and Gran Chaco, the country's largest. On the other side of the country, near the town of Rurrenabaque, lie the Madidi and Manuripi Heath reserves, in the heart of a protected area larger than France, parts of which still lie untrodden by any human foot at the beginning of the 21st century.

It may come as a surprise to discover that Bolivia has a better developed and more responsibly run conservational tourism industry than her giant neighbour, Brazil. Though this is still in its infancy, Bolivia, like Guyana, can offer efficiently run specialist natural history and birding trips to areas with as many as 700 different species of birds and 130 species of mammals. Trips can be organized from a number of key centres. The capital, La Paz, lies firmly in the upper reaches of the Andean plains and, though trips to anywhere in the country can be arranged from here, only the cloud forests of the Yungas are in the immediate vicinity. Santa Cruz, although unattractive, is far closer to the Amazon proper and is a more convenient base. Noel Kempff Mercado and Amboró are a short journey away.

Rurrenabaque, on the banks of the Río Beni between the Beni savannahs and the lowland forests of the Alto Madidi park, is popular with backpackers. Trinidad, halfway between Santa Cruz and Rurrenabaque, is the access point for remote and little visited regions of the lowland forests, notably Beni, Ríos Blanco y Negro and Isiboro Sécure National Parks.

Bolivia

Official language: Spanish, Quechua, Aymara
Capital city: Sucre
Amazon gateway cities: Santa Cruz (*see* p.152) and Rurrenabaque (*see* p.170)
Currency: *boliviano* (Ns) of 100 centavo

Highlights

1. Flying in a light aircraft over the rainforests of the Noel Kempff Mercado National Park.
2. Hike to Mercado Arco Iris and El Encanto waterfalls in the Noel Kempff Mercado National Park.
3. Sleeping out in the rainforest in Amboró National Park.

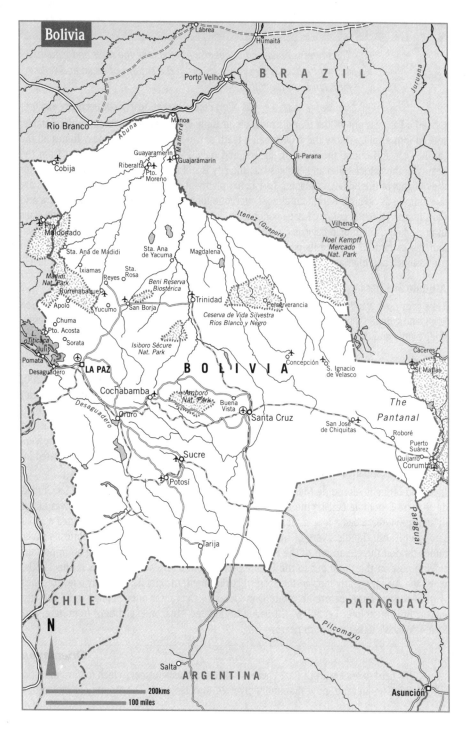

Bolivia

Lábrea
Humaitá
B R A Z I L
Porto Velho
Manoa
Rio Branco
Abuna
Ji-Parana
Guayaramerin
Cobija
Riberalta
Pto. Moreno
Guajarámarin
Itenez (Guaporé)
Vilhena
Pto. Maldonado
Noel Kempff Mercado Nat. Park
Sta. Ana de Madidi
Sta. Ana de Yacuma
Magdalena
Ixiamas
Reyes
Sta. Rosa
Madidi Nat. Park
Beni Reserva Biostérica
Burrenabaque
Apolo
Yucumo
San Borja
Trinidad
Perserverancia
Chuma
Pto. Acosta
Sorata
Ceserva de Vida Silvestra Rios Blanco y Negro
Isiboro Sécure Nat. Park
L. Titicaca
Juli
Pomata
Desaguadero
LA PAZ
B O L I V I A
Concepción
S. Ignacio de Velasco
Cáceres
St Matias
Cochabamba
Amboró Nat. Park
Buena Vista
Oruro
Santa Cruz
The Pantanal
Desaguadero
San José de Chiquitas
Roboré
Puerto Suárez
Quijarro
Corumbá
Sucre
Potosí
Paraguai
Tarija
CHILE
N
PARAGUAY
Pilcomayo
Salta
ARGENTINA
200kms
100 miles
Asunción

*The towers of many churches rise from among the roofs and gardens,
and white houses gleam like jewels in the pattern of green and yellow
farm lands on the hillsides*

Lt. Col. Percy Fawcett, early 20th-century explorer

Once La Paz was one of the world's most picturesque cities. Its setting is still unforgettable: tucked into a valley below the 6,000m-high teeth of Mount Illimani. But today fumes fill the rarefied air and choke the winding streets, and ugly, ramshackle houses detract from the beauty of the colonial tiles and cobbles. Yet the city is still more than a mere starting point for the delights of the Bolivian Amazon. La Paz has plenty of character. Indigenous languages are as common as Spanish here, and almost everyone looks Indian. Bowler-hatted Aymara and Quechua sell brightly coloured hats, ponchos and alpaca-wool jumpers from myriad little stalls in the old city, and Indian beggars crowd around the massive walls of the Iglesia San Francisco and the cathedral. Despite its poverty, most of La Paz's tour operators are organized and professional, and offer a wide variety of different trips to the Amazon and Yungas.

Altitude Sickness

Take your time wandering around the city when you first arrive. La Paz sits 3,600m above sea level, and giddiness, nausea and tiredness are common during the first few days. Drink plenty, sleep plenty and, if you feel really lousy, have a cup of coca tea.

History

The environs of La Paz were the cradle of Andean civilization. Between 800 BC and AD 1200, the ruined city of Tiahuanaco, an hour or so away, was the centre of the greatest pre-Incan Andean empire. Little remains today, and the city stands on barren plain surrounded by thousands of shards of pre-Columbian pottery. Lake Titicaca, just beyond Tiahuanaco, was the place of cosmic creation; the Inca Adam, the first emperor, and the principal divine powers were said to have been born here, and the islands of the sun and moon are still venerated by the Incas' descendants.

Inca gold brought Alonso de Mendoza, the first Spaniard, to what was to become La Ciudad de Nuestra Señora de La Paz; the Río Choqueyapu which still flows under the city was full of it, and the Aymara had a long-established mining community here. The city remained a small settlement until the discovery of silver in Potosí, some 400km to the south. Potosí's silver mines funded the expansion of the Spanish empire, and La Paz soon became an important staging post on the route out to the Pacific. Aside from a series of rebellions in the 1780s, when the Aymara nearly toppled the Spanish government, the city has had only a few brushes with history or fame: before he wrote Don Quixote, Cervantes once applied to be the city mayor; British explorer Percy Fawcett begun his ill-fated Amazon expeditions from here, and Raquel Welch's father was born nearby.

Orientation

It's hard to get lost in La Paz. There is only one principal street, which follows the fetid Río Choqueyapu, now thankfully diverted underground. The street goes by various

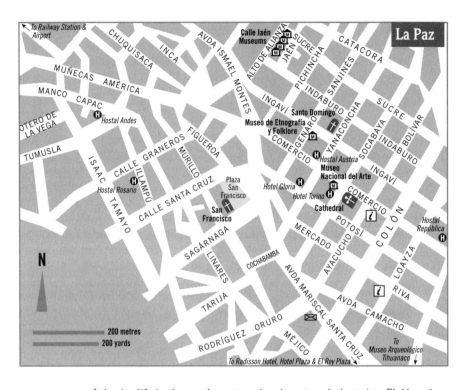

names: It begins life in the north west as the airport road, Autopista El Alto, then becoming Avenida Montes, before joining Figueroa near the Iglesia San Francisco, to become Mariscal Santa Cruz. It enters the centre of the newer part of town as the Prado (Avenida 16 de Julio), then becoming Villazón and finally, Avenida 6 de Agosto. As it follows the course of the river, and La Paz is in a valley, this main thoroughfare lies downhill of all the streets that surround it to the northeast and northwest.

La Paz (© 02–)	Getting There and Around
	by air

International: John F Kennedy International Airport is in the ugly suburb of El Alto, a 20-minute taxi ride from the centre. Flights to Miami with American Airlines and Varig; to Rio de Janeiro and São Paulo via Santa Cruz (with onward connections to the rest of Brazil, Europe and the USA) with Varig or LAB Bolivian Airlines; to Buenos Aires (with onward connections to Europe) with Aerolíneas Argentinas or LAB; to Santiago (via Arica and Iquique) with LanChile; to Quito (via Guayaquil) with Saeta or LAB; to Manaus, Cuzco, Asunción, Bogotá, Lima, Montevideo, Caracas, Córdoba, Mexico City, Cancún and Panama City with LAB.

National: Santa Cruz, Cochabamba, Rurrenabaque (Reyes), Trinidad, Sucre, Riberalta, Guayaramerín and Puerto Suárez with LAB or Aerosur.

Airline addresses: **American Airlines**, Plaza Venezuela 1440, Edificio Hermann,

Planta Baja, ℗ 351360; **LAB Bolivian Airlines**, Av. Camacho 1456–60, ℗ 371027, toll-free ℗ 0800 4321; **Varig**, Av. Mcal de Ayacucho, mezzanine, Oficina 3.c, Loayza between Camacho and Mercado, ℗ 314040; **Aerolíneas Argentinas**, Av. 16 de Julio, Edificio San Pablo, Piso 2, Oficina 202, ℗ 351711; **LanChile**, Edificio 16 de Julio, El Prado, Planta Baja, ℗ 358377; **Saeta**, Plaza del Estudiante 1931, ℗ 377595; **Aerosur**, Colón at Irala, ℗ 367400, toll-free ℗ 0800 3030.

by road

Buses: For Lake Titicaca/Peru: from Tranportes Manco Capac (℗ 350033), José Maria Aliaga 670 or Transtur 2 Febrero (℗ 377181), José Maria Aliaga 287 (near the cemetery). For the Yungas and Rurrenabaque: from Barrio Villa Fátima off Tejado Sorzano, on the northwest edge of the city. For Santa Cruz, Cochabamba and all other destinations: from the main bus terminal, Plaza Antofagasta, 10 mins by taxi from the city centre.

Car rental: Oscar Crespo Maurice, Av. Simón Bolívar 1865 (Miraflores suburb), ℗ 220989, ✉ 242608; has 4x4 vehicles.

Taxis can be hailed, or call Bolivia Radio Car, ℗ 330505 or Movil del Sur, ℗ 792020.

La Paz (℗ 02–) **Tourist Information and Useful Addresses**

Tourist office: Edificio Mcal. Ballivián, Piso 18, Calle Mercado 1328, ℗ 367463.

Changing money: Visa/Mastercard cashpoint: Banco Boliviano Americano, Av. Camacho at Loayza. Camacho is one block north of Av. Mariscal (the Prado).

Visa extensions: Av. Camacho 1433 (*open weekdays 9–12*).

Internet: La Paz's large backpacker contingent guarantees a wealth of internet cafes. One of the best is on Socabaya, right next to the cathedral.

Embassies and consulates: Australia Av. Arde Edificio Multicentro mezzanine, ℗ 359357; **Brazil** Cap. Ravelo 2334, Edificio Metrobol, ℗ 430303; **Canada** Av. 20 de Octubre 2475 (plaza Avaroa), ℗ 431215; **Colombia** Calle 9 Calacoto 7835, ℗ 784491; **Chile** Av. H Siles 5873, ℗ 785275; **Ecuador** Edificio Hermann, piso 14, ℗ 321208; **Peru** Av. 6 de Agosto, Edificio Alianza mezzanine, Oficina 110, ℗ 352352, and Av. Arce 2732, ℗ 433424; **USA** Av. Arce 2780 at Cordero, ℗ 430251; **Venezuela** Edificio Illimani, Av. Arce 2678, pisos 4 and 5, ℗ 431365.

Most consulates and embassies are open only between 9am and 12pm.

Conservation: The government departments responsible for the protection of Bolivia's wilderness areas are: **Dirección Nacional de la Conservación de la Biodiversidad Unida de Vida Silvestre**, Calle Batallón Colorados, Edificio El Condor, Piso 15, Oficina 1504, ℗ 315139, ✉ 316230, and the **Servicio Nacional de Areas Protegidos**, Calle Batallón Colorados; Edificio El Condor, Piso 13.

The Sights

Apart from some interesting museums, there's little to see in La Paz. The gloomy 16th-century **Iglesia San Francisco** (Sagárnaga at Mariscal Santa Cruz) is one of the city's oldest churches. The façade is decorated with carved tropical fruit and rainforest birds. The stained-glass windows of the massive 19th-century **cathedral** (Plaza Murillo) are typically Latin American, showing a series of military dictators and generals being blessed from on high. The best views of the city are from the top of the valley on the El Alto road. A taxi there will cost around $10.

The city's most interesting series of **museums** are next door to each other on one of the city's finest colonial streets, **Calle Jaén**, off Alto de Alianza, one block northeast of Montes. They have the same opening hours (*Tues–Fri 9.30–12 and 2.30–5.30, weekends 10–12.30*) and can be visited on one $4 ticket, purchasable at any of them. On Saturdays admission is free. The best by far is the **Museo de Oro** (*Museo de Metales Preciosos Pre-Columbianos*). There is little pre-Colombian gold and silver left in the world, and this museum houses some superb pieces from Tiahuanaco and the Inca empire. Displays are very well lit and displayed against black. Bring tungsten film or a blue filter for photographs. The others are also worth a peek: the **Casa de Don Pedro Murillo** contains a collection of colonial furniture, art and musical instruments in the house of a 19th-century Bolivian revolutionary later lynched by the Spanish. At the **Museo Costumbrista Juan de Vargas**, there are dolls, figurines and photos from old La Paz. Bolivia is one of very few landlocked countries in the world to maintain a navy. This is due to a combination of melancholy and wishful thinking, as the rather sad exhibits bewailing the loss of the country's Pacific territory to Chile at the **Museo del Litoral** (Museum of the Coast) attest.

Other museums include the **Museo Arqueológico Tiahuanaco**, Tiwanaku at Zuazo, two blocks from Av. 16 de Julio (the Prado) (*open Tues–Fri 9–12 and 2.30–6*): a small collection of mummies, pottery, ceramic sculpture, metal tools and textiles from the advanced Tiahuanaco civilization. The Incas modelled themselves specifically on Tiahuanaco, so these artefacts, mostly from around 1,500 years ago, mark the beginnings of a story that culminated in the Inca empire. There is a collection of art and iconography from the Potosí school of painting at the **Museo Nacional del Arte**, Calle Comercio at Socabaya (*open Tues–Fri 9–12 and 3–6*), in a grand former palace; and the **Museo de Etnografía y Folklore**, Ingavi at Genaro Sanjinés (*open Mon–Fri 8.30–12 and 2.30–6*) displays weavings, wickerwork, artefacts and photos from Bolivia's Andean and Amazon Basin tribes.

La Paz (℡ 02–)   ***Shopping***

Although you'll find nothing from the Amazon, La Paz is the best and cheapest place in the region (along with Cusco in Peru), to shop for arts and crafts. Best buys include alpaca- and llama-wool jumpers, traditional multi-coloured Quechua and Aymara Indian hats, carpets, bags and leather items. Stalls and shops piled high with these line the **Calle Sagárnaga** and the small arcade immediately to the north of the San Francisco church.

L.A.M. and Artesanías Maranatha (Sagárnaga 233 and 271) sell some of the better items, but even the cheapest stalls are well worth checking out. Many of the wool jumpers sold in La Paz have non-colour-fast dyes—be sure to ask.

Alpaca Export, Calle Linares 868, ℰ 231330, and **Suri Export**, Calle Juan de la Riva 1439, ℰ 413663, are more expensive but offer higher quality, and sell Bolivian crafts for export.

For herbal remedies try the **Mercado de Hechicería**, where you can even buy a llama foetus to bless your new house with.

La Paz has plenty of hotels to suit all but the royal wallet—even the Radisson is reasonably priced. New options are always springing up, especially on Calle Sagárnaga.

expensive

Radisson Hotel Plaza, Av. Arce 2177, ☏ 316161, ☐ 316302. One of the city's six five-star hotels with sauna, gym with massage service and a very good restaurant.

Hotel Plaza, Paseo El Prado 1789, ☏ 378311, ☐ 378318, *plazabolivia@usa.net*. Almost indistinguishable from the Radisson, with a spa, and a good penthouse restaurant with one of the best views in the city.

El Rey Palacio, 20 Octubre 1947, ☏ 393016, ☐ 367759, *hotelrey@wara.bolnet.bo*. Smaller, more personal and cheaper than the Radisson or Plaza. Free English-language newspapers, and one of the city's better restaurants.

moderate–inexpensive

Hotel Gloria, Calle Potosí 909, ☏ 370010, ☐ 391489. Conveniently located almost opposite the San Francisco church, with good views from the top rooms. The ground floor has the best vegetarian restaurant in La Paz.

Hostal Rosario, Av. Illampu 704, ☏ 316156, ☐ 375532; *turisbus@ caoba.entelnet.bo*. A very popular, small, mock-colonial hotel. The restaurant serves good continental breakfasts and evening meals, and there's a sauna.

Hostal República, Calle Comercio 1455, ☏ 357966. A colonial building that was once the home of a Bolivian president. Very helpful staff, a small library of used books, two airy courtyards and a small garden.

cheap

There are numerous cheaper options dotted around the old town; on or close to Calle Sagárnaga, and north towards the Plaza Vicente Eguino.

Hotel Andes, Manco Capac 364, ☏ 323461. The best of the cheaper options, in a faded 1950s block. Luggage storage is available and continental breakfast is included.

Hostal Austria, Yanacocha 531, ☏ 351140. Rock-bottom prices and relative cleanliness make this a backpackers' favourite; come early in the day.

Torino, Socabaya 457, ☏ 341487, is cheaper still. Large, bare and sometimes dusty rooms in a crumbling colonial mansion, with a small book exchange.

The **Radisson**, **Rey Palacio** and **Rosario** (*see* above) have some of the city's best restaurants, whilst the Plaza has the finest view. All serve a mixture of European and Bolivian dishes. The trout in white wine at Rosario is particularly good. Other good places include:

Vienna, Zuazo 1905, in the new part of town, serves predominantly European cuisine in a formal setting. Popular with businessmen.

El Palacio de Pescado, Muñecas América, in the old part of town, has fresh river fish from Lake Titicaca and the Amazon River (flown in from the Beni).

Nuevo Oruro, Ingavi 773, is a carnivores' favourite: the huge *Plato de la Casa* has four kinds of meat. There are good views and murals.

La Québecoise, 20 de Octubre 2355, one block northwest of the Plaza Avaroa in the new part of town, serves French Canadian and US dishes for those missing home.

Mamma Mia, 20 de Octubre 2090, near the Plaza Avaroa on the corner of Aspiazu. One of La Paz's best Italian restaurants, with pasta, pizza and fish dishes.

Around Calle Sagárnaga there are numerous cheapies: try **El Montañés** (between Linares and Illampu) and the **Peña Naira**, near the Iglesia San Francisco.

vegetarian

The **Hotel Gloria** (*see* above), has a vegetarian buffet on the first floor. There's plenty of choice, and dishes change from day to day. The *almuerzo* (set lunch) is very good value and includes fresh fruit juice. *Open for lunch only.*

Entertainment and Nightlife

Bars (dress smart casual): **Cambrinus**, 20 de Octubre 2453 at Plaza Avaroa has piano music, good beer and a good atmosphere; at **Arabia**, 6 de Agosto 2415 on the corner of Belisario Salinas, watch the Bolivian yuppies singing karaoke; **Montmartre**, Calle F. Guachala 399 at 20 de Octubre, is the place to be seen in La Paz, and has live bands at weekends.

International Bars: **Britannia**, Calles 15 and 16 in Barrio Calacoto, is a bizarre English theme bar; **Bavaria**, 20 de Octubre at Avaroa, has expensive snacks, good German beer and opens early; **X-Presión Café Art Bar**, Zoilo Flores 1334, has a Brazilian night on Wednesdays and live music at the weekends.

Clubs: Discoteca La Pampa, Av. Santa Cruz, and **Forum**, Víctor Sanjines 2908, are popular with young locals and play throbbing dance music and salsa. **Peñas** is far more fun with live Andean music, food and dancing. **Naira**, Sagárnaga 161, has Andean music for tourists, starting at 10pm. **Marka Tambo**, Jaén 710, is more traditional. **Las Cuatro Estaciones**, 20 de Octubre at Pérez has more of the same on Fridays and Saturdays only.

Cinemas: Catch up on the latest from Hollywood (no European arthouse here) at the Cine 16 de Julio, Av. 16 de Julio at Plaza Estudiante, ✆ 376099; or Cine 6 de Agosto, Av. 6 de Agosto 2284, ✆ 323829.

Tour Operators in La Paz   *La Paz (✆ 02–)*

All of the tour companies listed below have English-speaking and often multilingual guides (usually French, German and Hebrew, as well as English).

Academia Nacional de Ciencias de Bolivia, Av. 16 de Julio 1732, ✆/⊕ 350612, Casilla 5829. The government department responsible for granting permission for visits to the Beni Biological Research Stations (*see* p.161).

America Tours, Av. 16 de Julio 1490, Edificio Avenida Planta Baja, Oficina 9 (opposite the Monje Campero cinema at corner of Calle Bueno), ✆ 374204, ⊕ 328584, *AlistairM@ hotmail.com*. Very well-run, small-scale tours from Rurrenabaque to Chalalan Lodge (*see* p.171), from around $80–$100 per person per day, and backpacker-orientated mountain biking from La Paz to Coroico and beyond, from $30 per person per day.

Ecological Expeditions, Sagárnaga at Murillo 189, ✆ 314172, ✆ 365047, *ecological@bo.net*, Casilla 1705. Mid-range tour company with trips to Rurrenabaque and environs (*see* p.170), Amboró and Noel Kempff Mercado National Parks (*see* pp.162, 164).

Explore Bolivia, Galería Sagárnaga 339, Primer Piso, Oficina 1, ✆ 378421, ✆ 391810, *explobol@ceibo.entelnet.bo*. Bolivia's leading adventure tour operator with a wealth of different mid-price trips in the Amazon and Yungas, including trekking on Inca roads; rafting expeditions on the Ríos Tuichi and Coroico (*see* p.170); tours of the Beni lowlands near Rurrenabaque (*see* p.170); Isiboro Sécure National Park (*see* p.160); birding, fishing and photography tours in the Beni and Mamoré Amazon lowlands (around $70 per person per day); Jesuit Mission tours near Santa Cruz (*see* p.158). Other options include 4x4 expeditions to the desert, lakes and volcanoes of Los Lípez; sea kayaking on Lake Titicaca; treks to La Ciudad de Piedra; and a tour in the footsteps of Che Guevara.

Fremen, Calle Pedro Salazar, 537, Plaza Avaroa, ✆ 414069, ✆ 417062, ✆ 417327, offers upmarket river cruises on the Río Mamoré near Trinidad (*see* p.158).

Magri Turismo, Calle Capitán Ravelo 2101, Edificio Capitán Ravelo, ✆ 434747, ✆ 434660, *magri_emete@megalink.com*, *www.bolivianet.com/magri*, Casilla 4469. Upmarket trips around Bolivia, and to the Jesuit missions near Santa Cruz.

The Northeastern Lowlands

Though northeastern Bolivia is the country's agricultural heartland with perhaps the greatest rate of deforestation on the continent, large areas, some of the most beautiful in the entire Amazon Basin, still lie undisturbed by the tractors and regimented lines of soya bean. In the rainforest gardens of Amboró and Noel Kempff Mercado National Parks near Santa Cruz, remote waterfalls form rainbows against the greenery, and streams meander in the shadow of giant trees, their soft verges imprinted with jaguar and tapir spoor. Noel Kempff encloses a table-top mountain a fifth the size of Massachusetts, tropical savannahs with maned wolf, and forests of gliding king vultures and harpy eagles. Spectacled bear still forage in the misty, crumpled hills of Amboró's cloud forests together with over 700 species of birds. The blue-throated macaw, one of the world's rarest parrots, nests in the forest around Trinidad, on the outer limits of an unexplored wilderness of secret nature that stretches unbroken into the lowlands of Brazil.

Santa Cruz

Steamy and slightly sleazy Santa Cruz, surrounded by vast soya plantations that are eating into the lowland forests at a furious rate, doesn't feel much like the rest of Bolivia. The conservatism and reserve of the Andes evaporates in the heat of the lowland plains, and the cultural residue that remains feels almost Brazilian. Young men swagger, women wear shorts and flirt, and the streets are filled with the fumes of four-wheel drives and American sedans.

Santa Cruz has always been a more European city than its Andean counterparts. The town was settled some 150 miles from its present site by Spanish cattle ranchers in the late 16th century. They moved to higher ground after repeated attacks by local tribes, renaming their city Santa Cruz de la Sierra and cultivating the fertile soil that lay in the environs. Santa Cruz supplied Bolivia with sugar, cotton, rice and fruit throughout colonial times and up until the

1800s, when improved transport between La Paz and the Pacific undermined the city's importance and sent it into decline. Mule tracks were the only link with the highlands until the 1950s, when a road brought a boom in trade, both licit and illicit. The city has grown tenfold since then, ensconced itself in luxurious suburbs and shanty towns and peopled its streets with various migrants—Mennonites fleeing from Belize and Mexico, peasants from the Altiplano, American missionaries and oil workers, and a bevy of opportunists and would-be tycoons.

The city's first cinema produced such a fervour of excitement that a guard with a loaded rifle had to be present at every performance lest locals killed each other in an argument over the plot. Today, seediness and danger are associated with drug-trafficking and smuggling, but these pastimes go largely unnoticed by tourists. Santa Cruz is not a dangerous place. The only unpleasant encounter you are likely to have is during the Mardi Gras carnival, when belligerent children run riot with water pistols filled with garish, permanent dyes; foreigners are a particular target. Although it has some comfortable hotels and fairly good restaurants, Santa Cruz is a hub rather than a destination in its own right.

Santa Cruz (℗ 03–)   **Getting There and Around**
                                                                 by air

International: American Airlines, Casco Viejo Planta Alta, Oficina 111, ℗ 361414, have connections between Santa Cruz and Miami. Varig, Junín 284, ℗ 349333, fly to Miami (via Manaus), Cuiabá, São Paulo and Rio de Janeiro. LAB, Warnes at Chuquisaca, ℗ 344411, fly to Miami, Lima, Buenos Aires and Córdoba, Montevideo, Rio de Janeiro and São Paulo, Asunción, Caracas, Bogotá, Mexico City and Cancún, and Panama City. Lanchile, Libertad 144, ℗ 335940, have flights to Arica and Santiago.

National: LAB (*see* above) and Aerosur, Avenida Irala at Colón, ℗ 367400, have daily connections to La Paz and frequent connections to Puerto Suárez, Cochabamba, Sucre, Trinidad (connections here for Rurrenabaque (Reyes) which is close to Rurrenabaque), Riberalta and Guayaramerín.

by rail

International: The **railway station** is on Avenida Brasil at the third *anillo*, a short taxi ride from the centre. When it comes to buying train tickets, queues are unruly, demand is high and the ticket office keeps no regular hours. Try to get there before 8am. There are rail connections three times a week to Argentina (15hrs) and daily except Sunday for Puerto Quijarro and the Brazilian border (20hrs). Brazilian visas must be obtained in Santa Cruz (*see* consulates, above). The faster Ferrobus with couchettes leaves on Friday and Sunday and takes 12hrs.

by road

The **bus station** is on the edge of the first *anillo*, a 10–15-min walk from the centre. Several buses a day make the gruelling journey to the Argentinian border at Yacuiba (20–24hrs) and depart for La Paz (16–20hrs) and Sucre (18–20hrs). Buses for Cochabamba (8–12hrs, via Buena Vista for Amboró) leave at least hourly (with connecting services to Sucre, Oruro and Potosí). Buses depart daily for Trinidad but are frequently cancelled during the wet season (Dec–April); journey times can be anything between 12hrs in the dry to two days in the wet. Buses from Trinidad connect to Rurrenabaque, Rurrenabaque (Reyes) and Riberalta, via an equally long and unreliable haul. **Minibuses** leave when full from the corner of Calle Riva and Cañoto north of the main bus terminal, for Warnes (1 hr) and Buena Vista (about 2hrs).

Car rental: Barron's Rent-a-Car, Av. Cristóbal de Mendoza, 286, Zona El Cristo, ✆ 338823/420160, *www.bolivianet.com/rentacar*, and Localiza, Independencia 365, ✆ 372223. Both rent reliable cars and four-wheel drives.

Santa Cruz (✆ 03–)   ***Tourist Information and Useful Addresses***

Tourist office: Edificio CORDECRUZ, Av. Omar Chávez, ✆ 368900, is inconveniently housed in government offices south of the bus station. It does little more than dish out pamphlets and bus and train times.

FAN (*see* p.157) provide information on Amboró and Noel Kempff Mercado National Parks. They speak English and offer tours to both. **Associación Hombre y Naturaleza** (*see* p.157) provides information on conservation in the Gran Chaco National Park of the Bolivian Pantanal. They also offer tours here.

Medical centre: Clínica Lourdes, Rene Moreno 334, is reliable and efficient; they will give shots. Hypodermics can be bought at the nearby *farmacía* on the corner.

Internet: Café Liberty, Calle Warnes 38, next to the Entel office.

Changing money: The *casa de Cambio* on the eastern side of the plaza will change traveller's cheques. The Banco de Santa Cruz, Junín 154, gives slightly better rates. The Banco Boliviano Americano, René Moreno 366, has a Visa/Mastercard cashpoint.

Immigration office: in front of the zoo north of the centre at the third *anillo*, ✆ 438559, ✆ 368400 (*open Mon–Fri 8–12 and 12.30–6.30*).

Consulates: Argentina Banco de la Nacíon Argentina, Piso 3 ✆ 347133; **Brazil** Av. Busch 330, ✆ 344400 (**note**: there is no consulate in Puerto Quijarro or Puerto Suárez; get your visa here); **Chile** Barrio Equipetrol, Calle 5 Oeste 224, ✆ 331043; **Paraguay** Edificio Oriente, Piso 5, ✆ 366113; **United States** Barrio Guemes, Calle 6 Este, ✆ 330725.

The City

Santa Cruz is a regular mesh of modern streets, spreading concentrically in *anillos* (rings) from the central plaza. The **bus station** is six blocks south and four blocks west of the plaza along Independencia and Lemoine, at the edge of the first *anillo*. The **airport** and **railway station** are a 10–15-minute taxi ride away. The centre retains a colonial feel, with shady arcades and a few pre-20th-century buildings, including an 18th-century cathedral that looks like it could withstand a nuclear barrage. There are a few museums that serve to while away empty hours. The **Cathedral Museum** (*open Tues and Thurs 9–12 and 3–6*) houses relics from the Jesuit missions and a minuscule book of the Lord's Prayer the size of a fingernail. The **Casa de la Cultura**, also on the plaza, is one of the city's most elegant buildings, with a small collection of Bolivian art. The **Natural History Museum**, eight blocks south of the plaza on Irala (*open daily 9–12 and 3–6*) is full of stuffed rainforest animals, and large impaled insects and arachnids. The **Museo Etno-Folklórico**, on an island in the Parque Arenal, has a few remnants from lowland tribal cultures and a mural by the celebrated Bolivian artist Lorgio Vaca. The **Parque Zoológico** (*open daily 9–5*), with its depressing array of caged big cats, harpy eagles, monkeys and macaws, is a taxi ride north of the centre at the third *anillo*.

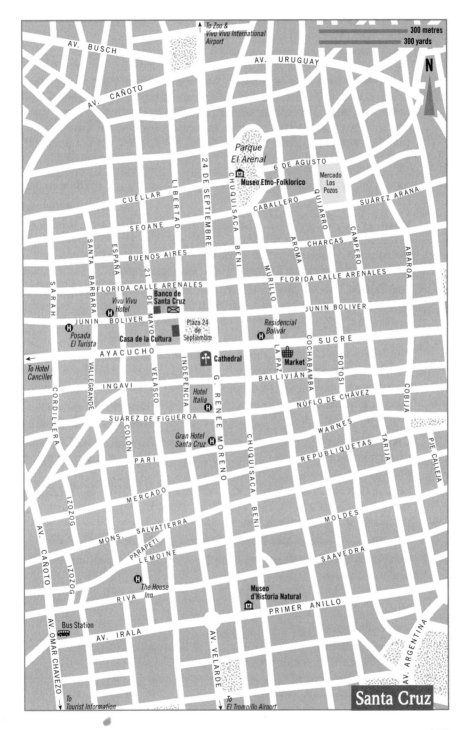

Santa Cruz

Arte Campo, Calle Monseñor Salvatierra 407, on the corner of Vallegrande, is one of the best places in the country to buy traditional Indian craftwork made by indigenous peoples of the Santa Cruz department. All the money generated goes to them. Santa Cruz is one of the cheapest places in the Americas to buy slide **photographic film**. FotoRelieve, Ingavi 256 between Velasco and Colón, sells Fuji film, including Velvia, Provia and Astia, and stores it properly. Their processing is reliable and cheap. Buy **camping equipment and supplies** at Piscinas Pocolín, Calle Arenales 48, ✆ 363582.

luxury–expensive

Yotaú, Av. San Martín 7, Barrio Equipetrol, ✆ 367799, ✆ 363952 (reservations), ✆363370 (sales), *yotauven@bibosi.scz.entelnet.bo*. The most upmarket hotel in Santa Cruz. A complex of modern air-conditioned flats with saunas, balconies and all mod cons, arranged around a swimming pool. Staff speak English.

Los Tajibos, Av. San Martín 455, ✆ 421000, ✆ 426994, *lostajib@bibosi.scz. entelnet.bo, wwwbolivianet.com/lostajibos*. Slightly cheaper, with a pool, tennis courts, gym and air-conditioned rooms. Their tour agency offers trips to Amboró and the Jesuit Missions and arranges trips to Noel Kempff Mercado through FAN (*see* p.157).

The House Inn, Colón 643, near the bus station, ✆/✆ 362323. Two pools, air-conditioned suites and a restaurant.

Canciller, Calle Ayacucho 220, ✆ 372525/364847, ✆ 361710, *canciller@daitec. scz.com*, is central, geared to business travellers, and the cheapest in this category.

moderate–inexpensive

Gran Hotel Santa Cruz, Calle Pari 59, ✆ 348811, ✆ 324194, *hsancruz@ mitai.urs.bolnet.bo*. In a well-restored, bright and airy 1930s building in the centre; air-conditioned rooms, good service and a pool.

La Quinta, Calle Arumá, Barrio Urbarí, ✆ 522244, ✆ 522244, *hotel.laquinta@ samerica.com*, Casilla 1270. With a small pool, mock-colonial rooms, a sauna, gym and restaurant. A five-minute taxi ride from the centre.

Viru Viru, Calle Junín 218, ✆ 335298, has rooms with air-conditioning or a fan.

Hotel Italia, Calle René Moreno 167, ✆ 323119, is central, with plain and simple air-conditioned rooms.

cheap

Hotel Sarah, Sarah 85, between Ayacucho and Junín, ✆ 322425, ✆ 372524. Basic, small rooms with a fan and TV.

Residencial Bolívar, Calle Sucre 131, ✆ 342500, Popular with budget travellers, with a pleasant hammock-filled courtyard.

El Turista, Junín 455. Box-like rooms, but the cheapest decent place in town. The friendly and helpful owners will let you store luggage.

Santa Cruz has some surprisingly good restaurants which also cater for vegetarians.

La Castañuela, Velasco 308 on the corner of Pari. A Spanish restaurant in a beautiful colonial house. Discreet service from aloof waiters in dinner jackets. The food is delicious—try the *gazpacho*—and the wine list is by far the best in town (*moderate*).

El Falcón, Independencia at Pari, has a menu from a different country nearly every day. The polyglot Argentinian owner, Cesaré, has some fascinating stories to tell about South America during the military years (*inexpensive*).

La Tabernet, Calle Moreno, on the corner of Chávez, serves delicious pizzas said by locals to be the best in town. For breakfasts, *licuados* (milk shakes) and good coffee, head for **El Tinto,** Calle Ingavi 323 between Colón and Vallegrande. **Cuerpomente,** Calle Pari between Colón and Velasco, with another branch at Sucre 525, is one of the best vegetarian options anywhere in the Amazon, with delicious and plentiful buffet food. It is also an Ouspenskian esoteric bookshop and yoga centre. *All inexpensive*

Tour Operators in Santa Cruz   *Santa Cruz (☎ 03–)*

Anavin, 24 Septiembre 185 (between the plaza and Florida), Local 4, ☎ 352009, @ 360788, *anavin@bibosi.scz.entelnet.bo*. Upmarket one- and two-day trips to Amboró National Park and the Jesuit Missions circuit, and five-star accommodation in the Bolivian Pantanal, cost $100–$250 per person per day, depending on numbers.

Asociación Hombre y Naturaleza, Calle Tacuarembó 2065, ☎/@ 436968, in Warnes (30km from Santa Cruz), Av. Circunvalación Lado Norte, Distrito 13, Rotonda salida a Montero, ☎/@ (0923) 2239, *hynb@bibosi.scz.entelnet.bo*, *www.paisvirtual.com/ong/ comercial/hynb/index.html*. A Spanish-Bolivian conservation NGO offering trips to Gran Chaco National Park in the Bolivian Pantanal (*see* p.168).

FAN, Calle Isoso 384, ☎ 337475, @ 329692, *ecoturismo@fan.scbbs-bo.com*, *www.scbbs-bo.com/fan/*, Casilla 2241. Trips to Noel Kempff Mercado (*see* p.164).

Fremen, Cañoto, corner of 21 de Mayo, ☎ 338535, @ 360265, *vtfremen@caoba.entelnet .bo*, *www.andes-amazonia.com*. Luxury cruises on the Mamoré from Trinidad (*see* p.159).

Gama Tours, Arenales 566, ☎ 340921, @ 363828, *gamatur@roble.scz.entelnet.bo*. Natural history, birding and general tours to Amboró, with a reputation for ecologically sound practice.

Magri Turismo, Calle Capitan Ravelo 2101, Edificio Capitán Ravelo, P.O Box 4469, ☎ 434747, @ 434660, Warnes at Potosí, ☎ 345663, @ 343591, *magri-srz@scz.logic. com.bo*, *www.bolivianet.com/magri*. Upmarket trips to the Jesuit missions.

Neblina Forest Tours, Calle Mojos 246, ☎/@ 336831, *neblinaforest@daitec.scz.com*. The newly opened Bolivian branch of the prestigious Ecuadorean wildlife and birding tour company, managed by Tim Miller of FAN. Offers specialist natural history and birding trips to Amboró and market FAN's trips into Noel Kempff Mercado. From $100 per person per day.

Rosario Tours, Arenales 193, ☎ 369656/369977, @ 369656, *tucan@cnb.net*, Casilla 683. Trips to Ríos Blanco y Negro reserve, Beni National Park and the Jesuit Missions.

T and T Sudamérica, Calle Junín 338, ☎ 363498, @ 331497. A Brazilian-run company offering trips to the Laguna Pistola 4hrs from Santa Cruz (good for bird-watching), Ríos Blanco y Negro and Amboró. Around $70 per person per day. Good value.

Around Santa Cruz: the Chiquitano Jesuit Missions Circuit

The Jesuit *reducciones* of the Chiquitos near Santa Cruz are the only ones in South America not to have been destroyed after the expulsion of the order in 1767. The nomadic tribes of the Amazon and Pantanal were brought here by the missionaries, clothed and put to work on plantations. Though their indigenous identity was undermined, the Indians who lived here were saved from the ravages of the Brazilian *bandeirantes* who captured and enslaved so many of their compatriots (*see* also pp.88–9). The art on the various churches is particularly fine, a fusion of indigenous and Baroque Christian themes. Howler and black spider monkeys rub shoulders with the Madonna and Child, Amazon fruits hang next to vines (symbolizing Christ) and nectar-sucking bats and toucans decorate Baroque pillars and colonnades. There are seven towns in the mission circuit, with churches dating from the late 17th century. The most impressive buildings are found at **Concepción**, with a church designed by Martin Schmidt between 1753 and 1756; **San Javier**, the first of the mission towns, established in 1691 (the indigenous peoples of this mission were famous for their beautifully carved musical instruments); **San Rafael** and **San Miguel**, both with fine gold leaf on their altarpieces; and **San José de Chiquitos**, which was one of the first to be built of stone. Transport in the region is irregular and uncomfortable; the easiest way to get to see all the mission towns is on an organized tour. For **operators**, *see* La Paz, p.151, Santa Cruz, p.157, and Trinidad, p.159.

Getting Around and Where to Stay

Buses leave from Santa Cruz's bus station for San Javier (1 hr), Concepción (5hrs) and San Ignacio (11hrs). Concepción and San Ignacio both have **airports**. Inquire at the Santa Cruz tourist office for flight details.

There are a couple of options if you want to stay in San Javier. For **Cabañas Totaitu** book through Totaitu Tours, Av. Irala 421, Santa Cruz, ✆ (03) 34470, ✉ (03) 344700, *totaitu@em.daitec.bo.com*, *www.totaitusez.com*. Comfortable *cabañas* and air-conditioned rooms, with two pools, a good restaurant, tennis and volleyball court and 'ecological' horse-riding excursions. There's good hiking, and the hotel rents mountain bikes (*expensive–moderate*, depending on season and whether it's a weekend). The **Gran Hotel Concepción**, on the central plaza, ✆ (03) 324192, ✉ (03) 364723, has fan-cooled rooms, a patio with carved pillars and a small garden (*inexpensive*).

Trinidad

Hot, sticky and reeking of stagnant water and open sewers, Trinidad festers in the lowland forest and savannahs of northeastern Bolivia; charitable people would call the town dull. Pass through quickly on your way to the prehistoric sites nearby or the remote parks, home to one of the world's rarest birds, the blue-throated macaw, before catching a plane, or a river boat downstream. Tourist attractions are not Trinidad's strong point—almost everything worth seeing is out of the city. If you are interested in river fish, Luís Torres in the **Universidad Técnica del Beni** has one of the best collections of preserved and living tropical fish in the country. There's also a small **zoo** on the site. The very helpful **tourist office** is on the ground floor of the Prefectural building, Joaquin de Sierra at La Paz, ✆ 21722. If you need to change money, the **Banco Mercantil**, near the plaza, and the **Banco Sur** change traveller's cheques, and money-changers on 6 de Agosto change dollars.

LAB (Bolívar, between 18 de Noviembre and Santa Cruz, ℃ 20595) and/or Aerosur (Cipriano Barace 51, ℃ 20765, 🖅 21296) **fly** to La Paz, Santa Cruz, Riberalta, Cobija, Puerto Suárez, Cochabamba, Rurrenabaque (Reyes). The main **bus station** is at the corner of Pinto and Rómulo Mendoza 1km east of the main plaza. Buses leave regularly for San Borja, Rurrenabaque and Santa Cruz. **Bikes, mopeds and jeeps** can be hired easily in town. The Mamoré, Bolivia's principal Amazon tributary, is 13km away at Puerto Barador. Guayaramerín is about a week away by irregular **boat**. Ask in the Trinidad tourist office or at the docks in Puerto Barador.

Tour Operators in Trinidad *(℃ 046–)*

Paraiso Travel, Av. 6 de Agosto 138, ℃ 20692/20946, 🖅 20692, *paraiso@sauce.ben. entelnet.bo*, Casilla 261. They employ the only bilingual specialist natural history guide based in Trinidad, Lilián González (most of La Paz and Santa Cruz agencies use her). With notice, Lilián can organize trips into the Ríos Blanco y Negro Reserve, staying at the Perseverancia hacienda (*see* p.160), and possibly to Isiboro Sécure. Paraíso themselves only offer one-day tours and trips to Las Lomas and along the Río Mamoré. About $85 a day all-inclusive.

Fremen, Av. 6 de Agosto 140, ℃/🖅 21834 (in La Paz, *see* p.152; in Santa Cruz, *see* p.157), *vtfremen@caoba.entelnet.bo*, *www.andes-amazonia.com*. One of the leading tour operators in the country, with boat-based trips along the Mamoré and Ibaré Rivers on their new flotel, the *Reina de Enin*. The trips last four to six days, and include stops in indigenous villages, exploration of gallery and inundated forests (navigated in small boats) and night camps in the wild. The flotel can accommodate 40 people in air-conditioned cabins and there's a small pool on board. Vegetarian and diabetic food is available. Guides speak English and German and have good knowledge of forest fauna and flora. Expect to pay $100 per day, all-inclusive.

The **indigenous people** of Trinidad have exciting plans to set-up an **eco- and ethno-tourism agency** offering trips to the Chimane Forest Reserve. Guides will be Spanish-speaking only. Contact the tourist office for the latest details. Expect to pay $50 or less, all-inclusive.

Gran Moxos, Av. 6 de Agosto 146 at Santa Cruz, ℃ 22240, the plushest and priciest in town, with air-conditioned rooms and cable TV, but no pool. **Taruma**, km 6 carretera asfaltada Trinidad-Santa Cruz; ℃ 22252, 🖅 20030; air-conditioned cabins with private baths, overlooking a pool. Private lake, trips along the Mamoré and other rainforest excursions. Good value. **Mi Residencia**, Manuel Limpias 76; ℃ 21535; 🖅 22464. Very comfortable, with air-conditioned rooms, a travel agency and a pool, half a block from the main plaza. **El Bajio**, Av. Nicolás Suárez 520, ℃ 22400, air-conditioned rooms, pool and a sauna (*all moderately priced*).

Eat out at the delightfully situated **Balneario Topacaré** at Laguna Suárez, an artificial lake and popular beauty spot 5km from town. The restaurant serves local specialities. Tasty fresh river fish is available at **Pescadería El Moro**, Bolívar at 25 de Deciembre. Vegetarians will have to make do with pizza—try **La Casona** on the plaza.

Around Trinidad

The **Llanos de Moxos**, one of the Amazon's most enigmatic wonders, consist of over 100km of canals, tumuli and giant animals sculpted out of the earth by the Beni Indians of the Paititi tribe 5,500 years ago—perhaps their fame bred the Paititi myth associated with the Incas. The **Santuario Chuchini** (*open daily 9–5; adm US$10*) is an ecological reserve and small museum built on one of the most accessible tumuli. The rainforest and savannah here is full of others, together with oxbow lakes and canals that echo with the calls of hundreds of raucous macaws and black howler monkeys. Apart from these, there are plentiful puma, spectacled caiman, capybara and black spider monkeys and marmosets. Bungalows here cost $60 a night including food, and the park has a $10 entrance fee. Bring mosquito repellent.

San Ignacio de Moxos is a predominantly Mojeno Indian crossroads hamlet that bursts into life between 30 July and 2 August. The **Fiesta del Santo Patrono** is one of the liveliest events in the lowlands, and is infinitely preferable to the damp and irritating Bolivian carnival celebrations. The streets of the little village fill with brightly clad dancers, Indians in huge macaw-feather head-dresses, and traditional masked processions. This is also a good time to buy arts and crafts, especially Indian hammocks and reed-weavings. San Ignacio has an interesting restored **Jesuit mission** dating from 1689. There are unexcavated Mojeno archaeological ruins nearby in the Arroyo Tiyere and at Lázaro at the confluence of the Apere and Matos Rivers. The village lies close to the **Isiboro Sécure National Park** and the **Indigenous Territory of the Isiboro Sécure** (TIPNIS). It may be possible to organize trips here with local Indians, but check safety with the tourist office in Trindad before doing so. The huge Laguna Isirere, just north of the town, has a floating reed island, and is surrounded by tropical forest.

Minibuses leave when full for San Ignacio de Moxos from the Trinidad bus terminal (3hrs). There are a few plain guesthouses dotted around the plaza, the best of which is the **Plaza Hotel**, Plaza Principal, Acera Sud, ✆ 2032. Prices double during the festival.

National Parks Near Trinidad

There are three important protected areas near Trinidad. All are remote, with little tourist infrastructure, which means that though they are fairly difficult to visit the wilderness is pristine and wildlife remains largely undisturbed (at least in the areas not damaged by illegal logging and hunting).

The 14,000km^2 **Ríos Blanco y Negro Wildlife Reserve** (*Reserva de Vida Silvestre Ríos Blanco y Negro*) is situated in the midst of Bolivia's largest area of lowland tropical wilderness. The two rivers that drain the reserve mark the transition zone between the lowland rainforest and savannah of the northern Beni department, and the deciduous dry chaco scrub and thorn forests that stretch into Paraguay to the south. The park is an important refuge for large mammals. There is little accommodation here; the **Perseverancia hacienda**, built by rubber-tappers in the 1920s, is accessible only by plane. The **Lake Taborga Biological Station** is idyllically situated on a lake in first-growth tropical rainforest between the Ríos Blanco and Negro, to the west of the reserve. Accommodation is basic but is more than made up for by the remote and magical location replete with wildlife. Guarayo Indians act as guides.

Even fewer tourists make it to the vast **Isiboro Sécure National Park**; though the forests at the heart of the park are pristine, there has been much illegal logging and disorder in recent years. This is Bolivia's lawless wild frontier, where conflicts between peasants and indigenous

Threats to the Forest and Local Indigenous People

In these backlands, threats to the forest and environmental abuse are at their most acute. The region's Indians have been largely responsible for bringing this to the attention of the government, but there is still a long way to go. Whilst indigenous people are long gone from Santa Cruz, Indians from around Trinidad have been at the vanguard of the Latin American indigenous awakening and the protection of local forests. In October 1990, 800 Moxo, Chimane and Guariní set out from Trinidad to walk the 330 miles to La Paz in protest against the government's failure to prevent the extraction of mahogany from a 400,000-acre area of the Chimane forest. As they climbed through the mountain passes, they were joined by thousands of highland Indians. The president, Jaime Zamora, came out to meet them, and agreed to their demand for the withdrawal of loggers, and the granting of title to four million acres of the Amazon forest, much of which has now become the Chimane Forest Reserve. This was a major breakthrough—until then, these people, who had lived in the forest for millennia, had had the same civil and legal status as plants and animals. Unfortunately, little subsequent protection has been offered to the Indians by the government, and they continue to be ruthlessly persecuted by settlers and loggers, especially in the Isiboro Sécure National Park.

Other regions are suffering too, and for similar reasons—the DEA and big business agriculture have forced *campesinos* off their plantations, and they have had nowhere to go but virgin territory. There is plenty of illegal logging and hunting going on in the Ríos Blanco y Negro reserve. In the lawless chaos that has ensued, even unscrupulous westerners masquerading as 'conservational tourism' operators are attempting to get a slice of the rainforest pie; there are reports that a German and English couple based in Trinidad offer trips into the Ríos Blanco y Negro Reserve as a front for the skin trade, so be wary when choosing a guide and, if you witness any unscrupulous practices, report them to the local authorities—FAN in Santa Cruz (*see* p.157); Conservation International (*see* p.177); or one of the following:

The Dirección Nacional de la Conservación de la Biodiversidad Unida de Vida Silvestre, Calle Batallón Colorados, Edificio El Condor, Piso 15, Oficina 1504, ✆ (02) 315139, ✉ (02) 316230

The Servicio Nacional de Areas Protegidos, Calle Batallón Colorados, Edificio El Condor, Piso 13, in La Paz.

people rage, and the presence of the *gringo* is often associated only with the hated Drug Enforcement Agency, and therefore deeply resented. Tourists should seek advice from tour operators (*see* below), the federal government or their embassy before venturing here.

The forests and savannahs of the 334,200 hectare **Reserva Biosférica del Beni** and the 1.2 million hectare **Reserva Forestal Chimane** Indian reserve which adjoins it are currently accessible only to those willing to rough it. The only accommodation is at the **Biological Research Station**, in semi-deciduous forest on the edge of the Beni savannah in real pioneer country. It is possible to stay here, either as a volunteer or a visitor. Facilities are basic and you must bring your own food. Expeditions further into the adjoining parks may get easier with the establishment of the Indian conservational tourism company in Trinidad (*see* above).

Paraiso Travel in Trinidad can arrange trips to Ríos Blanco y Negro (*see* p.160). **Rosario Tours** and **T and T Sudamérica** (*see* Santa Cruz, above) can arrange bespoke trips to Perseverancia and environs in the Ríos Blanco y Negro, and to the Beni savannahs. They require at least two weeks' notice and charge about $100 a day per person, all-inclusive (except transport from Santa Cruz to Trinidad.) **Hombre y Naturaleza** are also based in Santa Cruz (*see* p.157). They charge around $100 per person per day to stay at Lake Taborga plus transport—either by light aircraft or overland. **Explore Bolivia** (*see* p.152) offer a seven-day boat and camping tour in Isiboro Sécure, using indigenous guides, for around $130 per person per day. To book stays at the **Beni Biological Research Station**, contact Carolina Zurmarán, Outreach Programme, Beni Biological Station, Bolivian Academy of Natural Sciences, P.O Box 5829, La Paz, or enquire at the Trinidad tourist office. Enquiries about visiting the park with indigenous people should also be made here.

Amboró National Park

....then the sun came up. The small and large animals were happy; and arose from the banks of the river, in the ravines, and on the tops of mountains, and all turned their eyes to where the sun was rising.

The First Dawn, *Popul Vuh* (the sacred book of the Quiché Maya)

Amboró's misty and crumpled foothills, monolithic crags of plunging sandstone and rainforests of giant cecropia and cedar are renowned the world over as a wildlife enthusiast's paradise. Giant eagles still hover high above the canopy in remote regions of the park, searching for monkeys and sloth to pluck from the trees. South America's only bear hunts alongside puma and jaguar in Amboró's cloud forests and tapir and giant otter still swim in her meandering rivers. Dawn is a magical time along Amboró's steep-banked rocky creeks and warm, silty rivers: forest birds wake, unfurl their wings and begin to sing in chorus, led by the loud jeer of scarlet macaws, and the cackle of green parrots. Agouti and paca forage on the shores of Amboró's soft sandy beaches, ever watchful for puma and jaguar, and the rich golden light of the morning sun gradually pierces the crown of the giant cedar trees, warming the browns of the rivers, the reds of heliconia flowers and the myriad shades of rainforest green. Bird lovers are particularly drawn here; the most ambitious hope to catch a glimpse of the unicorn bird, an elusive currasow the size of a pheasant, coloured irridescent blue, with a horn on its forehead. Others are searching for the red-fronted macaw or the Bolivian recurvebill. The latter was only recently rediscovered, in the upper Saguayo valley, the habitat of the unicorn bird, and is found only there. The park is an island in a sea of agriculture, a last vestige of the huge forests that once mantled the lower slopes of the country's northeastern Andes and marched northwards to the Orinoco. The suburbs of Santa Cruz are less than 90 miles southeast, along one of Bolivia's busiest roads. This makes access, at least to the park's boundaries, straightforward, and thus it may come as a surprise to learn that conservational tourism is in its infancy here. There are no jungle lodges, only rustic huts, and visits are usually day trips. Nonetheless, for wildlife enthusiasts and birders visiting the northeastern lowlands, a trip to Amboró is a must. And those willing to rough it will find Amboró one of the cheapest and most convenient places to visit in the entire Amazon.

History and Conservation

Amboró was declared a park in 1973 to protect a wilderness area that lies at the extremities of three distinct ecosystems—Andean cloud forest, lowland Amazon forest and chaco thorn scrub. Following scientific investigation in the park by the great Bolivian biologist Noel Kempff, and the discovery of unique birdlife by British ornithologist Robin Clarke, the park was expanded to cover 630,000 hectares in 1985. Since then, it has been threatened on all sides by agriculture and settlement; the greatest single threat to the survival not only of the Amazon but of the livelihood of the *campesino* (peasant farmer). As big business buys up available alluvial land, *campesinos* are forced to settle in wilderness areas. Forest is chopped down and turned to pasture. But, as the *campesinos* have no written entitlement to this newly settled land, once it has been adapted for pasture it is bought from the state by big business. The *campesinos* are once again displaced; they move on to fresh wilderness, and the cycle continues.

In Amboró's case, many coca-growing *campesinos*, displaced from the Chaparé region of Bolivia by the United States Drug Enforcement Agency in the early 1990s, settled in lowland areas of the park, practising slash-and-burn agriculture that ate into Amboró's rainforests. Attempts to put a stop to the destruction led to heated protests, and eventually the government reneged and gave the *campesinos* nearly 200,000 hectares of land, designating it as the *Area Natural de Manejo Integrado*. Amboró's remaining 44,200 hectares are theoretically inviolable, but by 1999 *campesino* land was almost completely denuded of forest and fields were pressing right up against the park's borders. With few park guards and underfunded conservation programmes, Amboró is under constant threat. Organizations like FAN and Hombre y Naturaleza are struggling to implement a conservational tourism programme that will offer *campesinos* an alternative source of income, but these projects are still in their infancy.

Visiting Amboró National Park

There are two principal access points to the park: **Samaipata** to the south, with trails leading into the cloud forests, and **Buena Vista** to the north, close to the lowland forest. Many **buses** for Sucre and Cochabamba, leaving from the main bus station in Santa Cruz, stop at Samaipata. Micros leave from Calle Riva, a block north of the bus station. To **visit the park independently** from Samaipata, visit the tourist office in the village (© (0944) 6129). They can contact the park guards, who will let you camp at their hut, and help you find a guide.

Samaipata, which, at over 1,660m, is far cooler than Santa Cruz, is a quiet little village with an interesting set of pre-Inca ruins, **El Fuerte**, on a hilltop 10km away (taxis can be hired in the village). It isn't really a fort at all, but an enigmatic ceremonial centre, with a complex of channels, sculpted seats and carvings cut out of a single giant slab. There's little for outsiders besides the quiet—just a small archaeological museum, and a tiny Japanese garden on the hill.

Buena Vista is another quiet little village with life focused on a plaza, overlooked by a beautiful 18th-century Jesuit church designed by Martin Schmidt. The Chiragiuano Indians who once worshipped here are, alas, long gone. **Independent guides** can be hired here from the BID office on the dirt street south of the main plaza for about $15 a day; no English is spoken and most are entirely ignorant about the flora and fauna. Taxis will take you to the park boundary on the southern bank of the Río Surutú. Wade across and you are in the Area Natural de Manejo Integrado. A two- to three-hour walk through little villages, past football pitches and cashew and banana plantations, brings you to the Río Saguayo, a quietly flowing river shrouded by rainforest giants. The first hut is on the far bank, and you can camp here.

In **Samaipata**, there are a few basic hostels, the best of which is the comfortable, self-contained **Cabañas Helga** (*moderate–inexpensive*), near the Landhaus restaurant. The Dutch-owned **La Vispera** (*inexpensive*), about a kilometre from the plaza and looking out across the valley, and the more upmarket **Achiba Sierra Resort** (*moderate*), Km 113, carr 4 a Cochabamba, ✆/@ (03) 862101 (or book in Santa Cruz, Calle Igmiri 506, Barrio Urbari, ✆ (03) 522288, @ (03) 522255, Casilla 1020) with a pool. Both rent horses and camping equipment and arrange one- to seven-day excursions into the park and in the hills near Samaipata. About $70–$100 a day all-inclusive.

In **Buena Vista**, the village itself has only basic accommodation options, the best of which are the **Nadia**, just off the plaza, and the **Sumuque**, Km 100 Cochabamba Road, ✆/@ 09322080. The **Amboró Eco-resort**, Km 103, Nueva Carreterra-Cochabamba, Buena Vista, ✆ 422372, ✆/@ 09322048, *bloch@bibosi.scz.entelnet.bo*, 2km out of town, offers a comfortable, if fortified, alternative with a pool, bar, good restaurant, jacuzzis, comfortable air-conditioned rooms or *cabañas*, a butterfly farm and a small area of forest. Dirk Haussman takes trips into the park during the dry season (May–Nov) and rents horses and mountain bikes. A more intimate and cheaper option is the **Flora y Fauna Lodge**, ✆ 01 943706, 7km from Buena Vista on the dirt road to the Río Surutú (*moderate*), owned by English ornithologist Robin Clarke who offers excellent natural history and birding trips into Amboró conducted by him or Guy Cox, another bird-loving Englishman, who can also be reached through the Amboró Eco-Resort or through helpful Rosario, at Rosario Tours in Santa Cruz (*see* p.157).

For **tour operators**, *see* La Paz, p.151 and Santa Cruz, p.157, and Trinidad, p.159.

Noel Kempff Mercado National Park

> *And like a downward smoke, the slender stream*
> *Along the cliff to fall and pause and fall did seem.*
>
> Tennyson, *The Lotus Eaters*

Huanchuca, a 2,000 square mile table-top mountain rises sheer from the surrounding plain, countless waterfalls cascading from its edges into virgin forests and tropical savannahs that stretch to a limitless horizon. Black-water rivers covered with giant waterlilies spill into oxbow lakes whose mirrored surfaces are broken only by river dolphins, caiman and giant otters coming up for air. This is the Taj Mahal of the Amazon's readily accessible national parks. If you are planning to visit only one place in the Bolivian Amazon, let it be here; few regions in the world can compete with it for sheer diversity of awe-inspiring natural wonders, habitats and biological variety.

Geography and Conservation

Noel Kempff and the forests that surround it are a fortress of green against the genetically modified soya and ranch lands that are rapidly spreading east from Santa Cruz and west from Rondônia. It lies in the northeastern extreme of Bolivia, 450km from Santa Cruz, on the border of Rondônia state in Brazil. The park is centred on Huanchaca, a 1,800ft-high sandstone ridge baked red by the sun, ravaged by powerful electrical storms and covered in wild grasslands and forest islands that are home to unique plants and animals. Originally only Huanchaca was protected, but the park was expanded in posthumous honour of the great Bolivian biologist Noel Kempff. The boundaries now enclose more than three million acres of the savannah and rainforest that surround the mountain's base, and the two major rivers that flow through them: the Iténez (Guaporé) on the Brazilian border, and the Paraguá at the park's western extremity. Both are black-water tributaries of the Río Mamoré, a tributary of the Madeira, which finally flows into the Amazon proper near Parintins in Brazil.

Noel Kempff himself was the first great Bolivian to explore and champion the meseta. The second was Hermes Justiniano, a pilot and photographer who fell in love with the forests, waterfalls and rivers of Noel Kempff Mercado, and has dedicated his life to protecting them. His efficient and dedicated NGO, Fundación Amigos de la Naturaleza (**FAN**), is now the country's leading conservation organization and is responsible for protecting 6.5 million acres in two Bolivian National Parks and a biological reserve. Through their employee Tim Miller, an American biologist and expert birder, FAN offer a range of conservational tourism, natural history and birding trips from their two comfortable jungle lodges, Los Fierros, in the heart of the lowland forest and savannah, and Flor de Oro on the banks of the Río Iténez. Generous support from the Nature Conservancy's Parks in Peril programme and the Swiss government has helped to make Noel Kempff the best-protected park in Bolivia. All money generated goes towards salaries for park guards, cooks and lodge staff, who are mostly locals, and environmental education for Bolivian and Brazilian communities who once raided the park for timber.

Wildlife in Noel Kempff Mercado

The park encompasses five important ecosystems: humid tropical evergreen forests, gallery forests, subtropical thorn scrub similar to the Paraguayan chaco, savannah wetlands similar to the Pantanal, and the seasonal forests and dry savannahs typical of Central Brazil. Here however, apart from some light selective logging around the Río Paraguá, the ecosystems remain primordial and untouched. Wildlife is abundant and economically important tree species such as mahogany, cedar, roble oak and Brazil nuts are still common.

Birds: A quarter of all existing bird species in the neotropics can be found in Noel Kempff; apart from harpy eagles, hyacinth macaws and a wealth of guans and currasows, there are more than 20 species of parrot, multicoloured tanagers, and at least seven cracids, a neotropical family with many endangered species. Rarities you stand a fair chance of seeing include the following: zigzag heron, white-browed hawk, bare-faced currasow, starred wood quail, red-throated piping guan, ocellated crake, hyacinth macaw, crimson-bellied parakeet, long-tailed potoo, horned sungem, rufous-necked puffbird, black-girdled barbet, rusty-necked piculet, flame-crested and snow-capped manakin, pale-bellied tyrant-manakin, snethlage's and zimmer's tody-tyrant, rufous-sided pygmy-tyrant, white-banded and white-rumped tanagers, coal-crested finch, black-and-tawny and grey-and-chestnut seed-eater.

Other vertebrates: Recent biological inventories suggest that Noel Kempff is one of the few places on the continent where larger vertebrates are increasing in number: Brazilian tapir, jaguar, giant armadillo and giant anteater are as common here as they are anywhere. The endangered maned wolf hunts the park's savannahs, and two threatened species of river turtle, the tracaya and tataruga, nest here. Giant otter, river otter, river dolphin, black and spectacled caiman are frequently seen on the rivers and black howler monkey, spider monkey and several species of tamarin and marmoset are common in the forests around the base of the mountain.

Tour Operators and Lodges in Noel Kempff Mercado

The easiest and most convenient way to get to Noel Kempff is through **FAN**, Calle Isoso 384, Santa Cruz, ✆ 337475, 🖷 329692, *ecoturismo@fan.scbbs-bo.com, www.scbbs-bo.com /fan/*, Casilla 2241. Expect to pay around $120 per person per day, plus the cost of getting to the park (around $150 each if the plane is full). Any agencies in Santa Cruz or La Paz offering trips to Noel Kempff will be operating through FAN, so it's best to go directly to them (for La Paz and Santa Cruz tour operators, *see* pp.151 and 157).

FAN have two lodges in the park, **Flor de Oro**, a comfortable converted ranch on the bank of the Río Iténez close to the Brazilian border (it is possible to cross here if you get your Bolivian exit stamp in Santa Cruz), and the more rustic and remoter **Los Fierros**, a hundred miles or so south, in selectively logged forest on the edge of an extensive area of savannah. Both lodges have *cabañas* with private bathrooms and separate dining areas. Flor de Oro has solar-powered electricity. Food is plentiful, tasty staple fare. If you are a vegetarian give Tim Miller at least a week's notice, and check that you have been catered for before you leave. FAN also maintain a number of overnight camps for longer treks and expeditions. **Campamento Ahfeld** is near the waterfall of the same name on the Río Paucerna and marks an overnight stop on the journey to Arco Iris Waterfalls (*see* below). Both these camps are reached by boat from Flor de Oro. There is also a rustic camp in primary forest at the edge of the savannah near Los Fierros, on the track to the El Encanto waterfall.

A Typical Dry Season Itinerary

Day one: A two-hour flight in a light plane will take you over lowland forest and across savannah to the edge of the Huanchaca escarpment, before flying low over Arco Iris and Ahfeld waterfalls to land at Flor do Oro camp. After lunch, explore the gallery forests that line the Río Iténez and the savannah near Flor de Oro, where you'll see birds like hoatzin, toco toucan, scarlet macaw and animals like silvery marmoset and coatimundi.

Day two: A canoe trip to oxbow lakes near Flor de Oro, where pink river dolphin and spectacled caiman are frequently seen, followed by a backwater trip through small creeks and lakes frequented by water birds like rufescent tiger heron, sunbittern and the southern screamer. You may see the elusive giant otter. Travel by boat to Las Torres, a rocky outcrop that affords breathtaking views across gallery forests to the Huanchaca plateau, where jaguars have been spotted.

Day three: The third day is spent on foot, exploring the periodically inundated savannahs and tall tropical rainforests that lie between Flor de Oro and Lago Caiman. More than 300 bird species have been recorded; bird lovers have the opportunity to see rare species like horned sungem, black and tawny seedeater, red-necked araçari and the endangered snow-capped manakin. You also have a high chance of seeing black spider monkey, Brazilian tapir and white-lipped and collared peccaries. A stiff climb up the meseta passes through four different types of forest and culminates in the Mirador de los Monos—Monkey Look-Out Point.

Day four: Another spectacular flight across the meseta takes you to Los Fierros lodge, one of South America's hotter wildlife spots. Jaguar, puma and ocelot hunt here at night and 350 species of birds have been recorded in the environs, including scarlet macaws, channel-billed toucans, chestnut-eared araçari, long-tailed potoos, and blue-throated piping guans.

Day five: A walk through the savannahs, home to the rare, long-legged maned wolf, takes you to the top of the meseta for a breathtaking view of the rainforest; steam rises and forms drifting clouds which periodically burst, a heavy downpour falling silver in the slanting light. The twilight journey back offers the best chance yet to see a large cat.

Day six: The final full day at Los Fierros is spent in areas of the savannah and tropical forests rich in black spider monkeys and raptors, on the way to one of the park's most enchanting waterfalls, El Encanto. Harpy eagles have been seen in these forests, and both species of peccary are common. The falls themselves plummet 80 metres into a deep blue pool, from an amphitheatre of terracotta sandstone.

Day seven: Walk the trails around Los Fierros, before flying back to Santa Cruz.

Wet-season extras: Though the wet season offers the chance to explore flooded forests and inundated savannah near the two lodges, the best reason to visit at this time of year is to see the magical waterfalls of the Río Paucerna and their surrounding habitats. This is an adventure in remote country—the boat and walk are a long haul, and the Ahfeld camp where you will overnight is rustic. As this area is very rarely visited, you stand a good chance of seeing rare birds and animals, including zigzag heron, tapir, jaguar and giant otters. After a day's boat ride, you'll arrive at Ahfeld waterfall, a horseshoe of gently cascading steps of soft white and lush green; there are few places in the world more idyllic for a swim. The next morning is spent walking to **Arco Iris Waterfalls**, the most breathtaking in the park,with water plunging in a veil of mist and forming a perfect rainbow against a 60m high monolith of red sandstone.

Specialist birding tours and bespoke options: A two-day extension to the Jesuit Mission settlements (*see* p.158) and bespoke tours can be arranged with FAN. FAN also have excellent birding guides and good facilities, including scopes, powerful halogen lamps and professional recording equipment. Flor de Oro also has a small library of field guides.

Visiting Noel Kempff Independently

It is possible to get to Noel Kempff independently and set-up your own camp at Flor de Oro, Los Fierros or the more rustic sites near El Encanto and Ahfeld. These four camps are excellent bases for extensive hikes or mountain biking (FAN have some decrepit bikes at their lodges). No cooking is allowed near the waterfalls themselves or on the top of Huanchaca and FAN will require you to have a local guide from the community of Florida with you at all times during your stay in the park. Visit the office before you leave Santa Cruz to register your visit and make all arrangements. You won't be allowed into the park unless you do this. The easiest way to get there is to rent your own four-wheel drive (see 'car rental', Santa Cruz, p.154). FAN will then provide you with free directions and a map. Public transport is limited: during the dry season (May–Nov), a bus travels from Santa Cruz to Piso Firme near the border with Brazil. Although it is possible to stay here, you should get off the bus at the turning to Florida, a 35km hike off the 'main' road. After 34km, turn right at the fork in the road and walk the last kilometre to the village, where you will find basic food and accommodation, and a park guard station where you must register. Malaria is rife, so take prophylactics. Los Fierros is a half-hour boat ride and a 40km walk from here. The wet season route is even more difficult: take a bus from Santa Cruz to San Ignacio de Velasco. Get off at Santa Rosa de la Roca (9 hours from Santa Cruz), where there is basic accommodation. From here, walk to the El Carretero trucker's restaurant, about five minutes outside Santa Rosa towards San Ignacio, and hitch a ride north into the park; it is a logging route and the main road into Brazil. Aim for the community of La Mechita, where there is basic food and lodging, and then for the La Florida turn-off the next day.

The Bolivian Pantanal and Gran Chaco

Bolivia's share of the world's largest wetland is peppered with the thorn and scrub forests associated with the Paraguayan Chaco, and small areas of tropical forest, making it higher in biological diversity than its Brazilian counterpart, as well as wilder and less explored. The country's largest protected area is the vast Gran Chaco National Park, contiguous with the Ríos Blanco y Negro wildlife reserve and the territories of the Guarayos and Sirionós tribes.

A number of La Paz and Santa Cruz tour operators offer trips here (*see* pp.151 and 157), the best of which are managed by the Spanish/Bolivian NGO **Hombre y Naturaleza**, who maintain two lodges in the area. The most luxurious is the **El Tumbador Biological Station**, on the shores of the Cáceres lagoon near Puerto Suárez in the heart of the Pantanal. This is tropical wetland and the forest of the Amazon is broken by lakes and savannah here, as in the Pantanal a short distance away in Brazil. The open space makes spotting wildlife easy; jaguar, Brazilian tapir, two species of peccary, giant armadillo, anteater, greater rhea and road-runner are regularly seen. The stay here includes trips on the Río Paraguay (around $120 per person per day plus transport to Puerto Suárez). The **San Matías Angel Sandoval Ecological Centre** is more rustic, and and is devoted to ethno-tourism as much as conservational tourism. Facilities are found in the small village of the same name, and profits go towards educating the local people about conservation and sustainable tourism. Tiny San Matías is lost in the midst of four distinct Pantanal ecosytems: semi-deciduous lowland cerrado woodland, sub-humid high woodland, seasonally flooded forest, and seasonally flooded pampas wetland. The wildlife found here is typical of the Pantanal. Disruption has been fairly minimal: even jaguar are still quite common. Around $100 per person per day.

Puerto Quijarro and the Brazilian Border

Bolivia's border with Brazil is marked by the disreputable contraband town of Puerto Quijarro, squatting at the end of the Santa Cruz railway line. Though tourism has barely begun here, it is possible to organize rough and ready trips into the Pantanal. Make inquiries with Blanca de España at the **Hotel Santa Cruz**, Av. Brasil, Puerto Quijarro, ✆ (0978) 2113/2044. Most of the hotel's trips are operated by Bismarck Zaccharías, who lives next door, and who has a boat on the Río Paraguay. Sheep and goats come too, and are slaughtered for food along the way. You will see no other tourists—it is wild down here. Expect to pay $40–100 per person per day, for a week to 10-day trip, depending on the size of your group. Other hotels include the excellent three-star **Oasis**, Calle Argentina 4, ✆ 2159. Cheaper places can be shifty; try the **Hotel de La Frontera**, Rómulo Gómez; ✆ 2010.

Puerto Quijarro   ***Getting There and Getting to Brazil***

LAB (no office), and Aerosur (Av. Bolívar 69, Plaza Principal; ✆ (0976) 2155), **fly** between Santa Cruz and Puerto Suárez (10km from Quijarro) several times a week.

Taxis meet the sluggish **trains** that take nearly 20hrs to crawl across the plains from Santa Cruz (every day except Sunday). The border is two kilometres away. **Buses** will take you from here to Corumbá (Brazilian immigration office in Corumbá, Praça da República, between Rua Antônio João and Antônio Maria Coelho).

Note: Be sure to have a Yellow Fever vaccination certificate showing that you had an injection at least ten days previously, or you won't be allowed into Brazil.

Northwest Bolivia

A road journey from La Paz to the forests of northern Bolivia is one of the continent's most exhilarating and terrifying experiences. Buses and lorries race each other at a hair-raising pace down a narrow dirt road, tearing along past snowy crags and cliffs of sheer brown granite towards the cloud forests of the Yungas 80km away and more than 3km below. As the temperature lifts, the stunted cacti of the paramo become lush shrubs and the air thickens as the road twists its way around jungle-covered spurs that drop precipitously into forested valleys littered with the carcasses of tiny cars. Life, it seems, is cheap in this wild and lawless part of the country. The foothills of the Andes are peppered with little gold-mining towns, like Guanay, where the intrepid and desperate blast the banks of the Río Beni away with powerful hoses in a frantic search for gold, turning the river mud-red and polluting it with mercury.

There are a few tourist towns: laid-back and gentle **Coroico**, nestled in the green and misty lower slopes of the Andes, is an ideal place for a break to rest the nerves after the journey down. Beyond it lie the ripples of the lower Andes, shrouded in forest, that flatten into a lowland sea of rainforest-green extending into Peru. This tract of wilderness, full of rare wood and Brazil nut trees, has been demarcated as one of South America's largest protected areas, the Manuripi Heath Reserve. Together with the contiguous Tambopata-Candamo Reserve in Peru, this has perhaps the greatest biodiversity on earth. Easier to reach is the Alto Madidi Park, which stretches west from the river port at Rurrenabaque, whose once friendly community has been alienated in recent years by the incessant bartering of Western backpackers.

The Yungas

The transition zone between the Andes and the lowland rainforests is known as the Yungas—a land of forested mountain ridges, coca plantations, orchards and twisting Inca trails. Its green slopes are washed by plentiful rain and drained by fast-running brooks and winding rivers that eventually find their way to the Amazon. Though the Yungas begin near Lake Titicaca, in picturesque villages like Sorata, we concentrate here only on those towns or regions lying on significant Amazon tributaries.

The orange groves and corrugated roofs of **Coroico** are perched on an Andean spur at a balmy 1,760m on the road between La Paz and the Amazon lowlands, making the little town the ideal spot for a rest. It's famous for walks in the surrounding hills and for beautiful views. **Mapiri and Guanay**, two gold-mining towns, are the Wild West of Bolivia—full of pistols, ne'er-do-wells, and spit and sawdust bars overflowing with drunk miners and whores. The only reason to come here is to end a trek between the mountains and the Yungas, in which case, it is probably wise to arrive the day you wish to leave. Both are connected to La Paz by road. Guanay is connected to Rurrenabaque by boat—contact the Agencia Fluvial when you arrive. Expect to pay around $20 for the 6–8-hour trip.

Inca Trails in the Yungas

The altiplano and the lush cloud forests of the Yungas are criss-crossed with Inca and pre-Inca trails that offer wonderful hiking opportunites of varying length and difficulty. The views along the way are invariably wonderful, whichever route you choose, and there are numerous waterfalls and rivers to cool off in as the cold of the mountains turns to the warm humidity of the high Amazon. The chances of seeing wildlife and rare birds is higher here than on Peru's famous Inca trail simply because there are far fewer walkers. All of the following walks are offered by **Explore Bolivia** (*see* p.152), who can supply precise itineraries. Mules and porters are available, the camp food is as good as it gets in Bolivia and vegetarians can be catered for. Expect to pay around $100 per person per day. The following is but a taster.

The **La Cumbre trail** is a two- to four-day trek from the altiplano through indigenous villages, paramo and cloud forests to Coroico, and the most popular walk in Bolivia. The **Takesi trek** also runs from the mountains to the Yungas, and follows a fine stretch of Inca road for over 40km. It takes three days. The **El Chorro trail** is the best preserved Inca road in the Andes; the six- to seven-day **Camino de Oro** is tougher going, cutting through some little disturbed valleys before emerging into the scarred gold-mining settlements near Guanay. The slightly longer **Mapiri trail** is tougher still, and is available from Explore Bolivia as a bespoke option only (form your own group and give them plenty of notice). There is no better walk for seeing cloud forest wildlife—the trail passes through some little-walked areas requiring a machete.

Explore Bolivia offer two **rafting** trips in the Yungas—on the Río Coroico and the Río Tuichi. The former is a light three-day trip, the latter one of the most exciting adventures on offer in the Bolivian Amazon: a 14-day expedition which descends from the altiplano, through cloud forest and gold-mining areas, and culminates in the Amazon lowlands at Rurrenabaque. Half of the trip is spent rafting; the rest is hiking and rainforest walking.

Coroico (℡ 0811–)   **Where to Stay and Eat**

Coroico is tiny, and one of the delights of being here is whiling away the hours admiring the views and popping in and out of the little cafés and restaurants.

El Viejo Molino, ℡/℻ 6004. The best place in Coroico, if not Bolivia: very relaxing; wonderful views, great food, a sauna, jacuzzis, swimming pool and gym. A kilometre from the centre on the Caranavi road (*expensive*).

Hotel Prefectural, off Av. Thomas Manning on a road leading to the river; ℡ 212604. These are the rooms with the view—though little else, not even locks on the door or private baths. Bring a padlock or a door wedge (*inexpensive*).

Hostal Sol y Luna, 15 mins from the centre on a south fork off the road to Cerro Uchumachi. The best cheap option in Coroico—home grown veggie food and coffee, a swimming pool, free massage and beautiful views (*cheap*).

Hotel Esmeralda, Julio Zuazo Cuenca, 400m from the centre. Very good, cheap vegetarian restaurant, and a patio with superb views over the valley. Rooms come with or without bath, and there's a pool (*cheap*).

Rurrenabaque

Only ten years ago, Rurrenabaque was a sleepy little river town full of hummingbirds and friendly locals. Then a road was built to La Paz, and the backpackers started to come, demanding ever-lower prices and creating tourist ghettoes. Now the place is full of cheap hotels, pulsating, ramshackle clubs and travel agencies offering jungle trips at prices at which they barely break even. On these rock-bottom trips rapport between tourists and locals can be far from good, and ecological concerns have gone out of the window—the anaconda you are 'guaranteed' a sighting of has probably been kept in a box hidden behind a bush.

Nonetheless Rurrenabaque is still a tiny place (there are only two streets), and has some delights in its more distant environs. **Chalalan Rainforest Lodge** is one of the best anywhere in the Amazon, and Bolivia's newest national park, Alto Madidi, offers a catalogue of potential wonders that could put it in the Manu or Tambopata league when it is finally explored. The best of Rurrenabaque's travel agencies may be persuaded to take you there, at a price, and with advance notice. You can change US$ cash only in shops or hotels throughout the town. Contact Conservation International, Rurrenabaque, ☎ (0892) 2419, about conservation issues.

Rurrenabaque (no tels)   ***Getting There***

TAM and LAB **fly** between Rurrenabaque (Reyes) and La Paz several times a week and Rurrenabaque (Reyes) and Santa Cruz once a week. Both have offices in Rurrenabaque. The TAM office in La Paz is on Plaza del Estudiante 1931, ☎ (02) 366654, ✉ (02) 362697. For LAB *see* La Paz, p.148. **Buses** for La Paz leave daily (via Yolosa for Coroico), a 20-hr journey down one of the world's most terrifying and spectacular roads; sit on the left on the way down. Buses for Trinidad run daily (via San Borja and San Ignacio de Moxos): an equally gruelling, bumpy 10hrs, but with no precipitous drops. There is a twice-weekly bus for Guayaramerín (Brazil), 15 sweaty hours. There are no regular **boats** up- or downstream from Rurrenabaque. It may be possible to hitch a ride with a cargo ferry to Riberalta. Ask at the docks or at the Hotel Tuichi.

Rurrenabaque (no tels)   ***Where to Stay and Eating Out***

The choices are few; both hotels and snack-bars are cheap and backpacker-orientated.

Taquara, on the plaza, has musty fan-cooled rooms with private baths, yet is far and away the best in town. The **Santa Ana**, Calle Vaca 10, near the main plaza, is the next best hotel, with fan-cooled rooms with private baths. The best of the absolute cheapies is the **Hotel Tuichi**, Calle Abaroa, with thatched-roof rooms with or without a bath. The **Hotel Rurrenabaque**, Calle Abaroa, is much the same, but has a cheap dormitory.

The **La Chocita restaurant** on the waterfront serves excellent river fish. The restaurant **El Tambo** dishes up backpacker fare like pancakes with syrup, yogurt and fruit.

Tour Operators in Rurrenabaque

There have been repeated complaints about a Rurrenabaque guide, Israel 'Negro' Janco, who was accused of drugging and raping a tourist in 1997 and sexually assaulting another the following year. This is not the same Negro who works for Agencia Fluvial. After a brief period away from Rurrenabaque, he is said to be working in the town once again. For further details contact South American Explorers (*see* p.25 for website). In view of these complaints, we can only recommend one tour company in Rurrenabaque, the **Agencia Fluvial**. Book through the Tuichi Hotel, ☎ (083) 2999—the town's telephone exchange; at present there are no private phones in Rurrenabaque. Owned by veteran tour operator Tico Tudela, they offer professionally run, good-value tours with safe and reliable guides.

A Typical Rurrenabaque Rainforest/Savannah Itinerary

The Rurrenabaque environs are best visited in the dry season between May and November. At other times the savannahs are flooded and it is difficult to see wildlife.

Day one: Travel up the Río Beni in a motorized canoe to the Río Tuichi, a smaller tributary with creeks leading into the forest. Here camp is made under a plastic sheet on a river beach. Take some tape to seal up the holes in the tour company's mosquito net.

Day two: Canoe in a dug-out along a creek off the Río Tuichi, looking for turtles and primates. Camp is made at lunchtime; a swim with river dolphins and a short trail walk follows. Supper and searching for caiman with a torch conclude the day.

Day three: A tiring 5–6-hour walk through the forest, cutting through dense undergrowth with a machete, fording streams and looking for animals and traditional medicines. Supper is followed by a night beach walk in search of jaguar.

Day four: Back in the canoe along the Tuichi and Beni for 3 or 4 hours. The afternoon is spent piranha-fishing in an oxbow lake, or walking through some tropical savannah in search of anacondas. Supper is followed by another night walk or caiman spotting.

Day five: A dawn walk and return to Rurrenabaque.

Two further days in the savannah can be added to this trip, affording a far greater chance of seeing Amazon wildlife, including greater rhea, jabiru stork and anaconda.

Captured Animals

Some of the tour companies have been encouraged by backpackers to capture wild animals for photographs—particularly sloths, crocodiles and anacondas. This has not only led to unnecessary trauma for the animals, but also to the practice of keeping animals in boxes in the wild to 'guarantee' a sighting and spread the reputation of the company. A number of anacondas have died this way. Please try to discourage the practice.

Alto Madidi National Park and Chalalan Rainforest Lodge

Though it is threatened by damming and polluted by the gold mining run-off from the upper Río Tuichi, the Alto Madidi National Park is still one of the potentially highest reservoirs of tropical biodiversity on Earth, spanning numerous mountain and lowland ecosystems from high paramo to varzea and gallery forest. All the important large Amazonian mammals live here, together with a wealth of birds (Conservation International claim that there are 1,000 different species), reptiles and amphibians, many still uncatalogued, some perhaps new to science.

Conservation International are so concerned about the welfare of the park that they are concentrating much of their Latin American campaign efforts here, and are keen to develop conservational tourism in the area. They have already made inroads with **Chalalan**, one of the Amazon Basin's most beautifully crafted and idyllically situated lodges, in partnership with the local indigenous community. Access to the remainder of the park is very difficult.

Chalalan Rainforest Lodge: (book through America Tours in La Paz (*see* p.151), or Conservation International in Rurrenabaque, *see* p.170). A stay at Chalalan is one of the most memorable rainforest experiences available in the Bolivian Amazon. Beautifully crafted and carved cabins built in the traditional Tacana Indian style watch over an oxbow lake in primary forest off a tributary of the Río Tuichi. Rooms are mosquito-proofed and food is prepared from rainforest produce. Twenty-five kilometres of signposted trails surround the camp (these can be walked with or without a guide) and a series of creeks and rivulets make perfect dug-out canoeing, by day or night. The lodge was built by, and is run in partnership with, Quechua-

Tacana Indians from the village of San José de Uchipiamonas. Other activities focus on their culture and include traditional dance and learning about rainforest medicine and agriculture. The lodge is five hours by boat from Rurrenabaque. Booking through America Tours guarantees that you won't have to organize transport when you get to Rurrenabaque. Expect to pay around $60 per night for the lodge and $100 for transport from Rurrenabaque.

Other tours: Explore Bolivia offer a number of tours in Madidi, including a 14-day rafting expedition down the Río Tuichi (*see* p.170). Agencia Fluvial in Rurrenabaque may be willing to organize a bespoke tour into the remotest regions of Madidi, given a few days notice. Expect to pay around $120 per person per day.

Onward towards Brazil

The only reason to come to **Guayaramerín** on Bolivia's northern border is to cross into Brazil. If you get stuck here in the dry, take a water taxi to the Isla Suárez, which has some broad sandy beaches, forest walks and clear-water streams. The island is named after the ruthless rubber baron Nicolás Suárez, who kept Indians as whores for his guests in Cachuela Esperanza, 45km north of the city, on the Río Beni. The site can be visited through a local tour operator—the river is beautiful here, tumbling over small rapids, and there's a small, restored church near its banks. **Amazonas Tours**, Av. Federico Román 680, ✆ (0855) 3515, ✉ 4000, and **Cris Tours**, ✆ (0855) 2312, or in Guajará Mirim, ✆ (069) 541 3473, both offer tours to the environs of both Guayaramerín, and its Brazilian counterpart, Guajará Mirim. Trips include day tours of Cachuela Esperanza, visits to river beaches and light rainforest walks.

If you want to change money in town, the waterfront touts give good rates for cash dollars and Brazilian reals. The Hotel San Carlos, Av. 6 de Agosto at Santa Cruz, ✆ (0855) 2419, ✉ 2150, will change American Express traveller's cheques. It is a delight after a long journey, with a pool, sauna and air-conditioned rooms. Breakfast is included in the price (*inexpensive*). There are a few other seedy budget options dotted around the plaza and near the airport, the best of which is the **Santa Ana**, Calle 16 de Julio.

Guayaramerín   ***Getting There and to Brazil***

LAB and Aerosur have regular **flights** between La Paz, Santa Cruz and Guayaramerín. Both have offices in the airport, which lies 500m southeast of the plaza. There are **buses** five times a week for La Paz, a long, long haul (35hrs) with a break in Rurrenabaque (15hrs); buses for Cobija (14hrs) depart three times a week and for Trinidad (26hrs) once a week. **Cargo boats** leave for Puerto Barador (Trinidad) nearly every day. The trip takes a week and costs around $50 with food.

Getting to Brazil: Motor taxis ply the Río Mamoré between Guayaramerín and Guajará Mirim constantly. The Brazilian Consulate (*open Mon–Fri 9–12*) is one block east of the plaza—visas are issued the same day; Bolivian exit stamps should be collected at the Immigration Office on the waterfront. The Brazilian Immigration office is on the waterfront in Guajará Mirim.

Note: Be sure to have a Yellow Fever vaccination certificate showing that you had an injection at least ten days previously, or you won't be allowed into Brazil.

The Pando Department and Manuripi Heath National Reserve

Bolivia's youngest and remotest department, tucked away between Peru and the Brazilian state of Acre, has little tourist infrastructure. Trips into the lowland rainforests and savannahs that dominate the region, and to the little protected Manuripi Heath National Reserve, are difficult to organize, but this may change. Conservation International have ambitious plans to create a giant international park linking Manuripi Heath and Alto Madidi in Bolivia with Bahuaja-Sonene and the Tambopata-Candamo Reserve Zone across the border in Peru. Independent travellers using the back door route to Brazil and Peru near Cobija can also make a difference by encouraging locals in Cobija to begin expeditions into the forest, thus increasing awareness of conservational tourism as a potential source of income. For the present this is just for pioneers—head for Cobija and ask around.

Cobija, a small, sweaty frontier town, seems to be fighting a losing battle with the forest. Its edges are slowly being reclaimed by creepers and rainforest weeds. The main source of income here is from the harvesting of brazil nuts, and Cobija sees few foreigners. There are a few touts who will **exchange cash** US$ or Brazilian reals for Bolivianos. The *casa de cambio* on 11 de Octubre at Cornejo charges commission on traveller's cheques. The **Immigration Office** on the main plaza opens sporadically; the Brazilian consulate (*open weekdays 9–12.30*) is on Calle Beni at Molina. The **Hotel Pando**, a block south of the Brazilian consulate, has fan-cooled rooms with a private bath (*inexpensive*).

Cobija   *Getting There and to Brazil and Peru*

Flights for Cochabamba, La Paz, Santa Cruz, Trinidad and Guayaramerín, depart five times a week with LAB or Aerosur. Daily **buses** to Riberalta (12hrs) connect with services to La Paz (30hrs); Rurrenabaque (12hrs) and Guayaramerín (3hrs).

To Brazil and Peru: Brasiléia lies just across the river Acre from Cobija. Get an exit stamp from Bolivian immigration in Cobija and then take a taxi from the central plaza across the bridge and to Brazilian Polícia Federal. The bus station (*rodoviária*) has onward connections to Rio Braco (Acre) and then to the rest of Brazil. Those wishing to get to Puerto Maldonado in Peru should take a bus to Assis Brazil. Further details can be found on p.130.

Note: be sure to have a Yellow Fever vaccination certificate showing that you had an injection at least ten days previously, or you won't be allowed into Brazil.

Ecuador

Within the borders of South America's smallest Latin republic lie sweeping beaches of golden sand, rainless deserts, towering snow-capped volcanoes, swathes of cloud and lowland rainforest. In the highlands, Indian markets aimed squarely at the tourist flourish alongside traditional indigenous culture. In the Amazon, tribal peoples still consult shamans, and swig manioc wine in forest filled with one of the greatest varieties of plants and animals on earth. Ecuador enjoys a reputation for being one of South America's safer tourist destinations, a reputation based more on the attributes of its neighbours than the country itself. Yet the country has, nonetheless, had an unhealthy quota of dictators and military coups and today, it teeters between stability and economic ruin. Popular discontent with government policy is high and culminated in yet another coup in early 2000. It may come as some relief to learn that this is of little concern for the traveller; crime against tourists is low and, though certain areas of the capital are best avoided, the greatest annoyance is likely to come from industrial action forcing buses to stop running or banks to close.

Tourist infrastructure in Ecuador is well developed, with a wealth of choice that surpasses many of the Amazon's larger countries. Indigenous tourism is an ever-growing industry, with a number of tribes inviting visitors to their tribal lands. Facilities for natural history enthusiasts are excellent: the country boasts two of the finest birding lodges in the world. Despite this, Ecuador has the most pressing and acute environmental problems on the continent: petrochemical and cattle-ranching industries are even given access to national parks by a government which makes all the right noises and yet continues to promote serious damage to forests it is determined to open up to industry and progress. This has been actively encouraged by the oil multinationals and cattle-ranchers have been directly or indirectly responsible for much of the destruction in Ecuador's Amazon.

Quito

The winding streets and steep hills of Ecuador's Andean capital cower beneath the threatening gaze of nearby volcanoes. As recently as 1999, the largest, Pichincha, hurled ash over the city, carpeting the cobbles, the concrete office blocks and the colonial tiled roofs with a warm grey volcanic snow. When there's no ash, Quito can be a pleasant place for a brief stopover before heading for the forest. On a cloudless day, the setting is magnificent. To the west, Pichincha

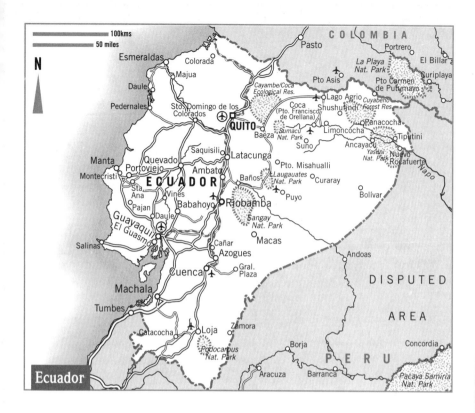

Ecuador

towers nearly five kilometres above sea level and Cotopaxi's perfect cone, hovering on the southern horizon, is nearly a kilometre higher. To the south, the steep, cobbled streets of the old colonial quarter, a UNESCO world heritage site, snake past heavy Spanish churches up a hill crowned with a statue of the virgin. Though belching buses and traffic hold-ups can be frustrating, facilities in Quito are generally good. Most of the city's decent hotels and restaurants (in any price range) are based here, together with tour companies, embassies and bars. The area is easy to negotiate on foot, but care should be taken when wandering around the old quarter, and in general at night. Quito is well-connected internationally and all of the major jungle centres can be reached by plane within a couple of hours, and by bus in about a day.

History: Quito and the Conquest of the Inca Empire

The Quito region has been populated for at least 10,000 years. Fishtail projectiles found near to the city suggest that the first occupants were a semi-sedentary people who hunted wild horses in the fertile grasslands of the Ecuadorean altiplano. The area was later dominated by the coastal Valdivia people, who traded with tribes throughout the country, including the Amazon, and subsequently by the Quitus who gave their name to the capital.

By 1470, the smaller kingdoms around Quito had been incorporated into the Inca empire by the Yupanqui and Tupac Yupanqui dynasties. Quito resisted conquest longer than the smaller settlements, but by 1492 it had been established as the headquarters of the northern empire,

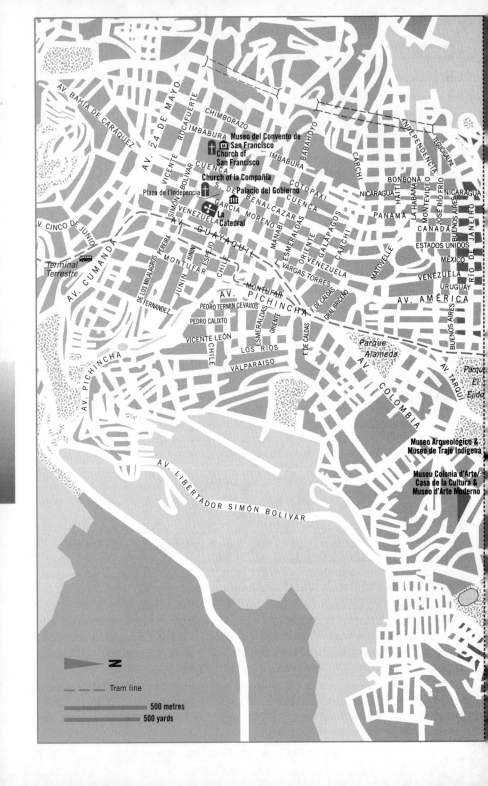

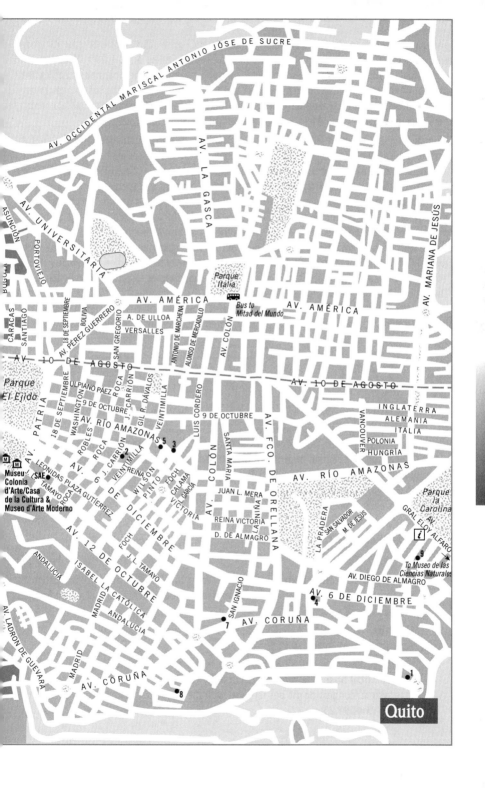

Quito

under Huayna Capac. As Quito's strength and influence grew, the empire became divided, with Huayna Capac's illegitimate son Atahualpa ruling Quito, and Huascar (supposedly Atahualpa's brother), ruling Cusco in Peru. This split was to be the downfall of the entire empire. By the time Francisco Pizarro arrived in 1533, the division had erupted into civil war, with Atahualpa gaining the upper hand. When Pizarro stumbled across him in Cajamarca, Atahulapa had just returned victorious from a campaign against his brother.

After tricking the Inca with false courtesies, the Spaniards captured Atahualpa and held him for ransom. During the same period, Atahualpa's forces captured Huascar and, unconcerned that the Spanish were a genuine threat to the inca empire, Atahualpa ordered him killed. Pizarro organized a mock trial for Atahualpa, accusing him of plotting to wipe out the Spanish. The Inca was baptized and then strangled. In 1533 Pizarro stepped into the void to claim Cusco and the empire for Spain. To appease those loyal to the Incas, Pizarro crowned a puppet emperor, Manco, and began to control the southern portion of the Inca empire from Cusco (*see* p.110 for more Inca history.) Quito held out bravely against the Spanish under the Inca general Rumiñahui until late 1534. When the Inca were finally forced to flee, Rumiñahui razed it to the ground, leaving a wasteland of smoking rubble and corpses to Sebastián de Benalcázar. The rubble was used to rebuild the city and, in 1535, the resurrected, colonial Quito became an *audiencia* under the Viceroy of Peru, administered from the new colonial capital, Lima. The city was a small outpost until the 18th century, when what is now called the old city was laid out in its current form.

Quito (℗ 02–)   ### Getting There and Getting Around

by air

The **airport** is 15 minutes from the New Town centre by taxi (about $5).

International: Quito is one of Latin America's transport hubs and is well served by many of the world's largest carriers. A full list of the addresses of international airline offices can be obtained from the tourist office. The following have agents or offices in the capital: Air France ℗ 527374; American Airlines ℗ 260900; British Airways ℗ 228933; Continental ℗ 461493; Iberia ℗ 441509; Japan Airlines; ℗ 564074; KLM ℗ 432088; United ℗ 254662; Varig ℗ 437137.

National: TAME, Amazonas 13–54 at Colón, ℗ 509382/3/4/5/6/7/8; *tame1@ tame.com, www.ecua.net.ec/tame,* fly to Coca, Lago Agrio, Loja and Macas.

by road

Buses and collective taxis leave regularly from the Terminal Terrestre is located at the south end of the Old Town. Details of buses to jungle centres are given under the relevant sections.

Car hire: Localiza, Av. 6 de Diciembre 1570 at Wilson, ℗ 505986. Avis, Av. de las Americas, CC Olímpico, ℗ 284559.

Taxis are cheap, about $2 from the bus terminal to the New Town, and run on metres. **Local buses** are very cheap, but follow confusing routes. The **Trole** is a tram-type system, connecting the bus terminal with the New Town along Av. 10 de Agosto. It costs about $0.25.

Tourist office: Corporación Ecuatoriana de Turismo (CETUR). Eloy Alfaro 1214 at Carlos Tobar, ℗ 514044, and at the airport. Helpful, English spoken

Changing money: Most hotels will exchange US dollars in cash. Banco Guyaquil and Banco Popular have branches throughout town with Visa/MasterCard cashpoints and will change traveller's cheques. There are plenty of money changers all over town and at the airport which have longer opening hours than banks.

Internet: There are hundreds of different Internet cafés on the corner of JL Mera and Calama and nearby. If you want a beer as well, try The Turtle's Head (*see* p.183).

Embassies and consulates: USA, 12 de Octubre at Patria, ℗ 562890, UK, González Suárez 111 at 12 de Octubre, ℗ 560670, Brazil, Amazonas 1429 at Colón, Ed. España, piso 10, ℗ 563086; Peru, El Salvador 495 at Irlanda, ℗ 468410; Venezuela, Chile 329 at Aguirre, piso 2, ℗ 326579.

South American Explorer's(SAE): Jorge Washington 311 at Leonidas Plaza, ℗/✉ 225228, *saec@amauta.rcp.net.pe. www.samexplo.org*, (*open Mon–Fri 9.30–5*). A wonderful repository of information on all aspects of travel and adventure in South America, focusing particularly on the Andean countries. Great library.

Indigenous peoples: Co-ordinador de las Organisaciones Indígenas de la Cuenca Amazonica (COICA), Alemania 832 at Mariana de Jesús, (Casilla Postal 1721753); ℗/✉ 553297, *coica@ecua.net.* Information on indigenous issues throughout all the countries of the Amazon Basin, compiled by indigenous peoples in a centre run by indigenous peoples. Connections throughout South America. **CONFE-NIAE** (Confederación de Naciones Indígenas de la Amazonia Ecuatoriana), Av. 6 de Deciembre at 159 Pazmino, Edificio. Parlamento, Piso 4, Of. 408, ℗ 543973, ✉ 220325.This is also run by indigenous people and is the best place to come for the very latest on indigenous issues in the Amazon, from an indigenous perspective.

The Sights of Colonial Quito

Quito has no pre-Columbian architectural wonders as Rumiñahui's sacking of the city wiped away almost all vestiges of its Inca past. Quito's sights are colonial.

The **Plaza de la Independencia** is the best point from which to begin an exploration. The most dominant building on the plaza is the **cathedral** (*open daily 8–10 and 2–4*), with green cupolas, a Moorish roof and a few Inca stones incorporated into its façade. Sucre, a hero of Ecuadorian independence, is buried inside and the walls are adorned with some fine 17th-century paintings by the Quito School. The 17th-century church, **El Sagrario**, just around the corner, is a dazzling golden festival of Iberian American Baroque. The northwest side of the plaza is dominated by the 18th-century **Palacio de Gobierno** (*open daily 9–12 and 3–6*), which has a huge mural of Orellana travelling down the Amazon on the first floor. The **church of San Francisco** (*open daily 9–11 and 3–6*), on the plaza of the same name, is the largest church in the city, and is said to be the first built by the Spanish in South America. The interior is more remarkable than the exterior, with a delicately carved ceiling, choir and altar piece covered with gold leaf. There is a small museum attached, devoted to the paintings of the Quito School. The finest church in the city is probably the Jesuit **church of La Compañía**, (*open daily 9.30–11 and 4–6*), a block from the Plaza de la Independencia. During the colonial era,

Quito kept up close artistic relations with both Spain and Europe, with the educated and cultural Jesuits as one of the principal conduits of influence. The beautiful carved stone sculptures on the façade and interior were worked by two different Jesuits in the mid-18th century.

Museums: Quito has several museums and art galleries, a handful of which are housed in the Casa de la Cultura in the Parque El Ejido. The best is the joint **Museo Arqueológico** and **Museo de Traje Indígena** (*open Tues–Fri 9–5, Sat, Sun 9–3*) which contains an impressive and extensive collection of clovis and other flints, ceramics and gold, covering the various cultures and civilisations of pre-Columbian Ecuador. A video describing Ecuador's indigenous groups is useful to see before exploring the Museo de Traje Indígena which houses a collection of their jewellery and traditional dress. Also here is the **Museo Colonial y de Arte and Museo de Arte Moderno** (*open Tues–Fri 9–5 and Sat, Sun 9–3*), with colonial, modern and contemporary art including some iconographic paintings from the Quito school and the **Museo de Instrumentos Musicales** (*open Tues–Fri 9–5, Sat, Sun 9–3*) which houses the second largest collection of musical instruments in the world. Other museums in Quito include the **Museo Amazónico**, Centro de Cultura Abya Yala, 12 de Octubre 1430 at Wilson, (*open Mon–Fri 8.30–12.30 and 2.30–6.30, Sat 9–12*), with jewellery and clothing from various Ecuadorian Amazon tribes, especially the Achuar, and a small collection of rainforest fauna and flora. Displays highlight the detrimental effects of mining and oil exploration in the forest. There is also a very good bookshop (mostly Spanish). At **Vivarium**, Reina Victoria 1576 at Santa Maria, (*open Mon–Sat 9–1 and 2.30–4, Sun 11–6*), you can see a collection of endangered species, mostly South American reptiles and amphibians, including poison dart frogs, boas and caiman. A breeding programme aims to reintroduce species to the wild. The small **Museo de Ciencias Naturales**, Rumipamba 341 at Los Shyris in the La Carolina Park (*open Mon–Fri 8.30–4.30, Sat 9–3*), covers the country's geography, flora and fauna, and geology.

Shopping

There are many artisan and souvenir shops of variable quality and price along Av. Amazonas and the streets running parallel to it, in the New Town. The **Fundación Sinchi Sacha**, Reina Victoria 1780 at La Niña, © 230609/52724, ✆ 567311, operate a small museum and shop to promote awareness of indigenous cultures. All profits support their environmental, developmental and cultural projects. **Libri Mundi**, Calle Juan Léon Mera 851 at Veintimilla, © 234791, is a multilingual bookshop stocking a large range of environmental and cultural books specific to Ecuador and the Amazon.

Quito (© 02–)   ### Where to Stay

Quito has several excellent, reasonably priced and well-equipped hotels. Our recommendations are located in the New Town, close to many agencies and restaurants. There are many budget hotels in the Old Town; getting to them without using a taxi can be an edgy experience, even during the day.

expensive

Hotel Quito, Av. González Suárez 2500, © 544600/234110, ✆ 567284, *hoquito@ibm.net, www.bestwestern.com/thisco/bw/70200/70200-b.htm/*. Bars, discos, a gym, swimming pool, casino, good restaurant and all mod-cons.

Hilton Colón, Av. Amazonas at Patria, © 560666, ✆ 563903. Themed restaurants, polished glass and impersonally sleek service.

Sheraton Quito, Av. Naciones Unidas at República de El Salvador, ✆ 970014, ✉ 433906, *sheraton@uio.satnet.net.* A predictably modern business hotel.

moderate

Hotel Sebastián, Almagro 822, ✆ 222300/222400, ✉ 222500, *sebast1@hsebastian.com.ec.* An environmentally aware luxury hotel, with filtered air (great idea given the Quito's pollution), tap water, and an excellent restaurant which uses organic vegetables. Used by a number of the country's leading ecotourism and birding operators, notably Neblina Forest Tours and Nuevo Mundo.

Hotel Café Cultura, Robles N-21-B at Reina Victoria, ✆ 504078, ✆/✉ 224271, *info@cafecultura.com, www.cafecultura.com.* Individually styled rooms with plenty of character. Café attached. Booking centre for Cuyabeno River Lodge and El Otro Lado near Baños (*see* p.187).

inexpensive–cheap

Hostal Sierra Nevada, Joaquín Pinto 637 at Cordero, ✆ 528264/224717, *snevada@accessinter.net, www.qni.com/~mj/snevada.* Ask for rooms on an upper floor so you don't have to look at the generator.

La Casona de Mario, Andalucía 213 at Galicia, Barrio La Floresta, ✆ 544036. Very friendly family atmosphere, kitchen access and nice garden.

Crossroads Café and Hostal, Foch 678 at Juan León Mera, ✆/✉ 234735, *brummel@uio.satnet.com.* Private rooms and hostal-style accommodation in the centre of New Town. Rooms are large and clean but spartan.

Quito (✆ 02–)   *Eating Out*

The new part of town overflows with fast food joints, but there are also a few decent places to eat. The best are in the expensive hotels (**Quito** and the **Hilton,** *see* above).

expensive–moderate

Rincón de Francia, Roca 779 at 9 de Octobre. One of the best restaurants in the city, serving French cuisine in very smart surroundings.

inexpensive–cheap

La Paella Valenciana, República at Almagro. Huge paellas and delicious fish.

La Choza, 12 de Octubre N34-551 at Cordero, ✆ 230839. Typical Ecuadorean cuisine, try the *cuy* (roast or barbecued guinea pig). Popular with the well-to-do.

The Turtle's Head, La Niña 626 at Amazonas. A bar and restaurant very popular with travellers and locals and run by Bert Crutcher, an affable Scot, who can arrange trips all over Ecuador. Great at any time of the day.

Café Colibrí, Joaquín Pinto 619 at Amazonas, has delicious and plentiful food, including a decent cup of tea and slices of buttered toast.

La Vid, (Juan León Mera between Cordero and Colón). Popular with the locals and extremely cheap.

vegetarian

Restaurante 'El Holandes', Reina Victoria 600 at Carrión, ✆ 522 167. Excellent vegetarian platters from around the world, the Indonesian is superb. Very cheap.

Bars and clubs: Zoo, La Niña E7-29 at Reina Victoria. Trendy spot for Ecuador's young and wealthy. The Indian bouncers on the door won't let anyone in if they look remotely like an Indian. **Cali Salsateca**, Almagro at Orellana. Good for salsa.

Cinemas: There are a number of multiplexes in town, including Multicines CCI, Amazonas at Naciones Unidas and, Cinemark Siete, América at Av. de la República

Tour Operators and Lodges in Quito
Quito (✆ 02–)

Amazon Jungle Resort Village, Coruña 2623 at Gonzáles Suarez, Dept 6, PO Box 1707.9107, Quito, *www.ecuadorexplorer.com/selva/index.html.* Luxury rainforest lodge in the Cuyabeno Wildlife Reserve.

Cabañas Aliñahui, Isla Fernandina N43-78 at Tomás de Berlanga, ✆ 253267, ✆ 253266, *alinahui@jsacha.ecuanex.net.ec.* The best rainforest lodge in the Tena region, in a buffer zone for the Jatun Sacha biological station, *see* p.186. From $90 per person per day.

Cabañas San Isidro, Carrión 555-C between JL Mera and Reina Victoria, ✆ 547403/ 465578, ✆ 228902. Simple, comfortable cabins in the cloud forest near Baeza. Good birding and trail walking. Around $60 all inclusive. Transport available from Quito to the lodge.

Emerald Forest Expeditions, Av. Amazonas N24-29 at Joaquín Pinto, Casilla 17-07-9633, ✆/✆: 541543, *emeraldforest@ecuadorexplorer.com, www.ecuadorexplorer.com/emerald.* Tours to Pañacocha Lodge on the lower Río Napo (*see* p.200). One of the best companies in Ecuador. Expect to pay around $50 per day all-inclusive.

Latin Tour, Av. Amazonas N24-03 at Wilson, ✆/✆ 222266, *mauri@internet.net.* A large company aimed at backpackers, offering a range of tours to different parts of Ecuador and specializing in the Cuyabeno Wildlife Reserve. From $50 per person per day.

Metropolitan Touring, República El Salvador N36-84, ✆ 464780, ✆ 464702, *www.ecuadorable.com.* The biggest tourist venture in Ecuador, with its own skyscraper and tours all over the country, including some of the best options for Cuyabeno. Prices per person on the Flotel Orellana river cruiser are around $200 (single cabin) and $160 (double), including all food, guides and excursions. Reductions are possible in the low season. Prices at their lodges near Lago Agrio run from about $130 per person per night. Aguarico trekking costs between $120 and $160 per person, per day, depending on the size of the group (the smaller the better). Flights are not included in any of the above prices.

Misahualli Jungle Hotel, Ramírez Dávalos 251 at Paez, ✆ 520043/504872. Luxurious lodge opposite Misahualli town on the upper Río Napo. From $80 per person all inclusive (flights extra.) *See* p.196.

Nuevo Mundo Tours, Av. Coruna N26-207, ✆ 564448/553826/553818/509431, ✆ 565261, *nmundo@telconet.net, www.nuevomundotravel.com.* Ecuador's most ecologi-cally-conscious large tourist venture, with Cuyabeno lodge-based trips from $100 to $140 per person per day, also fishing trips for $200; both include transport from Quito (lodges) and $200 (angling). Also act as an agent for Tiputini Biodiversity Station (*see* below).

San Rafael Lodge, Av. de los Shyris at Rep del Salvador, Edificio Onix, Oficina 10A, ✆ 469846/224961, ✆ 469847. Comfortable cabins near the country's highest waterfalls in cloud forest near Baeza. Around $60 per person per day. Transport from Quito is available. (*See* p.193).

SierrAzul Rainforest Lodge, Paul Claudel N41-16 at Isla Floreana, ✆ 264484, ✉ 449464, *azul2@azul.com.ec*. A very comfortable, American-owned lodge in the cloud forest near Baeza (*see* p.192). Spectacled bear and mountain tapir have been seen here, as well as giant antpitta and 150 other species of birds. Expect to pay around $75 per person per day, all-inclusive. Transport from Quito (by 4x4) can be arranged for around $20.

Yachana Lodge, Francisco Andrade Marín 188 at Diego de Almagro, ✆ 543851/541862, ✉ 220362, *info@yachana.com*, *www.yachana.com*. A lodge on the upper Río Napo near Misahualli, owned by FUNEDESIN, an NGO working with indigenous peoples in the Ecuadorean Amazon. From $90 per person per day. *See* p.197.

Adventure Tours, Kayaking and Rafting

Adventour, Calama 339 between Reina Victoria and Juan León Mera, ✆ 524715, ✉ 223720, *info@adventour.com.ec*, *www.adventour.com.ec*. A broad-based company that offers a range of activities and tours with a focus on water adventure sports. Their speciality is four- to five-day multi-adventure packages, including excellent rafting, trekking, mountain climbing and biking trips. These include kayaking in Cuyabeno and climbing the Reventador Volcano near the San Rafael Falls (*see* pp.194 and pp.192). All tours include equipment, bilingual guides and food. Expect to pay about $100 a day.

The Biking Dutchman, Foch 714 at Juan León Mera, ✆ 542806, ✉ 567008, *dutchman@ uio.satnet.net*, *www.ecuadorexplorer.com/dutchman*. This Dutch-Ecuadorean company provides a variety of high-quality (downhill only) mountain biking tours. Two are offered into the Amazon Basin: a two-day trip from Quito to the 4000m Papallacta Pass and down to San Rafael Falls and a five-day trip which includes biking on Cotopaxi volcano, before heading down through Baños and into the Amazon for a jungle hike. Accommodation is flexible and depends on individual budgets. For mid-range accommodation, expect to pay around $50 per person.

EuroVIP's, Amazonas 1023 at Joaquín Pinto, ✆ 522490. Booking agents for Magic River Tours, a Lago Agrio-based company who offer canoe and kayak trips in Cuyabeno. From $50 per person per day. Transport to Lago Agrio and park entry fees extra. *See* p.197.

Expediciones ROW, Foch 721 at Juan León Mera, ✆/✉ 239224, *row@uio.satnet.net,*, *www.travelecuador.com/row.htm*. white-water rafting and kayaking throughout Ecuador, most notably in Macas (*see* p.189) and a multi-adventure crossing of Ecuador from the Amazon to the Pacific, on water, four and two feet. From $150 per person per day.

Surtrek, Av. Amazonas 897 at Wilson, Casilla 17-03-064, ✆ 561129/231534, ✉ 561132, *surtrek1@surtrek.com.ec*, *www.surtrek.com*. A variety of adventure and ecotourism activities in the Oriente, focusing on the Cuyabeno Wildlife Reserve, as well as trips throughout the country, including climbing and rafting (not on Amazon rivers), aimed at the backpacking market. Expect to pay around $50 per person per day, all inclusive.

Yacu Amu Rafting, Av. Amazonas N24-03 at Presidente Wilson, ✆/✉ 236844, *yacuamu@rafting.com.ec*, *www.ecua.net.ec/yacuamu*). Rafting trips throughout Ecuador, from $150 per person per day.

Yuturí Jungle Adventure, Av. Amazonas 1324 at Colón, ✆/✉ 504037/503225 /544166, *Yuturí1@Yuturí.com.ec*, *www.Yuturílodge.com*. Ecuadorean-owned company, running two lodges on the Río Napo (*see* pp.199 and p.200). Costs between $180 and $310 per person for a four-day trip, do not include flights to Coca and depend on the lodge used.

Specialist Birding and Natural History Tours and Lodges

Neblina Forest Birding Tours, Casilla 17-17-1212, ✆ 407822, mobile ✆ 0970 3939, in USA ✆ 1 800 538 2149, *mrivaden@pi.pro.ec*. Package tours to top birding sites across Ecuador, including Sacha Lodge, Yuturí, Cuyabeno Reserve, and Tiputini Biodiversity Station, as well as other prime locations such as Mindo Cloud Forest Reserve on the Pacific western slopes. Neblina's Amazon Supreme Tour combining Sacha Lodge and Tiputini Biodiversity Station is one of Ecuador's (and the Amazon Basin's) best birding trips. Bespoke tours are also available and the company will book visitors in to virtually any lodge in Ecuador, or put birders in the best places for species of their choice. Tours include all transfers to and from the international airport, and are conducted by an experienced birding or natural history guide, sometimes of international stature: Robert Ridgely, author of the illustrious two-volume *The Birds of South America* can be booked on special request. Neblina have also set up the Fundacion Jocotóco, to protect an area in Podocarpus National Park where a new species, Ridgely's Antpitta, was recently discovered.

La Selva Jungle Lodge, 6 de Deciembre 2816, PO Box 17-12-635, ✆ 550995/554686, ✉ 567297, *laselva@uio.satnet.net*, *www.laselvajunglelodge.com*. Though fallen slightly from grace, this is still one of the most upmarket lodges in the Amazon, with an illustrious birding pedigree. Departures are either Wednesday for 4 days or Saturday for 5 days. Prices for 4 days and three nights are around $560, additional nights are $150 per night. Prices do not include transport from Quito to Coca. *See* p.200.

Sacha Lodge and La Casa del Suizo, Julio Zaldumbide 375 at Toledo, Casilla 17-21-1608, ✆ 566090/509504/509115, ✉ 236521, *sachalod@pi.pro.ec*, *www.sachalodge.com*. The first is the best rainforest and birding lodge on the Río Napo, and the second a luxury rainforest resort (swimming pool and cocktails), near Misahuallí (*see* pp.200 and p.196). From $120 per person per day, not including flights to Coca, for Sacha, and $90 for La Casa del Suizo.

Tiputini Biodiversity Station, c/o Dr Kelly Swing, Science Director, Universidad San Francisco de Quito, Casillo 1712841, ✆ 721046, ✉ 890070, *tbs@mailusfq.edu.ec*, *www.usfq.edu.ec/1tiputini/index.html*. In the USA, ✆ (01) 830 336 2720, *tiputini@aol.com*, or through Nuevo Mundo or Neblina Forest (*see* pp. 184 and 186). Tours (aimed at students of biological sciences) to a remote research station bordering the Yasuní Biosphere Reserve. The only place in the country with a canopy walkway, and the best for seeing large mammals.

Internships in Biological Research Stations

Fundación Jatun Sacha, Isla Fernandina N43-78 at Tomás de Berlanga, ✆ 250976, ✉ 451626, *jatsa\cha@jsacha.ecuanex.net.ec*, *www.jatunsacha.org*. A rainforest scientific research foundation that offers opportunities for volunteer interns to participate in research, community service, rainforest lodge maintenance and administration, plant conservation and agroforestry at their three research stations, Jatun Sacha near Tena, in the Amazon, Bilsa on the west coast and Guandera in the Andes. $30 a night for visitors, $20 for interns and researchers, in very basic accommodation.

Additional Birding and Natural History Information

CECIA (Ornithological Society of Ecuador), Casilla 1717906, Quito, ✆/✉ 244734.

Fundación Natura, Av. América 5663, ✆ 447341/4. The country's most prominent environmental NGO.

Visiting Indigenous Peoples

Tropic Ecological Adventures, Av. República E7-320 at Almagro, Edificio. Taurus, Dept 1-A, ✆ 225907/234594, 📠 560756, *tropic@uio.satnet.net, www.tropiceco.com* .The website is worth looking at for pictures of the various indigenous groups visited. Tropic run tours with four different indigenous peoples over several different communities in Ecuador. Although this style of tourism is its infancy, and things do not always run completely smoothly, the company have already won international awards for their advanced approach to ecotourism, and are doing great work to promote and consolidate indigenous culture within Ecuador and with foreign visitors. The company's founders, Welshman Andy Drumm (who works on the UN ecotourism) and his Ecuadorean partner are also trying to set up a centre for the assimilation and promotion of information about indigenous ecotourism in Ecuador. This may be open in early 2001. Tropic's most popular tours are five-day/four-night safaris on the Río Shiripuno with the Huaorani Indians (*see* p.201), which are occasionally cancelled due to adverse weather washing out the runway and tours with the Cofan people in Cuyabeno (*see* p.197), which run most regularly. Tours with the Siecoya and RICANCIE (*see* p.195) are also available. Expect to pay at least $200 a day. Accommodation is extremely basic.

Kem Pery Tours, Av. Joaquin Pinto 539 at Av. Amazonas, ✆ 226583/226715, 📠 568664, *kempery@ecuadorexplorer.com, www.ecuadorexplorer.com/kempery.home.* Sensitively managed tours to Cuyabeno with Siona Indians and the Napo with the Huaorani from around $60 (plus $20 tax payable to the Huaorani community for use of their land.) Airfares are extra.

Safari Ecuador and Bolivia, Calama 380 and Juan León Mera, ✆ 552505, 📠 223381, *david@safari.com.ec.* Wonderful and good-value tours to Huaorani villages near Coca and the Yasuní Biosphere Reserve, from around $60 per day, all inclusive (except for airfares.)

Baños

Quito's favourite weekend getaway lies hidden in a steep-sided valley of patchwork fields, crisscrossed with paths and rushing streams. It became popular earlier this century as a spa town. Now the hot springs that first drew settlers here have become a veritable complex, with thermally heated swimming pools, showers, a sauna and crowds of screaming school kids. Baños is the gateway for the central Oriente which, though not as important a tourist centre as the north, still has a few places of interest. The town is tiny; it's possible to walk from one end to the other in less than twenty minutes, and there's little to do but soak in the thermal baths, eat, sip coffee and breathe the cool mountain air.

Two of the four sets of hot baths are in the centre of town. Both are useful reference points for finding your way around: the Santa Clara baths are three blocks south of the cathedral, on 16 de Diciembre. The Baños de la Virgen (and Piscinas Modernas) are very close to the Santa Clara baths. The El Salado baths are 1½km from the centre off the road to Ambato (and Quito). The Santa Ana baths are on the road to Puyo on the eastern outskirts of town.

Baños (✆ 03–)   **Getting There and Around**

The town has no airport. The **bus station** lies on the road to Quito and Puyo, next to the river on Av. Amazonas and Baños is about 2 hours' drive from Quito on a well-paved road. For all journeys to the Oriente, sit on the right. The views are wonderful. Buses leave for Quito (3–4hrs) every 15 mins, and regularly for Puyo (2hrs), with some continuing to Tena (5hrs) or Coca (12hrs). There are regular direct buses for Macas and Sucúa (7hrs), or change at Puyo. **Rent 4x4s** at Cordova Tours, Maldonado at Espejo, ☎ (03) 740923 (one of the few places outside Quito where this is possible) or **rent mountain bikes** at Alexander, 12 de Noviembre and Montalvo.

Baños (☎03–)   *Tourist Information and Useful Addresses*

Tourist office: Second floor of the bus station. Maps and pamphlets. English spoken

Internet: There are many Internet cafés dotted around town; try the one on Martínez, between Thomas Halflants and Alfaro, next to the Casa Hood.

Baños (☎03–)   *Where to Stay and Eating Out*

As Ecuador's top tourist town, Baños has more than 90 hotels mostly in the budget category. Even these tend to have private bathrooms and hot water.

expensive–moderate

Luna Runtun, Caserío Runtun, Km 6, Casilla 28-02-1944, ☎ 740882, ✉ 740376, *runtun@ecuadorexplorer.com, www.lunaruntun.com* is a luxury resort on a hill overlooking Baños with travel agency, sports facilities, creche, Internet and a gourmet restaurant. **Hotel Sangay**, Plazoleta Isidro Ayora 101 (next to the Baños de la Virgen), ☎ 740490, *sangay@ecuadorexplorer.com*. The second most luxurious place in Baños, with a pool, sauna, tennis courts, billiard tables and a restaurant.

inexpensive–cheap

Hostería Monte Selva, Thomas Halflants at Montalvo, Casilla 808, ☎ 740566/740244. *Cabañas* with a great view across the valley, a sense of space, and a shady garden with small waterfalls and tropical plants. Walking trails leave from behind the hotel up the hill that backs Baños and there is a gym, two pools, sauna, bar and restaurant and horse-riding. **Hotel Palace**, Montalvo 20–3, ☎ 740470, has a Turkish bath, pool, tropical garden, sauna and jacuzzi, and spacious old-fashioned rooms.

The best of the cheapies are **Las Orquídeas**, Rocafuerte at Thomas Halflants, ☎ 740387, which is spacious and well-maintained with private bathrooms, or the **Plantas y Blanco**, Martínez at 12 de Noviembre, southeast of the cathedral, Casilla 1980, ☎/✉ 740044, a very popular budget travellers' hotel, with a steam and aromatherapy bath, rooftop café, and good value breakfasts. Rooms and dormitory beds.

Baños has dozens of restaurants, with a good variety of cooking and atmosphere. The following options are all inexpensive or cheap.

Le Petit Restaurant, 16 de Diciembre at Montalvo. Parisian-owned French restaurant with delicious food and coffee at reasonable prices. For good pizza or pasta try **Scaligeri**, Alfaro at Ambato, or **La Fornace**, Martínez at Halflants, which serves the best in Baños, cooked in a genuine pizza oven.

Tour Operators in Baños   Baños (☎03–)

Be very careful when choosing a Baños tour company. There are countless in town, but we feel that we can strongly recommend only one. For the latest, contact the SAE (*see* p.181).

Vasco Tours, Eloy Alfaro between Montalvo and Martínez, Casilla 18-02-1970, ✆/✆ 740017. This is also the only agency in Baños recommended by SAE. Vasco's Juan Medina is justly renowned as the town's most professional and ecologically sensitive tour guide. The company offer some far-flung destinations: three-day trips to their Bosque Protector Venecia (on the same road as Jatun Sacha near Tena); four-day trips leaving from Coca to Ananguococha Lake on the edge of Yasuní National Park (also used for birdwatching by Selva and Sacha Lodges). This includes a visit to an indigenous shaman, five- to ten-day camping trips along the Shiripuno and Cononaco Rivers with the Huaorani and five to ten days trekking through Llanganates National Park, following the Río Jatunyacu (Upper Napo) from its source down to the Tena area. Prices are $45–55 per person per day. SAE members get $10 per day discount. English is spoken.

Cautionary notes: Various other companies offer tours to the Cuyabeno Wildlife Reserve, near Lago Agrio. Baños is a very long way from the Cuyabeno and, as the town has no airport, trips there and back involve two solid days in a bus or 4x4. There are plenty of reputable tour companies who arrange fly-in tours from Quito, and even a few in Lago Agrio itself. We have also heard some worrying stories about Sebastian Moya which suggest that he is best avoided.

Rafting

Baños's rafting guides are the most dangerously under-qualified in Ecuador. Several tourists have died in recent accidents and, though dozens of agencies in town offer excursions, we would not recommend going with any of them. There are better and safer companies operating out of Tena (Ríos Ecuador, *see* p.195) and Macas (ROW, p.191 and p.185). Those who decide to throw caution to the winds should ensure that the guides are licensed by AGARE (Associación de Guías para Aguas Rápidas Ecuatoriana).

Mountain Biking and Horse-riding

Mountain biking around Baños can either be done alone locally (*see* bike hire, above), or through a tour company for journeys farther afield. The most popular organized route follows the verdant canyon of the Río Pastaza down to the edge of the Amazon flatlands at Puyo. The views, and the bird life in the cloud forest along the way are wonderful. Numerous trails along the way lead to waterfalls, the largest and most visited of which is El Pailón del Diablo. The beginning of the path is well-marked by Coke stands. Almost as many people rent horses and lead excursions around Baños as rent mountain bikes. Dos Locos and La Gringa are based at Casa Hood behind the market on Martínez. They do half-day and full-day tours to the community of Runtun on the lower slopes of Tungurahua, stopping at thermal baths along the way. Check the aAnimal's state of health before.

Macas

Tiny Macas sits on the edge of forests that stretch unbroken into Peru and beyond, and encompass Shuar and Achuar territory. Sangay, one of the country's highest volcanoes, sputters in the midst of thick forest to the town's northwest. The Río Upano, rushing through canyons and over boulders before passing the town, has some of the best white-water sections in South America, and tourists are still a relatively rare sight, with just a handful of tour operators. Excursions include multi-day rafting adventures and visits to the Shuar and Achuar Indians, the latter perhaps best done through the **Shuar-Achuar Indian Federation** (Federación de Centros Shuar-Achuar, Domingo Comín 17–38, Moraona Santiago, ✆/✆ (07) 740108; in

Quito, ✆ (02) 504264), the only official representatives of traditional Shuar and Achuar Indians living in the area. They are based in **Sucúa**, 23km from Macas. Applications to spend time in traditional villages are discussed by a group of *caçiques*, who then conduct interviews before making a decision. The process takes a couple of days. The Hostal Karina (*cheap*), on the plaza, provides the best accommodation, and Shuar crafts are for sale opposite the Federation.

| *Macas (✆07–)* | *Getting There and Getting Around* |

The **airport** is at the western end of Cuenca. There are flights to Quito three times a week. Macas is connected to Baños (via Puyo) and Cuenca but the road requires a 4x4 and there are no car hire facilities in town. The bus terminal is at the corner of Guamote, and 10 de Agosto. There are several buses daily for Cuenca (12hrs) with connections to Loja (an extra 5hrs). Sit on the left from Cuenca and the right to Cuenca for great views. Buses leave hourly for Sucúa (1hr or less) and regularly for Puyo, for connections to Tena and towns in the northern Oriente (5 hrs, 4 more to Tena). There are daily buses to Baños (8hrs), or go to Puyo and change there.

| *Macas (✆07–)* | *Where to Stay and Eating Out* |

There are few options in Macas. Most hotels are damp and dreadful, and all are *cheap*.

Peñón del Oriente, 837 Domingo Comín at Amazonas, ✆ 700124, is the best and most modern hotel, with private bathrooms with hot water showers. The **Orquídea**, 9 de Octubre at Sucre, ✆ 700970, has clean, spacious rooms with showers.

There are very few restaurants to choose from in Macas. **El Jardín**, Amazonas at Comín, is the best of the very few in town. The **Prashad**a, near the plaza, offers good international food, or try **La Randipampa**, on the Plaza, for Cuban food and cigars.

Tour Operators and Lodges in Macas   *Macas (✆07–)*

Aventuras Tsunki, Bolívar between Amazonas and Soasti (a block and a half west of the plaza); ✆/✉ 700464, *tsunki@ma.pro.ec*. Offer a variety of tours of varying physical difficulty, including a three-day/two-night cultural trip to a Shuar community in the Cordillera Cutucu southeast of Macas, a three-day hike through mountainous rainforest in the Sangay National Park, and a six-day camping odyssey, meeting the Shuar, canoeing on remote rivers and visiting an oilbird cave. Expect to pay between $50 and 70 per person per day.

Ikiaam, 10 de Agosto, second floor (opposite the bus station), ✆ 700457. Tours in the Sangay National Park, including the long and arduous three-week slog to the summit (by special arrangement only). Around $50 per person per day.

Carlos Arcos, ask at Tuntiak Expeditions in the bus terminal, ✆ 700082. A respected Shuar guide offering trips to Indian villages and sacred sites. From $60 per person per day.

Kapawi Ecolodge and Reserve, Luís Erdaneta 1418 at Av. del Ejército, Casilla 09-01-8442, Guayaquil, ✆ (04) 285711/280173, ✉ (04) 287651, *eco-tourism1@canodros.com.ec*, *www.canodros.com*. Kapawi is one of the most beautifully located and constructed lodges anywhere in the Ecuadorean Amazon. Each of its 14 cabins is built entirely from natural materials in Achuar Indian style and back on to a lagoon deep in Achuar Indian country, whose serenity is broken only by surfacing caiman and fishing osprey. The lodge is run by a company called Canodros in association with the Achuar federation, FINAE, and is located in primary rainforest, just a few kilometres upstream from the Peruvian border. It is only accessible by light aircraft. In 2011, ownership and responsibility for the lodge reverts to the Achuar. In the meantime, no hunting takes place within the land set aside for ecotourism operations, and a small tax is paid to the tribe for the use of their land. There is a flexible programme of excursions, although they generally start far too late to see much wildlife. Every visit includes a trip to a local Achuar village, with a chance to meet one of the families and enjoy a swig of manioc beer (fermented with saliva). Achuar household rules should be strongly adhered to: it is considered offensive to refuse the manioc beer, walk into the female portion of the house, or make physical contact with women or children. These community rules are not always enforced by guides and it is crucial that they are maintained if the project is to live up to its intentions of respecting Achuar culture and traditions. The lodge may be beautiful in an area rich in wildlife, but it is let down by its poor guides. Guests can be met at Quito or Macas airport. Expect to pay from $200 per person per day plus a $10 fee to the Achuar community visited. Transport is extra.

Rafting

The following companies run camping trips on the Río Upano from November to April, that combine white-water rafting (on Class III to IV rapids) with forest hikes. The longer tours pass through the spectacular Cañón de Namangosa, whose towering walls are watered by columns of cascading waterfalls. Trips need to be booked in Quito, as all food is brought from there.

Expediciones ROW, (through their office in Quito, *see* p.185) A professionally-run, safe and reliable company, affiliated with US River Odysseys West. Tours are accompanied by a Shuar who guides visits to his peoples' communities along the river. Cultural sensitivity is emphasized. ROW also combine rafting with a few days at Kapawi Lodge.

Yacu Amu Rafting, (through their office in Quito, *see* p.185). Yacu Amu offer basically the same package as ROW without visits to Shuar communities, and are considerably cheaper.

Loja and Podocarpus National Park

Podocarpus National Park, named after the only equatorial conifer in the Americas, that grows here, stretches across the top of the Andean plateau and down into the Oriente, protecting large areas of cold and dank paramo, scrubby elfin forest and warm and misty cloud forest. A host of rare animals live here: spectacled bear, mountain tapir, jaguar, puma and Andean mountain cat, together with 560 different birds, including rare or endangered species like the Andean condor and the striking orange, black and yellow-billed grey-breasted, mountain toucan. Like many of Ecuador's national parks, the park is being heavily exploited, in this case by gold mining, logging and agriculture. The government employs only 8 park guards, not enough to police an area of over 146,000 hectares. Podocarpus (admission US$10) lies only half an hour away from the strikingly dull highland town of **Loja** making access relatively easy. The botanical garden is the only worthwhile sight in the town, with separate areas for medicinal, edible, endangered and endemic plants, and a large and wonderful orchid collection.

Loja (℡ 07–)   *Getting There and Getting Around*

Loja is well connected to Quito by **air**, but the journey to or from the airport, 35km out of town, is longer than the flight. There are several **buses** a day to Quito (12hrs), twice-daily to Macas and Sucúa (10–12hrs).

Car hire: Localiza, Av. Paquisha, Km 1, ℡ 935455, ℻ 930379.

Tourist office: CETUR, Calle Valdivieso 08–22 at 10 de Agosto, just off the south-eastern corner of Parque Central, © 572964; *open Mon–Fri 10–4.*

Information on Podocarpus National Park: Fundatierra, Corner of Bolívar and Miguel Riofrio (on the 2nd floor above a pharmacy), Casilla 1101–91, © 584741/576808, *rodrisol@usa.net.* A new NGO operating in various locations around Loja, including Podocarpus. Fundatierra work towards environmental education, taking groups of Peruvian and Ecuadorean students around the Botanic Gardens.

Biotours: Colon 14–96 and Sucre, ©/✆ 578398, *biotours@loja.telconet.net.* The only agency in Loja that organizes tours to the Amazon sector of Podocarpus, with interesting four-day hiking treks from the Andes to the Amazon. Unhelpful owner.

All the following hotels are inexpensive or cheap.

Hotel Ramses, Colon 14-31 and Bolívar, © 571402, ✆ 581832, is a new hotel and the best in town, with modern rooms and restaurant, all amenities included. The **Hotel Vilcabamba International**, Av. Manuel Aguirre and Pasaje La Feue, © 562339, ✆ 561483, was once Loja's top hotel, now fraying at the edges. **Hotel Acapulco**, Sucre 07–61 at 10 de Agosto, © 570651, ✆ 571103, is the best cheapie in town so long as you remember to ask for a light and airy room.

Food is not Loja's strong point, and you can expect all restaurants to be closed by 8pm, at least in low season. However, vegetarian snacks and incredible fruit juices are available at **El Jugo Natural** (Calle Eguiguren 14–20). Carnivores should not miss out on the excellent, good-value lunch at **Gran Hotel Loja**, next to the Hotel Vilcabamba.

The Northern Oriente

At the base of the Andes, near Baeza, ranges of smaller mountains like rise up from flatlands to create a landscape riven by steep valleys full of carved boulders and waterfalls, and cut by fast white-water rivers that provide some of the best kayaking and rafting in South America. Most of the forest on the hills has long been chopped down and turned into pastoral land, tended by indigenous Quechua farmers, who have heavily colonized the area. But a few patches remain, most notably the Llanganates National Park, which rises high into the Andes. As the mountains flatten east of the towns of Tena and Misahuallí (the principal tourist centres in the region), the cloud forests diminish and are replaced by cattle ranches, amid a few islands of primary Amazon forest and thick jungle. The fast-flowing mountain rivers broaden and darken as they begin to wind their way towards Brazil. Ecuador's largest river, the Napo, links Misahuallí with Coca, and the series of rainforest lodges that line its banks combine the standard fare of trail walks and canoe trips with the opportunity to meet with and learn about Quechua Indians.

Baeza and San Rafael Falls

The little crossroad town of **Baeza** lies nestled in the Quijos Pass, its old colonial quarter gradually dying as residents move out to the uglier, modern part of town. The hills around offer some pleasant walks and reasonable birding, though much of it is pastoral, and a few agencies offer kayaking on the Río Quijos. The only attraction of any real note near Baeza are the **San**

Rafael Falls, where the Río Coca thunders 145m over forest clad cliffs that are home to Andean cock-of-the rock, spectacled bear and flocks of iridescent fiery-red and electric blue tanagers. The trail to the bottom of the falls is steep and hazardous and is best done in the company of a guide. The park guard may oblige for a small fee.

Baeza and San Rafael Falls   *Getting There*

The main highway from Quito to the northern Oriente divides at Baeza. The northern section continues to Lago Agrio and Coca, the southern to Tena and Misahuallí and the southern Oriente (via Puyo). It is not possible to rent a car in the Oriente. The bus stop is officially outside the Hotel Jumandí in the colonial part of town, but **buses** tend to pull off on the main road through town. Tena buses leave from outside the Hostal San Rafael. The following services are available at least twice a day: Tena (2hrs); Quito (3hrs); Misahuallí (3hrs); Lago Agrio (6–7hrs); Coca (9–10hrs).

There are two ways to get to San Rafael Falls; the easiest is to book a three-day/two-night package available through Adventour (p.185) and San Rafael Lodge (p.184). The less convenient, but far cheaper, way is to take a bus from Quito or Baeza towards Lago Agrio, and ask to be let off at Cascadas de San Rafael, five minutes from the guard's hut.

Lodges near Baeza and San Rafael Falls

SierrAzul Lodge (book through their office in Quito, p.185). A comfortable American-owned lodge in misty, orchid filled cloud and montane forest that is home to spectacled bear and mountain tapir. Accommodation, food and tours are high quality and guides are multilingual. SierrAzul can be reached on a rough side road from Cosanga, between Baeza and Tena. Drivers will need a 4x4. Transport is available from Quito. There is excellent birding at SierrAzul: giant and moustached antpitta, Andean potoo, at least 14 east Andean tanagers and 150 other species of birds have been recorded around the lodge. A bird checklist is available.

Cabañas San Isidro (book through their office in Quito, *see* p.184). Located on the same road as SierrAzul, and offering much the same with less luxury and a slightly cheaper price. Birding is equally good, if not better. In addition to those species listed under SierrAzul, possible species include black-billed mountain toucan, white-faced nunbird, and greater scythebill.

San Rafael Lodge (book through their office in Quito, p.184). Rustic but comfortable cabins in forest 20 minutes walk from the falls. Transport from Quito available. If you just turn up here (with your own food and a sleeping bag), it is at least half the price.

Trekking in the Cayambe-Coca Ecological Reserve

There are two popular treks in the Cayambe-Coca Ecological Reserve, which protects areas of montane forest in the hills around Baeza and the San Rafael Falls.

Oyacachi to El Chaco: A three-day trek through the cloud forests of this little-visited national park, from Oyacachi in the Andes down to El Chaco, on the Baeza-Lago Agrio road. The route is beautiful, with original Inca paving in parts, and affords many opportunities to see rare animals like puma, ornate hawk-eagle and Andean cock-of-the-rock. The going is tough: the path can be hard to find, and in places streams must be crossed via a cable and pulley system, which hikers must supply themselves! Fortunately, the difficulty of access to this area has helped to preserve the forest. It is possible to hire guides for the trail in Oyacachi for around $20 per day (including food). Getting to Oyacachi is difficult. Take a bus from Quito's principal bus station to Cayambe. Taxis or motorbikes will take you on to the village for around $5.

Reventador Volcano: Slightly less arduous is the ascent of this active and steaming 3,460m volcano on the edge of the Cayambe-Coca Ecological Reserve. It takes one day to reach a refuge at the base of the volcano's cone, and another day to reach the summit and return to the road. Views are spectacular from the top, but it is often covered in cloud. It is best to attempt the hike through Adventour (p.185) or San Rafael Lodge (p.184).

Kayaking

Class III to IV kayaking is available on the Quijos and Cosanga Rivers, with some stunning scenery. Sadly, the Cosanga is currently under heavy development as a new oil pipeline is being constructed between Tena and Baeza. No agencies offer this trip, but comprehensive information on kayaking is available from the SAE (*see* p.181).

Tena, Archidona and Llanganates National Park

Tena is a pleasantly sleepy town straddling the rivers Tena and Pano, with plenty of tour companies offering trips to Quechua Indian villages, lodges on the upper Río Napo, or kayaking or rafting on the exciting rivers in the area. The Parque Amazonico on a river island is about the only tourist attraction in Tena, with picnic spots, swimming and a self-guided trail.

Archidona, 15km north of Tena, is a small village with a museum of indigenous culture. The **Jumandí Caves** lie 6km further on, and harbour one of the largest colonies of common and hairy-legged vampire bats in Ecuador, together with large stalactites and stalagmites and a host of speleological excresence. The caves are prone to flooding and should be visited with caution and a guide. These are available through Amarongachi Tours (p.195) or in Archidona village.

The 220,000ha of Llanganates National Park, rise high into the Andes south west of Tena, encompassing cloud and elfin forest and high paramo. This is the legendary hiding place of the Inca Atahualpa's huge ransom in gold, spirited away by loyal subjects after his murder by Francisco Pizarro (*see* p.180). Today the only gold to come out of Llanganates has been washed out by mercury and high-powered water jets. Despite destruction in the peripheral areas, the park still protects rare animals like spectacled bear, mountain tapir, jaguar, Andean condor, Andean gull and Andean mountain cat. All are almost impossible to see on most tours to the park, as these visit areas already damaged or frequented by colonists or gold miners.

Tena, Archidona and the Jumandí Caves   ***Getting There***

The bus terminal is 1km south of the river. Ignore the touts inside. Regular buses leave Quito's Terminal Terrestre for Tena; the best company is Baños. Small buses leave Tena frequently for Misahuallí and Archidona from 15 de Noviembre in front of the main terminal. There are also frequent connections to Coca, Lago Agrio, Puyo and Baños.

Tena (© 06–)   ***Tourist Information and Useful Addresses***

Tourist office: CETUR, Bolivar at Amazonas, © 886536.

Tena (© 06–)   ***Where to Stay***

All accommodation in Tena is cheap and cheerful, and the water supply in most hotels sporadic. The best is **Los Yutzos**, Cesár Rueda, set in its own beautiful gardens away from the main street and overlooking the river (*inexpensive*). Or there is the **Hostal Turismo Amazónico**, Amazonas between Calderón Municipio and JL Mera, which is much better inside than outward appearances would suggest (*cheap*). The food in Tena is unremarkable and the choice is limited. There is good fish at Chuquito's on the eastern side of the plaza.

Tours Operators for Llanganates National Park   *Tena (©06–)*

Vasco Tours (*see* p.189). The only reputable company in Ecuador to offer trips into remote areas of Llanganates, with ten-day trekking tours following the Río Jatunyacu (Upper Napo) from its source down to the Tena area.

Amarongachi Tours, Av. 15 de Noviembre 438, Tena, ©/✉ 886372. Hiking, swimming, canyoning and natural history walks in the foothills of Llanganates, which are strong on adventure and weak on appreciation of flora and fauna. Around $25–35 per person per day.

Shangri-La Lodge (book through Amarongachi Tours, *see* above). Fairly comfortable cabins on a cliff overlooking the Río Anzu. Forest walks, inner-tubing, and medicinal plant trail walks are available. Expect to pay around $40–55.

Cabañas Pimpilala (contact through Rios Ecuador, p.195). Rustic cabins owned by Quechua Indian, Delfín Pauchí, who seems genuinely concerned that visitors leave with an appreciation and understanding of his culture. Delfín and his family lead hikes to sacred natural sites within Llanganates, and explain the mythology related to them. They also offer light adventure tours like canyoning and forest hiking. The best deal in Tena at only $30 per person per day.

Sacharicsina, Calle Tarqui, Tena, © 886250/887181. Tours of varying length to indigenous communities around Tena, and rafting on the Río Jatunyacu.

RICANCIE (Red Indigena de Comunidades del Alto Napo para la Conviviencia Intercultural y el Ecoturismo), 15 de Noviembre 774, Bellavista Alta, Casilla 243, Tena, ©/✉ 887072, or through Tropic Ecological Adventures in Quito, *see* p.187). RICANCIE is a network of ten Quechua communities who have independently decided to set up ecotourism projects rather than cut down more of their forest. Each community has a specific focus, be it nature, native culture or medicinal plant gardens, and all are coordinated from the office in Tena. Visits are flexible to the tourist's needs, but normally combine one or two nights in one of the 'cultural' communities with others in a community with access to undamaged forest. One of the 'cultural' communities, Capirona, was a prime mover in the establishment of Ecuadorean indigenous ecotourism in the early 1990s. As well as showing tourists traditional forms of song, dance, and crafts, the villagers invite visitors to take part in a community *minga* (work-day), which involves the whole village working together on a project that is considered of benefit to all. This is followed in the evening by a presentation of song and dance, at which tourists are expected to contribute something from their own culture. The *cabañas* at Salazar Aitaca offer more intimate contact with rainforest and rivers. As well as a system of forest trails where the Indians explain traditional plant usage, a waterfall close to the cabins crashes into a canyon that is full of the busy squawking of rare oilbirds. Facilities in the villages are basic, the food is plain, and the administration often disorganized. Expect to pay between $30–60 per person per day.

Rafting and Kayaking around Tena

Rios Ecuador, second floor of Cambahuasi Hotel (near the bus terminal) Tena, ©/✉ 887438, *info@riosecuador.com*. One of Ecuador's best rafting companies, and the only one in Tena with professional qualifications. Standard trips include the Jatunyacu (Upper Napo, Class III), the Anzu (Class II), and the Misahuallí (Class IV). Around $60–$70 per person per day.

Twenty years ago, Misahuallí was Ecuador's jungle frontier, the last stop on the road for travellers looking for a cheap Amazon experience. Increasing settlement along the Upper Napo has led to large-scale deforestation, and today little primary forest remains. It's still easy to arrange a cheap jungle tour, but the chances of seeing wildlife other than birds and butterflies are pretty slim, and for a taste of purer rainforest you'd be better off in Coca, Lago Agrio or Macas. The only real attraction in the Misahuallí area is the AmaZOOnico Animal Rescue Centre, a rehabilitation centre for rainforest mammals that have been captured or injured. These include tapir, coati and various monkeys, some of which are free-roaming. Sadly, funds are low due to lack of visitors, and there are reports that the animals do not receive the care they require.

There are plenty of hotels in Misahuallí, but it's much better to stay in Tena as far as choice, quality and things to do are concerned, and though Jatun Sacha biological research station (see p.186) is only across the river from Misahuallí, it is, bizarrely, easier to reach from Tena.

Misahuallí (© 06–)   **Getting There**

Misahuallí is only half an hour from Tena by local bus and all transport from other parts of the country passes through there. Motor canoes leave from Puerto Misahuallí for Coca, five hours downstream on the Río Napo. It costs about $7.50 one way, and is more pleasant and scenic than the bus, although there's little chance of seeing wildlife.

Misahuallí (© 06–)   **Where to Stay and Eating Out**

Misahuallí Jungle Hotel, (arrive, or book in advance through their office in Quito, p.184). Located on an island just across the river from the town. Rooms and food are of variable quality, but the hotel grounds contain some of the best forest in the immediate vicinity of Misahuallí. Don't be fooled by the apparent placidity of the river (*moderate*).

El Albergue Español, Casilla 254, Tena, ©/✆ 584912. Balconied rooms overlooking the Río Napo, with private bathrooms and a restaurant with vegetarian options. Rainforest trips can also be arranged (*inexpensive*).

Tour Operators in Misahuallí   *Misahuallí (© 06–)*

Ecoselva, on the plaza, postal address: Casilla 2–52, Tena. Principal guide Pepe Tapia González speaks English and has a biology background. He is linked to and approved by the Rainforest Roadshow in Britain. Prices from $20–30 per person per day.

Viajes y Aventuras Amazonicas, on the plaza, attached to **Hotel La Posada**, efficiently run by Maria del Carmen Santander. Standard canoe trips along the Napo and rain forest hikes are distinguished mainly by excellent food. Around $50 per person per day.

Lodges on the Río Napo near Misahuallí

La Casa del Suizo (through the Sacha Lodge office in Quito, p.186). A luxury rainforest resort, an hour from Misahuallí. Caged animals shatter any claims they may have to be ecotouristic, and reflect poorly on their owners, Sacha Lodge. The lodge offers soft Amazon immersion, with gentle hikes and canoe trips, and is ideal for families with young children..

Cabañas Aliñahui, (through their office in Quito, p.184). Rustic cabins in a beautiful setting overlooking the Río Napo and Sumaco Volcano. The most ecofriendly operation in the Tena area and a haven for animals, with 531 species of birds and 750 species of butterflies recorded on site. The lodge offers trail walks and trips down the Río Napo in canoe to visit indigenous communities or the AmaZOOnico centre for animal rescue (*see* p.196).

Jatun Sacha Biological Station (through the Fundación Jatun Sacha, *see* p.186). A privately owned 2,000ha research station aimed principally at young interns and students, but open to visitors who wish to explore the forest without guides, along a series of marked trails. The precarious canopy rope-walk (and 30-metre-high bird tower) are not for the faint-hearted. Accommodation and food are very basic. The money generated funds a non-profit organization, working to educate Ecuadorean students about the value of their rainforest.

Yachana Lodge, (through their office in Quito, *see* p.185). A lodge nestling in a surviving tract of primary forest three hours downstream of Mishuallí, offering cultural exchange trips with Quechua Indians, together with the standard package of trail walks and canoe trips. Yachana is run by FUNEDESIN, a non-governmental organization that is attempting to combine income generation for local indigenous people with conservation of the forest. As part of their agricultural project, most of the ingredients of the predominately vegetarian food are grown here. No red meat is served as FUNEDESIN are opposed to cattle-ranching in the Amazon. The highlight of a visit to Yachana is the opportunity to meet a Quechua *pahuya* (medicine man), a central figure within Quechua communities.

Lago Agrio and the Cuyabeno Wildlife Reserve

The forests around Ecuador's northern borders are some of the oldest in the Amazon Basin: part of an area of humid tropical forest that remained unchanged by the last Ice Age and which has perhaps the highest biodiversity in the country. Though parts are protected, at least on paper, by the Cuyabeno Wildlife Reserve, much has been scarred and poisoned by unregulated multinational oil companies and large scale cattle ranching. Millions of plants and animals have been destroyed by gas burning, or poisoned by the run-off from the *piscinas*; large shallow pits, scraped out of the forest by bulldozers and filled with toxic run-off high in heavy metals like cadmium and lead. The indigenous peoples that once thrived here have also suffered. In the 1970s and 1980s, the Cofan, Siona and Secoya were forced to abandon their nomadic lifestyles and settle in marginalized and poverty-stricken communities at the edge of Lago Agrio town. Today both environmentalists and Indians look to ecotourism to protect the forests that remain and Cuyabeno has become a popular destination, with high quality rainforest lodges and adventure and cultural expeditions led by indigenous groups.

Lago Agrio

The principal town of the northern Oriente lies in the midst of devastated forest, twisting pipes and spouting oil wells and offers a graphic illustration of the moral priorities of oil industry employees in the Ecuadorean Amazon. The only reason to come here is to get out fast and head for the Cuyabeno Wildlife Reserve.

Getting There

The airport is a 5km cab or bus ride from the town centre. There are daily flights from Quito. The town is linked by road, best tackled with a 4x4, to Quito, via Baeza. There are no car rental companies in Lago Agrio. There are regular **buses** to Quito (10–12hrs); Coca (3hrs); Baeza (7hrs) and Tena (9hrs).

Tour Operators and Lodges in Cuyabeno Wildlife Reserve

Amazon Jungle Resort Village, Coruña 2623 and González Suarez, Dept 6, PO Box 1707.9107, Quito, *www.ecuadorexplorer.com/selva/index.html.* Three-to six-day luxurious lodge-based tours, with visits to Secoya and Cofan communities, canoe excursions, light trail-walking and fishing.

Metropolitan Touring (through their office in Quito, *see* p.184). A large tour company offering a variety of cruises, lodge-based trips and forest hikes: the Aguarico Trekking trip takes visitors on a week-long expedition through Cuyabeno, accompanied by Cofan guides. Three nights are spent in the Cofan community of Zabalo, a centre of indigenous-driven ecotourism. They also run the **Flotel Orellana**, a Mississippi-style paddle-wheeler that plies the Aguarico and Cuyabeno Rivers. Two- to four-night excursions are offered, with activities including visits to a Cofan community centre, a parrot salt lick, paddle-canoeing, trail-walking by day and night and fishing for and swimming with piranhas. Flotel accommodation and food is very good, and after-dinner talks by naturalists are a nightly feature of every tour. The company run the **Aguarico Lodge,** on the river of the same name, and **Iripari Lodge** (meaning 'yellow parrot' in Cofan) at Lagartococha, which are both comfortable (but less so than the **Flotel**), and built of wood and thatch, with solar-generated electricity, waste treatment and shared toilets and showers. Cofan Indian guides lead hikes into the rainforest, with visits to Imuya Lake, with its floating islands of vegetation, pink dolphins, and catch-and-release fishing. Iripari Lodge has a semi-tame ocelot and a tapir, both allegedly rescued from Coca market.

Tropic Ecological Adventures (through their office in Quito, p.187). Tours with the Cofan people run by their chief Randy Borman. International award-winners for responsible tourism.

Specialist Wildlife and Birding Tours

Neblina Forest (through their office in Quito, *see* p.186). Best birding tours in the country.

Nuevo Mundo (through their office in Quito, *see* p.184). Ecuador's most enlightened ecotourist operator, with a variety of lodge-based, and adventure trips, including four- and five-day trips into Cuyabeno, based at their Cuyabeno River Lodge, offering the standard mix of rainforest walks led by native guides and canoeing, with lectures focusing particularly on the sustainable use of forest resources. Accommodation is in thatched roofed huts with en suite bathrooms. Food is excellent. The nine-day ecofishing excursion offers anglers the chance to catch and identify some of the estimated 800–2,500 species of fish found in the Amazon Basin. Ecofishing involves using barbless hooks to avoid harming the fish, and the participation of a trained ichthyologist to aid in identification. Once caught, the specimens are weighed, measured, photographed and released. With so much uncertainty over the exact number of species in the rivers of Cuyabeno, there's a good chance of discovering a new one.

Canoeing in Cuyabeno

Adventour, (through their office in Quito, *see* p.185). Sea-kayaking on the Cuyabeno lakes.

Magic River Tours, Vilcabamba at 18 de Noviembre, Casilla 17-03-1671, Lago Agrio, ✆ (06) 831003 (or book through EuroVIP's in Quito, p.198). A variety of five- to 14-day trips by motorless canoe. Up to five hours per day are spent paddling, always on lakes or quiet, narrow rivers. Longer trips and upstream voyages are undertaken in a motor canoe, but the emphasis of the tours is on quiet enjoyment of the environment. All tours are led by English- or German-speaking guides and an Indian. These tours also combine opportunities for hiking, demonstrations on the use of medicinal, hallucinogenic and otherwise useful forest plants, piranha fishing, night walks, and visits to Siona and Secoya communities and the Cofan village of Zabalo. Life jackets, rain gear, boots, camping equipment and dry bags are all provided. Expect to pay between $55 per person per day (for the longer trips) to $70 (for the shorter).

Coca and Yasuní National Park

Coca, once known as Puerto Francisco de Orellana, is without doubt the most maligned Amazon town in Ecuador, and not without reason. Its overwhelming raison d'etre is oil, and the substance penetrates every fibre of the town's existence. Rainbow-stained pools gather on the mud streets, and a roaring illegal trade in endangered species is conducted in the town's market. Despite all this, Coca is a tourist town, albeit accidentally. Its squalid quays are the access points for some of Ecuador's finest rainforest lodges, for camping safaris into Huaorani communities, and for the wilds of Yasuní National Park which is gradually being opened up to tourism. Most visitors to Coca book their tour and flight through one of the better lodges or tour companies in Quito, and spend no longer in town than it takes to drive from the airport to a waiting canoe. There are a few accommodation options for the curious and tight-budgeted.

Coca (✆06–)   ***Getting There and Around***

Most lodges on the Napo will arrange flights for visitors and meet them at the airport, before transferring them out of Coca as quickly as possible. In really bad weather planes can't take off or land, leaving people unable to either get in or out. There are daily flights from Quito. There are also regular buses (or local *rancherias*, converted trucks with church pews screwed on the back) several times a day to Quito (12hrs), with either Transportes Baños or Putamayo, Lago Agrio (2hrs), and Tena (7hrs), a miserable journey along a grim road. Launches leave every day from the municpal jetty for Misahualli. There's a ticket office opposite the Emerald Forest office on Calle Napo.

Coca (✆06–)   ***Where to Stay***

The best of a very poor bunch are the **Hostería La Misión**, La Misión, ✆ (02) 553674, ✉ (02) 564675, ✆ (06) 880260/1, Coca's newest, cleanest and smartest hotel (*inexpensive*) and the **Hotel Auca**, Napo, ✆ (06) 880127 which is central and reasonably clean, and fills up before dark. Both have adequate restaurants.

Lodges on the Río Napo near Coca

These are ordered according to their distance from Coca, and only those we feel able to recommend are listed.

Yariña Lodge (through Yuturí Jungle Adventure, Quito, p.185). Only an hour downstream of Coca at a cost of $40 per day per person. Rustic accommodation, bird tower and walks in primary rainforest. Good value.

Sacha Lodge (through Neblina Forest Tours, or Sacha's office in Quito, *see* p.186). Sacha Lodge opened in the early 1990's and was unashamedly modelled on **La Selva** (below). After nearly a decade, it has overtaken its rival and established itself as the country's premier rainforest destination for birders and natural history enthusiasts. It is possible to see as many as 250 species in a week from the 43metre-high observation platform which looks out over the canopy, the mini-platform over the lake, or the extensive system of trails and flooded creeks. A select few include the endangered cocha antshrike and zigzag heron, boat-billed heron, Salvin's currasow, Spix's guan, chestnut-fronted and red-bellied macaw, the regionally endemic orange-crested manakin, and ornate hawk-eagle. A full bird checklist and good reference books (including *The Birds of South America* and *The Birds of Colombia*) are available at the lodge. The main buildings of palm-thatch and wood sit over a still black-water lake surrounded by varzea forest. Baby caiman hunt freely under the elevated walkways and a small birding tower looking out across the lake allows for extra-curricular birding at dusk and dawn.

Morning trail-walks are conducted by both a naturalist and a local guide both of whom are bilingual and knowledgeable about ecosystems, the fauna and flora, and the traditional and medicinal use made of them by local peoples. There's a high chance of seeing Amazon dwarf squirrel, paca, agouti, nine-banded long-nosed armadillo, caiman lizard, night monkey and pygmy marmoset on a morning walk, as all their haunts are well known to guides. Early after-noons are free for birding or swimming with the piranha and turtles in the black water lagoon, and a visit to the on-site butterfly farm follows, together with more trail walks or canoe trips in the early evening. Longer excursions include canoe outings to the northern bank of the Río Napo (which has some species not found around the Sacha Lodge), or to the Yasuní parrot clay lick on the edge of the national park of the same name.

La Selva Jungle Lodge (through Neblina Forest Tours p.186, or La Selva's office in Quito, *see* p.186). La Selva was one of Ecuador's original rainforest lodges, and for years led the way in establishing ecological standards for Amazon tourism. Today it seems to have fallen somewhat from grace. Like Sacha, La Selva's principal buildings, *cabañas*, boardwalks and birding towers are made from natural materials. Only the lounge and dining areas have electricity, but candles are provided in the rooms, which makes La Selva quieter than Sacha (which uses a motor generator), and less intimidating for animals. The buildings and boardwalks may be in a fairly poor state of repair, but the food is unequalled on the Río Napo. A system of trails and creeks run through the surrounding forests, which are particularly rich in bird and insect life, and walks on these, bird-watching from the canopy tower and side trips to parrot licks, oxbow lakes and other parts of the Napo's forests, comprise the bulk of La Selva's menu of standard activi-ties. The bizarre 'Light Brigade' tours are overpriced and disappointingly unadventurous. All the lodge's excursions are conducted by a Quechua guide and an English-speaking naturalist, and a science programme run in conjunction with Harvard provides all-round biological expertise in the form of resident dons and students. The lodge is still wonderful for birding: at least 530 species have been sighted here. The list is phenomenal and includes: (once resident) zigzag heron, orange-crested manakin, long-tailed potoo, 7 tinamous, 19 parrots, 7 jacamars, 11 puff-birds, 7 toucans, over 50 antbirds, 8 cotingas and 34 tanagers. Many of these are admittedly thin on the ground, but birders can still expect as many as 250 species in a week.

Yuturí Lodge (book through Yuturí Jungle Adventure or Neblina Forest Tours, both in Quito, pp.185–6). Accommodation and price closely resemble Pañacocha.

Pañacocha Lodge (book through Emerald Forest Expeditions, Quito, see p.184). Pañacocha itself, the piranha lake, is a grand and almost perfectly circular sheet of dark water, whose shores and surrounds play host to some of Ecuador's most abundant wildlife. It lies an hour's ride up the sublime Río Panayacu. The Pañacocha Lodge is basic, with no electricity or hot water, but the food is exceptionally good and service and environmental sensitivity are of an equally high standard. The main guide, Luís García, is part Cofan Indian, and his enthusiasm for and extraordinary understanding of the rainforest and its people is infectious.

The lodge has a birding tower built around a huge ceiba tree about 50 metres from the dining area. Common sightings finclude blue and yellow and red and green macaw, blue-crowned motmot, white-tailed trogon, purple-throated fruitcrow, black-headed parrot and black-mantle tamarin monkeys. Jaguarundi and night monkey are frequently seen here at dusk or during the night. Hoatzin, American swallow-tailed kite, rufescent tiger heron, white-eared jacamar, pauraque, orange-backed troupial and multitudes of kingfisher, toucan and araçari are regular sights on the Río Panayacu. One of the best lodges in Ecuador. Around $60–70 a day.

Note: Emerald Forest was the only reliable company operating in the Pañacocha area at the time of writing; some operators in Coca have been accused of drunkenness and incompetence.

Yasuní National Park

Yasuní National Park is Ecuador's largest and most controversial protected area, and a repository of such exceptional diversity of species that it has been classified as a UNESCO World Biosphere Reserve. Over a million hectares of low-relief rainforest drained by countless tiny rivers and streams that gently wind their way towards the Río Napo, twisting through swathes of varzea forest and black-water swamps. Significant portions of the park have remained undisturbed by human beings for decades, and sightings of larger mammals and birds are commoner here than in any other part of Ecuador. Capybara, Brazilian tapir, and three-toed sloth are relatively easy to spot on the river banks, red brocket deer roam the humps and hollows of the dry forest, and nowhere in the country is more likely to produce a jaguar sighting. The rivers teem with fresh water dolphin, and several species of caiman.

Yasuní is a huge park, but it only exists on paper. Despite being officially protected by Ecuador's Ministry of the Environment, and internationally recognized for its ecological significance, the park is divided up into 'blocks' for oil extraction. One of these, Block 16, lies in the park's heartland. Environmentalists are worried not only about possible pollution, but feeder roads that could bring waves of settlers into the park, disrupting the ecosystems and the long-suffering Huaorani who live nearby. Such is the concern that UNESCO threatened to review Yasuní's status as a World Biosphere Reserve. Perhaps this shocked the government into action. In 1999 the boundaries of the National Park were redrawn, eliminating some of the areas despoiled by petroleum companies and including a greater area of pristine forest. An accompanying declaration was made, stating that that 40 per cent of the total area of Yasuní National Park, Huaorani Territory and the Cuyabeno Wildlife Reserve to the north will be off limits to any kind of development or tourism in perpetuity. This is, however, a fragile agreement, which may not survive the violent change of government that occurred in early 2000.

Visiting the Huaorani

The Huaorani are among the proudest and most independent of all the Amazon's tribal people, long aware of the presence of foreigners around their territorial lands, and long dismissive of them. They made international headlines in the early 1990s when they tried to prevent international oil companies from drilling within their territory. One of the courageous leaders of their protest movement, Moi Enomenga, was made famous by Joe Kane's book, *Savages*. Moi is now a seasoned campaigner for his tribe's rights and, like many of his fellow Huaorani, has turned to ecotourism to generate awareness of his tribe's cause and traditional culture outside Ecuador, and much-needed income to ensure the protection of tribal lands at home. Visitors to Indian communities are expected to live like Huaorani, which affords a rare insight into their culture.

As well as allowing visitors to share in their songs and customs, their language, face-painting and fire-starting, making nets from stripped and braided reeds, and using blow-guns, visitors witness the damage done to Huaroni lands by oil companies, which guides are only too keen to demonstrate. It also means no toilets, showers or beds, and sleeping in hammocks in thatched huts in the forest. Food is basic; barbecued fish, fruits and game.

Walking with the Huaorani in the forest is an awe-inspiring experience. These are the true professors of the rainforest, with a depth and complexity of knowledge that exceeds even that of the most illustrious western field biologists. The hikes are well-paced and lead through a variety of ecosystems, with plenty of stops to learn about the manifold uses a plant has, or to spot a bird or animal, before reaching a ridge that affords panoramic views out over the mottled and endless green of the Amazon. Guides will take interested visitors to pumping sites where huge flames of gas burn bright, thickening the clean forest air with soot, or to the road to the Río Shiripuno, which illegally bisects their territory and is lined with pools of black sludge dumped by oil men. All tours are accompanied by both a Huaorani and a bilingual guide.

Tour Operators and Lodges in Yasuní

Safari Ecuador and Bolivia Tours (through their office in Quito, *see* p.186). Responsible and well-run tours on the Napo with the Huaorani, with a good chance of spotting many birds and animals.

Kem Pery Tours, (through their office in Quito, *see* p.187). Expeditions into the park with the Huaorani.

Sacha Lodge and La Selva (*see* pp.199 and 186). Visit Anangucocha Lake in the park for specialist birding trips.

Tiputini Biodiversity Station (book through their office in Quito, or Neblina Forest Tours, p.186, or Nuevo Mundo Tours, *see* p.184). This 650ha biological research station on the edge of Yasuní is run by the University of San Francisco in Quito. It lies in an area of forest which has been completely undisturbed for over twenty years and at the time of going to press had the only canopy walkway in Ecuador. If you are serious about wildlife, there is no better place to visit in the country. Birding is wonderful, four species of araçari, golden collared toucanet, Salvin's currasow, blue dacnis, black-tailed trogon and spangled cotinga can all be seen within the vicinity of the lodge, as can herds of collared peccary. This is the only place in Ecuador where you are likely to see a jaguar. The centre is first and foremost a research station and though tourists are allowed to visit they must come in small, carefully screened groups. Accommodation is in huge rooms with desk, fans and candles. There's generator driven electricity for a couple of hours each day. Food is meagre; bring some snacks.

Tropic Ecological Adventures (through their office in Quito, *see* p.198). Five-day/four-night safaris on the Río Shiripuno with the Huaorani Indians, with Moi Enomenga, a seasoned campaigner for his tribe's rights (*see* above), as guide. Tropic won the TODO! 1997 Award for Responsible Tourism for this tour. Huaorani trips can be cancelled due to bad weather.

Vasco Tours (through their office in Baños, *see* p.189). Four-day trips leaving from Coca to Anangucocha Lake on the edge of Yasuní National Park. This includes a visit to an indigenous shaman. There are also five- to ten-day camping trips along the Shiripuno and Cononaco Rivers with the Huaorani.

Brazil and Colombia

The forest is magical in Brazil. The frontiers of the country's wild lands, where the modern world eats into the ancient trees, seem to exist in mythical as well as real time. Here the Universe of Nature still dwarfs tiny man, the battle between Cowboys and Indians is more than a childhood game and older civilizations still struggle to keep their ways of being from drowning in the flood of ongoing conquest. Vast swathes of trees grow, primeval and undisturbed, in areas never paddled through, or trodden, even by an indigenous foot. Aeroplanes pass over villages whose people are unaware of the arrival of Europeans in the Americas. They speak in languages which have no word for nature; for them it is part of the internal as well as the external landscape, and within their forests lurk animals as yet unknown to us. Contacted tribes talk of a black and white cat the size of a tiger, a jaguar with a tail like a beaver that lives by remote oxbow lakes and a shaggy ape-man with a terrible roar who shuns humans.

Tourism is in its infancy in giant Brazil, which has not noticed the progress made by its little neighbours. The entrance points to the Brazilian Amazon are as seedy as the wilderness is sublime: frontier towns and cities that still struggle to assert their identity over the forests that surround them, centuries after they were founded. Indian is a dirty word in Manaus, for example. Almost everyone is trying not to be one. Ecology and conservation are feared and for the most part loathed, for the forest must be tamed for Manaus to feel civilized. Belém has gone further; much of the forest in her environs has been chopped down and the city feels itself to be more modern. Manaus makes a better base for rainforest exploration. The more Indian the town, the more it seems to be harmonious with the Amazon. São Gabriel da Cachoeira comfortably nestles in its hills, and the Ticuna and Tucano Indian villages of the Solimões and Rio Negro, scruffy and poor though they may appear, are reclaiming the culture they have lost over the centuries. Tefé and Santarém are quieter bases from which to plan a trip. The former is a paradise for birders. The latter is close to Óbidos where artefacts dating back 12,500 years have been discovered in forest caves. Parintins is livelier, at least during the Boi Bumba festival in late June, the Amazon equivalent of the Rio carnival.

Brazil	Colombia
Official language: Portuguese, and over 200 indigenous dialects and languages	**Official language**: Spanish, and over 180 indigenous dialects and languages
Capital city: Brasilia	**Capital city**: Bogotá
Amazon gateway city: Manaus (*see* p.206)	**Amazon gateway city**: Leticia (*see* p.218)
Currency: *real* of 10 *centavos*	**Currency**: *peso* of 100 *centavos*
Highlights	
1. The *fazendas* of the Pantanal, and the transpantaneira road and environs at dawn.	3. Relaxing on a river beach in São Gabriel da Cachoeira or Santarém.
2. Staying with the Ticuna or Tucano Indians.	

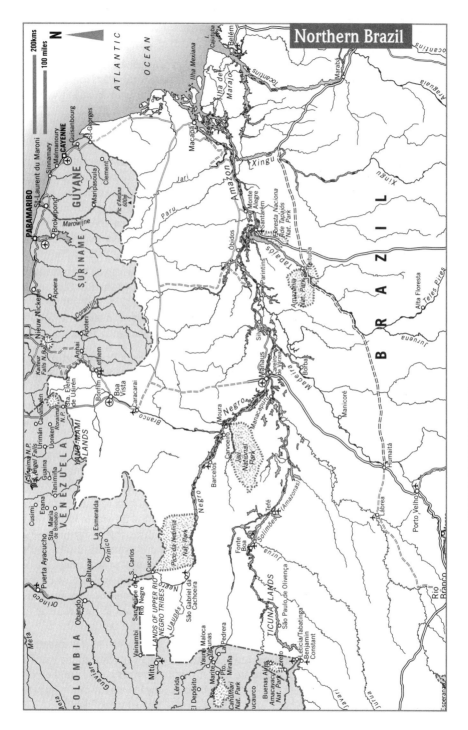

Northern Brazil

205

Note on the Colombian Amazon

Most of the Colombian Amazon is unsafe to visit at present. As those areas which are not dangerous are most easily accessible from Brazil, we have included them in this chapter. Leticia, a Colombian town which is twinned with Tabatinga in Brazil, offers some very good lodge- and tour-based trips along the Rio Javari and in the Amacayacu National Park. These areas are overflowing with rare birds and primates.

Manaus

Despite the tourist office's attempts to reinvent their city as an Amazon paradise, Manaus remains a seedy, down-at-heel river port. Along the bustling waterfront and among the hundreds of river boats docked at the floating harbour, a stock of colourful characters ply their trade: bible-touting evangelists, scantily clad whores, smugglers and street vendors. Up past the ugly concrete blocks and tax-free shops, the neoclassical 19th-century opera house, its mosaic dome the colours of the Brazilian flag, dominates the city like a tropical version of London's St Paul's cathedral.

Manaus is named after a long-extinguished Amazon tribe. Though what you see today is the product of the 19th-century rubber boom, the city was built on the trade in 'Red Gold', as the Portuguese called captured Indians. This practice of theirs is why there are so few tribes living along the margins of the Amazon and Negro Rivers. Manaus remained an official slaving port up to and beyond Independence, and an unofficial one long after the ban in 1888.

Manaus *(© 092–)*   *Getting There and Around*

The **airport** is 14km out of town. Airport departure tax on international flights is about $25. There are connections to Caracas, Georgetown, Bogotá and La Paz. Manaus is well connected to Miami and all of Brazil's major cities through Varig, Av. Santos Dumont, © 0800 99700; Vasp, Av. 7 de Setembro 993, © 621 1258 and with smaller Amazon towns like São Gabriel da Cachoeira via Rico, © 981 1553.

When weather permits, **buses** run from Manaus north to Presidente Figueiredo and Boa Vista, where there are onward connections to Guyana and Venezuela. The *rodoviária* (main bus station) is 7km from the town centre.

There are regular **boats** to destinations all over the Amazon from Manaus. Services are quicker in the wet than the dry. International services run all the way to Iquitos (up to a week), while national services include Porto Velho (4 days), Tefé (3 days), Tabatinga (5 days), São Gabriel da Cachoeira (4 days), Parintins (1 day), Santarém (2 days), Belém (4 days), and Boa Vista (2 days). Bring a hammock and rope (available from Casa des Redes on Rua dos Andrades), some bottled water and supplementary food, insect repellent and a good book. Watch your bags well as theft is common. Details of departures are published in the **Jornal do Comércio** newspaper, or ask at the booths at the entrance to the floating docks or the ENASA office on Marechal Deodoro 61.

Manaus's **local bus** network is extensive and cheap but bewildering if you speak no Portuguese. The **main terminal** is on Marques da Santa Cruz next to the Praça da Matriz, near the cathedral. There are several **shuttle services** a day from the Hotel Tropical which lies on the river beach Praia da Ponta Negra to the city centre, stopping on Doutor Moreira. The hotel (*see* p.210) has details. Staff all speak English.

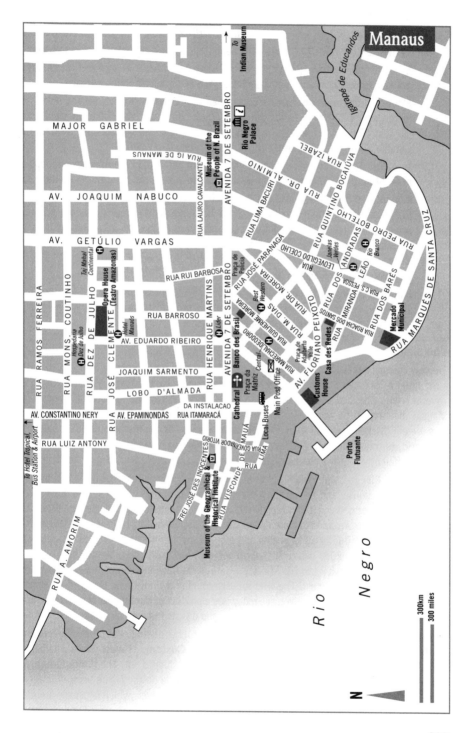

Manaus

MAJOR GABRIEL

AV. JOAQUIM NABUCO

AV. GETÚLIO VARGAS

RUA RAMOS FERREIRA

RUA MONS. COUTINHO

RUA DEZ DE JULHO

RUA RUI BARBOSA

RUA BARROSO

AV. EDUARDO RIBEIRO

JOAQUIM SARMENTO

LOBO D'ALMADA

AV. CONSTANTINO NERY

RUA EPAMINONDAS

RUA ITAMARACÁ

DA INSTALAÇÃO

RUA LUIZ ANTONY

RUA A. AMORIM

To Hotel Tropical,
Bus Station & Airport

RUA IG DE MANAUS

RUA LAURO CAVALCANTE

Museum of the
People of N. Brazil

To
Indian Museum

AVENIDA 7 DE SETEMBRO

Rio Negro
Palace

RUA DR. ALMINO

RUA LIMA BACURI

RUA QUINTINO BOCAIÚVA

RUA IZABEL

RUA PEDRO BOTELHO

RUA MARQUÉS DE SANTA CRUZ

Igarapé de Educandos

RUA JOSÉ PARANAGA

RUA DR MOREIRA

Praça de
Policia

Best
Western

RUA M. DIAS

RUA MARCHAL DEODORO

RUA GUILHERME MOREIRA

LEOVÉGILDO COELHO

ANDRADAS

LEÃO

Janelas
Verdes

Rio
Branco

RUA DOS

RUA MIRANDA

RUA ROACHA DOS SANTOS

RUA C.S. PESSOA

RUA DOS BARÉS

Mercado
Municipal

Praça de
Adalberto
Valle

AV. FLORIANO PEIXOTO

RUA

Casa des Redes

Customs
House

Taj Mahal
Continental

Hospedaria
Dez de Julho

Opera House
(Teatro Amazonas)

Hotel
Manaús

RUA JOSÉ CLEMENTE

RUA HENRIQUE MARTINS

AVENIDA 7 DE SETEMBRO

Banco des Brasil

Líder

Cathedral

Praça da
Matriz

Main Post Office

RUA LIMA

Local Buses

RUA GOVERNADOR VITORIO

RUA VISCONDE DE MAUA

FRE I JOSÉ DES INOCENTES

Museum of the Geographical &
Historical Institute

Porto
Flutuante

Rio Negro

300km
300 miles

N

207

Tourist office: EMAMTUR, Av. 7 de Setembro 1546, © 633 2850. Very inefficient.

Thérèse Aubreton of Alternatur (*see* p.211) has written a helpful and informative **pocket guide** to Manaus, published in English and available from her office.

Money changing: Banco Bradesco and Banco do Brasil, who have several branches in the centre of town, have Visa cashpoints. Banco do Brasil changes traveller's cheques (American Express are best) but better rates can be found at the Casa de Câmbio Cortez, Rua Guilherme Moreira 315 (*open 9–3 weekdays*).

Internet: There's only one public facility in town, way out in the Amazonas shopping mall ('*Amazonas Shopping*' in Portuguese), a ten-minute cab-ride from the centre.

Consulates: France, Av. Joaquim Nabuco 1846, Block A, Sala 02, © 233 6583. Note that visas for Guyana (French Guiana) are best obtained in Brasília or another South American capital city. They take several weeks to come through from Manaus as passports are sent to Brasília. Venezuela, Rua Emilio Moreira, 214, © 233 6004. Visas for Venezuela take two days. USA, Rua Recife 1010, Adrianopolis, © 633 4907, UK and Eire, Av. Eduardo Ribeiro 520, © 622 3879.

National parks of Brazil: IBAMA, Rua Ministro João Gonçalves de Souza, Hwy BR-139, Km 1, Distrito Industrial © 237 3710, can provide information on national parks in Brazil and are responsible for issuing permits.

The Sights

The few colonial streets that spread out from the Teatro Amazonas on Praça São Sebastião are a reminder of Manaus's brief dalliance with wealth and luxury. Eduardo Ribeiro, the state governor who presided over these golden years, was determined to make 19th-century Manaus the envy of the world. He spared no expense: trams were running in Manaus before they were in Manchester or Boston and her streets were lit by the first electric street lights in the world. Extravagance begot extravagance and rubber barons eager to compete in statements of affluent vulgarity gave their horses vintage wine or bought lions as guard cats.

In the 1890s, Ribeiro commissioned Portuguese architect Domenico de Angelis to build an Italianate opera house, and to surround it with a series of stone-cobbled streets filled with elegant houses, plazas, and gardens replete with ornate fountains and gilded cherubs. After the doors to the **Teatro Amazonas** (*open Mon–Sat 9–4.30*) opened in 1896 Caruso sang here, and Pavlova danced. But for all its beauty and cost the theatre was used for little more than a decade. In the early 20th century, the rubber economy collapsed. Seeds smuggled by Englishman Henry Wickham to His Majesty's Gardens at Kew and thence to Malaysia were producing a higher rubber yield. The wild rubber economy dwindled and died and the doors to the Opera House closed. What you see today is the product of careful restoration. There are regular performances, which sell out very quickly, and an arts festival every April.

The city has a few other noteworthy reminders of its rubber-boom heyday. The **Palàcio da Justiça** was reputedly modelled on Versailles, and the **Customs House** (Praça Adalberto Valle) on that in Delhi. It was prefabricated in England and shipped out. The **Punta Flotante**, where the river boats dock in a riot of bawdiness, was made on the Clyde before the First World War. Boats still rise and fall with the annual tide of the river, which is usually around 15m (45ft), but has been as much as 30m (96ft). Tons of exotic fish are carved and chopped up on marble slabs in the **Mercado Municipal** (*open daily 8–6; mornings are the best time*). The building is splendid—a cathedral in wrought iron designed by Eiffel. The beautiful **church of São Sebastião**, on the square near the Opera House, dates from 1888.

Museums: The **Indian Museum** (Museu do Indio), on Duque de Caxias 356 (*open Mon–Fri 8.30–11.30 and 2–4.30, Sat 8.30–11.30*) contains a collection of artefacts and models (mostly from the tribes of the Rio Negro), including the Ticuna, Wai Wai, Tucano and Yanomami. The **Museum of the Geographical and Historical Institute** (Museu do Instituto Geográfico e Histórico do Amazonas), on Bernardo Ramos 117 (*open Mon–Fri 2.30–5*) displays a hodge-podge of fossils, stuffed animals, artefacts and books in Portuguese. At the **Museum of the People of Northern Brazil** (Museu do Homem do Norte), Av. Sete de Setembro 1385 (*open Mon–Fri 9–12 and 1–7*), exhibits are devoted to the history and way of life of the Amazon mixed-race peasants (*caboclos see* p.230).

Beaches: Manaus has two sandy beaches on the outskirts of the city. **Praia da Ponta Negra**, which lies upstream of the city's pollution, is the most popular and the most heavily developed. Buses leave from the local bus terminal on Marquês da Santa Cruz. The beach can also be reached on the Hotel Tropical's shuttle bus, ✆ 658 5000. **Praia Amarelinho** is a little too close to the centre to avoid pollution and is not recommended.

Peripheral attractions: INPA Science Park, Alameda Cosme Ferreira, 1756, Aleixo, ✆ 643 3192, *www.cr-am.rnp.br* (*open Tues–Fri 9–11 and 2–4, Sat and Sun 9–4*) conducts research into all aspects of the Amazon and maintains a small park that's good for a taste of rainforest flora and fauna before you head out to the real thing. The **City Zoo**, Estrada Ponta Negra 750, (*open Tues–Sun 9–5*) is maintained by the army's tropical warfare unit. The animals, which were kept for years in criminally small cages, have finally been moved to a new, larger home. This is still too small as the animals' distressing repetitive behaviour patterns indicate. Take bus nos.120 or 207 (buses are marked for Ponta Negra). The remote and well-maintained little **Museum of Natural History**, Cachoeira Grande suburb (*open Mon–Sat 9–5*), not far from INPA, is one of the city's little-known treasures. The main building houses cases full of hundreds of preserved Amazon insects and butterflies, together with stuffed specimens of a selection of the river's bizarre fish. You can also see live versions, including the enormous, endangered pirarucu, a primitive osteoglottid that breathes air.

The **Mindu Municipal Park,** Rua Perimetral, Parque Dez suburb, ✆/🖨 236 7702, *manaus.pegasus.com.br/mindu/mindu.htm*, (*open Tues–Sun 7.30–5*), is an environmental education centre and 33ha ecological reserve with a system of trails, elevated walkways, a little amphitheatre and orchid gardens. You may glimpse one of the world's rarest monkeys, the pied bare-faced tamarin, a subspecies of bare-faced tamarin thought to live only near Manaus and threatened with extinction. The **Encontro das Águas** (Meeting of the Waters) is an awe-inspiring sight: this is the point where the black coffee waters of the Rio Negro meet and flow side by side with the coffee-with-milk waters of the Solimões, forming the Amazon. To see it, catch a Vila Buriti bus (no.713) to its final stop about 15km from Manaus. From here you can catch a free ferry across the river and back every half hour. Alternatively, if you plan to leave Manaus by river, any downstream boat will take you through it.

Manaus (✆ 092–) **Where to Stay**

Apart from the Tropical, there are no great hotels in Manaus, though there are some luxurious ones and some familiar chains with all mod cons.

Top of the bill is the Varig-owned **Hotel Tropical**, Estrada da Ponta Negra 9015, ✆ 658 5000, ✉ 658 5026, lying outside the city centre on the river beach, Praia da Ponta Negra (*see* p.209). There's a luxurious swimming pool with a wave machine and cocktail bar, a mini-zoo and one of Manaus's finest restaurants (not that there's much competition). The **Novotel**, Av. Mandií 4, ✆ 237 1211, ✉ 237 1094, and **Best Western**, Rua Marcílio Dias, 217, ✆ 622 2844, ✉ 622 2576, provide familiar options, though the former is a long way from the centre. **Taj Mahal Continental**, Av. Getúlio Vargas 741, ✆ 622 1010, ✉ 633 1010, has panoramic views of Manaus and the adjacent Opera House. Its revolving restaurant is surprisingly cheap and has one of the city's best menus. Next to it is a postage-stamp-sized rooftop pool.

The **Hotel Manaos**, Av. Eduardo Ribeiro 881, ✆ 633 5744, ✉ 232 4443 is notable principally for its location, right opposite the Opera House. The **Central**, Doutor Moriera 202, ✆ 622 2600, ✉ 622 2609, with a reasonable restaurant, lives up to its name. The **Líder**, Av. 7 de Setembro 827, ✆ 633 1326, ✉ 633 3393, is more upmarket with clean, modern rooms and a sauna. The tiny **Janelas Verdes**, L. Coelho 216, ✆ 233 9423, is cheaper, more intimate and serves good breakfasts.

Many of Manaus's cheap hotels charge by the hour for some of their clientele. The following are almost the only exceptions: **Hospedaria Dez de Julho**, 10 de Julho 679, ✆ 232 6280, ✉ 232 9416, clean and only a stone's throw away from the Opera House. **Hotel Rio Branco**, Andrades 484, ✆ 233 4019, verges on sleaziness but is nonetheless fairly clean, central and very popular with backpackers.

Manaus (✆ 092–)   **Eating Out**

Away from the more expensive hotels, food in Manaus tends to aim at filling the gap not delighting the palate. Pizzerias, ice-cream parlours and *churrascarias* (for hunks of grilled meat) are easy enough to find. The only **local specialities** are the river fish, which are delicious. Unless your conscience can digest eating an endangered species, avoid pirarucu (*see* p.23). Restaurateurs have been banned from selling it, fishermen have been banned from catching it, but plenty of people here still insist on eating it.

The **Hotel Tropical**, ✆ 658 5000, has the best restaurant in the city with an international menu and local specialities including Amazon river fish. If you're looking for something more central, try the **Taj Mahal's** revolving restaurant, ✆ 622 1010. The **Xalaco**, Av. Pedro Teixeira, ✆ 238 1688, specialises in river fish. **Vegetarians** should head for **O Naturalista**, 7 de Setembro 752, 2nd Floor. Food is varied, wholesome, and good value (*open 12pm–2pm*).

These are Manaus's real delight. They are dotted all over the city centre and serve a bewildering variety of delicious tropical fruit juices. If you're a novice, here are some recommendations: *camu camu* (great for vitamin C); *tapareba* (mild and refreshing); *cupuaçu* (bizarre, pungent and delicious); *cacao* (whose nuts are used to make chocolate); *cajú* (whose nuts are roasted to produce cashews); *graviola* (also known as *guanabana*) and *açerola* (a very refreshing cherry originally from Madeira).

Visiting the Rainforest from Manaus

Very few come to Manaus to see the city, and you are almost certainly going to be more interested in the forest that beckons on every horizon. Be aware, though, that Manaus is not the best place in Brazil from which to visit it. It may be convenient, but you will pay more than you would upstream in Tabatinga or Leticia and the forest you'll visit will be more disturbed. Large animals, especially cats, have long fled despite the tall stories of some guides. Nor will you see any traditional Indian tribes. Despite this, some agencies offer well-organized trips that serve as a good introduction to the forest, and a few that can take you to more remote areas.

Tour Operators in Manaus   *Manaus (℗ 092–)*

Alternatur, Rua Coronel Salgado 63, 69110-450, ℗ 234 5915, ✆ 233 7470. The best mid-price option in Manaus, offering a range of lodge-based tours, river cruises on the Rio Negro, and bespoke canoe expeditions to other destinations. Book a month in advance. Alternatur also offer sports fishing and birding tours (*see* below, p.213). About $100 a day.

Amazon Indian Turismo, Andradades 311, ℗ 633 5578. This agency offers a range of trips from two to ten days, mostly on the black-water Rio Urubu. All the guides are either indigenous people or have grown up in the forest. The jungle lodge the company uses is maintained by Waipixana Indians. Trips tend to be quite rough—you'll be camping in the jungle and sleeping in hammocks. But what they lack in comfort they make up for in adventure and price: $60 to $70 per day all-inclusive. Little English is spoken.

Amazon Nut Safari, Av. Beira Mar 43, Bairro São Raimundo, ℗ 671 3525/5134, ✆ 671 1514, offer some of the best tours available to the Analvilhanas Islands. Tailor-made and fixed itinerary options from around $90 a day. Their nine-room lodge, Apurissawa (*see* p.212), is one of the best ones in the area for seeing wildlife.

Companhia de Aventuras, c/o José Savio or Rosana Rosa Costa, Benjamin Lima 620, Vila Militar, São Jorge (outside the centre), ℗ 625 1592, mobile ℗ 987 3926. Run by a Brazilian army major, this company offers interesting encounter trips with indigenous people near Tabatinga and climbing expeditions to Brazil's highest mountain. They also offer jungle survival training at all levels. Strongly recommended: $150 a day upwards.

Green Planet Tours, in the lobby of the Hotel Aquarius, Guilherme Moreira at Andrades, ℗/✆ 232 1398. A budget travel option that conducts bespoke tours around Manaus. Make sure you know exactly what you are getting before you commit.

Natsafaris, Flávio Espírito Santo NE 1, Kissia II 69040-250, Manaus, ℗ 656 2017/656 5464, *www.naturesafaris.com*. Operate in conjunction with the King Island Lodge in São Gabriel da Cachoeira, one of the finest in the region (*see* p.215). Useful website.

Orquídea Amazônica, José Paranaguá 243, Centro, Manaus. ℗ 234 8149, mobile ℗ 984 0398. Offer a range of one-day tours around Manaus and more interesting, longer two- to five-day river boat tours, using a traditional Amazon two-storey river boat with hammocks. Overnight stays are in the Maloca Jungle Lodge. Tailor-made tours to more remote areas, such as the northeast of Amazonas State including the Hill of Six Lakes on the border of Pico da Neblina National Park. Prices are fixed according to itineraries; around $70–90 a day.

Swallows and Amazons, Quintino Bocaiúva 189, Andar 1, Sala 13, ℗/✆ 622 1246. A foreign-owned river boat and jungle lodge tour company with a high profile and an even higher opinion of themselves. If being treated courteously is important to you, look elsewhere.

River Cruises

River cruises are generally more comfortable and more sedate than rainforest trips, unless you choose to stay at one of the luxury lodges. They include canoe trips along rainforest creeks, and often visit *caboclo* (*see* p.230) villages.

Alternatur (*see* above, p.211)

Amazon Clipper, ✆ 656 1246, ✉ 656 3584. Moderately comfortable cabin-based river cruises on the Rio Negro. Cold-water showers (which is not so bad in the Amazon heat).

Ecotour, ✆ (011) 3063 0856. Offer comfortable cruises on the Amazon on river boats with air-conditioned cabins. Tailor-made itineraries, mostly up the Rio Negro range from one to seven days, with an option for sport-fishing. They take in the usual sights and begin with a city tour.

Lodges near Manaus

There are more than a dozen lodges within a days boat ride from Manaus. Most staff speak English and conditions are fairly comfortable. If you are looking for wild country, avoid any lodges in the January Ecological Park.

Acajatuba Jungle Lodge, bookable through most of the Manaus agencies including Anaconda Turismo, ✆ 233 7642, ✉ 232 9492. A small, rustic lodge in secondary forest four hours from Manaus on the shore of a large black-water lake. Around $90 a day.

Aldeia dos Lagos, Itaparinga road, near Silves, ✆ 622 4289. A small, basic lodge near Silves, 250km from Manaus. Linked to a WWF programme working with local *caboclo* people. Tours from here include canoe trips along creeks in the forest and visits to *caboclo* villages.

Amazonat Resort, Rodovia Am 10, Km 160, Zona Rural, Manaus, ✆/✉ 633 3227, *amazonat@internext.com.br*. This luxurious and beautiful naturist resort in a small private reserve offers a real Adam and Eve experience. Facilities include two pools, a volleyball court, 24km of rainforest trails and they say there aren't too many mosquitoes.

Amazon Lodge, Lago do Juma, São Jorge, Manaus–AM, 69000-000, ✆ 656 3357, ✉ 656 3878. 80km from Manaus, with wheelchair access, shop, restaurant, kayak and dive equipment rental and a swimming pool. Rooms have en-suite kitchens and bathrooms and are fan-cooled. One of the more ecologically committed lodges. Around $100 a day.

Amazon Swiss Lodge, ✆ 233 1764, ✉ 633 2322. Two to three hours by road and a 30-minute boat ride from Manaus on the Rio Urubu. The location is not visited by many Manaus operators, making it fairly good for wildlife. Camping out in the forest can be arranged.

Amazon Village, bookable through Gran Amazon Turismo, ✆ 633 1444, ✉ 633 3217. A medium-sized lodge in not-so-wild secondary forest close to Manaus. Comfortable cabins, good facililities, overlooking a black-water lake on the Rio Negro. Around $120 per day.

Analvilhanas Creek Lodge, through SAF Participaçoes e Turismo, ✆ 233 6168, ✉ 234 2947. Luxurious 35-bungalow lodge on a creek off the Rio Urubu near Silves. Air-conditioned rooms have roof patios with forest views, mobile phones, mini-bars and en-suite bathrooms. There's a pool and a good restaurant. Book well in advance. Around $220 a day.

Apurissawa Jungle Lodge, book through Amazon Nut Safari (*see* p.211). Small lodge in the Analvilhanas archipelago. When the forest floods the lodge is surrounded on all sides by water and river dolphins can be heard surfacing near the rooms. One of the better lodges in the area.

Ariaú Jungle Towers, through most of Manaus's travel agencies or Rio Amazonas Turismo, Hotel Mónaco, Silva Samos 41, ✆ 234 7308, ✉ 233 5615. More an overpriced jungle theme park than a jungle lodge: an enormous complex in the Analvilhanas Islands that includes a business centre, heli-pad and a glass pyramid to bring in the wealthy New Age crowd. Not great for the serious wildlife enthusiast, nor conservationists, but fabulous for kids. Around $200 a day.

Boa Vida Jungle Resort, Rio Ituxi 68, Vieiralves–69.053-530 Manaus, ✆ 633 2501, @ 232 2482. A luxurious resort an hour's drive from Manaus with a small birding tower. A soft rainforest option but good for those with little time who crave comfort. Around $200 per day.

Malocas Jungle Lodge, through Orquídea Amazônica (*see* p.211). Further from Manaus than most lodges, which means there's a greater chance of seeing wildlife. The lodge consists of four *malocas* (Indian longhouses); one is made in the traditional Indian style with space for 30 hammocks, another has 12 rooms with private bathrooms. There's no electricity (a bonus if you want to see animals), and the water comes from an artesian well. Around $80 a day.

Birding

Birding-Brasil, Rua das Samaúmas 214, Conj Aquariquara-Aleixo suburb, ✆ 644 3792, @ 644 3792. An English-run company that offer tailor-made birding trips all over the country. Service and guides are excellent. Prices are high: about $100 upwards a day. Book in advance.

Alternatur (*see* above, p.211) also offer birding trips and require advance notice.

Sports Fishing

The Rio Negro and the lakes that lie close to it are one of South America's best spots for fishing **peacock bass.** Unfortunately many Manaus agencies do not practise catch-and-release fishing, and others, particularly large, foreign-owned enterprises, show wanton disregard for the interests of local people. The only agency we can recommend is **Alternatur** (*see* p.211 for contact details). Fishing takes place on the Upper Rio Negro around Barcelos and above.

A Typical One-day and Three-day Itinerary

One day won't take you anywhere near the genuine wild and is probably not worth the $50–100 expense unless you really are pressed for time. You'll visit the **Meeting of the Waters** (*see* p.209) and the **January Ecological Park**, a disappointing 9,000ha reserve that is geared up to receive large numbers of tourists. Longer tours head up to one of the lodges in the **Analvilhanas of the Rio Negro**, a beautiful archipelago of forested river islands and *igarapés* (creeks) that begin some 90km upstream of Manaus. Few head down the Rio Solimões as there are more biting insects. But the Rio Negro is a black-water river, which means that it is surrounded by relatively infertile soil, and as a result has a diminished diversity of plants and animals. A standard trip to the Analvilhanas will run more or less as follows:

Day one: An early morning departure will take you up the Rio Negro to one of the lodges. In the afternoon, visit a *caboclo* (peasant) community and learn how they grow manioc, fish and survive the annual rise and fall of the Rio Negro. After this, fish for piranhas. Supper will be followed by a canoe trip to look for caiman with a halogen lamp.

Day Two: A guide will take you for a forest walk explaining the various plants (and perhaps animals) along the path, including their traditional medicinal uses. In the afternoon, explore *igarapés* and if the river is high, *igapós* (flooded forests) where the chances of seeing animals is highest. Supper is followed by more caiman-spotting or spear-fishing.

Day Three: After breakfast, you'll walk through a different forest ecosystem, perhaps visiting an oxbow lake, before returning to Manaus after lunch.

Presidente Figueiredo

This small rainforest resort around 200km from Manaus on BR174 is a popular getaway for the Manaus middle-class. Few foreigners ever visit and little English is spoken. Though crowded at weekends, in the week it can be pretty quiet. The main attractions are the beautiful waterfalls, natural swimming-pools and undergound rivers and caves, all of which can be visited with a guide. Some are a few hours from the resort, and offer the best chance of seeing animals.

Presidente Figueiredo (☎ 092–)   ***Where to Stay and Eating Out***
Maroaga, Rio Uatumã, 1927, ☎ 324 1176, ✉ 324 1110, offers a bar and sauna (*expensive–moderate*). **Iracema Falls**, BR 174, ☎ 324 5500, has cold-water showers and TVs (*moderate*). **Pousada da Jibóia**, Rio Copaíba 69, ☎ 324 1228, has shared bathrooms (*inexpensive*). All three have air-conditioned rooms.

Parintins and the Boi Bumba Festival

Our God, Tupa, ordered the forest people to come together around a big fire and bring their bows and their arrows because today would be the beginning of the festival. We are showing the world the festival of a people who bring the symbol of a bull with a heart on his brow. Beat the drums so the bull arrives soon bringing magic and splendour, beat them so the crowd reverberates and smiles and sings.

Mailzon Mendes, *Festa de Um Povo*, music for the Boi Bumba festival

There's only one reason and one time to come to the little town of Parintins halfway between Manaus and Santarém: for Boi Bumba—northern Brazil's biggest festival, held on the weekend before June 24. This is a spectacle that rivals 'carnaval' in Bahia or Rio and, like them, it is an explosion of jubilation from the poor of mixed-race Brazil. Two competing schools of men and women, wearing either Indian body paint and little else, or elaborate Indian costumes of feathers and skins, gyrate to pounding rhythms as they parade through the giant bull-shaped Bumbódromo stadium, cheered by 40,000 frenetically dancing spectators. They are judged winners according to their dance and music which recounts the triumphant victory of a caboclo slave and his beautiful wife Catirina over their cruel and greedy landowner.

Catirina and the Ox

Catirina was the archetypal Brazilian woman, a sensual mixture of Amazon Indian, African and Portuguese. Her husband, Francisco, was devoted to her and would do anything to please her. When she became pregnant with their first child, she developed an irresistible craving for ox tongue and begged her husband to sacrifice his master's finest bull (*boi*). Francisco was terrified, knowing it would mean certain death for both of them, but did as she asked and Catirina had her treat. The landowner soon discovered that his prize bull was missing and swore that the lovers would die at the hands of his Indian slaves. Francisco, desperate, called on the help of a Catholic priest and an Indian shaman, who worked together through the night and managed to persuade God to resurrect the bull. When the landlord came to exact his revenge, he could do nothing. The *caboclos* had triumphed.

The bad news is that you may as well forget about formal accommodation during Boi Bumba. Hotels are booked up six months in advance. The good news is that myriad boats descend on the city for the festival, and you can sling up a hammock and sleep on board for the duration. Ask around the agencies in Manaus and Santarém. If you want to try a hotel against the odds, the best are the **Uyrapuru**, ✆ 533 1834 and the **Ilha Bela**, ✆ 533 2737. Both are *inexpensive*, with air conditioning and TVs.

Up the Rio Negro

Nestling next to a set of swirling black-water rapids that form a small waterfall in the dry season and surrounded by the forest-veiled dark sandstone hills of the Guiana Shield, **São Gabriel da Cachoeira** is one of the Brazilian Amazon's most picturesque little towns. There's a strong Indian presence here—the tribes of the upper Rio Negro have long used the town as a base to defend their lands from goldminers and road builders. The broad white sand beaches, slow pace and enchanting surroundings ensure that life is sweeter, safer and more relaxed here than in Manaus. The town is an ideal base for exploring seldom visited regions of the Rio Negro forest, including indigenous lands that have recently been opened to tourists by the tribes themselves. And there's a wonderful back-door route to Venezuela just to the north.

São Gabriel da Cachoeira (✆ 092–)   ***Getting There***

Rico (✆ 652 1553) **fly** between Manaus and São Gabriel, via Barcelos and Santa Isabel do Rio Negro three times a week. There are irregularly timetabled **boats** (weekly departures) between Manaus and São Gabriel, via Barcelos, taking about five days upstream and three down. To visit Morro dos Seis Lagos, catch the Cucuy bus from outside the Uaupés Hostel in São Gabriel and ask the driver to drop you at Ia'Mirim.

São Gabriel da Cachoeira (✆ 092–)   ***Where to Stay and Eating Out***

São Gabriel's best hotel, the **King Island Lodge**, ✆ 471215, *natsafari@man. sol.com.br,* on an island downstream of the rapids, is also one of the most tranquil, delightful jungle lodges in the Amazon Basin. The views are unforgettable. The bedrooms look out over private white sand beaches, across the black waters of the Rio Negro to the forest and the plunging crags of the Bela Dormecida mountain. Breakfast is included in the cost of the room, and excursions along the Rio Negro, to indigenous communities or to the Pedra do Cucuy, can be organized. Guided trips for birders are available with advance warning. *The Birds of Venezuela* is in their library.

There are two or three indistinguishable cheapies along the waterfront downstream of the rapids, the best of which is the **Uaupés**. Apart from the **King Island Lodge**, food is restricted to the handful of cheap eateries on the waterfront.

Morro dos Seis Lagos (Hill of the Six Lakes)

Legend has it that a dragon inhabits one of the six coloured lakes that pockmark this rocky hill that rises from the forest some 100km north of São Gabriel. One very dry year, so locals say, three soldiers undergoing jungle training found a cave in the bottom of the lake, with huge reptilian footprints pressed into the soft mud. They heard a rumble from the darkness and ran for their lives. With a little daring and plenty of packet food, you can sleep out next to the lake of the dragon and, if you live to tell the tale, be rewarded with spectacular views from the top of the hill over turquoise lakes and a sea of forest that stretches unbroken for thousands of miles. Few people other than local Tucano Indians and occasional army trainees ever venture here, and the surrounding forest is pristine and home to many rare animals and birds including jaguar, tapir, ocelot and king vultures. The journey begins at the Tucano village of **Ia'Mirim**, a two-hour bus ride from São Gabriel along the road to Cucuy. Guides can be organized here through the *caçique* (community leader) or the local school teacher, Professor José. After an overnight stay in the village *maloca*, sleep is broken by an early canoe ride through a sandy *igarapé* (creek) full of electric blue morpho butterflies, tiny manakins and diurnal bats. After a couple of hours you reach the hill and begin the tough scramble up. A gap in the trees gives tantalizing glimpses of the views to come; finally, a break in the path looks out over the first lake, a turquoise sink-hole in the rock several hundred metres below, surrounded by thick forest that stretches blue-green to the horizon. Camp and a swim are at the Lake of the Dragon, an hour further on. Ia'Mirim has no facilities and locals speak only Portuguese. The only drinking water available is rainwater collected off the roofs as the lake water is unsafe to drink and you must bring all your own food for your stay here, and additional food for you and two guides in the forest. Packet food and fruit are available in São Gabriel.

Cucuy

Cucuy is a tiny frontier town overlooked by the **Pedra da Cucuy**, a 400m hulk of dark brown, sprinkled with lush green and surrounded by a sea of unbroken forest. The Rio Negro is only about a kilometre wide here, and is as still as the surface of a mirror. Cashew and cupuaçu trees grow on the banks and the main street is lined with little houses whose gardens are filled with luxuriant bougainvillaea.

Getting There and to Venezuela and Colombia

Buses for Cucuy leave from São Gabriel twice a week from outside the Uaupés Hotel. **Launches** can be hired in Cucuy for about $120, for the three- to four-hour journey to San Carlos de Rio Negro in Venezuela or San Felipe on the opposite bank, in Colombia. From San Carlos there are twice-weekly **flights** to Puerto Ayacucho (*see* p.250). San Felipe has flights every two weeks to Iniridia and from there are regular flights to Bogotá. An exit stamp must be obtained from the Policia Federal (on the main street near the Hotel Uaupés) in São Gabriel—there are no offices.

Lodges in Cucuy

If you want to stay around for a while, and see the forest, you will be better off at **El Kiosko**, ✆ (0856) 62032/3, or ✆ (092) 471 1245, a beautifully situated, comfortable and welcoming jungle lodge on the Colombian side of the Rio Negro at Cucuy, offering interesting forest tours well off the beaten track at a very reasonable $45 including all food and accommodation. Book through the owner, Mattias Vasques Gonzales (the Colombian consul) at the Colombian consulate, opposite FOIRN and next to IBAMA in São Gabriel. He is a very friendly character full of fascinating information on the area, its tribes and its history. A typical El Kiosko itinerary would include canoe trips along the creeks, rainforest walks to the Pedra de Cucuy or along an old rubber-tappers trail, and a journey upstream to the meeting of the Negro and Orinoco Rivers at La Casiquiare. The lodge also offers 15-day safari tours in the Colombian Amazon and visits to Colombian Aruak and Kuripako indigenous communities.

Birding around São Gabriel da Cachoeira and Cucuy

São Gabriel, the Rio Tiquié, Picos da Neblina National Park and Cucuy are a pioneer's paradise, little explored by professional or amateur birders. There are certain to be many new species here. Aside from those listed below under Pico da Neblina, specialities include tawny-tufted toucanet, grey-legged and barred tinamous, cherrie's antwren, scaled flower piercer, chestnut-crested and grey-bellied antbirds and Pelzeln's tody-tyrant. Wire-tailed and blue crowned manakin, yellow-hooded blackbirds, blue-backed tanagers, rufous breasted wren, black nunbird, long-tailed sylphs and scissor-tailed hummingbird have been seen around the Ilha dos Reis (King's Island) alone. The Tiquié boasts rarities like yellow-knobbed and lesser razor-billed currasow, citron-throated toucans and harpy and ornate eagles.

Pico da Neblina National Park

IBAMA (Av. 7 de Setembro s/n), in São Gabriel or Companhia de Aventuras in Manaus (*see* p.211) can organize expeditions to the remote forests and mountains of the Pico da Neblina National Park bordering Venezuela. The park is Brazil's second largest, and the third largest in Latin America, consisting of a range of little explored ecosystems from Rio Negro savannahs to lowland rainforest, montane and cloud forests through to the bare rocks at the top of **Pico da Neblina** (3,014m) and **Pico 31 de Março** (2,992m), Brazil's two highest mountains. There is a greater diversity of flora and fauna here than in any other part of Brazil and it may possibly rival even Manu and Tambopata in Peru. Among them are rare mammals like the black-faced uacari, the bush dog, and plentiful jungle cats including jaguar and tapir. Rare birds include the endangered ornate and black hawk eagles, Guianan cock-of-the-rock, and black currasow. Access is difficult and the going is tough, involving extensive canoeing and walking over a ten-day to two-week period, and there are lots of snakes.

Staying with the Tribes of the Upper Uaupés and Tiquié Rivers

Equally as rewarding and as arduous is a stay in one of the indigenous communities along the Upper Uaupés and Tiquié Rivers and tributaries of the Rio Negro that flow from the highlands of the Colombian Amazon. Anyone wanting to get genuinely close to the reality of modern tribal life will find this experience unforgettable—as long as they speak Portuguese or Spanish. The best part of the stay is hearing stories from members of the community and learning about their lives. Guests share the same space in a simple adobe hut with an Indian, usually Tucano, family, sleeping in hammocks and eating with the whole community every morning in the *maloca* longhouse. Afterwards you'll be encouraged to take part in the chores of daily life—grinding manioc into flour, fishing, or, as the Indians are far too polite to insist you help, you can explore the forest with them on foot or by canoe.

The Rio Negro forests are very different from their counterparts around the Amazon proper. From the river they look similar—a network of rivers and *igarapés* (creeks) with lush trees hanging low over the water. But on foot the difference soon becomes plain. The thick muddy earth of the Amazon forest floor is nowhere to be seen; instead there is an intricate filigree of tiny rootlets, soaking up all detritus like a giant loofah and rendering the path springy underfoot. A space where the forest has been cleared to leave only scrub and silt confirms that the Rio Negro forests maintain a giant but fragile interdependence, and are perhaps all that prevents northern Brazil from becoming a vast desert. Botanical studies have shown that the symbiotic fungi and bacteria that live in the rootlets never return once they have been destroyed.

In the evening the Indians will tell you about the forest and their daily life. Amazon Indians were famous among the conquistadors for their oratory and their descendants are still wonderful story tellers. Life in an Indian community, thousands of miles from the polluted city, may seem paradise, but remember there are no soft beds, warm showers or lavatories, and when life is communal there is little privacy. The biggest problem for many visitors is the food. Indians eat highly spiced boiled fish once a day, for breakfast, washed down with warm, fermented, manioc goo. The easy answer for outsiders is to bring packet food from São Gabriel and then to take all of the plastic packaging away with them (*see* also p.23). Any visits to the tribes of the Upper Negro should be booked through **FOIRN**, Av. 7 de Setembro s/n, opposite IBAMA in São Gabriel da Cachoeira. Contact Estevão Lemos Barreto, ✆/✉ 471 1349.

West of Manaus along the Amazon

Tefé is the biggest town between Manaus and Leticia but it barely qualifies as a village by US or European standards. The area near it is wilder than the forests near Manaus, making Tefé an attractive alternative as a base for exploration. Infrastructure is little developed here. There's a pleasant river beach, and a small Franciscan convent where nuns sell handicrafts, but the real attraction is the **Mamirauá Sustainable Development Reserve**, (Caixa Postal 38, 69470-000, Tefé, AM, Brazil) *www.cnpq.br/mamiraua/mamiraua.htm*, set up with British support, to protect huge areas of varzea forest at the confluence of the Solimões and Japurá Rivers, near Tefé. With a total area of 1,124,000ha, up to 80km of forest can be submerged between these two important Amazonian rivers in the wet season. Thousands of water birds and black caiman gather here. Tefé has a handful of inexpensive hotels, all of which are fairly basic. The **Anicelis,** on Santa Teresa, is air-conditioned. Boats and planes (Varig) stop here regularly on their way to or from Manaus or Tabatinga/Leticia.

Tabatinga and Leticia

Tabatinga in Brazil and Leticia in Colombia, which have merged together to become one town, are two of the best places from which to explore the rainforest. You are in the very heart of what remains of the core Amazon here—a sea of unbroken green stretches for thousands of miles. The Amazon, known in these parts as the Solimões, takes some 20 minutes to cross in a speedboat, yet it is 3,200km from its source. Ticuna Indian villages, and the Eden of undisturbed rivers and forests that surround them, lie close by, as does the Rio Javari, whose fertile environs are full of oxbow lakes, *igapós* (flooded forest) and *igarapés* (creeks) that are home to rare birds and animals in high concentrations. The towns themselves are less inspiring, but the locals are friendly and laid back, and life is more relaxing here than in Manaus or Iquitos. Tabatinga is a typical frontier affair, with barking dogs, black vultures and the constant buzz of teenagers on mopeds, mostly displaying to each other in a fossil-fuelled courtship dance along the same stretch of red-dirt road. Leticia is more salubrious. Most of the streets are paved, there are a few comfortable hotels and even a shady plaza that erupts with a riotously irreverent parakeet chorus at evensong. It's hot—the towns lie very close to the equator and the afternoon sun hits you like a hammer. Don't let this put you off a jungle trip though—the forest is a cool and wonderfully relaxing wild garden full of brightly coloured flowers.

Hitoma Safeama, ✆ (098) 527019, a Huitoto Indian shaman, at communidad Km 7 beyond the airport in Leticia, conducts Ayahuasca ceremonies and teaches tourists about medicinal plants. You can stay in the village for about US$10 a day. Bring a hammock, hammock mosquito net (available on the wharf in Tabatinga), bottled water and T-shirts, notebooks or pens for the children. All money generated goes towards rebuilding the community's *maloca*.

Tabatinga (© 092–) and Leticia (©098–)   *Getting There and Around*

There are no **roads** connecting Tabatinga to the rest of Brazil, or Leticia to Colombia. Tabatinga and Leticia are connected by boat to Manaus, downstream, and Iquitos in Peru upstream. Most **boats** dock in Tabatinga. Boats to Iquitos leave three times a week and take about eight hours. Tickets are sold at the Loreto ticket booth on Rua Marechal Mallet. Manaus river boats are currently scheduled to leave on Tuesdays, Wednesdays and Thursdays, but timetables are unreliable. The journey takes three to five days. Bring a hammock (available on the wharf in Tabatinga), bottled water, snacks, a thick book and insect repellent. Tickets are available at the dock.

There are daily **flights** to Bogotá from Leticia with either Satena (office in airport terminal). Avianca (Carrera 11 at Calle 8) or Aerorepública (office in airport terminal). Tickets are also on sale at the various travel agencies in the centre of Leticia. Expect to pay around $70. Varig connects Tabatinga to Manaus via Tefé three times a week. The Varig office is on Av. da Amizade at Av. Internacional. Tickets to Manaus are around $100. Expect to be very thoroughly searched when leaving Tabatinga.

Cheap VW **shuttle buses** ply between the two towns every few minutes. In Tabatinga you can catch them on Av. da Amizade; in Leticia, at the corner of Calle 8 and Carrera 10. They run until the early evening, after which you can hail a **taxi**.

Red tape and visas: When you arrive in Tabatinga, you'll be expected to find Brazilian immigration at the Polícia Federal (*open 9–1pm*), next to the post office at the far, Brazilian, end of Av. da Amizade. Although no one will hassle you in ultra-laid-back Tabatinga or Leticia, if you don't get the appropriate stamp it will cause you considerable problems further into Brazil. You don't need a Colombian entry stamp to visit Leticia. If you want to move on to Bogotá, then head for the Colombian consulate on Av. da Amizade in Tabatinga, or Colombian immigration (DAS) on Calle 9 between Carrera 8 and 9. There's a Peruvian consulate on Carrera 10.

Tourist Information and Useful Addresses

There's **no official tourist office** in Tabatinga, though there are plans to open one. If you need advice, helpful Joaquím at the town hall speaks excellent English. Leticia's **tourist office** is on Carrera 11 between Av. Victoria Regia and Calle 12. They are very helpful, and speak some English.

The **Amacayacu National Park Office**, Carrera 11, 12–45, ©/✉ (098) 592 7124, where you can buy permits to visit the park for about US$5, lies a few doors upstream.

Changing money: The Banco do Brasil in Tabatinga has a Visa cashpoint and will change traveller's cheques at poor rates. There's an exchange counter on the corner of Calle 8 and Carrera 11 in Leticia that will exchange reals or US$ for pesos. The Banco Ganadero on Carrera 11 has a Visa cashpoint.

Internet: Infocentre, Av. Amizade 1581, Tabatinga © 412 2851.

FIUPAM: Duarte Coelho 10, Porto Bras, Tabatinga © 412 2949. Information on indigenous rights on the Amazon (*see* foreword, p.1).

Leticia is a cleaner, larger town and has a greater choice of hotels and restaurants. None is anything special.

The **Anaconda**, Carrera 11 between Calles 7 and 8, ℗ 592 7119, ✆ 592 7005, is the plushest and priciest hotel in Leticia, with air conditioning, a pool and a reasonable restaurant. The **Amazons Hotel**, Calle 8 #10–32, ℗ 592 8026, and the **Parador Ticuna**, Carrera 11, #6–11 provide cheaper alternatives with air-conditioned double rooms, fridges and TVs. The Amazons has a pool. The best of the cheapies are the **Amazonas Hostal**, Carrera 6 # 11–84, ℗ 592 7069, the best value place in Leticia with a travel agency in the lobby offering very ordinary tours. The friendly **Marina**, Carrera 9 #9–29, ℗ 592 7121, is frayed at the edges but has poky but clean rooms.

Untidy Tabatinga does have one nice, kitsch little hotel with very friendly and welcoming staff: the **Pousada do Sol**, General Sampaio, ℗ 412 3355, with a sauna and a pool. There are a couple of fish restaurants nearby.

Tour Operators in Leticia and Tabatinga *Tabatinga (℗ 092–) and Leticia (℗098–)*

There are two types of agency in Tabatinga and Leticia. Most offer fairly touristy and expensive trips to the Isla de los Micos, Puerto Nariño and Amacayacu National Park; these are not bad if you want a light introduction to the region with minimum inconvenience, though you can visit Amacayacu and Puerto Nariño with more freedom and for a cheaper price if you travel independently (*see* below, p.221). Most agencies are connected with one of Leticia's hotels and have an office in the lobby. The more adventurous agencies and independent guides offer lodge-based tours and forest expeditions into remoter regions of Amacayacu and the Rio Javari (Yavary in Spanish). No specialist natural history or birding guides are available.

Amazon Jungle Trips, Av. Internacional #6–25, PO Box 199, Leticia, ℗ 592 7377. The best option (and the best-value option) in Leticia, offering a variety of adventure, bespoke and lodge-based tours. Antonio Cruz speaks excellent English. João, one of his guides, has incredibly sharp ears and eyes, and a deep knowledge of the forest. He speaks Spanish and Portuguese.

Anaconda Tours, Hotel Anaconda, Leticia, ℗ 592 7119, ✆ 592 7005. Offers standard tours to Amacayacu, Isla de los Micos and Sacambu Lodge at a high price. English spoken.

Elvis Cuevas, Av. Internacional, #6–06 at Calle 7, Leticia ℗ 592 7780. An independent guide with well-organized bespoke trips to Amacayacu and indigenous communities nearby.

Traveller's Jungle Home, 86 Rua Marechal Rondon, Tabatinga. Forest trips at budget-travel prices taken by Tony Mowgli and his French wife. English and French spoken.

OIATTUR, Ticuna Indian agency offering trips into their tribal lands in Brazil (*see* p.221).

Isla de los Micos (Monkey Island)

This tiny island 40km upstream from Leticia, which is featured on most tour trips, supports a surprising number of rare birds and primates. Together with several thousand non-indigenous yellow-footed monkeys, introduced by an American entrepreneur hoping to make money selling them to labs, there are five species of macaw, five nightjars, undulated tinamou and hoatzin. There's a network of trails and a pricey but comfortable lodge on the island, which was closed at the time of writing. Check for details with the Leticia tourist office.

The 3,000 square kilometre Amacayacu National Park is the best place in the region to get a taste of the rainforest if you want to **travel independently** or cheaply. You can get here without using a travel agency and stay at the **Matamata Hostel** in dormitory accommodation for around $30, including food and park guides. In the wet season, many trails are flooded but the park guards can arrange canoe trips through the flooded forest. The park is a great place for birders, with nearly a third of Brazil's species represented including zigzag heron, orange-breasted falcon, crested eagle, and nocturnal curassow. If you want to stay close to the park but crave a slightly more comfortable room head for **Puerto Nariño**, a small, principally Ticuna Indian, town that lies a further 15km upstream. The simple family-run **Brisas del Amazonas** has cheap rooms and a small restaurant, and can organize tours in Amacayacu and to the Tarapoto oxbow lakes. This is a good place to see giant water lilies and river dolphins.

Staying with Ticuna Indians

The Ticuna were one of the first Amazon Basin tribes to have the misfortune of meeting a white man. When Francisco de Orellana made his river odyssey down the Napo in 1541, the first Indians he encountered were a group of Iramarai, probably Ticunas. Orellana placated the suspicious chief with gifts of Spanish clothing. The Indians in turn fed the expedition for a month and were rewarded by a trick ceremony in which they formally annexed their lands to Spain. Today the Ticuna are thoroughly accustomed to their conquerors. Things have got better for them since Fernando Enrique Cardoso demarcated their tribal lands in the 1990s, affording the tribe long-needed legal protection, but now the Ticuna are eager for greater control of their financial affairs and cultural image in Brazil and abroad. In 1999 they decided to open some of their vast lands that stretch downstream from Tabatinga to Tefé and set up their own agency to coordinate trips. It would take a lifetime to explore all the wonders that lie here—there are areas where even the Ticuna seldom if ever go—but just a taste will be enough to cast its spell over you. The Rio Tacaná that links the village of Belém do Solimões with Tabatinga, for instance, is an Eden of heavily scented forest flowers and orchids, huge cecropia trees and buriti palms hiding tiny Ticuna villages. Red and grey river dolphins cavort around the canoes, and parrots, macaws and egrets fill the trees that hang down into the black waters. In the dry, the white beaches are piled with basking black and spectacled caiman.

The Tacaná is only one of hundreds of rivers in the Ticuna lands. Near São Paulo da Olivença, the site of a cruel massacre by the Spanish in 1701, there is a network of oxbow lakes and *igarapés*, the furthest of which are said to be the home of an animal as yet unknown to the white man. The onça de agua is a fearsome black cat with a broad paddle-like tail and webbed feet, a little smaller than a jaguar, which spends most of its time in water. Other real or perhaps mythical beasts live deeper in the Ticuna forests. The yawaruna is another cat the size of a tiger with a huge black head and a white splash under its chin. The mapinguari is a shaggy man-ape with a terrible roar that attacks humans unprovoked.

OIATTUR, Manuel Lizardo (president), Duarte Coelho 10, Porto Bras, Tabatinga, ☎ 412 2949, run by Ticuna Indians, are the only authority that can give you permission to visit Ticuna lands in Brazil. Whatever anyone says to the contrary, any attempts to go independently will result in quick, summary ejection. It is best to visit OIATTUR a few days before you plan to visit. Staying with the Ticuna is very good value—expect to pay less than $30 a day all-inclusive. Tourism is very new to the Ticuna; life progresses slowly and things take a long time

How You Can Help to Preserve Ticuna Culture

OIATTUR are eager to use the money generated by ecotourism to preserve and revive Ticuna culture. At the moment families live in separate houses in most villages, wear western clothes and no longer practice traditional customs. The *caciques* (community leaders) hope this will change if tourists show an interest in Ticuna culture and beliefs. So, if you feel you wish to, you can play an active role in reviving a small part of one of the world's threatened cultures. You can also help preserve the wildlife treasures that lie in Ticuna lands. Unscrupulous Brazilians have at times approached Indians for jaguar pelts and other animal skins. Tourists who will pay money to see a big cat alive have already helped to change attitudes all over the Amazon, and there is no reason why this should not happen here. A visit to the Ticuna Museum in Benjamin Constant (*see* below) will give you some idea of Ticuna culture and how it has changed since the arrival of the conquistadors.

to get done. Accommodation is hammock-based and very simple. There is no bottled water, so bring a water filter if you can. If you're a vegetarian you will have to live off manioc flour and occasional fruit unless you bring extra provisions from the small supermarkets in Tabatinga or Leticia. Only Portuguese, Ticuna and a little Spanish are spoken.

Benjamin Constant

Away from the scruffy market on the docks, Benjamin Constant is a quiet village of tiny houses with gardens of brightly coloured flowers and is worth the 20-minute speedboat ride from Tabatinga, if only to visit the **Ticuna Indian Museum**, Av. Castelo Branco, 396, ✆/✉ 415 5624. This well-planned and laid-out museum has original Ticuna costumes, once used in tribal dances, drums and ritual paraphernalia, photographs of the tribe shortly after they were evangelized at the turn of the century and displays on Ticuna art, language and culture. You can also hear traditional music and there is a small shop selling beautiful wicker- and basket-work made in the nearby villages. The museum doubles up as the tribe's administrative headquarters, so if you have any questions about Ticuna culture and the curator, Xnina Fernandes, is free, she will be happy to answer you in Portuguese. The best place to stay in town is the **Hotel Benjamin Constant**, Getúlio Vargas 36, ✆ 415 5638, ✉ 415 5310, next to the wharf.

Rio Javari

A canoe trip on the Javari at dawn is an unforgettable experience. Silver hatchet fish startled by the paddles hurl themselves into the boat, wriggling at your feet, and caiman call to each other with deep resonant booms. This is one of Brazil's best places for Amazon wildlife. In the dry season the river's sandy beaches are covered in huge black caiman, and red and grey dolphins are plentiful all year round, often following the tiny canoes and surfacing close by with a gasp from their blow holes. There are even Amazonian manatee in the Rio Cambo.

Lodges near Benjamin Constant

There is only one lodge in the region, the **Sacambu Rainforest Lodge**, run by Amazon Jungle Trips (*see* p.220). Sacambu is one of the most beautifully situated, intimate lodges in the entire Amazon Basin. It is built over the Rio Sacambu, which flows underneath the rooms during the wet season, and faces a small beach of white-pepper sand often used by basking caiman. Behind is a small oxbow lake full of giant water lilies, passion flowers and water hyacinth. Manatee often visit here and there are flocks of hoatzin in the trees. As you eat supper, you can watch river dolphins surface yards away, and monkeys cavort in the trees close by. The lodge is built of traditional materials with palm thatched roofs and lighting is by 12-volt battery or gas lamps.

A Typical Five-day Rio Javari Itinerary

Day one: Leave Leticia in the early morning for an excursion on the Amazon River, visiting floating reed islands that are home to wattled jacana, black-banded crake, green ibis and capped and agami heron. After an optional visit to the Ticuna Indian Museum in Benjamin Constant, head down the Javari to Sacambu Lodge. An afternoon canoe trip ends at sunset and at night-time you'll be looking for the red eye-shine of caiman with a powerful halogen lamp.

Day two: Breakfast is followed by a canoe ride to oxbow lakes near the lodge to look for hoatzin, giant otter and giant water lilies. In the forest surrounding the lakes you will almost certainly see at least two species of monkey, together with blue and yellow, red and green and scarlet macaws. In the wet season there is a good chance of seeing bird-eating spiders which escape from the floods into crevices in dead trees. The afternoon is spent on the Camboa or Chita Rivers, where you will see horned screamer, black-collared hawk and, possibly, Amazonian manatee. A jungle hike gets you back on terra firma to become acquainted with some of the plants of the forest and possibly some terrestrial mammals and reptiles.

Day three: Travel up the Rio Javari for 75km, stopping at Palmari to visit some *caboclo* settlements and the San Antonio lake. At the settlements you'll learn about living in the forest, growing manioc, fishing, hunting and coping with the annual 15m rise and fall of the river. This will be a good day for seeing primates. There are at least seven species living in the region, including white-lipped marmosets.

Day four: During a long hike through virgin forest you may see smaller mammals like paca and agouti and, with luck, larger ones like tapir or even jaguar. With prior notice, you can spend two more nights in the forest, the last spent at a salt lick visited by all the large mammals.

Day five: Back along the Rio Quixoto, a tributary of a tributary of the Rio Javari. In the dry season, cats are occasionally seen on the sandy beaches between here and the Sacambu Lodge, which is where you will lunch. Then it's back to Leticia.

East of Manaus Along the Amazon

Picture a provincial, rather dull Mediterranean market town: the odd tiled house, a few squares with palm trees, a scruffy market and lots of mopeds. Now imagine a perfect Mediterranean beach: a 2km crescent of fine white sand, some shady parasols of thatched palm, and clear blue water. Transport both to the Amazon, adding a dash of humidity, a freshwater sea, lianas, cecropias and a horde of neotropical birds and butterflies, and you have **Santarém** and the beaches in its environs. The city is built at the junction of the blue Tapajós and the coffee-with-milk Amazon—their waters meet and swirl together about a kilometre off the bustling city quay. Beyond, towards Belém, lies an archipelago of forested islands that stretches for a hundred miles to the northern bank of the river. The Tapajós is only a minor tributary of the great river, but it carries more water than the Mississippi and is 30km wide at Santarém, giving

The Tribes of the Javari

The Upper Río Javari and its tributaries are home to the greatest density of uncontacted tribes in the Amazon, together with large groups of Matsés, Matis, Kurubo and Mayoruna. This has long been an area of conflict between Indians and outsiders. As recently as 1984 there were fatal clashes between previously uncontacted tribes and Petrobras, the Brazilian state oil company and, later, loggers and drug smugglers were involved in further bloodshed. In December 1998, after a prolonged campaign by the Javari Valley Indigenous Council and Survival International, an area of the Upper Javari as large as Belgium was demarcated as a protected indigenous area by presidential decree.

the city a maritime feel. Further upstream, towards Itaituba, it is lined with a series of beautiful beaches that seem even more idyllic set against the blue water and its green forested banks.

In 1922, torrential rain washed tons of mud off the streets of Santarém, exposing stone tools and fragments of pottery that had lain buried for several millennia before the arrival of the Portuguese. The ceramics were as fine as anything that had been found in the Americas—a panoply of exotic shapes covered in elaborate plant and animal motifs, spiral scrolls and bosses. We know very little about the civilization that produced them but Anna Roosevelt has recently added to the mystery by showing that some artefacts predate anything so far found in North America (*see* **History**. p.83).

European Santarém began life as a Jesuit mission in 1661, later becoming an assembly town used for the 'settlement', in reality enslavement, of Indians who were an ostensible threat to the Portuguese or to tribes friendly to the empire. In the 18th century, the town became a popular base for European naturalists like Henry Bates and was even settled, for a short while, by confederate refugees from the American Civil War. Some English surnames survive still in modern Santarém. 19th-century Santarém was full of rubber wealth, and would have stayed that way but for Englishman Henry Wickham (*see* **History**. p.83). The city became a backwater until the construction of the Santarém-Cuiabá highway, when it underwent a small financial renaissance. But the forest reclaimed the road and now Santarém is busy only as an intermediate port between Manaus, 595km (369 miles) upstream and Belém 836km (518 miles) downstream, and looking to ecotourism to provide its livelihood in the future.

Santarém (✆091–)   ***Getting There and Around***

Santarém has **flights** to Belém, Manaus and Cuiabá via Tavaj, Travessa Dos Mártires 161, Centro, ✆ 522 1418, and Penta, Travessa 15 de Novembro 183, ✆ 522 2220 and daily via Varig, Tv. Siqueira Campos 277, Centro, 523 2488. At the time of writing this book, there was **no road transport** along the BR163. This may change. **Boats** regularly sail upstream to Manaus, via Óbidos and Parintins and downstream to Belém and Macapá. Ask at Docas do Pará, 1½km west of the market along the quay.

Tourist Information and Useful Addresses

Tourist office: Comtur, Floriano Peixoto, 343, ✆ 523 2432, *santarem@.etfpa.br*

Changing money: Banco do Brasil, Av. Rui Barbosa for exchange and Visa cashpoint.

The Sights

The **cathedral church of Nossa Senhora da Conceição** lies on the south side of Praça Monsenhor José Gregorio. The original was built by the German Jesuit chronicler João Felipe Betendorf, champion (or exploiter, depending who you ask) of the Indians, who was largely responsible for introducing chocolate to Europe. The six-foot-high crucifix inside was a gift from the German scientist Karl von Martius who was shipwrecked on the Amazon in 1819. There is a fine collection of Santarém ceramics from the mysterious civilizations that first inhabited the region in the **Centro Cultural João Fona** (*open Mon–Fri 8–5*), on the Praça Barão de Santarém. Santarém also boasts one of Brazil's finest collections of indigenous art and artefacts—in the **Centro de Preservação da Arte Indígena** (*open daily 9–12 and 1–5*) in the village of Alter do Chão 35km from the town centre.

Santarém (© 091–)   *Where to Stay and Eating Out*

Santarém's hotels are all a little frayed. The best, with pool, air-conditioned rooms and restaurant is the **Hotel Tropical**, Av. Mendonça Furtado 4120, © 523 2800, @ 522 2631, 1½km from the centre along Av. Rui Barbosa. The **Santarém Palace**, Av. Rui Barbosa 726, © 523 2820, @ 522 1779, five blocks from the waterfront along Tv. 15 de Agosto, is a notch down in quality and price. You can stay even less expensively at the **New City**, Tv. Francisco Côrrea 200, © 522 3764, @ 522 4719, which can organize river trips. The best cheapie is the **Hotel Grão Rios**, in a little alley of Av. Tapajós between Travessa dos Mártires and 15 de Agosto, with air-conditioned rooms some of which have a river view. The **Brisa**, Lameira Bittencourt 5, © 522 1135, is another budget option with rooms with a river view with or without air conditioning.

Santarém is no place for gourmets. Most of the **restaurants** serve café-style food or set menus and are dotted along the waterfront in the centre. River fish is your best bet, at the **O Mascote**, Praça do Pescador, four blocks east of the cathedral on the quay or at the **Night-Day**, Av. Mendonça Furtado s/n, Praça da Libertade.

Rainforest Trips from Santarém   *Santarém (© 091–)*

There are only two operators currently organizing trips to the forest from Santarém. All other tour operators in town book adventure trips through them and take a commission. This may change as Santarém has plans to expand its ecotourism activities. Ask at the tourist office.

Santarém Viagens and Aventuras, Raimundo Fona 864, ©/@ 523 2037, a ten-minute taxi ride from the centre, offer trips all over the Brazilian Amazon, including canyoning on the Rio Tapajós, climbing Pico da Neblina, 17-day mountain bike trips to Belém and Cuiabá along the disused Transamazônica road, and white-water rafting on the Tapajós. The agency is run by an eccentric Frenchman who plans to walk the entire length of the Amazon from mouth to source in 2000—this means he may not be around to organize tours.

Santarém Tour, Av. Adriano Pimentel 44, Centro, or through the Hotel Tropical, © 522 4847/523 1836, @ 522 3141, is another foreign-run company offering land and river tours along the Tapajós as well as to Tapajós National Forest, Maiçá Lake, Fordlandia and Belterra.

Around Santarém

Maiçá Lake is not so much a single lake as a natural canal and lake system that begins about 30 minutes downstream from Santarém as an outlet of the Amazon River. It eventually makes its way back to the main stream after winding through a flood plain of gallery forest some of which has been felled for pasture. This is a good place to see river dolphins and waterfowl, and to get a taste of *caboclo* life on the Amazon.

The **Igarapé Açu**, in front of the city, is a natural Amazon canal with giant water lilies, caiman and waterfowl including capped heron, egrets, jacanas and gallinules.

In 1934, Henry Ford bought 2,500,000 acres of land near the mouth of the Rio Tapajós and built **Fordlandia and Belterra**, rubber plantation towns, that would be, he hoped, as well-run and productive, as any of those operated by the British in Malaysia. But even Ford could not conquer the Amazon: the neat rows of rubber plants were attacked by violent Amazon parasites; *serengueiros* neglected the neat rows of Detroit houses, ignored the American cinema and sports club, and lived off their week's pay for months, refusing to work until the money had run out. After losing $30,000,000 Ford gave up, and sold his dream to the Brazilian government who turned Fordlandia and Belterra into an agricultural research station. A visit to the two plantation towns is a bizarre experience—the vision of neat and cosy small-town USA, of *American Graffiti* or *Edward Scissorhands* (complete with fire hydrants) clashing with the untamed beauty of the Amazon. Tour agencies in Santarém offer trips to both sites. Belterra is closer to the city. Boats to Itaituba stop at Fordlandia and you can sling up a hammock in the old school building or the ruined factory.

Alter do Chão, a 2km sweep of white sand bank that backs a blue lagoon, 35km from Santarém on the Rio Tapajós, is one of the Amazon's best river beaches. At weekends it gets very crowded and finding a room in the simple *pousadas* can be a problem. There is an excellent **indigenous art museum** in the village next to the beach (*see* above, p.225),as well as four cheap *pousadas* and a few basic restaurants and some snack bars serving fried fish, beer, artificial drinks and fruit juices along the beach. The dry cerrado habitat around Alter do Chão is home to narrow-billed woodcreeper and rusty-backed antwren.

The only town worth stopping at on the river between Santarém and Belém is the little town of **Monte Alegre**, its colonial stucco and modern concrete perched on a bluff overlooking the Amazon. This is the principal region excavated by Anna Roosevelt (*see* **History** p.83), and the hills behind the town are full of 10,000-year-old rock paintings. The surrounding marsh land and seasonally flooded lakes is pioneer birding territory. There are a few simple hotels in the town and one Portuguese speaking guide: Nelsi Sadeck, Rua do Jaquara 320.

West from Santarém, **Óbidos** marks the point where the inland sea that once covered the Amazon Basin burst through the Guyana Shield to drain into the Atlantic and form the great Amazon River system. It is the narrowest and deepest point on the river. The Amazon is only 2km wide here—narrower than it is at Iquitos over 2,500km upstream. The town itself is a collection of neat tiled buildings and small parks. The 17th-century **Forte Pauxis** has intact ramparts and a cannon poised to blast out across the river. There are several small, inexpensive hotels and restaurants on the quay. Boats leave daily for Manaus and Santarém.

Amazônia (Tapajós) National Park and Itaituba

The Amazônia (Tapajós) National Park, encompassing 600,000ha of high, semi-humid tropical forest south of Santarém, is about the only national park in the Brazilian Amazon readily accessible to tourists who don't want to plan a full-scale expedition. It is also one of the few areas in Brazil with formal legal protection. The park's rivers form a network of *igarapé* channels, some with crystal-clear water, punctuated with waterfalls and sections of rapids. All the Amazon's

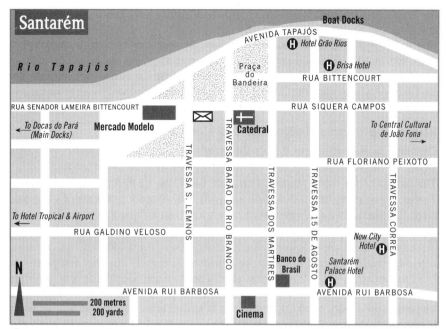

Santarém

Boat Docks

AVENIDA TAPAJÓS

Rio Tapajós

Praça do Bandeira

🄷 Hotel Grão Rios

🄷 Brisa Hotel

RUA BITTENCOURT

RUA SENADOR LAMEIRA BITTENCOURT

RUA SIQUERA CAMPOS

← To Docas do Pará (Main Docks)

Mercado Modelo

Catedral

To Central Cultural de João Fona →

RUA FLORIANO PEIXOTO

TRAVESSA S. LEMNOS

TRAVESSA BARÃO DO RIO BRANCO

TRAVESSA DOS MARTIRES

TRAVESSA 15 DE AGOSTO

TRAVESSA CORREA

← To Hotel Tropical & Airport

RUA GALDINO VELOSO

New City Hotel 🄷

Santarém Palace Hotel 🄷

N

Banco do Brasil

AVENIDA RUI BARBOSA

AVENIDA RUI BARBOSA

200 metres
200 yards

Cinema

large vertebrates, including anaconda, jaguar and black caiman, inhabit the park, as well as some highly endangered species. Tassel-ear and silvery marmosets, tiny monkeys as large as your hand, can be seen on the Ramel da Capelinha trail, 29km inside the park along the road that bisects it beyond the Tracoa entrance. Lesser anteater, tapir and giant armadillo may also be seen. Rare birds abound. The spectacular and highly endangered golden parakeet occurs at Uruá, 12½km before the Tracoa entrance. Other endemics include white-crested and red-throated piping guans, harpy eagle, razor-billed currasow, dark-winged trumpeter, gould's toucanet, bar-breasted piculet, spix's woodcreeper, chestnut-winged foliage gleaner, saturnine antshrike, ornate antwren and snow-capped and flame-crested manakins.

The park is 300km upstream of Santarém, on the west bank of the Tapajós, near the ugly gold-mining and cattle-ranching town of **Itaituba**. It is possible to visit independently, but by far the easiest way to visit is through one of Santarém's tour operators (*see* above, p.225). Birding-Brasil in Manaus (*see* p.213) undertake bespoke birding tours here with lots of advance warning. If you want to go it alone, you will need to get a permit to visit from IBAMA, Av. Tapajós 2267, Santarém, ✆/📠 (091) 523 2964. IBAMA can also book accommodation in the park, at one of the two simple lodges at Km 83 and Km 117 along Highway BR230.

Santarém is linked to Itaituba by boat (18hrs) and plane (45mins, *see* p.24). The best hotel in Itaituba is the cheap Juliana Park, ✆ (091) 518 0548, on the waterfront. Highway BR230, cuts across the southern corner of the park 65km from Itaituba. Cars can be hired from Jaci, ✆ (091) 518 3025. From Itaituba it is possible to continue along the Transamazônica to Belém or Porto Velho; a long, hard, and frequently cancelled bus ride.

Alta Floresta

The clear-water Rio Cristalino near the ranching town of Alta Floresta is surrounded by beautiful first growth forest and is well worth exploring. There is good catch-and-release fishing on the Rio São Benedito. Varig flies to Alta Floresta several times a week from Belém (via Santarém and Itaituba) or Cuiabá. There are sweaty, long bus connections north to Itaituba and south to Cuiabá. The best hotels are the Floresta Amazônica, Av. Perimetral Oeste 2001, ✆ (065) 521 3601, @ 521 2221, with air-conditioned rooms, a pool and sauna (*moderate*) or the basic Estoril, Av. Lucovico da Riva 2950, ✆ (065) 521 3298, cheap and friendly. The restaurants at the Floresta Amazônica and the Lisboa Palace Hotel (Av. do Aeroporto 251) are about the best in town. Feitiço, Av. Ariosto da Riva 2846, serves good pizza.

Rainforest and Fishing Lodges near Alta Floresta

Cristalino Jungle Lodge, book through the Floresta Amazônica hotel (*see* above). Wonderful forest trails and boat trips on the clear Rio Cristalino. About $100 per person per day.

Thayamaçu Lodge, Carlos Munhoz, Thayamaçu Lodge, Rua C2 #234, Caixa Postal 04, Alta Floresta, Mato Grosso 78.580–000, ✆/@ (065) 521 3587. Peacock bass fishing in a luxurious lodge. Cabins are near a lovely waterfall in primary forest. An idyllic spot. Book in advance.

Belém

Belém is a hodge-podge of tower blocks, crumbling Portuguese churches and palaces in Mediterranean hues with white stucco sweltering on the humid southern bank of one of the Amazon's mouths. Though the city has character, and in places almost verges on elegance, it's a bit of a dump at heart, rather like its namesake in modern Israel. You may not want to go out of your way to visit but, if you're passing, it's worth popping in for a glass of *cupuaçu* juice and a stroll around the old colonial centre. If you're thinking about using Belém as a base for visiting the rainforest, think again. Nowhere is more symptomatic of Brazil's head-in-the-sand parochialism than this state capital; thousands are spent on lavish brochures advertising the meagre delights of the city, while facilities for visits to the forests of the Amazon are almost non-existent. If you want to get out into the wild it is easier to visit the Ilha do Marajó (*see* below), the world's largest river island, covered in farms, forest and feral buffalo. Other islands also lie within easy reach of Belém. Many, like Algodoal, have fine sandy beaches.

History: Indian Slavery

The wooden **fort of Nossa Senhora do Belém** was founded in 1616 as a military outpost after the Portuguese had routed French settlers and their allies the Tupinambá and reclaimed the lower Amazon. The fort soon developed into a settlement of mud and thatch, which became capital of the autonomous state of Pará. The forest was cleared for sugar cane and tobacco plantations and, as they had done all over colonial Brazil, the Portuguese forced Indians to work them. The suffering was appaling: whole tribes were re-settled close to Belém to provide slave labour to the colonists only to be were wiped out by smallpox and dysentery. In 1655 King João IV was finally moved to pass laws entrusting the welfare of the Indians to the Jesuits in an attempt to put a stop to slavery. Though this resulted in some improvement, the Jesuits were themselves responsible for many Indian deaths and much cultural destruction: tribes were re-settled in *aldeias* near the city, contact brought devastating European diseases, and the Indians were forced to abandon much of their culture under the threat of the whiplash. Even this mixed blessing did not last. The Portuguese of Belém demanded that slavery be re-introduced and Indians again perished from overwork, beatings and the ravages of European diseases. About a sixth of the entire population of non-Andean South America was wiped out— one of the greatest genocides as a percentage of total population in world history.

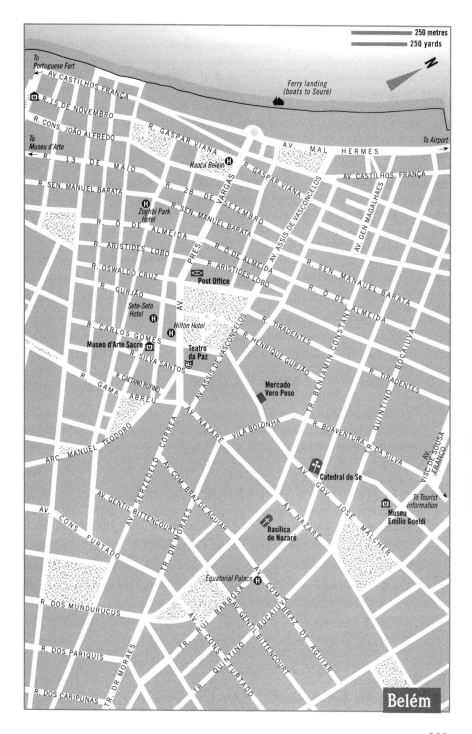

250 metres
250 yards

To
Portuguese Fort
AV. CASTILHOS FRANÇA

Ferry landing
(boats to Souré)

R. 15 DE NOVEMBRO

R. CONS. JOÃO ALFREDO

R. GASPAR VIANA

AV. MAL HERMES

To Airport

To
Museu d'Arte
R. 13 DE MAIO

Haoca Belém

R. GASPAR VIANA

AV. CASTILHOS FRANÇA

R. SEN. MANUEL BARATA

R. 28 DE SETEMBRO

R. SEN. MANUEL BARATA

AV. GEN MAGALHÃES

Zoghbi Park
Hotel

R. Ó DE ALMEIDA

R. ARISTIDES LOBO

R. Ó DE ALMEIDA

R. SEN. MANUEL BARATA

R. OSWALDO CRUZ

R. ARISTIDES LOBO

R. Ó DE ALMEIDA

R. GURJÃO

PRES. VARGAS

Post Office

R. ASSIS DE VASCONCELOS

Sete-Seto
Hotel

AV.

R. TIRADENTES

R. CARLOS GOMES

Hilton Hotel

R. ASSIS DE VASCONCELOS

R. HENRIQUE GURJÃO

TR. BENJAMIN CONSTANT

R. TIRADENTES

Museu d'Arte Sacre

R. SILVA SANTOS

Teatro
da Paz

BOCAIUVA

QUINTINO

R. CAETANO RUFINO

R. GAMA ABREU

Mercado
Vero Peso

R. BOAVENTURA DA SILVA

ARC. MANUEL TEODORO

AV. ASSIS DE VASCONCELOS

AV. NAZARÉ

VILA BOLONHA

AV. VISC. DE SOUSA FRANCO

AV. SERZEDELO CORREA

AV. COM. BRAZ DE AGUIAR

Catedral de Se

To Tourist
information

AV. GENTIL BITTENCOURT

AV. GOV. JOSÉ MALCHER

Museu
Emílio Goeldi

AV. CONS. FURTADO

TR. DR. MORAES

AV. NAZARÉ

Basílica
de Nazaré

R. DOS MUNDURUCUS

Equatorial Palace

AV. COM. BRAZ DE AGUIAR

R. DOS PARIQUIS

TR. DR. MORAES

AV. RUI BARBOSA

R. CONS. FURTADO

QUINTINO BOCAIUVA

AV. GENTIL BITTENCOURT

R. DOS CARIPUNAS

Belém

The Cabanagem *Caboclo* Rebellion

Indian women fared little better than the men who were put to work on the Portuguese plantations. Prostitution, sexual slavery and rape were commonplace and the children that resulted were put to work as slaves by their own fathers. By the 18th century enslaved Angolans had joined the diminishing numbers of Indians and the colonists' bastard children and a mixed-race underclass known as began to emerge. These were known pejoratively as *caboclos*. After Brazilian independence, the *caboclos* of Belém rose against the descendants of the settlers that had long exploited them and drove them from the city, declaring an independent state. But the rebels unwisely captured a British ship laden with arms that had docked in Belém shortly after the rebellion began. The crew were killed, incensing the British government, who sent the Royal Navy to Belém. When Eduardo Angelim, the leader of the *caboclo* government, refused to negotiate, the British blockaded the port, paving the way for troops from São Paulo to re-take the city. Nearly a third of the region's population were massacred and the city was returned once more to the descendants of the Portuguese. Many of these went on to become rubber barons. The city expanded threefold in the 19th century during the rubber boom, christening itself the 'Marseille of the tropics' and laying out spacious palm-lined avenues and an elegant theatre to rival the Opera House in Manaus.

Belém (℗ 091)   *Getting There and Around*

Belém is connected by **air** to Paramaribo, Cayenne and Georgetown in the Guyanas via Suriname Airways, ℗ 211 6038/212 7144 and Miami through Varig, ℗ 0800 997000. Varig, Transbrasil ℗ 0800 171171, and VASP, ℗ 0800 998277, have connections to all the major cities within the Brazilian Amazon and the country as a whole. There are regular, comfortable **bus** services to São Luis and onwards to the Brazilian coast (Fortaleza, Recife, Salvador and so on).

Regular **boats** leave from Belém upstream to Manaus (five days), usually calling at Santarém, Óbidos and Parintins on the way, and to Macapá on the northern bank of the Amazon, 24 hours away. There are various companies with booths at Escadinha port. The smaller operators tend to be cheaper and offer a better service.

Car hire: Avis or Hertz, at the airport. Both speak English.

Taxis are cheap, plentiful and safe in Belém. There are plenty at the airport, around the docks and at the bus station. If you prefer to take public transport, the **Marex-Patroni bus** will take you from the airport to the bus terminal or city centre. If you're arriving at the bus terminal take buses marked Aeroclube or Cidade Nova 6.

Belém (℗ 091)   *Tourist Information and Useful Addresses*

Tourist office: Paratur, ℗ 223 2130, ✉ 223 6198, Praça Kennedy, near the waterfront at the end of Travessa da Piedade.

Changing money: Banco do Brasil and Bradesco have branches all over Belém with Visa cashpoints.

Internet: Convert Photo Centre, Iguatemi Shopping Mall, on Padre Eutiquio.

The Sights

Wander around near the quays around Av. Hermes to see the best of Belém's colonial buildings and the old **Portuguese fort**, but watch your wallet. The fort, near the Porto dos Lanchas, is now one of the city's finest restaurants. The pink and stucco **Teatro de Paz**, opposite the Hilton on the Praça da Republica, is the city's answer to the Manaus Opera House. The **Palácio Antônio Lemos** (between Praça Dom Pedro II and Praça Felip Patroni) is another monument to the rubber boom. It now houses the city art museum with a collection consisting mostly of antique French furniture. The **Palácio Lauro Sodré**, next door, now houses the state museum. Once the city's seat of government, it was invaded by *caboclos* during the Cabanagem rebellion, when the state governor was killed on the front steps. The **Basilica da Nossa Senhora de Nazaré** (on the Praça Justo Chermont, ten minutes by taxi from the centre) is an important Brazilian pilgrimage centre. The mural on the façade depicts the arrival of the Portuguese in Brazil. There is a **museum of sacred art** in the cellar. A short walk away is the **Museu Emílio Goeldi** (Av. Magalhães Barata 376, ten minutes by taxi from the centre, *open Tues–Thurs 9–12 and 2–5, weekends 9–5)*. There's a small **zoo** here, and a pleasant rainforest garden with wild deer, agouti, paca, sloth and monkeys. It is well worth a visit.

Belém (℡091–)   **Where to Stay**

expensive

The **Belém Hilton**, Praça da República at Av. Presidente Vargas, 882, ℡ 242 6500, ✆ 225 2942, is the city's best hotel. The upper floors have views out over the city to the Amazon and the forests beyond. The restaurant is mediocre. The **Equatorial Palace**, Av. Braz de Aguiar 612, ℡ 241 2000, ✆ 223 5222, is cheaper and has a small pool on the roof and a better restaurant. **Novotel**, Av. Bernardo Sayão 4804, ℡ 249 7111, ✆ 249 7808, 6km from the centre, has all the familiar comforts.

moderate

The **Manacá**, Travessa Quintino Bocaiúva 1645, ℡ 223 3335, ✆ 2226227, near the centre in a pleasant renovated colonial building. Rooms with air conditioning or fan. **Zoghbi Park** near the Hilton at Padre Prudêncio 220 ℡/✆ 241 1800, has impersonal air-conditioned rooms with a view over the city and river. If you want to be on the waterfront, try the **Itaoca Belém** at Av. Presidente Vargas 132, ℡ 241 3129, ✆ 241 3434/2082. Rooms have air conditioning.

cheap

Budget travellers see the worst of Belém. The best of the bunch are the **Sete Sete**, Travessa 1 de Março, ℡ 222 7730, near the Praça da República, with air-conditioned rooms and TVs, and the **Fortaleza**, Travessa Frutuoso Guimarães 275, with spacious rooms and a very basic shared bathroom.

Belém (℡091–)   **Eating Out**

Belém specialities: Though lackadaisical about many things, Belém seems to care about its food. Regional specialities include *pato no tucupi*, duck cooked in manioc (cassava) juice and *maniçoba*, a stew of bacon, pork, Brazilian sausage and calves' hooves, which takes a week to prepare. There's *feijoada*, too, Brazil's national dish, an equally carnivorous camp-fire style stew combining pork, beef and Brazilian beans. The crowning glories of Belém cuisine, however, are the river fish, the tropical fruit juices and the cakes made with Amazon fruits like *cupuaçu* and *cacao*. The fish, all of which are delicious, are usually served simply—grilled or lightly fried. Try *filhote* or *dourada*, the two most highly prized.

O Círculo Militar, ✆ 233 4374, delightfully situated in the old fort near the Porto dos Lanchas, with views out over the Amazon, is one the city's best restaurants. It specializes in river fish, like the highly prized noble fish (*peixe nobre*) and the meaty *tambaqui*. The **Avenida**, overlooking the Basilica at Av. Nazaré 1086, ✆ 233 4015, has a view and a good fish-based menu, but the atmosphere is rather cheerless.

Lá em Casa, José Malcher 247, ✆ 222 9164, offers well-prepared regional dishes under a mango tree and the **Lacuticho**, Bernal Couto 40, specializes in food from Minas Gerais, including *frango com ora-pro-nobis* (chicken with regional vegetables) and *feijão tropeiro* (mashed brown beans with manioc flour, bacon and sausage).

Like Manaus, Belém is full of juice bars selling delicious tropical fruit juices pure or as *vitaminas* (with milk). Try as many fruits as possible; they are nearly all delicious. The easiest on the palate for the uninitiated are *graviola*, *camu camu*, *tapereba* and *cacao*, the fruit whose nuts are used to make chocolate. Stranger local specialities include *cupuaçu*, a pungent, pulpy relation of *cacao*, that becomes addictively delicious after the third or fourth try, *cajú*, the fruit of the cashew nut tree and *açaí*, a deep purple palm-fruit said to provide energy. All taste like nothing you'll ever had before.

Tours Operators in Belém
Belém (✆091–)

No companies in Belém offer trips into the rainforest. **Amazon Star Tours**, ✆ 241 8624, ✆ 212 6244, offer cruises on the river, and book lodges on several islands, including Marajó.

Around Belém: River Islands

Compared to the Ganges or Mekong, the mouth of the Amazon is relatively narrow—a mere 200 miles across. The flow of the river is too strong to form a muddy delta with rivulets slowly meandering through it. Instead fresh water is pumped far out into the Atlantic through two channels separated by the Ilha do Marajó, staining it with silt for hundreds of miles off shore, and dumping mud from the Brazilian forests on the beaches of the Guyanas. Other sand islands also lie in this fresh water sea, shifting position and size from year to year as the river changes its course and cuts sand from their shores and re-depositing it elsewhere.

Getting to the Islands and Where to Stay

Accommodation on the islands can be booked through Amazon Star (*see* p.232).

Marajó, Mosqueiro and Mexiana: regular boats leave from Belém in the early morning. Times and departure points vary throughout the year, and Amazon Star can best advise you of the latest. For **Algodoal**, take a bus to Marudá and catch the ferry.

Ilha da Marajó

Marajó is not so much a single island as a complex archipelago of shifting sands, richly forested islands and muddy rivulets coloured by flocks of scarlet ibis and snowy egrets. Its size is testimony to the might of the Amazon: its 48,000 square kilometres is 2km deep in river sediment carried across Brazil and left in the river's mouth over hundreds of thousands of years.

The island is highly fertile and much of the region around **Soure, Salvaterra** and **Cachoeira do Arari** has been turned into huge ranch lands grazed by beef cattle and Asian water buffalo, farmed for Brazilian mozzarella. The western portion is covered in some of the Amazon's densest and most handsome forest, much of which is sadly in the process of being cut down by *serengueiros* who can no longer make a living from tapping wild rubber. Life on Marajó is orientated to the flow of the river and the tidal canals that bisect the island; transport is usually by boat and the stilted houses that line the banks of the rivers are redolent of a lifestyle that has changed little since *caboclos* lived in the *cabanas* that gave their name to the Cabanagem Rebellion. Fishing is still important here, but feeding Belém's voracious appetite is bleeding the Arari Lake in the middle of the island dry of pirarucu and peacock bass, and aquarium fish are taken in huge numbers from the brooks near Soure and Ponte de Pedras. Crabs destined for Belém are caught in the mangrove forests that line the western fringes of Marajó and the Caviana and Janauca Islands. Shrimp, fish fry and young sharks thrive here too, helping to create an ecosystem that supports large colonies of waterfowl. Scarlet and wood ibis, southern lapwing, ash-throated crake, and sooty barbthroat can all be found in Marajó's wetlands.

Intricately designed **Marajó pottery**, replicas of which you can see for sale on the streets of Belém, has been found in the burial mounds of the Ananatuba civilization, suggesting that Marajó has been an important centre for ceramics since about 1000BC. We now know that pottery was produced near Santarém as early as 10,000 years ago, making this the oldest region of ceramic production so far discovered anywhere in the Americas. Original pieces can be seen in the **Museu Goeldi** in Belém (*see* p.231).

Around the Island

Souré, the main town on the island, is buffalo-run; when they aren't pulling carts or being ridden, they roam free like citizens through the streets and along the beach. You can hitch a ride on a buffalo cart or in a taxi to one of the many fine **beaches** around the town. The best is the Praia da Araruna, a 5km walk or a short taxi-ride away. The Ilha do Marajó Hotel, Travessa 2, ☎ (091) 741 1315, is the best hotel in Souré, boasting a pool, air-conditioned rooms, a tennis court and restaurant. If you want to see the interior of the island, you will either have to camp or stay at one of the *fazendas*, ranch houses in the centre of vast estates that border on the wild. Many offer horse-riding, sport-fishing (with your own equipment) and canoe trips through the creeks and waterways. Much of the research into Marajó's fauna has been undertaken at the Fazenda Bom Jardim which specializes in trips for wildlife enthusiasts. Accommodation is rustic but comfortable. The Fazenda Nossa Senhora do Carmo, has a similar standard of accommodation and offers buffalo riding, fishing and canoe trips through what is mostly secondary forest whilst the Pousada das Guaras near the village of Salavaterra is located in an ecological reserve in front of the Baia do Marajó and is a good place to see waterfowl. All can be booked through Amazon Star Tours in Belém (*see* p.232), for between $60 and $100 a day.

Other Islands and Resorts

The **Ilha do Mosqueiro**, close to Belém, is the city's weekend escape; the beaches are nothing special and there are a handful of hotels in the port town. More remote are the **Ilha da Mexiana** in the Marajó archipelago and the broad beaches of **Algodoal**, a bus and boat away on the Atlantic coast. **Salinópolis**, a resort on the Pará coast with broad sandy beaches washed by a murky sea, is popular with locals. There are plenty of hotels in the town; try the **Salinópolis**, Av. Beira Mar 26, ☎ (091) 823 1239 (*inexpensive*).

Boa Vista and on to Venezuela and Guyana

This ugly, modern frontier town between Manaus and Venezuela offers little to the tourist. It was the centre of the Yanomami massacres in the 1980s. Trips to near Mount Roraima are more easily organized from Santa Elena de Uairén across the border in Venezuela. Tour operators in Boa Vista include Amamturs, Sebastião Diniz 65, Centro Comercial, ✆ (095) 224 0004, and Anaconda Tours, Silvio Botelho 12, ✆ (095) 224 4132; both offer trips to the surrounding rainforest and savannah, and along the Rio Branco. Lago Caracaraña, also nearby, has fine white sand beaches. Boa Vista is well connected: several buses a day leave for Santa Elena, Lethem (in Guyana) and south along the BR174 to Manaus. Varig have daily flights to Manaus. If you get stuck here, try the Hotel Eusebio, at Cecilia Brasil 1107, ✆ (095) 224 6342 (*inexpensive*). There's a tourist office at Coronel Pinto 241.

Porto Velho and on to Bolivia

Porto Velho is even less inspiring than Boa Vista, a sprawling town that lies at the centre of the greatest de-forestation in the Brazilian Amazon. It is really only worth visiting if passing through to Bolivia. Accommodation is seedy and expensive. Try the Novo Hotel, Carlos Gomes 2776, ✆ (069) 224 6555 (*moderate*), Vila Rica, Carlos Gomes 1616, ✆ (069) 224 3433 (*expensive*), or the Amazonas, Carlos Gomes 2838 (*cheap*). Varig fly to Porto Velho from Manaus, Belém and other major Brazilian cities, several times a week. Buses run to Rio Branco (for Acre and Peru), Guajara Mirím (for Bolivia) and Cuiabá (the Pantanal). but the roads are rough. River boats leave for Manaus via the Rio Madeira three times a week and the trip takes three days.

The Bolivian border lies at **Guajara Mirím**, five hours from Porto Velho by bus. Guayaramerín, the Bolivian counterpart, lies on the opposite bank of the Rio Mamoré, and boats flit to and fro every few minutes. There are connections from here to Riberalta, Rurrenabaque and La Paz. Guajara Mirím is laid out in a grid pattern. There is a Bolivian consulate on Av. Costa Marques 495, open on weekday mornings. Bring two passport photos for Bolivian visas. If you need to stay try the fairly comfortable Lima Palace, Av. 15 de Novembro 1613, ✆ (069) 541 3421, (*moderate*), or the Tropical, Av. Leopoldo de Matos, ✆ (069) 541 3308 (*cheap*)

The Pantanal

Those who want to see Amazon wildlife come not to the Amazon but to the Pantanal. This is South America's Serengeti—a seasonally flooded plain of grass, lakes and forest islands, crawling with animals and has recently become a UNESCO World Heritage Site. Hundreds of caiman bask on the fringes of Pantanal lakes, herds of capybara hold up cars on her roads, anaconda hunt in her gullies and ditches, and her grasslands are overflowing with rare and endangered birds. The Chapada dos Guimarães table-top mountains rise steeply from the flat vastness of Pantanal, marking its northern border with a line of steep cliffs fringed with forests and splashed with the white of hundreds of waterfalls. In the south, shallow hills rise towards Bonito on the Paraguayan border, whose clear rivers and vertiginous caverns provide a cooling break from the heat of the Pantanal plain. The wetlands slope gently to the west, draining into the Rio Paraguay and giving the Pantanal two distinct seasons. In the wet animals huddle together on islands of high ground and locals brave the torrential rain to canoe across their lands. In the baking hot dry season, grasslands reappear, beef cattle graze alongside South American ostriches and gauchos herd them across vast ranch lands. Apart from beef, tourism is the Pantanal's main industry, and the infrastructure here is more developed than in the Brazilian Amazon. Cuiabá and Corumbá have some excellent travel agencies, and many ranches now function as tourist lodges.

History

As if to presage its fate, the Pantanal was first explored by a Spanish explorer called 'Cow Head' in 1543. He didn't like it much, complaining about plagues of mosquitoes and vampire bats and turned westward into the even more hostile Chaco, leaving the fate of the wetlands to the ruthless Portuguese. Apart from a few unsuccessful slaving raids, the Pantanal was left alone for nearly 200 years. Then gold was discovered in the north in 1719, and colonists from all over the empire descended on the wetlands for a slice of the pie. Cuiabá was established shortly after and Portuguese began scouring the area for native slave labour. The Indians understandably resented this invasion and two of the most courageous tribes, the Guaicurú and the Paiaguá, ferociously attacked the Europeans. In an unusual act of cooperation, the like of which would have preserved all the Americas from Europe, the two tribes combined their efforts and jointly attacked the Portuguese, thus maintaining control of the Pantanal for a century. In 1734 the alliance was broken after a devastating Portuguese ambush from Cuiabá decimated the Paiaguá; the tribes retreated into the depths of the Pantanal, to be ravaged by disease, punitive expeditions and inter-tribal conflict. Today only 200 Guaicurú survive and the Paiaguá have been reduced to a pathetic remnant living on a sad island reservation in Paraguay.

Other Indian groups fared even worse. The Parecis were used as slaving fodder in the mines of Cuiabá and only a fortieth of their pre-conquest number survive. The Bororó, a powerful warrior tribe, who lived to the east of Cuiabá, allied themselves with the Portuguese against other tribes. The tactic proved moderately successful; today the Bororó are one of the few tribes in the Pantanal that live by traditional means. After the gold rush, came economic decline and then the introduction of beef cattle. Today nearly 25 million head of cattle roam the wetlands of the Pantanal, owned by vast *fazendas* (ranches). With the advent of tourism, some of these turned their activities towards wildlife preservation rather than destruction.

Cuiabá

After the grimy cities of the Brazilian Amazon, Cuiabá will feel positively civilized. But clean streets and outdoor cafés don't make a city a tourist destination. Cuiabá is a place tourists pass through; in this case, on their way to the Pantanal or the Chapada dos Guimarães mountains.

Cuiabá (© 065–)   ***Getting There and Around***

Cuiabá is a major transport hub with daily Varig **flights** to all Brazil's major cities, and regular connections north to Santarém, via Sinopé, Alta Floresta and Itaituba. LAB have connections to Santa Cruz, Bolivia. The airport is a 15-minute taxi-ride from the centre.

Modern-day Destruction of the Pantanal

'The lands of my people were occupied by large land owners who have lands that go as far as the eye can see, full of well treated and well fed cattle. On my land, cattle is worth more than Indians. the cattle stomp on their gardens and tractors knock down their houses. The rivers are dirty with the waste from the large farms in the region: pesticides, mercury. They finished with our forests, they are finishing with what is left of our savannahs... For this reason young Guarani are killing themselves, they are searching for the end, hanging themselves.'

Marta Silva Vito Guarani. President of the Kaguateca Association for Displaced Indians, in an address to the US House of Representatives, May 10 1994

The tranquil beauty of the Pantanal belies the deep problems that threaten the region. Long after the Brazilian gold rush that brought in die-hard settler, a frontier mentality still exists. Law and order is in the hands of the landowners and their gun-wielding hired-hands. The seasonal burning of grasslands, hunting and voracious commercial fishing continue to exploit the region and the health of local residents and wildlife is threatened by mercury poisoning from gold-mining and agro-chemical pollution. The toll on the larger birds and mammals is already beginning to show. Ostensibly eco-friendly legislation has been passed by government and the region has even been given an environmental Police force—the Policia Florestal. When fishermen claim a fishing quota for every member of the family, including the baby, the Policia just wave them by, especially if handed a choice *dourado* to take home to the folks.

The buck stops with the landowners in the Pantanal, and if the flagrant abuse of environmental law is not enough to prove it then the fate of local tribespeople is. In September 1999 five young Guarani Kaiowa drank a lethal mix of insecticide and rum in the village of Panambizinho in protest at the gradual theft of their lands by colonists. This was the most recent of more than 300 such suicides that have taken place since 1985. Despite a 1995 federal act which recognized the tribe's right to 1,240ha of land, 300 Kaiowa are crammed into an area of barely 60ha, hemmed-in by electric fences that are patrolled by gunmen. Repeated protests, even by foreign pressure groups, have achieved nothing the gunmen still operate and police and government turn a blind eye.

The Brazilian government also have commercial ambitions for the Pantanal. By deepening the Paraguay River, they hope to open up the region to ocean-going ships, linking the interior of Brazil with Paraguay, Argentina, and the other countries of the South American common market, the Mercosur. This would be a disaster for the Pantanal: a deeper Paraguay River would drain the wetlands far more rapidly, greatly shortening the wet season, radically altering the ecosystem, and wiping out many of the animals. Only lobbying by environmental groups has prevented the scheme, which is backed by the US government, from going ahead. Whether UNESCO's decision in late 2000 to name the Pantanal a World Heritage Site will change any of this remains to be seen.

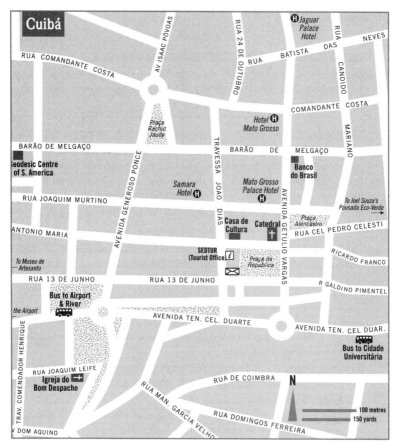

There are daily **bus** connections to Campo Grande (10hrs), Alta Floresta (13hrs) and Porto Velho (2hrs). Buses leave several times a day for Cáceres (for Bolivia, 3hrs), Poconé (2hrs) on the Transpantaneira and the Chapada dos Guimarães village (2hrs). **Car rental:** Avis ✆ 682 5077, Unidas ✆ 682 4052 and Localiza ✆ 624 7979.

Cuiabá (✆ 065–)`   ***Tourist Information and Useful Addresses***

Tourist office: Praça da Republica, ✆ 724 5830 (*open Mon–Fri 8.30–11.30, 2–6*).

Changing money: Banco do Brasil and Bradesco have offices all over town.

The Sights

The only hidden jewel in Cuiabá's mundane setting is the **church of Bom Jesus dos Passos**, which surveys the city from a hill. A pyramid and a small monument in the Praça Moreira Cabral mark the (supposed) exact **Geodesic centre** of South America. The **Museu de Artesanato**, 13 de Junho, (*open Tues–Sun 10–3 and 6–11*) 5km east of town, houses weapons and ornaments from the Xavantes and other Pantanal tribes and has a shop selling artefacts next door. The **Museu do Índio**, (*open Mon–Fri 8.30–11 and 2.30–5*) on Av. Fernando Correia da Costa, has exhibits from the Bororó, Carajás and Xavantes tribes.

expensive

Global Garden, Av. Miguel Sutil 5555, ✆ 624 1660, ✆ 624 9966, five minutes taxi-ride from the centre, is the most luxurious hotel in town. The **Veneza Palace**, Av. Col. Escolástico 138, ✆ 321 4847, ✆ 322 5212, is marginally cheaper, and more individual with a mock oriental lobby.

moderate

The **Jaguar Palace Hotel**, Av. Getúlio Vargas 600, ✆ 624 4404, ✆ 623 7798, *jaguarph@zaz.com.br*, is central with comfortable air-conditioned rooms and a pool, and includes breakfast in the price, while the **Hotel Fazenda Mato Grosso**, Antônio Dorileo 1200, ✆ 361 2980, is 7km outside the city, in 19ha of forest. Horse riding and paddle-boats are included in the price, there's a pool and the cheesy tiled-huts that house the rooms all have air conditioning and immaculate bathrooms.

inexpensive–cheap

The **Hotel Mato Grosso**, Comandante Costa 2522, ✆ 614 7777, ✆ 321 2386, *homat@nutecnet.com.br*, has garish décor but is central and has air conditioning. The best of the budget options is **Joel Souza's Pousada Eco-Verde**, Pedra Celestina 191, ✆ 623 4696, in a colonial house in the old part of town.

Though Cuiabá has some good options for meat- and fish-eaters, vegetarian, will be restricted to omelettes or pizza.

Regionalissimo, 13 de Junho, serves good fish dishes including grilled *piraputanga* and the regional *pacu assado com farofa de couve*, grilled fish with bacon and greens. The **Recanto do Bosque**, Candido Mariano 1040, serves huge hunks of meat, grilled or barbecued, with nearly twenty different types of salad. Pasta and pizza can be found at one of the Italian restaurants on Getúlio Vargas, the best of which are **Tavola Piena** and **Adriano** at Nos.985 and 676 respectively.

Visiting the Northern Pantanal from Cuiabá

Northern Pantanal trips are all based around the **Transpantaneira**, a dirt road that runs south from the gold-mining town of **Poconé**. The best way to visit, unless you particularly want a guide, is to drive this road by yourself, stopping at *fazendas* along the way. You'll need a good 4x4 (*see* car rental above), a flask of drinking water, binoculars and twice as much camera film as you think you'll use. The one petrol station is opposite the Pousada Pixaim at Km 60.

Wildlife on the Transpantaneira

The wildlife, especially birdlife, along the road is awesome, staggering in its quantity as much as its species diversity. The best time to be on the road is dawn at the end of September. Huge flocks of egrets, roseate spoonbills and cabeça seca, descend on the roadside gullies, mingling with jabiru storks and capped herons, in the glorious rich orange of the morning light. Capybara cross the road in troupes, together with greater rhea, marsh deer and the occasional anaconda, and a stay at one of the *fazendas*, particularly the Pouso Alegre (*see* below, p.239), offers a real chance of seeing a big cat. Birding from this road can produce over 100 species in a single day, including many herons, ibises and raptors, the endemic chestnut-bellied guan and the spectacularly noisy hyacinth macaw. Other specialities include the crowned eagle, bare-faced currasow golden-collared macaw, blue-fronted parrot, helmeted manakin, bearded tachuri, black-and-tawny seedeater, coal-crested finch, and scarlet-headed blackbird.

Fazendas on the Transpantaneira   Cuiabá (© 065–)

From the wildlife point of view, three *fazendas* stand out above the others.

Pousada São Sebastião do Pantanal, Centro de Estudos Ambientes, Transpantaneira Km 25, © 322 0178/321 0710, © 322 0178, a first-class establishment in beautiful wooded surroundings, with pool, good food, horse-rides and boat trips. Moderate to expensive prices.

Araras Lodge, Km 30, Transpantaneira, c/o André Turoni, Pantanal Explorer Expeditur, Av. Gov. Ponce de Arruda 670, Cuiabá, © 682 2800), has rustic air-conditioned rooms, excellent and food and a small pool. The swamp land immediately to the north of the *fazenda* is full of caiman and waterfowl. A walkway leads out across it to a large tree with a viewing platform built in the crown of the branches. At dawn this is one of the best spots for birds and wildlife in the Northern Pantanal. Aside from Pantanal regulars like marsh deer, capybara and ruffescent tiger-heron, this is part of a jaguar's territory. Around $80 per person.

Pouso Alegre, Km 33 Transpantaneira, © 626 1545 (in Cuiabá), © 968 6101 (at the *fazenda*), is charming, and only a little simpler than the nearby Araras Lodge; at only $40 including full board, horse-riding and guides, it is one of the real bargains on Transpantaneira. The long driveway is lined with trees nested by various species of parakeets, toucan and jabiru storks, and hyacinth macaw congregate in the trees in front of the pousada every afternoon. Giant anteater, and great rhea are common sights on the horse-riding trips.

Other options along the Transpantaneira

Pousada Piúval, Transpantaneira Km 10, © 721 1338, *piuval@vehiculum.com, www.vehiculum.com/piuval*, offers boat and walking trips, piranha fishing and horse-riding. The small observation platform is a good place to watch wildlife at dawn. Moderate prices.

Cabanas do Pantanal Lodge, Transpantaneira Km 42, c/o Rua Candido Mariano, 434, Cuiabá, © 623 4141, © 623 8880, *conftur@nutecnet.com.br*, clean basic *cabanas* lacking personality with a pool. Fishing trips, horse-riding and trail walking are offered.

Pousada Pixaim, Transpantaneira Km 60, © 721 2091, *pixaim@zaz.com.br*, lacks charm, but there are some facilities for kids, and the staff are friendly but speak only Portuguese.

Pantanal Mato Grosso Hotel, Transpantaneira Km 65, © 968 6205/614 7500, is uncomfortably large, touristy, and anonymous, but has a pool and air-conditioned rooms with TVs.

The Fazenda Hotel Beira Rio, Transpantaneira Km 65, © 321 9445/721 1861, © 321 9445, is ugly and large, but good for trek options.

Hotel Santa Rosa do Pantanal Porto Jofre, Transpantaneira Km 150, © 322 0513/0077. This once luxurious and still comfortable hotel lacks the charm of the *fazendas* but has some wonderful birding along the Cuiabá river and the trail leading to Porto Jofre and the campsite.

Chapada dos Guimarães National Park

Visitors to the sights near the Emanuel Pinheiro Road (MT251) will probably be disappointed by the indiscriminate building, litter, graffiti and lack of care and maintenance of the environment. To see the Chapada at its best it is necessary to get far off the beaten track.

The following sights are the ones usually visited on one-day Chapada tours. All are near the road and can be seen independently. The first sight along the road is the **Salgadeira**, an artificial waterfall with a pool at its base that would be a wonderfully romantic spot if it didn't have an ugly restaurant complex right next to it. The **Portão do Inferno** (Hell's Gate), nearby, is a sheer 80m drop into a dramatic sculpted canyon. A right turn onto a dirt road 6km after the Salgadeira takes you past an IBAMA research station and a complex of restaurants, beyond which is a short trail to the **Salto do Véu de Noiva** (Bridal Veil Falls), a sliver of water cascading 86m from an amphitheatre of red rock into the canyon below. Eight km before the village of Chapada dos Guimarães, where you're likely to stop for lunch, is the **Cachoeirinha**, another waterfall with a natural pool, and another little beach spoilt by a restaurant and bar. The **Chapada dos Guimarães Mirante** (viewpoint) is 8km beyond the village of Chapada (take the last road on the right out of the village and, after 8km, take the dirt road that leads a few hundred metres off it). A path leads down from a dirt car park to the edge of the meseta with a spectacular panoramic view dotted with farms.

There's a great deal more to the Chapada than the sights you see on the tour; you will have only skimmed the edge of a park that occupies 33,000ha, taking in savannahs and submontane forests that are home to a variety of endangered species. The rarest are the maned wolf, black-capped capuchin and harpy and crested eagles. To see these you'll need a great deal of luck, a tent and camping gear and an itinerary that takes you to the wildest parts of the park. A barely discernible dirt track, navigable only in a 4x4, leads to the **Cidades das Pedras** rocks, seven bizarrely eroded rock formations that jut out amongst the gnarled trees on top of the meseta. At the **Nascente do Rio Claro**, there is an incredible 300m drop affording hypnotic views over an interminable plateau of fields and rivers.

Birding in the Chapada

There are no specialist agencies offering birding trips in the Chapada, though Joel Souza, who is probably the best birding guide in Cuiabá (*see* p.241), can arrange bespoke trips if given notice. The park is home to harpy and crested eagles, crowned eagle and coal-crested and yellow-billed blue finch: all endangered species. Blue-winged macaw, also an endangered species, can be seen near the Portão do Inferno. Helmeted manakin occurs at the bottom of the Véu de Noiva falls and, on the road to the Porta do Fé religious centre towards the village of Chapada, you'll find horned sungem. Behind the centre itself are cinnamon-throated hermit, dot-eared coquette, pale-crested woodpecker and fiery-capped and banded tailed manakins.

Chapada dos Guimarães Village

UFO-spotters and crystal healers love table top mountains; and Chapada is no exception. Even if you are not convinced by populist New Age philosophy, you may still be tempted by Chapada's cool, tranquil air and healthy food. Life focuses on the small plaza, full of flowering trees and hummingbirds and looked over by the venerable **church of Nossa Senhora de Santana**, built in 1779. There are five buses a day between Cuiabá and Chapada.

Chapada (© 065–)   ***Where to Stay and Eating Out***

The best hotel is the *inexpensive* **Pousada da Chapada**, Rodovia MT 251, Km 63, Estrada Chapada dos Guimarães, Km 63, © 791 1171, ✆ 791 1299, a kilometre outside town towards Cuiabá, with its own pool and restaurant. More central are the cheaper **Rios**, Tiradentes 33, © 791 1126, and the budget **Quinco** on Praça Dom

Wunibaldo, ✆ 791 1284. The **Gaia Bar**, off the main plaza, serves some vegetarian food, the **Borboleta Casa de Chá** on Rua Fernando Corrêa, has good tea and cakes and the **Taberna Suisa**, on the same street, serves international food, weekends only.

Tours in the Pantanal and Chapada dos Guimarães *Chapada (✆ 065–)*

There are many agencies offering economical trips to the Northern Pantanal and the Chapada dos Guimarães from Cuiabá. Only a few, listed below, are any good.

Joel Souza Safari, Rua Pedro Pedro Celestino 391, ✆/✉ 624 1386, is run by probably the best wildlife guide in the Pantanal. Tours are economical at around $60 a day, with fairly basic but charming accommodation on *fazendas* that offer the best chance of seeing animals. Horse-riding and/or boat trips are included depending on the season. Bespoke birding tours to both the Pantanal and wilder regions of the Chapada are also available (request Joel as your guide.)

Confiança Turismo, Rua Candido Marian, 434, Cuiabá, CEP 78005-340, ✆ 623 4141, ✉ 623 8880, *conftur@zaz.com.br*, a professional and comfortable outfit offering standard tours to *fazendas* along the Transpantaneira, one-day trips to the Chapada dos Guimarães and sport-fishing trips on the Rio Paraguay. Around US$100–120 per day.

Pantanal Explorer/Expeditour, Av. Gov. Ponce de Arruda, 670 Cuiabá, ✆ 682 2800 run by André Thuronyi, who has been working in the Pantanal for twenty years. Most trips are based round the Araras Lodge (*see* above), though cruises on their small boat are also available in the wet season. Guide quality is variable—some of the newer guides are not well informed.

Ecoturismo Cultural, Praça Dom Wunibaldo, 57, Chapada dos Guimarães Village, ✆ 791 1393. The only agency that exclusively operate in the Chapada, and the best, with an imaginative range of tours to remote parts of the park. They will also help arrange accommodation.

The Southern Pantanal

Corumbá is a small city on the edge of the Brazilian Pantanal, basking in thick heat and cooled only by the Paraguay river which it overlooks and the intense cold brought by the winds that sweep down sporadically from the Andes. Life revolves around the quayside. The colonial buildings that crumble at the water's edge are a reminder of the days before the railway eclipsed the river port's importance and sent Corumbá into economic decline. In 1840, before the Amazon rubber boom, this was the largest river port in the world. It's hard to believe; nowadays the quayside is illustrious only in the wonderful sunset views it affords of the Rio Paraguay. Money now comes from licit and illicit cross-border trade with Paraguay and Bolivia. Most of this passes tourists by—travellers are ignored by the Corumbá underworld, and the city is a safe place to visit, with an unintimidating small-town feel.

Aside from the quayside view, there's little to see in Corumbá. The **Forte Junqueira** east of town on the waterfront is the city's oldest building, dating from 1772, and there is an English steamroller once used to flatten Av. General Rondon and a waterwheel from the old sugar mill in the **Praça da Independencia**, 4 blocks from the quayside along Rua Frei Mariano.

Corumbá (✆ 067–) *Getting There*

Corumbá is connected daily **by air** to Santa Cruz (with connections to Miami) and Cochabamba in Bolivia with LAB and Aerosur (offices in the airport or through Pantur). VASP, 15 de Novembro, ✆ 231 4468, is the only large Brazilian carrier connecting Corumbá with the rest of the country.

There are more than ten **buses** a day to Campo Grande, which has regular onward connections to Cuiabá, Iguaçu, Rio and São Paulo.

The 'death train', as it is affectionately known to locals, carries budget travellers, smugglers and Mennonites from Quijarro, in Bolivia, on the opposite bank of the river, to Santa Cruz. Though the scenery is beautiful the journey is not comfortable and takes up to 24 hours. Watch your bags like a hawk—opportunist thieves abound. **Trains** leave four times a week.

Corumbá (© 067–)   ***Tourist Information and Useful Addresses***

Tourist office: Emcotur, América 969, © 231 6996, (*open Tues–Fri 8.30–12 and 1.30–6 and Mon 1–6*). Helpful Ângelo at the Secretaria de Meio Ambiente e Turismo, © 231 6617, has studied ecotourism in the area.

Changing money: Banco do Brasil, Rua Delamare, near Praça da Republica.

Bolivian consulate: Rua Antônio Maria Coelho at the junction of Rua América, (*open Mon–Fri 8.30–1.30*).

Corumbá (© 067–)   ***Where to Stay and Eating Out***

Gold Fish, Av. Rio Branco 2799, © 231 5106, @ 231 5435, has rooms with all mod cons, centrally located by the river and offers fishing and river trips (*moderate*). The well-equipped **International Palace**, Dom Aquino Correia, 1457, © 231 6343, @ 231 6852, has a swimming pool (*moderate–inexpensive*). The **Santa Monica Palace**, Antônio Maria Coelho 345, © 231 3001, @ 231 7880, with all the amenities, can also organize tours to the Bolivian Pantanal (*inexpensive*).

Campo Grande

You will have to pass through Campo Grande, the Mato Grosso do Sul state capital, if you travel to Corumbá overland from Iguaçu or the cities of the Brazilian litoral. It's a dull, anonymous place: the star attraction is a new conference centre, but at least it is well connected to all the major cities in Brazil by air and bus. There are several anonymous accommodation options such as the Internacional, Alan Kardec, 223, © 784 4677, @ 721 2729, or Novotel at Av. Mato Grosso 5555, © 726 1177. The Hotel Pousada LM, 15 de Novembro 201, © 721 5207, is a comfortable, cheap option. All have restaurants. Vegetarians should head for Viva Vida on Av. Fernando Correia da Costa at Bahia. It is open only at lunchtimes.

Campo Grande (© 067–)   ***Tourist Information and Useful Addresses***

Tourist office: Rua Manuel Seco Tome, 143, Jardim dos Estados, © 725 4822.

Changing money: Plenty of branches of Banco do Brasil and Bradesco.

Ecotourism: Ação Guaikuru, São João 430, Vilas Boas, CEP 79051-010, Campo Grande MS, © 741 6726, @ 741 4455, *www.guaikuru.org.br*, are a charity dedicated to the sustainable development of the Pantanal.

Tours Operators in Campo Grande and Corumbá   *(© 067–)*

Campo Grande has only a few agencies, Corumbá many. All offer access to the Pantanal both by road and river and connections to Pantanal *fazendas*. Operators travel to three main areas: along the *estrada parque*, a dirt road that, like the Transpantaneira in the north, cuts through the wetlands, affording excellent opportunities for seeing animals, particularly capybara, anteaters, caiman and anaconda, the Rio Negro environs, where many of the best *fazendas* like the Santa Clara are situated, and Nhecolandia—an area of grasslands rich in wildlife to the east of the *estrada parque*. Upmarket agencies also offer fishing trips on the Rio Paraguay, whilst the reliable cheaper ones have good-value camping excursions, something to consider whatever your budget—a night in the open, waking to birdsong, is a wonderful experience.

Many agencies in Corumbá aim at the budget-travel market and the city buzzes with the sales patter of touts. Ignore it. Quality of service is often low and tourists do not always get what they are promised. Our list of reliable operators in Corumbá includes budget options. All speak English unless otherwise stated. There are no specialist birding operators that we know of.

Corumbátur, Antônio Maria Coelho 852, ✆/✉ 231 1532, The best upmarket agency in Corumbá, offering luxury cruises and sport-fishing trips on the Rio Paraguay, and stays at the more expensive *fazendas* in the Pantanal.

Pan Tur, América 969, ✆ 231 4343, ✉ 231 6006, offer comfortable Pantanal tours, and are agents for the Fazenda Xaraes (*see* below, p.244), and also for LAB and AeroSur airlines.

Pantanal Tours, R M Cavassa 61A, ✆ 231 5410, ✉ 231 3130, offer luxury fishing tours on large Paraguay river boats and expensive one-day Pantanal tours.

Green-track, Delamare 576, ✆ (067) 231 2258, *travel.to/greentrack, greentk@pantanalnet. com.br*, is one of the two best small-scale budget operators, running imaginative camping trips to Nhecolandia, an area particularly rich in wildlife, with some beautiful lakes and marshlands.

Walter Ley, ✆ 231 5525/231 9212/231 6547, is an independent guide with very good combination *fazenda* and camping trips. Nights are spent camping in Nhecolandia and at the wonderful Santa Clara and Leque *fazendas*. Prices are rock-bottom.

In Campo Grande

Pantatur, Av. Alfonso Pena 2081, sala 103, Vila Cidade, 79002-071, MS. ✆ 382 0052, offer three- to four-night packages to upmarket Pantanal *fazendas* and fishing trips.

Orlando Rondon, Rua Antônio Corrêa 1161, Bairro Monte Líbano, Campo Grande, ✆ 725 7853, organizes tours to the Fazenda Rio Negro (*see* below, p.244)

Fazendas in the Southern Pantanal

Pousada Santa Clara, for written reservations and enquiries, contact Jose Antônio do Carmo, Batista das Neves, N 523, 79 300-000 Corumbá, MS, ✆ 987 2290 (two days notice required for pick-ups), Corumbá office: Cuiabá, 757, Corumbá 79301-50 MS, ✆/✉ 2311532, the English-speaking agent is **Walter Ley** (*see* above). Without a doubt the best *fazenda* in the Southern Pantanal for birdlife, and one of the best for animals. Dozens of hyacinth macaw roost in the trees opposite the cabanas, giant otters live in the Rio Abobral, giant anteaters and cats are a regular sight and even the elusive maned wolf has been seen here. An incredible bargain at less than $40 a day all-inclusive. Only Portuguese is spoken, though Walter Ley includes the Santa Clara in his two-night programme (*see* above).

Pousada Arara Azul, ✆ 383 3709, is a very comfortable *pousada* in Nhecolandia near the Rio Negro. Second only to the Santa Clara for birdlife, and perhaps even better for animals. Book through Pan Tur in Corumbá or Pantatur in Campo Grande (*see* above).

Pousada Caiman, write to Roberto Klabin Hotels e Turismo, Andar 1, Pedrosa Alvarenga 1208, São Paulo, SP 045531, ✆ (011) 883 6566. This is the premier ranch hotel in the state, a five-star, luxury Pantanal Southfork. Prices are very high. Book through Pan Tur in Corumbá or Pantatur in Campo Grande (*see* above, p.243).

Fazenda Leque, book through Walter Ley (*see* above), a cheap, rustic *fazenda* offering horse-riding trips. Good for wildlife.

Hotel Cabana da Lontra, ✆ 231 9933/987 3311. In an area good for river birds and otters and great for fishing. Moderate prices. Book through Pan Tur in Corumbá or Pantatur in Campo Grande (*see* above, p.243).

Hotel Fazenda Xaraes, reservations: América 969, Corumbá, ✆ 231 6777, a comfortable but over-priced lodge on the Rio Abobral offering horse-riding and boat trips. Book through Pan Tur in Corumbá or Pantatur in Campo Grande (*see* above, p.243).

Pousada Jatoba, Rodovia BR 267, KM 15, Jardim, MS 79240-000, ✆ 686 7026, office: 251 1583, ✉ 251 1713, *jatoba@jardim.menthor.com.br*, is a comfortable *pousada* outside the Pantanal proper in the higher ground near Jardim. Good for families.

Fazenda Rio Negro, (*see* Orlando Rondon, above), one of the oldest *fazendas* in the southern Pantanal—its been in the Rondon family for over 100 years. Intimate and upmarket with good guides, horse riding and boat trips.

Bonito

Although Bonito describes itself as 'the ecotourism capital of Brazil', its hardly big enough to be capital of anywhere, and the jaguar pelt trinkets for sale in the tourist shops are testament to its commitment to conservation. The town was discovered by TV Globo in 1993, and has been swamped with Brazilian families every holiday since. This means that it is used to catering for childrens' whims. There are some interesting sights to explore in the surrounding hills and plenty of travel agencies in town, all of whom offer exactly the same tours at exactly the same price. Taxis are the only public transport, and as there's no transport available to visit the sights, it is well worth hiring a car, either here or in Campo Grande (*see* above, p.242). Bonito Rent-a-car, ✆ 255 1474, rent cars, dune buggies and motorbikes. The tourist office, Rua Pillad Rebua 1780, ✆ 255 1850, has a list of other agencies. There are numerous hotels in Bonito and you won't have trouble finding a room. The Olho d'Água, is on the edge of town on the Rodovia Bonito–Três Morros, Km 1, CEP 79290-000, Bonito, MS, ✆ 255 1430, ✉ 255 1470, *olhodagua@vip2000.net*. It is set in a woodland park, roamed by paca and agouti and full of tropical fruit trees.

The Rios Sucuri, Prata and Cristalina which have crystal-clear water and are full of silver dourado and cachara (tiger catfish). Fishing is strictly prohibited and the fish, unintimidated by visitors, swim with you as you snorkel. The **Abismo Anhumas** is one of several caves full of stalactites and stalagmites. The vigilante and cortina, a 6ft-high finger of apparently melting rock standing sentinel in front of a wall dripping with slender stalactites, are particularly impressive. Other caves include the **Gruta da Lagoa Azul**, in a fifty-metre-long blue pool pierced by shafts of sunlight and **Nossa Senhora Aparecida**, which is currently closed to visitors. **Bonito Aventura**, a small sanctuary about 7km from town, offers waterfall body surfing, snorkeling and trail walking. There's plenty of wildlife in the woodland, including ocelot, friendly woolly monkeys, coatimundi, paca, and razor-billed currasow. The little bar and restaurant serve good food and are a haven when not mobbed with raucous tourists.

Venezuela

I never saw a more beautiful country, nor more lively prospects; hills raised here and there, over the valleys, the river winding into different branches, plains without bush or stubble, all fair green grass, deer crossing our path, the birds towards evening singing on every side a thousand different tunes, herons of white, crimson, and carnation perching on the river side, the air fresh with a gentle wind.'

Sir Walter Raleigh, *The Discovery of the Large, Rich and Beautiful Empire of Guayana, with a Relation of the Great and Golden City of Manoa (which the Spaniards call El Dorado)*

Sir Walter Raleigh was a notorious liar, but he told the truth about Venezuela. The harsh drama of Peru or Bolivia's landscapes are softened here—the coves and bays of the northern coast kissed by a gentle Caribbean Sea and the incipient Andes lush with coffee—but they are no less grand. To the south table-top mountains known as *tepuis* burst through the canopy of the forests and the bush grass of the Gran Sabana, their brooding cliffs lightened by the white slivers of a hundred waterfalls. The most famous of these is the Angel Falls, whose fountainhead is a kilometre above its base, making it eighteen times higher than Niagara.

Venezuela is Africa-shaped and delineated by the basin of the great Orinoco River which cuts across the centre of the country. Its headwaters stretch towards Brazil like the end of a fish-hook, mingling with the Negro River through the Casiquiare Canal to create a natural waterway to the Amazon River. This is remote territory, much of it uncharted and inhabited by tribal groups who still maintain a lifestyle that many of their cousins in Brazil have forgotten.

Tourism is concentrated in two regions: the Canaima National Park that encompasses the Angel Falls and Gran Sabana; and Amazonas State, which is mostly rainforest. The former is most easily reached through Ciudad Bolívar or Santa Elena, and the latter through Puerto Ayacucho. Birders and biologists of all schools are coming to Venezuela in increasing numbers. A high diversity of habitats means very high species diversity, many of which are unique not only to Venezuela but to the area in which they are found. Each *tepui* is a separate biological kingdom, separated from the surrounding plains by sheer cliffs. Sports fishermen interact with the wildlife more directly; Venezuela is one of the continent's premium sites for her two greatest fighting fish, peacock bass and payara.

Venezuela

Official language: Spanish and indigenous dialects including Yanomamo
Capital city: Caracas (*see* p.297)
Amazon gateway city: Puerto Ayacucho (*see* p.250)
Currency: *bolivar* of 10 *céntimos*

Highlights
1. Flying over the Angel Falls.
2. Climbing Mount Roraima or Auyan Tepui.
3. Visiting the waterfalls of the Gran Sabana, particularly the Quebrada de Jaspe.

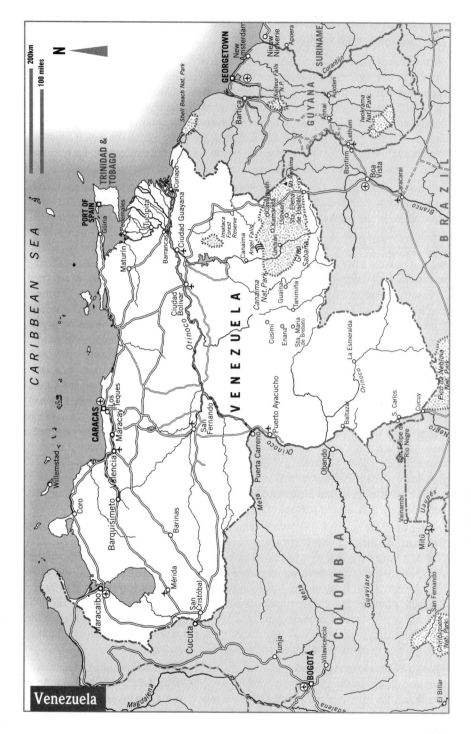

Venezuela

El Dorado and Other Myths

Southern Venezuela's landscapes have long inspired myths. The aboriginal groups of the Gran Sabana, collectively known as the Pemón, still consider the *tepuis* to be the symbolic homes of various archetypal spirits, the most ominous of which is the death spirit Canaima, after whom the national park is named. Canaima can adopt any form, hiding in the sides of the *tepuis* or under the rivers to attack his unsuspecting victim. Perhaps it is the spirit of Canaima who lurks mischievously behind the region's most famous myth—that of the Gilded Man, El Dorado, and his fabled kingdom, for nothing but death and ruin have come to those who pursued its promises.

Shortly after their brutal conquest and probably in a desperate bid to please the mercenary desires of the *conquistadors*, the Indians started to talk of a fabled land that lay somewhere in the depths of Venezuela or Colombia. They described a king who wore nothing but dust of pure gold over a coat of aromatic resin, both of which were washed off and discarded every day. This king ruled over a kingdom rich in treasure beyond belief. From the early days, El Dorado captured the imagination of hundreds of adventurers, many of whom perished in the forests of Canaima and the Orinoco, or returned to Europe broken and impoverished. The most famous casualty of all was the illustrious English buccaneer-nobleman and poet, Sir Walter Raleigh, who borrowed thousands to fund an ill-fated expedition; Queen Elizabeth herself empowered him 'to do Us service in offending the King of Spain and his subjects in his dominions to your uttermost power'. According to reports by a previous expedition, the city of El Dorado lay in the upper reaches of the Orinoco, beyond the mountains of Guyana on the shores of a vast lake called Parima. When Raleigh's expedition had struggled up the Orinoco and Caroni Rivers, through what is now Canaima, they found no lake. The previous expedition had been on the river in the wet season and the 'lake' had in fact been flooded forest. Parima was no more than the local name for one of the region's many rivers. Raleigh returned to face the wrath and scorn of Elizabeth's court. He later published an account of his travels which included a drawing of the great sea of Parima; such was his reputation that Raleigh's Lake Parima was still marked on maps until 1805. But Raleigh lost his head in his attempt to find El Dorado, both metaphorically, and literally; he was beheaded after his second attempt to find the city failed.

In later years the search for El Dorado turned to another ill-fated location, the Laguna de Guatavita in Colombia near Bogota. The stories focusing on this small Andean lake at least had some basis in fact; it had been the ritual centre of the Muisca Indians, whose chief, adorned with gold dust, would plunge into the water after throwing in gold offerings. From the 1560s, noblemen had been going bankrupt trying to extract gold from the muddy bottom, but it wasn't until Alexander von Humboldt had declared, after meticulous calculation that there must be at least 50,000,000 gold pieces buried in the ooze that the hysteria really took hold. Since then, the lake has been dredged, drained and dived by numerous individuals and companies, to no avail.

Though El Dorado is as lost today as it has always been, gold was eventually found in the Gran Sabana in the 19th century and in the Venezuelan Amazon in the 20th. And like Brazil, the discovery has brought little but misery to indigenous peoples and destruction the local area. Garimpeiros continue to cause environmental damage on a large scale, especially through their use of mercury and arsenic-based extraction techniques which pollute the rivers around the principal gold-mining towns, one of which is, appropriately enough, called El Dorado.

The primordial landscapes of Canaima continue to cultivate myths in the fertile minds of its visitors. Today hundreds come here to commune with extra-terrestrials, apparently led by a psychic commander in search of enlightened earthlings. UFOs are seen frequently flying low over the Gran Sabana, and shops in Santa Elena and Ciudad Bolívar sell maps showing the hottest spots for a Close Encounter.

The Venezuelan Amazon

A country nine or ten times larger than Spain, and enriched with the most varied productions is navigable in every direction by the medium of the natural canal of the Casiquiare…

Alexander von Humboldt

Though the Venezuelan Amazon is replete with wildlife, the real highlight of any trip is the scenery itself. It is peppered with table-top mountains called *tepuis*, and though these are smaller than those at Canaima and Roraima, they are equally as breathtaking. The plains south of **Puerto Ayacucho** are mostly thick with lush rainforest that swathes the flanks of the rocky crags that jut from the plain like worn teeth. The base of the most famous and dramatic of all, **Autana Tepui**, is visited on most standard tours. This rainforest Kailash is one of the world's holy mountains and has long been venerated by the Poroa, one of 13 tribes that live in the Venezuelan Amazon. They regard it as the broken stump of the severed world tree; an axis that connects the sacred to the profane, like Mount Sinai in the Judaeo-Christian tradition. Indians still climb its near sheer sides with their dead, leaving them to the eagles and the lightning storms that flicker over its flattened peak. The forests near Autana break into wild grasslands near the crumpled hills of the Guyana Shield before bursting into an even thicker growth of lowland and gallery forest further south, in the misty equatorial heat of the lower Orinoco. Here the river meanders in sluggish brown, mingling in wisps with the black Ventuari at the outpost of **Santa Bárbara**, where the course of the upper Orinoco runs from the east, from Yanomami Indian country where it loses a third of all its flow to the Río Negro via the 354km-long Casiquiare Canal.

This natural canal linking two of the world's great river systems is a useful measure of the extent of the Amazon's grasp. In theory, a canoe could enter South America at the mouth of the Orinoco in Venezuela and navigate its way to within a few kilometres of the headwaters of the Río Cuiabá and the Teles Pires, a tributary of the Amazon in the Brazilian Pantanal. The Cuiabá drains into the Paraguay which flows on to Buenos Aires in Argentina, so anyone who accomplished this journey would travel a distance far greater than that separating Spain and South America, and all on fresh water but for a few kilometres' walk.

So far none of Puerto Ayacucho's intrepid operators have this epic journey on their itinerary. Most take visitors white-water rafting on the Orinoco River a good deal closer to town, or to Autana Tepui, to visit a few indigenous villages and the narrow tributaries of the Orinoco that weave their narrow way through the forest and tropical savannah. A few go further afield and offer a three-week river odyssey along the **Humboldt Route**, taken by the famous German

19th-century biologist baron. This finishes in **San Carlos de Río Negro,** a tiny town deep in the heart of nowhere that provides a back door route to Brazil via the even tinier Cucuy a few hours' boat-ride down the Río Negro (*see* p.216).

Puerto Ayacucho

Puerto Ayacucho, the scruffy capital of the Venezuelan Amazon and the only town larger than a hamlet in the region, swelters sleepily at the edge of the nation. The Orinoco is a faster river in Puerto Ayacucho, rushing past the city in a series of broad boulder strewn rapids and providing the only terrestrial access to the wild south. Several professionally run tour operators offer trips of varying length and adventure downstream, using one of a number of rainforest lodges along the way. Some offer tours to Indian villages, and a few follow the Humboldt Route.

Eighty years ago Puerto Ayacucho didn't exist. Fifteen years ago it was a ramshackle frontier port that barely qualified as a town, linked to the rest of Venezuela only by a dirt track. This was paved in the late 1980s and the town has grown rapidly since. The main attraction now is the town's location, as the views out west from the giant boulders on the Orinoco's banks attest. Aside from this, Puerto Ayacucho holds only one tourist attraction: the excellent **Museo Etnológico de Amazonas** (Indigenous Peoples' Museum), on the central plaza (Av. Río Negro). This provides detailed information about the life of Venezuela's Amazon Yanomami, Yekuana, Piaroa and Guajibo Indians, with displays describing their lifestyle and customs. The **Cerro Perico** (west of town) and **Mirador** (south of the centre) are the best points from which to gaze at the Orinoco. El Mirador overlooks the Raudales rapids.

Puerto Ayacucho (℗048–)   ***Getting There and Around***

The airport is 7km south of town. There are regular flights to Caracas with LAV ℗ 21422, and to San Fernando de Apure and San Juan de Mapiare with Wayumi (Av. Evilio Roa) and Aguasya (Av. Río Negro). The bus station is east of town; there are regular departures for Caracas, Caicara, Puerto Ordáz, San Félix and San Fernando de Apure. There are regular ferries across the Orinoco and a long, inexpensive boat journey to Caicara; bring insect repellent and a hammock.

Puerto Ayacucho (℗048–)   ***Tourist Information and Useful Addresses***

Tourist office: Palacio de Gobernación, main plaza (*open Mon–Fri 9–11.30, 4–6*).

Changing money: The Banco de Unión on Av. Orinoco between Aguerrevere and 23 de Inero will change traveller's cheques and give an advance on a Visa card.

Puerto Ayacucho (℗048–)   ***Where to Stay and Eating Out***

Puerto Ayacucho's hotels are very ordinary. There are several jungle lodges nearby which are in far more beautiful surroundings and are as comfortable as any hotels in the town (*see* p.252). The best of the bunch in town are the **Hotel Guacharo's Amazonas Resort**, at the end of Evelio Roa, ℗ 210328, the only hotel with a swimming pool. Rooms are air-conditioned with TVs, and the restaurant is adequate; the **Hotel Apuré**, Av. Orinoco 28 ℗ 210516, is the next best option, with air-conditioned rooms and a restaurant. **El Jardín**, Av. Orinoco, ℗ 213373, has much the same but the restaurant is better. These are all moderately priced. Inexpensive options include the **Orinoco**, Av. Orinoco s/n, ✆ 210285, at the extreme northern end of town near the banks of the river; air-conditioned rooms. The best budget hotel is the efficiently run and friendly **Residencia Internacional**, Av. Aguerrevere 18, ✆ 210242, which has small rooms with air-conditioning or fans. The **Residencia La Cueva**, 23 de Enero, ✆ 210563, has clean rooms with air-conditioning or a fan.

There are no gourmet restaurants in Puerto Ayacucho; the town is small and sees few foreign visitors. Some of the cheap and cheerful Syrian- and Lebanese-run takeaways on Orinoco make delicious and authentic falafel and kebabs. The following are all inexpensive: **El Jardín**, (in the hotel), is the best of the town's few options. **El Capi**, Evelio Roa, two blocks east of Orinoco, serves a selection of simple, tasty dishes including burgers, some vegetarian options, good breakfasts and excellent fresh fruit juices and fruit salads. The staff are very friendly and accommodating. **Las Palmeras,** Av. 23 de Enero, serves decent pizzas and juices.

Tour Operators in Puerto Ayacucho
Puerto Ayacucho (✆048–)

Though there are some excellent lodges in the Venezuelan Amazon, these are mostly fairly close to Puerto Ayacucho or San Fernando. Most forest trips that stray further from civilization necessitate camping in tents or hammocks under mosquito nets, with perhaps a night spent in a comfortable lodge along the way. Food on expeditions is mostly simple fare, though the fresh fish will be among the finest you'll ever taste and the excitement of a night in the open in rainforest, together with the beauty of the scenery, make many forget the basic lifestyle.

We only list the companies we feel we can recommend. There are others in Puerto Ayacucho, some of whom have a reputation for sharp practice.

Cacao Expediciones, Piar 37, ✆/⊜ 213964, ✆ (02) 9771234, *cacaotravel@cantv.net*, *www.cacaotravel.com*. A professional country-wide company based in Caracas who have a good reputation for responsible tourism, and offer the standard four-day/three-night tour to Autana and two-day river tours on the Río Cuao, through rainforest and creeks near Samariapo, with the option of a light aircraft flight over the forest. Trips are basic, sleeping in hammocks (mosquito nets provided) in Indian villages, though one night is spent at the Campamento Garcitas (Orinoquia) (*see* p.252) within the Orinoquia Wildlife Reserve on the Autana trip. Between $80–$100 all inclusive. Bespoke trips available if you have your own group (minimum three people). Guides speak English.

Amazonia, Av. Río Negro 33A, in front of the Plaza de los Indios, ✆/⊜ 214926 (if the office is closed, leave a message with Expediciones Aguas Bravas). An experienced and adventurous local company who offer a wide range of tailor-made tours to the Venezuelan Amazon, including Autana and Cuao, and to the Gran Sabana and Andes around Merida. Longer expeditions up the Orinoco to San Fernando de Atabapo (four days) and along the Humboldt Route (21 days) require notice to organize. Rafting is also available. Between $80—$120 per person. Guides speak English.

Expediciones Aguas Bravas, Av. Río Negro, in front of the Plaza de los Indios, ✆ 210541/214458, ✆/⊜ 211529. The best rafting company in town, who conduct the occasional trip to Autana and one-day tours in the Refugio Yagrumo Cataniapo, a little reserve 50km from Ayacucho that offers a good foretaste of the rainforest. Expect to pay $40–50 for half a days rafting or the Yagrumo excursion, and $70 for Autana. English is spoken.

Turismo Yutaje, Bario Monte Bello 31, ✆ 210664, *turismoamazonas@cantv.net*. An established Puerto Ayacucho agency, run by enthusiastic and helpful Virgilio Limpias. Yutaje offer some of the most interesting deep forest excursions, including light aircraft and boat trips to the remote Yutaje Waterfall (three days) and to the Casiquiare Canal (seven days). Yutaje also offer the standard Autana trip and the Humboldt Route (17 days), and sports-fishing tours to catch South America's greatest fighting fish, the 40-inch payara (*see* below).

Tobogan Tours, Av. 23 de Enero 24, ✆ 214865, ✆/📠 214553, *tobogan@cantv.net*. One of the smartest local operators, with trips to Autana, the Humboldt Route and stays in the comfortable Campamento Camani (*see* p.253). Don't bother with the dull Amazonas Ideal tour.

Expediciones Guaharibo, Evelio Roja 39, between Av. Río Negro and Av. Amazonas, ✆ 210635, in Caracas ✆ (02) 952 6996. The most professional outfit in Puerto Ayacucho. Their VIP tour is one of the most comfortable of all those offered by Venezuela's Amazon tour companies, although it still involves camping in the forest.

Rainforest Lodges

Venezuela boasts some comfortable forest lodges. We have put them in two groups. Those close to the city, though not in pristine forest, offer comfortable alternatives to the city's uninteresting hotels. The remoter lodges are a short flight from the city, in the heart of the forest. Many are excellent destinations for birders. Some of the lodges are operated by tour operators in Caracas or Isla Margarita, who concentrate on three-day excursions from there via Puerto Ayacucho. They will arrange for a company representative to meet you in Puerto Ayacucho or alternatively, most travel agents in town can arrange your stay, although some may encourage you to opt for the lodge with whom they get the most favourable commission.

Close to Puerto Ayacucho

Amazonas Camp Calypso, in Puerto Ayacucho ✆ 210572; operator in Caracas, Calypso Tours C.A, ✆ (02) 545 0024/3065/6009, 📠 (02) 541 3036. At only 15km from Puerto Ayacucho's tiny airport, this luxurious resort is hardly in virgin forest. Rooms are under a single roof in an indigenous-style thatched *maloca* (*churuata*). Bathrooms are shared. Expect to pay $90 per person per night, including excursions.

Campamento Garcitas (Orinoquia), through Cacao Expediciones (*see* p.251). 20km from Puerto Ayacucho, within the Orinoquia Wildlife Reserve, whose dominant vegetation is tropical savannah, interspersed with sandstone monoliths in islands of gallery forest. The camp is named after the Orinoco River island that lies within its confines. The Indian-style cabins have private bathrooms. It is cheapest to visit Garcitas on a Cacao tour (*see* above).

Camturama Amazonas Resort, Puerto Ayacucho Km 20, ✆ 210572; in Caracas, ✆ (02) 941 8813, 📠 (02) 943 5160. The resort is very comfortable, with wonderful views of the Orinoco River. Facilities include a bar, disco and games room. Camturama is located in the borderlands between the savannah and forest. Upwards of $100 per day all inclusive.

Further South

Campamento El Yaví, operator in Caracas: Base Aerea Francisco de Miranda, ✆ (02) 993 5493/992 9395/991 7942; in Miami, USA, ✆ (305) 891 6524. One of the finest camps in the country, with nine very comfortable stone cabins with thatched roofs and private bathrooms, and a charming swimming pool with its own little waterfall, standing on top of a table-top hill commanding a view of the untouched savannahs and forest environs. The camp's name comes from the El Yaví *tepui*, and means jaguar in the Yavarana language. Excursions include flights by microlight, photographic and nature safaris and peacock bass fishing. Expect to pay $150 upwards for the standard package. The microlight and other extras cost more.

Campamento Camani, in Puerto Ayacucho book through Tobogan Tours (*see* p.252), main office (in Isla Margarita) ✆ (095) 627402, ✉ (095) 620989, *info@camani.com*; *www.camani.com*. Fifty minutes by plane from Puerto Ayacucho, in remote forest on a tributary of the Río Ventuari, near the village of San Juan de Manapiare. This is a comfortable, small-scale jungle resort with excellent facilities including a swimming pool, bar and restaurant. Though the electricity discourages some animals, rare birds like black currasow and rufous-winged ground cuckoos can be seen near the lodge. Expect to pay $100 per day all inclusive. Bathing under the falls of Tenqua or Caño de Piedra is a delight and the Cerro Churuata, 30 minutes away, affords wonderful views of the surrounding forest. Additional excursions, to Autana Tepui and the Ventuari are about $170 per person per day.

White-water Rafting

A few companies offer half-day white water rafting trips through the fierce, Class IV Atures Rapids, near Puerto Ayacucho; a hair-raising, exciting experience soothed in the smooth bits by the beautiful views across the grasslands to the hazy grey of the *tepuis*. The boats used come equipped with outboard motor, for safety, and no rowing is involved.

Birding in the Venezuelan Amazon

Venezuela is great birding country. The forests not only support species associated with the western Amazon (Manu in Peru, or La Selva in Ecuador), but also these associated with the *tepuis* of the upper Río Negro. Aside from generous numbers of guans, currasows, trumpeters, nightjars, potoos and rare raptors, the specialities include rufous-winged ground-cuckoo; Guianan cock-of-the-rock, orinoco soft-tail and yellow-crowned manakin.

Sports Fishing in the Venezuelan Amazon

Venezuela offers some of the continent's finest sport fish, including the payara, fiercer and stronger even than the peacock bass (*see* p.258)

Turismo Yutaje (*see* p.252), offer a variety of specialist fishing trips for payara and peacock bass on the middle Orinoco; about $100 upwards per person per day.

Capitán Barata-Puki Puki, operator in Caracas, Alptitour, ✆ (02) 283 1433/6677, ✉ (02) 285 6067. This 15m boat plies the Casiquiare Canal and Río Negro, along the Humboldt Route, and guarantees peacock bass along the way. Smaller boats explore inlets and creeks. Visits to indigenous communities are included on the trip. The fishing gear must be for 16lb minimum. Tours for a minimum of four people run between December and April.

Canaima National Park

Venezuela's largest national park dominates the southeastern corner of the country, a maze of rivers, crags and tropical rainforest that encompasses the eastern limits of the Venezuelan Amazon and the immense grasslands of the Gran Sabana. The park is dominated by 2 billion year-old-table-top mountains (*tepuis*) each a lost world, cut off from the surrounding plains by their sheer walls and harbouring unique plants and animals. Lightning clouds darken their vertical brows, bolts shoot across their tops, and the rain that falls there, a mile above the surrounding plains, tumbles in wispy cataracts from ledges so high that the water has formed clouds before it reaches the ground. The Salto Angel (Angel Falls), spilling over the flat top of Auyan Tepui, is the world's highest waterfall. As they leave the table-top mountains, these incipient rivers rush together and cut through the brown of the plains and the shallow hills, exposing sandstone, and sparkling red jasper. Tracts of tropical forest burst in tangled green where water settles, offering haven for scarlet macaws, toucans and capuchin monkeys that would be easy prey for the Sabana's predators in the exposed grasslands.

Route 10 between Ciudad Bolívar and Santa Elena offers a tantalising glimpse of this primordial scenery. To appreciate it fully, take a tour from either city, and explore the Sabana by 4x4, catch a light plane to the Angel Falls, or scramble up the highest *tepui* of all, Mount Roraima, that straddles the borders of Guyana and Brazil in the southeastern corner of the country.

The Angel Falls and Around

The world's highest falls drop from one of Canaima's tallest *tepuis*, and are best appreciated from the air. They begin in thin cataracts that foam from gashes in the top of Auyan Tepui, cascading for 979m (3,231ft) past the sheer craggy rock face. It is from the air that the first outsider saw the falls that came to bear his name. In 1935, while searching for gold, US bush pilot, Jimmy Angel, flew up the 'Devil's Canyon', that cuts into the side of Auyan Tepui and discovered the falls. It was not until two years later, after Angel crash-landed in a swamp on top of the *tepui*, that his claims were taken seriously; and not until 1949 that an overland expedition finally proved what Angel had long suspected: that he had been the first westerner to see the world's highest waterfall. The landscape around the falls is enough to explain why they were discovered so recently. Around the base of the *tepui* is an unbroken expanse of tropical forest that masks all but the narrow white waters of the Río Churún as it winds out across the plains. As it does so it is absorbed by the larger Río Carrao, which forms two further waterfalls: El Sapo, whose water curtain masks a shallow cave, and Hacha, which thunders over rocky steps, past dense rainforest into a broad lagoon.

This scene can be appreciated at leisure from the tourist village of **Canaima**, to the accompaniment of a cold beer, and is particularly beautiful in the late afternoon, when the low sun deepens the white of the falls and thickens the greens of the forest surrounds, and the tea-colourewde water int eh lagoon laps the pink beaches. The serenity of the lagoon can be disturbed in high season (July–October) when planes land every few minutes and the tranquil shore is alive with the cries of package tourists from the Caribbean resort of Isla Margarita. Prices rise accordingly and the accommodation can completely fill up. Those that plan to be there at this time may consider booking rooms well in advance.

Kavac, a remote congregation of twenty or thirty Indian-style tourist huts near the Pemón Indian village of Kamarata, on the other side of Auyan Tepui from Canaima, is the point of departure for those attempting the arduous and hot climb up the table-top mountain. Many Ciudad Bolívar agencies include it as an optional extra on the Angel Falls trips, visiting the La Toma falls and the Cueva de Kavac, a deep, waterfall-filled gorge, both located near the village.

When to go: The Angel Falls are at their fullest and most spectacular between June and November, particularly in August and September. Even then, seeing them in their full glory requires luck as they are sometimes obscured by its own cloud. In the dry season, between late December and May, they often shrink to a narrow sliver, that evaporates before reaching the ground. Boat access is only available in the wet season. Whenever you chose to go, you should aim to arrive after 10.30 and before 1pm, with 11am–12pm being the optimum time as the falls are in direct sunlight. At any time you will be sharing the view with other aircraft— the falls are the country's number one tourist attraction.

The Angel Falls — Getting There and Getting Around

There are two ways to see the falls, by air and by boat. Whilst a flight arguably offers the more impressive view, the boat trip is more of an adventure. A flight in past the falls followed by a boat expedition is the ideal option.

Flights can be arranged through tour operators in Canaima (around $100) or Ciudad Bolívar (around $180), or by approaching pilots at the airport in Ciudad Bolívar. If you choose the latter option, you will probably have to pay for a return ticket (around $160) even if you stay over in Canaima.

Boat excursions range from a cheap one-day rush to a more relaxed three-day two-night tour. The one-day tour begins before dawn and often entails arriving at the Mirador Laime (lookout point) when the falls are in the shade, with only half an hour to take in the view. The three-day tour usually includes a clamber behind the water curtain at El Sapo Falls, followed by a leisurely trip upstream with plenty of opportunities to see wildlife. Basic camp is made on Orquídea Island and the trip continues to the falls the next morning, culminates in a one-hour walk to the Mirador. Visitors usually have a few hours at the falls, in the best part of the day, before returning for a second night on Orquídea Island, and Canaima late the following morning. Most agencies can arrange extra nights at Orquídea Island. Even the boat trips can get crowded in the high season, and it is a good idea to check how many people will be on your tour before you decide who to book with. In any case, yours will not be the only boat on the river, and the camps on Orquídea Island, where everyone stays, can hold up to 200 people.

Many of the Ciudad Bolívar tour companies include a visit to **Kavac** in their itineraries and can arrange longer stays, with advance notice. Alternatively, charter flights can be arranged with pilots at Ciudad Bolívar airport, with a flight over the falls along the way. Expect to pay about $200 return.

Canaima and Kavac — Where to Stay and Eating Out

Canaima and Kavac are the only two villages with tourist facilities in the remote environs of the Angel Falls, with Canaima being the base for boat trips.

Canaima

Campamento Canaima, through the travel agency on site, or c/o Avensa Airlines, Caracas, (or any other Avensa Airlines office in Venezuela); in the USA ✆ 1 800 872 3533; and through travel agencies anywhere in the country. The smartest huts in town; guests can only stay here if they buy the whole Avensa tour package, comprising full room and board, a flight over the falls, a complimentary drink and a short boat ride on the lagoon; packages from $420–$800. Non-residents can eat here for around $20.

Campamento Ucaima, book through any agency in Ciudad Bolívar or Campamento Ucaima C.A in Caracas, ✆ (02) 693 0618, ✉ (02) 693 0825. Far smaller and more intimate than the Canaima camp, with thatched huts comprising rooms with private bathrooms Around $80 per night, all inclusive.

Parakaupa Lodge, book through any agency in Ciudad Bolívar. Basic but clean with private bathrooms, a restaurant and hammock space on verandas outside the rooms.

Wuey Tepuy, ✆ (086) 625955, or book through any agency in Ciudad Bolívar, or in Caracas, ✆ (02) 576 5271/5655/6992, ✉ (02) 576 6992. Basic rooms with private showers; the best of the village's cheaper options at around $30 per night all inclusive. Guided trips around Canaima available.

Campamento Hamaca, book through any agency in Ciudad Bolívar; or through Roymar Viajes y Turismo in Caracas, ✆ (02) 576 5271/5655/6992, ✉ (02) 576 6992. Very basic; from $15 per night.

camping

If you have your own tent it is possible to camp anywhere for nothing. A $5 permit must be obtained from the CVG building in the village, or from Inparques in Ciudad Bolívar (Casa del Gobernador, Av. Germania).

Kavac

Accommodation in Kavac is limited to a series of charming, but rustic large, indigenous style huts with earth walls. In the high season, the accommodation can get fully booked by tour companies, and it may be wise to book through one of them in Ciudad Bolívar—unless you have your own tent, you will be sleeping where they do in any case. Those who are travelling completely independently should bring extra food.

Tour Operators for the Angel Falls and Around

Most of the Angel Falls tour companies are in Ciudad Bolívar and offer much the same services: a one-day plane tour, or a three- or four-day boat tour with the option of visiting Kavac. All speak at least English and Spanish. All flights in and out of Canaima, food and accommodation and river transport are included in the prices quoted.

Climbing Auyan Tepui

Cacao Expediciones (*see* p.260), one of the most professional tour companies in the country, offer a trekking expedition to the top of Auyan Tepui. The itinerary is as follows:

Day one: A flight, that alone would make the trip good value, from Ciudad Bolívar over the *tepuis* of the Gran Sabana, the forests of Canaima and the Río Caroní and Angel Falls. Lunch in Kavac is followed by an afternoon hike to the Kavac Canyon and a swim.

Day two: A hot walk from Kavac to Guayaraca through a rainforest full of electric blue morphos butterflies and scarlet macaws, and across a series of rivers, culminates in fording the Río Okono before ascending to the first camp at Guayaraca.

Day three: The ascent to the second plateau at El Peñon begins by crossing savannah, continuing into thick forest around the base of the *tepui*. After a few hours, the vegetation changes back to dense bush, marking the beginning of Auyan's unique vegetation. Camp is made at the gigantic El Peñon rock.

Day four: An early tramp across a field of stone leads to the steep wall of the *tepui*. Ascent is made near a huge crevasse, and lunch is taken at the El Libertador rock, named after Simon Bolivar, whose statue was placed here. Camp is made a few hours further on under the rock of El Oso, the bear. The vegetation here is unique to Auyan Tepui: moor and swamp peppered with sundews, pitcher plants and islands of bushes.

Day five: The morning walk crosses a series of huge slabs that lead downhill to a tributary of the Río Churún, where the group stops for a swim, before crossing through the luxuriant vegetation of the valley that eventually leads to the Angel Falls. Pumas are often seen here.

Days six to nine: Return hike back to Kavac via Uruyen, a small Indian village.

Day ten: Return flight to Ciudad Bolívar.

The price (around $120 per person per day) includes flights, tents, porters (but not for private baggage) and all food and accommodation. The park fee (about $15) is extra.

Climbing Auyan Tepui Independently

Although Pemón Indians closed the *tepui* to walkers in 1995, it may now be possible to climb the mountain independently, hiring local guides. Cacao Expediciones (*see* p.251) or any Venezuelan tourist office should be able to advise you of the latest situation. Alternatively, it is possible to make enquiries locally: contact Tito Abati in Kavac or the more authentically Indian village of Kamarata, two hours walk away. The two-week (or more) round trip to the point where the Angel falls plunge of the *tepui* begins in the village of Kavac. Guides can be hired in Kavac for around $40 a day plus the same for a porter.

Walking to the Angel Falls from the Gran Sabana

Ruta Salvaje (*see* p.264), one of the region's best travel agents, offer one of Venezuela's greatest adventures: bespoke jeep, canoe and walking trips from the Gran Sabana to the Angel Falls. This affords an excellent opportunity to see the diverse ecosystems of the region and the animals that live there. The journey begins with a jeep tour of the Gran Sabana between Santa Elena and the village of Kavanayen, taking in several of the region's most beautiful waterfalls including the Quebrada de Jaspe (Jasper Falls). Walking begins on the second day, with a four-hour forest trek to the first camp (hammock accommodation). The next six days are spent in dense forest until arrival at the community of Kamarata. Motorised canoes continue from here to the Angel Falls camps, which are reached after three days. The company need a few weeks' notice to organize this expedition, which costs US$1,000 per person (maximum 12) including food, guides, equipment and all transport (including plane to Ciudad Bolívar).

Rafting from Kavac to Canaima

Cacao Expediciones (*see* p.251) offer a ten-day inflatable rafting expedition around Auyan Tepui through the narrow rivers, gallery forests and savannahs between Kavac and Canaima. The journey begins with a flight out over the Angel Falls, and takes in the fearsome Grade III-IV Chun Meru and the Gargantua del Diablo (Devil's Throat) Rapids (which can be circumnavigated by the faint-hearted), wonderful vistas of the Kuai Meru, the Amaruay and Auyan Tepui, and a wide variety of plants and animals (depending on the time of year.) Expect to pay around $100–150 per person per day.

The Río Caura

This remote black-water Orinoco tributary, littered with giant boulders and lined with beaches of fine white sand and lush gallery forest, is one of the cleanest and least spoilt areas of natural beauty outside of the depths of Venezuela's southern Amazon. The river's basin covers 30,000km^2 of rainforest that stretches unbroken but for Yanomami and Yekwana villages into Brazil, visited only by these Indians on their hunting trips. River dolphins, Amazon turtles, giant otters and Brazilian tapirs abound in this wildlife haven, and jaguars can sometimes be seen basking on Caura's broad beaches in the dry. *Tepuis* burst through the forest to either side, and at the Para Lagoon, five waterfalls, the tallest over 50m high, plunge into the inky waters in the heart of dens forest. Two companies specialize in trips to the Caura: Cacao Expediciones (*see* p.251), who maintain a small lodge at Las Trincheras, and Soana (*see* p.261) who offer camping safaris, spending some nights in beachside huts in the Yekwana community of El Playón.

Sports Fishing on the Río Paragua: Lake Guri and the contiguous Río Paragua are one of South America's premium destinations for those afflicted by peacock bass- and payara-mania. Peacock bass are already well-known as one of the world's greatest fighting fish, while the vampire-fanged payara has not yet achieved their formidable reputation, those who have caught the evil-looking fish often proclaim it to be stronger still, and more aggressive. Its appearance certainly suggests this: two rapier-like teeth as much as two inches long protrude from the lower jaw into a gaping mouth that can open nearly a foot wide. These formidable poke through even when the jaw is closed. Dearuna (*see* p.261) offer fishing trips based in the Peacock Bay and Uraima Falls lodges (best seasons Sept–April and Dec–May respectively). Peacock Bay (for bass) use 18ft Boston whalers equipped with 40hp outboards, trolling motors, fish-finders and rod-holders. Uraima (for payara) use 35ft dugouts with swivel seats and rod holders, for easy access to the rapids where the payara spend their time. Water-skiing is also available. Food and drink is good and plentiful at both camps. Both are a one-hour charter flight from Ciudad Bolívar, and can be booked through Dearuna (*see* p.261.)

Ciudad Bolívar

Beyond its proximity to the Angel Falls and its historical interest, this uncomfortably hot and architecturally undistinguished city has little to recommend it. A sunset stroll along the promenade that lines the Orinoco to watch the dolphins surface from the brown of the river, past the colonial buildings where Bolivar planned the liberation of South America, is pleasant, but spoilt by the heat, the din of the modern city and the unimaginative buildings that seem to crowd out any dreamy, imaginative reveries inspired by her history. Nonetheless, Ciudad Bolivar is the best jumping-off point for Canaima and the Angel falls, as well as being an important junction between the Amazon and the Gran Sabana. There are plenty of tour operators here, and transport links are excellent.

Ciudad Bolívar (✆085–)   ***Getting There***

There are daily flights to Caracas and several buses depart daily for Puerto Ayacucho (10hrs), Caracas (9hrs), Santa Elena (8–10hrs), and more than hourly to Ciudad Guayana (Puerto Ordáz) (1–2hrs).

Car rental: Budget, ✆ 27413/27431; *www.budget.com.ve/ciuboliv.htm.*

Ciudad Bolívar (✆085–)   ***Tourist Information and Useful Addresses***

Tourist office: next to the airport, ✆ 26491.

Changing money: Banco Unión, Dalla Costa, has a Visa cashpoint, and the Banco Consolidado, near the airport at the Centro Comercial Canaima will change American Express Traveller's Cheques.

Internet: Facilities at Expediciones Dearuna, in the Hotel Caracas (*see* p.261).

The Sights

Ciudad Bolívar was founded in 1764 as San Tomás de la Nueva Guayana. Its location at this particular point where the Orinoco contracts earned it the popular name of Angostura, the Spanish word for 'narrows'. For some forty years, it remained a backwater river port, until Simon Bolivar, the archetypal South American romantic man of action, expelled the Spanish from the town in 1817 and established it as his headquarters.

It was in Ciudad Bolívar that the hero of South American independence planned the re-conquest of Spanish America. Bolivar declared Angostura to be the new capital of the independent republic of Gran Colombia in the modern-day **municipal museum** on the plaza. Bolivar was educated and well-known in Europe: he studied Locke, Spinoza and Hobbes in Madrid, was an eyewitness to the final scenes of the French revolution in Paris, and took an oath in Rome to liberate Venezuela from Spanish rule. His agent organized loans and sent arms and equipment across the sea and up the Orinoco River to this tiny river port on the edge of the known world and the wilderness. English, Scots and Irish adventurers, the fearless cowboys and Indian lancemen of the Venezuelan *llanos,* and the indigenous horsemen of the Gran Sabana were all filled with inspiration by dashing, Byronic Bolivar, and rallied to his cause. This ragged and motley crew accomplished one of the greatest military feats of modern times: in just over a year, they routed the Spanish, crossing vast swamps, scaling the Andes and battling stifling heat, disease and hunger along the way. When he returned to the town, Angostura hailed him as the deliverer and father of his country. Bolivar soon passed a law by which the republics of Venezuela and New Granada united in a single state under his presidency, Gran Colombia. The **Casa de Congreso de Angostura** (*open daily 9–12 and 2.30–5*), the building where this law was passed, still stands today on the Plaza Bolivar. Angostura was re-named Ciudad Bolívar 16 years after the liberator's death in 1846.

Apart from its colonial history, the town is famous only for the bitters that bear its name. In 1800, when Alexander Von Humboldt was taken ill in Ciudad Bolívar, it was the prototype of Angostura bitters, mixed with honey and the bark of a local tree, that saved his life. Twenty four years later, a Prussian doctor called Siegert invented the modern formula in the modern-day **Consejo Municipal** (*between Plaza Bolívar and Parque Miranda*) moving the factory to the Port of Spain in 1875.

Other sights: The **Instituto de Cultura del Orinoco** (*open Tues–Sun 9.30–12 and 3–5*), halfway along the Paseo Orinoco near the Mirador, has Southern Venezuelan Indian crafts and an aquarium of Orinoco River fish. The **Museo Casa San Isidro** (*open Tues–Sat 9–12 and 2.30–5*), beyond the fort on Av. Táchira, is an old coffee hacienda, turned into a period piece museum. Bolivar reputedly wrote his impassioned Angostura speech during his stay here. The **Museo de Arte Moderno Jesús Soto** (*open Tues–Sun 10–5*), Av. Germania, is set in pleasant gardens and is devoted to Venezuelan modern art. **Jimmy Angel's plane**, rescued from Auyan Tepui, is propped up in front of the airport terminal building (*see p.254*). The **Museo Geológico y Minero** (open Tues–Sat 9–11.30 and 2.30–5), School of Mines, UDO University, Av. Principal, La Sabanita suburb, has displays of the rocks and minerals of the Gran Sabana and Canaima. The **Museo de Ciudad Bolívar** (*open Tues–Sat 9–12 and 2–5, Sun 9–12*), Paseo Orinoco at Carabobo, contains a small selection of historical items, including the first printing press and the first newspaper, interspersed with modern art. The **Zamuro**

Hill Fort, (open Tues–Sat 9–12 and 2.30–5), Paseo Heres, was built after the revolution (in 1902) to house a garrison. There's little to see inside but the views out over the city make it worth the trip.

Ciudad Bolívar (℃085–) — *Where to Stay*

Laja Real, Av. Andrés Bello at Av. Jesús Soto, ℃ 27953/27944. The plushest establishment in town, conveniently situated opposite the airport for trips to Canaima. The **Laja City,** Av. Bolívar, ℃ 29910/29919, is the Laja Real's cheaper sister. **Valentina,** Av. Maracay 55, ℃ 22145/27253, is quiet, conveniently close to the airport with comfortable air-conditioned rooms and a very good restaurant. The **Hotel Colonial,** Paseo Orinoco between Dalla Costa and Píar, ℃ 24402, ℮ 23080, is the only air-conditioned hotel with a river view, making it the most attractive, though not the most luxurious, place to stay in town. At the bottom end of the moderate price range.

There are a number of cheap and inexpensive options of varying quality along the Paseo Orinoco, all of which are safe, and some of which are grungy. The **Hotel Caracas,** Paseo Orinoco, ℃/℮ 22132, (mobile) ℃ (014) 985 1360, *expdearuna@ telcel.net.ve*, is the most popular choice with budget travellers, and the best of the cheapies if you don't mind this crowd. The large terrace offers a river view, and there's a bar serving snacks, a professionally run travel agent and internet facilities.

Ciudad Bolívar (℃085–) — *Where to Eat*

Tasca Ankares, in the lobby of the Hotel Valentina, Av. Maracay 55, is one of the best restaurants in the city, with delicious river fish. **Arabe-Venezolana,** Cumaná at the corner of Bolívar, has good Arabic food (including wonderful falafel), in air conditioned surroundings. Most of the cheap hotels along the Paseo de Orinoco have equally cheap restaurants, the best of which are: the **Hotel Italia, Hotel Caracas, Charly's.**

For vegetarian food head to peaceful **Gran Fraternidad Universal Fundación Dr Serge Reynard la Ferreira,** Dalla Costa at Amor Patria. They also offer yoga classes and have a small bookshop. Open lunchtimes only.

Tour Operators in Ciudad Bolívar — Ciudad Bolívar (℃085–)

Unless stated otherwise, all the companies listed below speak English and run tours that take in the standard sights around the Angel Falls (Gran Sabana). Some offer lodge-based trips to the Río Caura. Prices include all but the $10 entry fee to Canaima National Park and, if you're heading to the Angel Falls, airport tax (about $2), and are negotiable, especially if you bring your own group. If visiting the Angel Falls, check which lodge the company usually uses— some cut costs by booking guests into accommodation suitable only for those who don't crave comfort. There are a range of options in Canaima Village (*see* p.255) and most tour agencies will be happy to book clients into one that suits their requirements. Santa Elena, near the border with Brazil, is a better place from which to visit the Gran Sabana (*see* p.264).

Cacao Expediciones, Venezuela at Boyaca, ℃ 28727, in Caracas ℃ (02) 997 1234, ℮ (02) 977 0110, *cacaotravel@cantv.net, www.cacaotravel.com.* One of the most professionally managed and adventurous tour companies in the country, with a large range of imaginative tours around the country, using good equipment and facilities of high standard (though forest expeditions often involve camping and hammocks). The large selection on offer include boat trips to the Angel Falls, and one-day (or more) plane excursions; climbing Auyan Tepui (*see* p.256); rafting around Auyan Tepui; ten-day forest and savannah walk around Kavac; Gran Sabana tours; climbing Mount Roraima; jungle-lodge based trips on the Río Caura (*see* p.257) and a variety of Amazon and Venezuelan beach tours.

Auyantepuy, Boulevard Bolívar com Dalla Costa, Ctro Comercial Roque, Local 8, Ciudad Bolívar; ✆ 20748, mobile ✆ (016) 852465, ✉ 48668/28702; *www.venezuelaonline.com /travel/*; *tepuy@telcel.net.ve*. One of the more upmarket operators in Ciudad Bolívar, with the standard aeroplane and boat trips to Canaima (from $190 and $280 respectively), and Gran Sabana tours (around $90 per day), with a little added comfort.

Soana Travel, Bolívar 50 (at Dalla Costa), Apt., 454 Ciudad Bolívar 8001-4, ✆ 22030, ✆/✉ (014) 851 0373. A mid-range, family-run European and Venezuelan travel agency, with informal and friendly staff. The best choice for adventurous hikes and canoe trips on the Río Caura. Soana also take trips into the Gran Sabana (at around $70 a day) and Angel Falls, with an optional extra night in Kavac (about $260 for the standard trip and $80 extra for Kavac).

Cunaguaro Tours, in the lobby of the Hotel Italia, Paseo Orinoco, Ciudad Bolívar, ✆ 22041, ✆ mobile (014) 850344, ✉ 27810. As well as bespoke options at cheap prices, they offer the variation on the standard tour to the Angel Falls (with an extra night at Kavac) for $340 including the flight between Kavac and Canaima. They are one of the best value, if the most basic, options for Mount Roraima treks and 4x4 tours of the Gran Sabana (around $55 and $65 per day respectively). Professionally run tour company.

Dearuna Tours, Hotel Caracas, Paseo Orinoco, ✆/✉ 22132, ✆ mobile (014) 985 1360, *expdearuna@telcel.net.ve*. One-day flights to the Angel Falls for around $180 and three-day boat trips for around $260. Dearuna offer the usual variety of accommodation options in Canaima village, plus tours to the Orinoco Delta (about $70 per day), the Gran Sabana, and sports fishing on the Río Paragua (*see* p.258).

Neckar Tours, in the lobby of the Hotel Colonial, Paseo Orinoco, ✆ 24402/28167, ✉ 21315. Offer the standard boat and plane trips to the Angel Falls for around $280, with the added option of a night in Kavac. A range of bespoke rainforest treks near the falls include a wildlife hike between Kavanayen and Kamarata, using local guides (not biologists). Tours through the Gran Sabana are also available.

Gekko Turismo, Posada Casita, Av. Lijin Pulido, Urbanización 24 Julio, ✆ 014-9851683. German-run, budget travellers' favourite covering all the main sights of the Gran Sabana (around $60 a day), the Angel Falls (around $180 for the plane trip and $260 for the boat trip), and Orinoco Delta (about $70 a day).

The Imataca Forest Reserve

This selectively logged wilderness area is the most reliable site in South America for seeing harpy and crested eagles. Black-faced hawk, rufous-winged ground cuckoo, Guianan toucanet, capuchin bird, Guianan red cotinga and rose-breasted chat can also be seen here. Jaguar red-rumped agouti and Guianan saki monkeys. Any agency in Ciudad Bolívar will take you to Imataca on a bespoke trip, given a couple of week's notice. Alternatively, hire a car in the city and head east to Upata. From here, head 19km south to Villa Lola and then 30km east to El Palmar. There are a few hotels in the village, the best of which is the Parador Taguapire (*inexpensive*). You should be able to hire a guide either at the Parador or in the village itself.

La Gran Sabana

In the southeastern half of Canaima National Park, the forests that engulf Auyan Tepui disperse to become dark green islands in a sea of light green grass, and the dark brows of the *tepuis* brood on every horizon. They seem to grow in stature as they march towards Brazil and Guyana, culminating with Mount Roraima, whose harsh walls guard a biological kingdom that stands isolated, 1½km above the surrounding plains. The rivers that leave the *tepuis* wind their way through the grasslands in a meander of rapids and cataracts that expose the hard rock of the Guyana Shield: water thunders over the 150m-high Chinak-Meru Falls, and veils a shallow cave at Kamá-Merú. At the Quebrada de Jaspe (Jasper) Falls, it sparkles an almost fluorescent red as it rushes over a 50m-wide step of the semi-precious stone. Jasper litters the pebble beaches of the Río Yuruaní and the broken boulders of 2 billion-year-old sandstone lie strewn across the plains and rolling hills like the shattered remnants of giant black pepper corns, or burst through its flesh like darkened teeth. The easiest and most convenient way to see the sights of the Gran Sabana is through a tour operator in **Santa Elena de Uairén**, a quiet little town that is Venezuela's last outpost before the frontier with Brazil.

Mount Roraima

The seemingly impregnable natural fortress of Roraima soars above the surrounding plains, meadows and grasslands lapping its walls, waterfalls dripping from its 1550m-high sides. Its wind- and rain-sculpted summit is a maze of dark stone arches and bizarrely shaped monoliths interspersed with canyons of sparkling pink and white rock crystal. Wisps of fog play around the jumbled rock towers and atolls of carnivorous plants, lichens and mosses. The nutrients essential to life are washed down the sides of Roraima by the incessant rain, and glistening sundews, vase-like pitchers and specialised bromeliads supplement their diet in this stone desert with lured and trapped insects and spiders. Half of Roraima's plants and animals are found nowhere else on earth; at certain times of the year the *tepui's* plateau is covered with legions of tiny black toads that have never been forced by evolutionary pressure to hop or swim. Their closest relatives are probably African, drifting away from their Roraima cousins when the giant continent of Gondwanaland split to form Africa, Australia and South America. Several agencies in Ciudad Bolívar and Santa Elena (a closer and a more convenient starting point) offer trips up Roraima.

Santa Elena de Uairén

Santa Elena is a quiet, undistinguished little town near the border with Brazil. There is nothing to see here, but the atmosphere is more relaxed and a good deal cooler than in Ciudad Bolívar further north. The town looks to tourism for its livelihood. and is the best base for visits to the Gran Sabana and Roraima. Tours to either taken from Ciudad Bolívar usually spend the first day driving to Santa Elena, making it better value to catch a bus here and make arrangements with one of the town's well-equipped and well-run tour companies when you arrive.

Santa Elena de Uairén   ***Getting There and Around***

Flights to Ciudad Bolívar, El Paují, Caracas and Puerto Ordáz (Ciudad Guayana).

International **buses** leave daily for Boa Vista in Brazil (4hrs), some continuing to Manaus (at least 12 hrs). **Note** that when you book a bus ticket to Brazil, it is imperative that you have a valid Yellow Fever certificate, issued at least ten days prior to arrival. Otherwise you will have to be vaccinated in Santa Elena and wait ten days before being allowed into Brazil. Several national buses leave daily for Ciudad Bolívar (8hrs), Ciudad Guayana (7hrs) and Caracas (16hrs).

There are plenty of **taxis** in town. Expect to pay $10 to the Brazilian border.

There were no car rental agencies in town when this book went to press. For the latest, enquire at Ruta Salvaje Tours (*see* p.264).

Useful Information and Border Crossing

There is no **tourist office** in Santa Elena.

Changing money: Banco Orinoco, Bolívar at Mariscal Sucre, changes traveller's cheques. Ruta Salvaje (*see* p.264), and many of the shops in the centre (especially the gold shops) will exchange dollars in cash.

Internet: facilities at Ruta Salvaje (*see* p.264)

Brazilian consulate: opposite the petrol station near Ruta Salvaje, on Mariscal Sucre, the main road out of town to the north. Though it is theoretically possible to get a Brazilian visa here, it is quicker and easier to get one before arriving in Santa Elena.

Immigration: Venezuelan exit/entry stamps are given at the border.

Santa Elena de Uairén (© 088–)   ### Where to Stay and Eating Out

Unless stated otherwise, all the hotels, *cabañas* and guesthouses listed below have some staff who speak English.

moderate

Gran Sabana Hotel, Brisas de Uairén, Ruta a Brasil, Santa Elena de Uairén, © 951810; @ 951813, *hgransabana@hotmail.com*; *www.hotelgransabana.com*. Comfortable, modern business-style hotel with all the amenities. A little charmless.

Cabañas Friednau, Av. Principal Urb. Cielo Azul, © 951353. Private huts with en suite bathrooms. Organize trips to Mount Roraima.

inexpensive–cheap

Ya-Koo, Km 3, Vía a Sampay, © 951742/951332; or book through Ruta Salvaje Tours. Beautiful *cabañas* next to a rainforest island in the Sabana, with a view out towards the distant *tepuis*. Small, spring water-filled swimming pool, bar, and tasty breakfast and dinner (included in the price.) The best place in town in any category.

Cabañas Tavara, Km 2, Vía a Sampay, © (014) 863 4478, or book through Ruta Salavje tours. Comfortable, individual *cabañas* built on the hillside next to toucan-filled forest and just down the hill from Ya-Koo. Good food and good value.

Hotel Lucrecia, Av. Perimetral, a few minutes walk from the bus station, © 951130. Spartan but comfortable rooms opening onto an orchid-filled garden.

Vida Salvaje, Km 3, Vía a Sampay, book through Ruta Salvaje Tours. Rustic *cabañas* designed by a famous local artist with bizarre roofs and wonderful views.

La Casa de Gladys, Urdaneta 187, © 051171. Backpacker's favourite, and the best rock-bottom cheapie in town, with a communal patio and (bad) coffee served all day.

Hotel Luz, Raúl Leoni s/n, ☎ 951573. Another backpacker hotel, with its own budget travel agency. Friendly and helpful, but accommodation is basic.

Santa Elena is a centre for the harvesting of giant tropical ants, whose abdomens are eaten raw and wriggling, or squashed and made into a delicious piquant sauce. In May and June, at the beginning of the wet season, Pemón Indians in wellington boots can be seen everywhere, picking the inch-long new queens off blades of grass as they emerge from their nests, and throwing them into buckets that rustle and hiss with their squirming. Tourists squirm too, but adore the spectacle and the Indians get indignant when they try and photograph them. Asking to taste the ants before taking pictures will probably meet with a delighted response.

If ant sauce is not enough, then the Ya-Koo and the Tavara have Santa Elena's best restaurants, serving delicious regional and international food. These must be booked in advance by non-guests (*see* 'Where to Stay' above for details). Otherwise, most of the restaurants are little more snack-bars with little to distinguish between them.

Tour Operators in Santa Elena

There are half a dozen agencies in Santa Elena, offering much the same package. The following are the ones we feel most able to recommend.

Ruta Salvaje tours, Av. Mariscal Sucre at Akarabisi, ☎/⌨ 951134, *rutasalvaje@cantv.net*, *geocities.com/rutagransabana*. The best company in town, offering a variety of trips to the sights of the Gran Sabana and the Angel Falls in remodelled 1990s Toyota Land Cruisers (bring an inflatable pillow). Tours include: white-water rafting in inflatable dinghies, and body surfing on the Río Yuruaní; treks up Roraima and an exciting twelve-day overland trip taking in the sights of the Gran Sabana and then walking and canoeing through the forest to the Angel Falls (*see* p.254). The company's owner, the very helpful and friendly Ivan Artal, is a former champion dirt-bike racer. Ruta Salvaje can book any of the lodges in the Gran Sabana and have Internet facilities in the office.

Roberto's Mystic Tours, Ikabarú at Urdaneta, ☎ 951790, ☎ (014) 886 2901, *mystictours@cantv.net*. Two- to four-day 4x4 tours of the Gran Sabana for around $55 a day. Roberto and his colleagues have very good knowledge of local lore and are full of stories. Some of these can be found in his interesting Gran Sabana guidebook, available in English all over the town. The mystic aspect of the company includes a wholesale acceptance of New Age UFOlogy, with the Gran Sabana as one of the world's principal points of Close Encounter. Bespoke UFO tours are available, together with a map of where aliens and humans have met, and a portrait of their blonde-haired, blue-eyed alien commander. You may be reassured to know that the extra-terrestrial aspect of Roberto's Gran Sabana knowledge is an optional extra. He knows the Sabana from a more down-to-earth perspective as well as anyone in Venezuela.

Tayukasen Expeditions, in the lobby of the Hotel Luz, ☎/⌨ 951825. The budget travellers' option, with Roraima treks and Gran Sabana tours for around $45 a day.

The Guianas

In Georgetown, Guyana, the gutters brim with lotus flowers, reggae booms from car stereos and Bollywood films pack out the cinemas. Hindu temples, etched with Shiva's trident, the domes of mosques and the wooden spires of Anglican churches reach up for the heavens. Paddy-fields are tilled by Javanese around Niuw Amsterdam in Suriname and some of Totness's residents still have ginger hair and moustaches. Paramaribo streets are lined with wooden replicas of houses from a Pieter de Hooch painting. And in Cayenne, capital of the only remaining European enclave in the Americas, the music of Jacques Brel and Serge Gainsbourg wafts out of bars and pâtisseries, mingled with the smell of crêpes and Gauloises.

The three Guianas, it seems, are only in South America geographically. Yet a few miles behind this alien façade toco toucans call to each other in forests and savannahs that stretch to the banks of the Amazon, 800 miles away. This is 'the Interior', as it is known in all three Guianas, a world of thundering waterfalls, copper-coloured rivers and crags of ancient sandstone that serves as a fragile refuge for disparate tribal groups of Indians and African 'Maroons', who preserve a tribal way of life long lost in their West African ancestral homes. Forgotten for generations, this vast wilderness is now beginning to be exploited in Guyana and Suriname, by big logging and mining corporations and groups of *garimpeiros* who leave ugly scars on the landscape, and poison the rivers with mercury.

The interior of the Guianas are brimming with wildlife: 825 species of birds have been recorded in Guyana, 600 in Suriname and 829 in Guyane. These probably represent only 70 to 80 per cent of the real total and new species are regularly discovered.

When there aren't strikes or political problems, facilities in the Guianas are generally good. Trips to the Interior or the turtle beaches tend to be made from the capitals—Georgetown, Paramaribo and Cayenne. There are a number of modern, well-equipped jungle lodges, and specialist natural history guides. English is the first language of Guyana, is widely spoken in Suriname (whose first language is Dutch) and not spoken at all in Guyane, where no one understands anything except French.

Guyana
Official language: English
Capital city: Georgetown (*see* p.270)
Currency: *nuevo sol* of 100 *cents*

Guyane (French Guiana)
Official language: French
Capital city: Cayenne (*see* p.291)
Currency: *nuevo sol* of 100 *cents*

Suriname
Official language: Dutch
Capital city: Paramaribo (*see* p.283)
Currency: *nuevo sol* of 100 *cents*

Highlights
1. Karanambu Lodge, to visit the rehabilitated giant otters and Diane McTurk.
2. A flight to the Kaieteur and Orinduik Falls.
3. The old wooden buildings of Georgetown and Paramaribo.

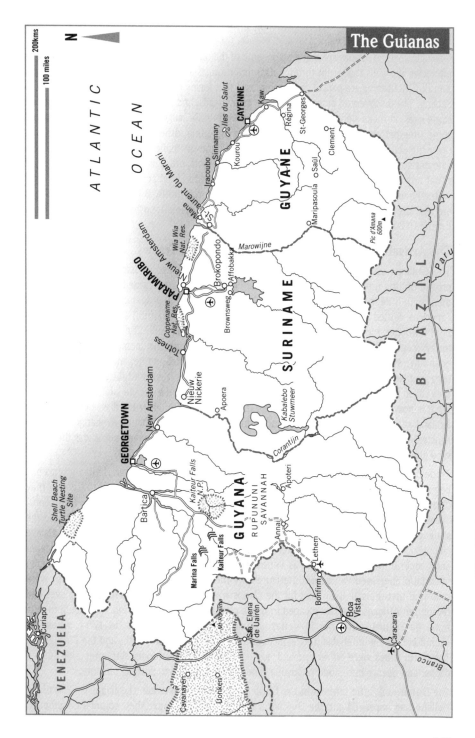

History

Geologically the Guianas are made up of some of the oldest rocks on the planet. The sandstone pinnacles and cliffs that erupt through its interior forests and plains to form the Pakaraima and Kanuku Mountains are part of the same massif that forms the *tepuis* of the Venezuelan Gran Sabana. The discovery of petroglyphs, stone arrowheads, and grinding grooves used to sharpen stone axes, in rocks along the rivers of Suriname's Interior, suggest that the first people arrived some time before 6000 BC. Over the following millennia, other Amerindian groups arrived. Over the centuries, these tribal societies expanded and diversified, weaving together an intricate network of trading alliances in which foodstuffs, tools, drugs, and dyes and a whole host of ritual objects were exchanged through a labyrinth of rivulets, across waterfalls, rapids and watersheds, and, where this was not possible, rainforest trails. By the time the Europeans arrived, the Caribs, vigorous and fierce hunters and warriors who had migrated north from Brazil in 1200 AD, had come to dominate this alliance.

The Arrival of the Europeans and the Carib Slave Trade

The Guianan coast was sighted by Columbus in 1498, when he discovered Trinidad, but proved of little interest to the Spanish or the Portuguese, who regarded it as hostile to settlement with little mineral wealth to exploit. In 1616, the Dutch, desperate for a foothold in the Americas, settled on a small island at the confluence of the Mazuruni and Cuyuni Rivers and built a wooden fort which they called Kyk Ober Al ('See Over All'). The ruins still can be seen today (*see* p.283). The Dutch, less militant than the Iberians, complemented the local economy, swapping axes and steel for forest products. Meanwhile, the British founded a tobacco plantation in 1630 in modern Suriname, following it with a full-scale colony which they called Willoughby Land in 1651. The French followed suit a decade later at Sinnamary, in what is now Guyane. Towards the end of the century, Willoughby Land was conquered by Holland and renamed Fort Zeelandia and formally ceded by the British in exchange for Nieuw Amsterdam (which became New York). The French clung on to Guyane but it was the Dutch who dominated the region, expanding trade with the indigenous peoples.

Trade became so lucrative for both parties that by the 1700s, the dominant Indian groups had begun to enslave the weaker in order to supply the Dutch with more of the goods they desired. Slavery of this sort had been practised long before the arrival of the Europeans. Treaties signed with the two most powerful tribes; the Caribs and Arawaks, exacerbated the situation, and the problem was worsened further when the Dutch began to use 'red slave labour' on their sugar estates and later to sell 'red slaves' along the coast. Caribs raided deeper and deeper into the inland as fas as Venezuela in their search for fresh slaves and demanded material of increased value from the Dutch. By the 1740s, Dutch and Spanish sources were reporting that the sole livelihood for the Caribs was the barter of captured Indian slaves and recaptured Africans who had escaped from the plantations. Portuguese, too, had begun to infiltrate the Spanish territories in Venezuela, also searching for slaves. In 1754, when the situation became untenable, the Spanish declared war against the Caribs and the Portuguese. The Carib tribes were either crushed, forced to work on missionary settlements or pushed deeper and deeper into modern Guyana. They never returned to Spanish territory.

The Dutch took little interest in the Carib war. Relations between the Spanish Crown and Holland had improved and the Dutch did not want to antagonize their colonial neighbours.

The red slave trade faded in importance as Africans were imported in increasing numbers to the sugar plantations. Soon trade in sugar had eclipsed that of rainforest products, and in 1784 they established a capital city, Starbroek, at the north of the Demerara RIver, to cater to ever-growing demand. Apart from the recapture of escaped Africans, trade relations with the Amerindians came to an end.

British Guiana: the Early Years

In 1803, the British decided that Starbroek would be a useful South American foothold for the burgeoning empire and promptly took it from the Dutch, renaming it Georgetown. It became the capital of the new country of British Guiana, a union of the Dutch states of Essequibo, Demerara and Berbice. Holland retained Suriname and French Guyane. In effect, especially for the Indians, the only thing that changed in British Guiana was the flag and the national language. The 'red slave' trade continued to decline, and the Indians continued to be occasionally employed as bush police to recapture runaway African slaves.

In 1833, much to the dismay of the planters, black slavery was abolished in British Guiana. The French followed suit in Guyane about 20 years later and the Dutch in Suriname a decade after that. Indentured workers from India, the Azores, the East Indies and China began to pour into Georgetown and Paramaribo. The Caribs lost their job as black slave hunters and even the Warao, squeezed off their coastal territory by the expansion of plantations, had retreated to the Interior. Contact between the forests and the colonial world diminished and, but for missions and the timber trade, would have altogether disappeared. By the end of the 19th century, after the massive influx of Asians and the growth of the African population, the forgotten indigenous peoples of British Guiana and Suriname only numbered four per cent of the population. Their lands were annexed to European crowns, in order to better protect them from Brazil, and international borders were delineated through the middle of tribal territories.

Guyana became independent from Britain in 1966; Suriname from Holland in 1975. Guyane became a French *département* in 1946 and remains part of France. Despite a vigorous independence movement, in recent referenda the majority have voted overwhelmingly to stay so.

Guyana

Like its neighbour Suriname, Guyana is a strip of stolen mud sandwiched between forest and ocean. The sea constantly threatens to reclaim its territory, battering the concrete fortifications that protect the coastal cities and pounding the sluice gates that drain the sugar-cane fields at low tide. Life in this narrow strip is a distinctly non-Latin American mix of Creole and Asian patois, reggae and Bollywood, Saivaite mantras and Anglican hymns. Behind the reclaimed mud looms a giant forest whose interior is unknown to most Guyanese. It is a land of extraordinary beauty: valleys of virgin green fed by thundering waterfalls and savannahs bordered by mountains with eagles' nests and jaguars' lairs hidden in their folds. The original Americans still live here, in tribal groups that were never officially conquered. Ignored for years by the coast, these Amerindians are becoming increasingly vocal as their lands are sold off to foreign developers.

Guyana, the nation, has an identity crisis, resulting from decades of pretending she's not in South America, and ignoring her forests and the heritage of those that live there. When Britannia ruled the waves the illusion was fairly easy to maintain; but when the British left in the late 1960s Guyana began to become introspective and divided, unsure whether it was part of the Caribbean or out on its own in syncretistic limbo. In the struggle for a sense of self, conflict arose between the East Indians and the Africans who between them make up over 90 per cent of the population. Successive governments flirted with communism and the country drifted into debt and disarray. It wasn't until the late 1980s that the Guyanese really noticed that they were sitting on the edge of a vast forest full of timber and gold. Years of squabbling and petty dictatorship left a pressing need to service the foreign debt and resulted in invitations for foreign investment which have chiefly been aimed at exploiting the natural resources. Guyanese, especially Amerindians, have reaped few of the benefits; lax environmental controls have led to a number of environmental disasters, notably at the OMAI mine in 1995. Amerindians, ignored by the coast for decades, have been particularly vocal in their protests. Their anger has helped to attract the attention of groups like the World Rainforest Movement and Conservation International who have made the world aware of Guyana's enormous biological importance.

Guyana's coastal swamps and beaches and her Interior are a haven for rare wildlife: three endangered species of turtle (green, olive ridley and giant leatherback) nest on her beaches and the country has more than 825 bird species in 77 of the 92 families that regularly occur in South America. Cotingas and antbirds are the most abundant, and spectacular birds that are fairly easy to see here include the harpy, crested and ornate hawk eagles; great horned and crested owls; Guianan cock-of-the-rock; red-bellied and red-shouldered macaws; Rio Branco spinetail and antbird. Waterfowl include scarlet ibis; roseate spoonbill and zigzag heron. All of the big cats are found in Guyana, and Karanambu Ranch (*see* p.279) the best place in South America for giant otters. Though new lodges and travel agencies are appearing all the time and facilities are good, tourism is new to Guyana. Even the spectacular Kaieteur Falls are little visited and most groups have the park to themselves. Conservational tourism, if carried out in a low impact fashion, can benefit the country's wilderness: Guyana currently has just two protected areas.

Georgetown

Few are aware that this tiny capital is home to the largest wooden building in the world: St George's Cathedral, designed by Arthur Blomfield, harks back to an age when this now crumbling city was the wealthy capital of an imperial British outpost. Now her wharves and quays are quiet and Guyanese sugar is little more than a famous brand name. Most modern Demerara sugar is manufactured in Mauritius. Georgetown may be poor and a little decrepit, but it is still one of the finest and most elegant cities in the Amazon region. Only Paramaribo and Cusco are more delightful. Though many of the elegant wooden houses that grace the streets have broken window panes and peeling paint, lotus flowers bloom everywhere and a gentle breeze sways the scarlet jacarandas and heavily scented frangipanis in the elegant botanical gardens. Facilities are good. The city has some excellent tour companies, good hotels and reasonable restaurants. Note that care should be taken at night, as intimidating beggars roam the streets. Tiger Bay is unsafe even during the day. Check with your hotel for the latest information.

Georgetown (© 02–)

Getting There and Around
by air

Georgetown has two airports, one for domestic flights and another (Cheddi Jagan) for international flights. Both are out of town. For the latter, allow 45 minutes for a taxi ride (about $30). Airport tax is $20 on international flights.

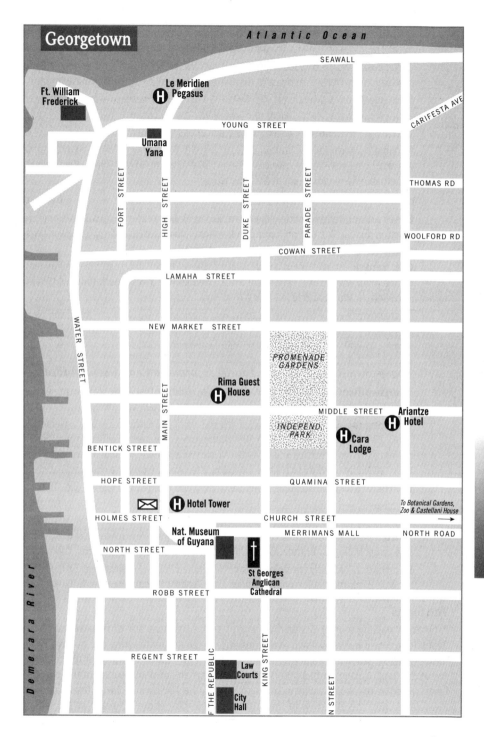

Georgetown

Atlantic Ocean

SEAWALL

Ft. William Frederick

Le Meridien Pegasus 🅷

CARIFESTA AVE

YOUNG STREET

THOMAS RD

Umana Yana

FORT STREET

HIGH STREET

DUKE STREET

PARADE STREET

WOOLFORD RD

COWAN STREET

LAMAHA STREET

WATER STREET

NEW MARKET STREET

PROMENADE GARDENS

Rima Guest House 🅷

MAIN STREET

MIDDLE STREET

Ariantze Hotel 🅷

INDEPEND. PARK

🅷 Cara Lodge

BENTICK STREET

HOPE STREET

QUAMINA STREET

✉ 🅷 Hotel Tower

To Botanical Gardens, Zoo & Castellani House →

HOLMES STREET

CHURCH STREET

Nat. Museum of Guyana

MERRIMANS MALL

NORTH ROAD

NORTH STREET

✝ St Georges Anglican Cathedral

ROBB STREET

Demerara River

REGENT STREET

OF THE REPUBLIC

Law Courts

KING STREET

City Hall

N STREET

BWIA (63 Robb St, ✆ 63661, ✉ 73016, *guyana@bwee.com*) flies to Miami, New York, Toronto, London and Frankfurt via Trinidad.

Guyana Airways (✆ 57337, ✉ 60032, *www.turq.com/guyana/guyanair.html*) fly to destinations in North America and the Caribbean as well as to the Guyanese Interior.

Suriname Airlines (Middle St, ✆ 54894/53473, *publicrelations@slm.firm.sr*) fly to Suriname, Guyane, Paris, Belém in Brazil (with onward connections).

LIAT fly to the Caribbean with onward connections to USA and Europe.

Roraima Airways (101 Cummings St, ✆ 59648/59653, ✉ 59646; *www.roraima airways.com*.) and Trans Guyana Aviation (158–9 Charlotte St, ✆ 73010) fly regularly to Lethem (via Mahdia). About $60 one way.

by road

Buses and collective taxis leave from Starbroek Market for destinations along the coast, including Corriverton/Springlands where a foot passenger ferry and river taxis-cross to New Amsterdam in Suriname.

Car rental: Budget Rent-a-Car: Ocean View Hotel International, Liliendaal, Georgetown, ✆ 223247. Union: Lot 24/25 Cauliflower Place, South Ruimveldt Park, ✆ 65364, in the USA ✆ (718) 848 6749.

Georgetown is easily navigable **on foot**. For longer journeys, **taxis** are cheap and plentiful and are easily booked through hotel receptions: E-Zee, ✆ 56926; David's Taxi Service, ✆ 70959; Roadrunner, ✆ 65759; Fat Boy: ✆ 53371.

Georgetown (✆ 02–)   ***Tourist Information and Useful Addresses***

Tourist office: 157 Waterloo St, ✆ 56699/50807/50817, ✉ 50817; *tag@solutions2000.net*; *www.interknowledge.com/guyana*. Helpful and efficient.

Changing money: Most hotels and shops will exchange cash in US dollars. Demerara Bank, 230 Camp and South Sts, ✆ 50610, the Amex representative here, has a foreign currency exchange service and a Money Master ATM. Globe Trust and Investment Co Ltd, 92 Middle St, ✆ 75141, gives a good rate for Amex traveller's cheques.

Internet: School of Computing, Middle St, between Main St and Carmichael St.

Embassies and consulates: **Suriname**, 304 Church St, ✆ 67844, *open 8–12*. Visas cost $40. Bring two passport photos; **UK**, High Commission, 44 Main St, ✆ 65881. **Brazil**, 308 Church St, Queenstown, Georgetown; *open 9–11*. Visas cost $20. Bring two passport photos. **France**, Consul, 7 Sherriff St, ✆ 65238. **Venezuela**, Thomas St.

Information on indigenous peoples: Amerindian Peoples Association, 71 Quamina St, ✆ 70275. Information on indigenous issues and Amerindian peoples in Guyana.

The Sights

A pleasant walking tour of Georgetown begins at the southern end of the Avenue of the Republic, where it meets Hadfield Street, historically the most interesting end of town, with the city's finest, and oldest buildings. The neoclassical **Parliament Building**, at the corner of Av. of the Republic and Hadfield St, is still the political and symbolic centre of the country. Emancipated slaves bought rights to land from here in the 1800s, and Cheddi Jagan, who led the country after the departure of the British in the 1960s, chose to keep it as the seat of government. **Starbroek Market**, the biggest market in the country (with the city's old Dutch name), stands a block west of the Parliament Building on Water St at Brickdam. You can buy anything from raw gold to raw plantain here, and it is a great place for taking black and white photographs, but watch your wallet. The former **Law Courts** and **City Hall** are possibly the most beautiful buildings in Georgetown: the Law Courts, on Av. of the Republic at Regent St, were designed by Castellani and are fronted by a decaying statue of Queen Victoria. The latter is a turreted, blue and white folly which looks like a minor German castle from the Rhine Valley remodelled in wood. **St Andrew's Kirk,** built in 1829, and standing obliquely opposite the Law Courts, is Georgetown's oldest surviving building.

On North Road at King St stands **St George's Anglican Cathedral,** grandest of the city's buildings, which, with a spire of more than 40m (132ft), is the tallest freestanding wooden structure in the world. The story of the building's construction, and much of the city itself, is depicted on its interior walls, memorials and stone tablets. Housed in an undistinguished building two blocks west of the cathedral, on North Road at Main St, the **National Museum of Guyana** is full of random bric-a-brac, hordes of stuffed animals, and a model of Georgetown before the Second World War (when a huge fire destroyed many of the finest wooden buildings), and some of the world's rarest postage stamps.

Main St is one of the city's most pleasant tree-lined streets. Many buildings have Demerara shutters (louvres with window boxes enclosed in fretwork). The **State House** is the official residence of the President, and formerly housed the British governor. The Prime Minister's house lies further along Main St. It was formerly owned by Booker Brothers, and it was said that the company director would watch the ships come in from the upper storey, and that the captains, aware of this, would ensure that the port sides were always painted.

On the High St, next to the Meridian Pegasus Hotel, stands the **Umana Yana**, a traditional Indian *maloca*, built by Wai Wai Indians for an indigenous conference in the 1970s. The name means the 'Meeting Place of the Peoples'.

The very Victorian **Botanical Gardens** lie a little out of town (five minutes from the cathedral by taxi on Homestretch Avenue at Vlissengen Road), but are well worth a visit. They are dotted with small, neat bridges and pavilions; giant water lilies cover the ponds and manatees will take grass from your hands. The small **zoo** houses Amazon fauna. The **Castellani House,** near the southwest corner, and designed by the eponymous Italian architect, now houses the national art collection. The gardens are not safe after dark.

Georgetown (✆ 02–)   **Where to Stay**

Georgetown has some comfortable hotels with good service and modern facilities, but they tend to be overpriced, particularly at the top end of the market.

luxury–expensive

Le Meridien Pegasus, Seawall Rd., Kingston, Georgetown ✆ 52853/52859, 📠 53703, *guypegasus@solutions2000.net, www.interknowledge.com/guyana /pegasus*, is the best hotel in town, though overpriced; Shell Beach Adventures and Timberhead Rainforest Resort have their offices in the reception (*see* p.276). **Cara Lodge**, Taitt House, 293 Quamina St, ✆ 55301/55304, 📠 55310, *caralodge@cara-hotels.com, www.carahotels.com*, is set in a 150-year-old colonial mansion house. There is a good restaurant. **Cara Suites**, 176 Middle St, ✆ 61612/61614, 📠 61541, *carasuites@cara hotels.com, www.carahotels.com*, has comfortable, business-orientated suites with cooking and internet facilities. No pool. **Main St Plaza**, 45 Main St, ✆ 70313, *mainstplaza@solutions2000.net*, *www.mainstplaza.com*, is a centrally located, modern complex of suites with restaurant and a pool.

moderate

Hotel Tower, 74–75 Main St, ✆ 72011, ✆ 56021; *hotel.tower@solutions2000.net*, *www.interknowledge.com/guyana/tower*. This hotel has seen better days but it is conveniently central; Wilderness Explorers have their office in the lobby. **Ariantze**, 176 Middle St, ✆ 65363 / 70152, ✆ 70210, *hughes@solutions2000.net*, has suites, a pool, restaurant and gym and live music at the Sidewalk Café and Jazz Bar.

inexpensive–cheap

Rima Guest House, 92 Middle St, ✆ 57401. The best cheap option in town, at the top end of the budget market. The **Palace de León Hotel**, 64 Cross St, ✆ 78686/58053 has simple rooms and a restaurant and bar. The **Palace de León Apartments**, 63 Croal St, ✆ 77019, offers self-contained apartments and a restaurant.

Georgetown (✆ 02–)　　　　　　　　　　　　　　　　　　**Eating Out**

All the restaurants below are moderately priced.

Bottle Bar and Restaurant, Cara Lodge, ✆ 55301/55304, offers excellent food in period surroundings; the restaurant and hotel are both in one of Georgetown's best preserved colonial mansions. Book in advance. At **Del Casa**, 232 Middle St, ✆ 52429, try the international and Creole cuisine in quiet, pleasant surroundings. No shorts or trainers. **Sidewalk Café and Jazz Bar**, Ariantze Hotel, 176 Middle St, ✆ 70152, has some local specialities, live jazz and Caribbean music. The **Palm Court Bar**, 35 Main St, ✆ 70008, offers excellent lunch specials in the city's yuppiest bar.

vegetarian

Back to Eden, David St, Kitty, Georgetown. Well worth the ten-minute taxi ride from the centre. Great value vegetarian lunches, juices and à la carte specialities, from a menu of West Indian and Creole food and curries. The best of the numerous branches.

Tour Operators in Georgetown　　　　　　　　*Georgetown (✆ 02–)*

Wilderness Explorers, Hotel Tower, 74–75 Main St, Georgetown, ✆ 77698, ✆/Voice Mail 62085, *info@wilderness-explorers.com*, *www.interknowledge.com/guyana/wilderness*. One of South America's top, (and most expensive) adventure travel specialists. Soft and hard adventure (including Kaieteur Falls overland), turtle nesting beaches, specialist birding, wildlife and bespoke trips, and stays at the country's best ranches and wildlife lodges can all be arranged with the company. Combined nature and/or birding trips to Guyana and Trindad/Suriname/ Guyane are also available. Most of the tours are arranged around six of the country's finest lodges and ranches (all described in 'Lodges and Ranches in the Interior', p.279). Wilderness Explorers also offer an expedition to a Wai Wai indigenous village in the south: there are only three Wai Wai Expedition trips a year. Participants are interviewed for suitability beforehand. Rates available from Wilderness Explorers only. The two-week trip involves staying in a Wai Wai village in the middle of forest and savannah lands, discovering their cultural, hunting and agricultural traditions and searching for wildlife with Wai Wai and tropical biologist guides. Animals and birds that have been seen on these trips include jaguar, tapir, harpy eagles and giant otters. Accommodation is in hammock camps along the way, and meals are supplemented with Wai Wai cooking. There are also expeditions to the Maparri Wilderness Camp, a simple wooden-framed shelter deep in the Kanuku rainforest. The Kanuku Mountains have been recognized by Conservation International as a pristine area of Amazon rainforest, still home to jaguar, puma, ocelot, margay, oncilla, jaguarundi, Brazilian tapir, and rarely seen animals like bush dog, kinkaju, and grison. Night boat trips expose the hiding places of black caiman and electric eels. Birding is very good (*see* harpy eagle trek, p.280). They have a bird checklist. Most Wilderness Explorers' trips are around $200 a day with a flight, $120 without. This includes all food, drink (including limited local bar), transport and accommodation. Meals and drinks in Georgetown are extra.

Shell Beach Adventures, Le Meridien Pegasus Hotel, Georgetown, ✆ 54483/4, ✉ 60532, *sbadventures@solutions2000.net*. Offer very similar options to Wilderness Explorers: ranch- and lodge-based trips at some of the region's best lodges (*see* p.279), Kaieteur overland and turtle nesting beaches, with a few specialist trips, including a 4x4 trip tracing the route of the 1992 Camel Trophy. Extensions to and from other countries including a Venezuela extension (meeting tourists in Curiape), a Suriname extension (you are met on arrival at Springlands) and a Tobago and Guyana combination tour. Unlike Wilderness Explorers, the company does not use professional biologists, but it is considerably cheaper: $100–$160 per person per day.

Rainforest Tours, Hotel Tower, 74–75 Main St, Georgetown, ✆ 72011/5, ✉ 56021. Tours to Kaieteur and Orunduik, Kaieteur overland and a hiking trip in the Pakaraima mountains, visiting Patamona Indian communities. Around $60–$120 per person per day.

Nature Tours, 45 High St, Kingston, Georgetown, ✆ 66109. Booking agent for Karanambu, Dadanawa, Timberhead, Baganara, Shanklands and Rockview, and plane trips to Kaieteur and Orunduik. Between $50 and $170 per person per day.

Wonderland Tours, 65 Main St, Georgetown, ✆ 53122, ✆ /✉ 59795. Plane trips to Kaieteur and Orunduik and Kaieteur overland.

Roraima Airways, 101 Cummings St, ✆ 59648/59653, ✉ 59646; *www.roraima airways.com*. Some of the cheapest day trips to Kaieteur and Orunduik from $150 (for the two) and $90 for Kaieteur alone.

Shell Beach Turtle Nesting Site

The Atlantic in Guyana is thick and muddy, and the beaches uncomfortable and ugly. This is probably why they provide one of the last undisturbed turtle nesting areas in the Caribbean, the **Shell Beach Turtle Nesting Site**, for at least four species of marine turtle, including the world's heaviest reptile, the magnificent giant leatherback. Though it is one of the largest and most widely distributed of all reptiles, the leatherback is rarely seen. But several times a year, usually between March and July, these giants haul themselves over the sand in the dead of night and dig rough holes with their powerful flippers and lay some 150 eggs.

Seeing a turtle is a matter of luck, patience and little sleep, but Guyana affords one of the best opportunities anywhere. **Audley and Violet James and their son Romeo**, an Arawak family who work closely with Shell Beach Adventures in Georgetown (*see* above), recently received the prestigious Neotropic Award from Conservation International for their work in protecting sea turtles. They are excellent guides and their ecotourism work is helping to ensure that there will be turtles nesting on Guyanan beaches for many years to come.

Standard Turtle Nesting Beach and Coast Adventure Itinerary

Day one: Travel up the Essequibo and Pomeroon Rivers to the village of Santa Rosa.

Day two and three: A three-hour trip on a small boat takes you to the Morouca savannahs and Dark Bush gallery and varzea forests. The Río Waini, home to freshwater dolphins, leads to the Atlantic Ocean and Almond Beach where camp is made.

Days four and five: Two nights with the James family, boating, fishing and trail walking, in search of scarlet ibis, and nesting green, olive ridley, leatherback, and hawksbill turtles. Accommodation is in mosquito-proof tents (bring plenty of repellent anyway).

This trip costs about $80 per person per day (for a group of 6–8) with Shell Beach Adventures (*see* p.275), and $130 with Wilderness Explorers (*see* p.274).

Jet Boating

These natural roller-coaster rides on the rapids of the upper Essequibo and Mazaruni Rivers are well worth the money. Lunch is included at the very comfortable Baracara Island Resort, on a small island with white-sand beaches in the Mazaruni. A day trip costs $70 or around $180 with an overnight stop at Baracara (all-inclusive). Contact Whitewater Adventure Tours, Kitty, ✆ 66614/52281, ✆ 65225, *wwat@solutions2000.net.*

Resorts near Georgetown   *Georgetown (✆ 02–)*

There are a number of rainforest resorts within fairly easy access of Georgetown.

Timberhead Rainforest Resort (✆ 53760/52853, ✆ 53702, or book through any of the larger agencies in Georgetown), is only 15 miles from Georgetown on a black-water creek that joins the Demerara River. The lodge is simple but comfortable, and set in a stretch of great birding territory close both to savannah and forest. Birders can expect as many as 200 species a day. The lodge also offers trail walking, canoe trips, uninteresting visits to local indigenous villages, and swimming in the creek. Around $90 per person per day.

Arrow Point (book through Roraima Airways, ✆ 59648, ✆ 59646) is only a few miles from Timberhead. Most time here is spent jet skiing on the creek. Don't expect to see any animals. Small, intimate and comfortable but overpriced at $100 a night (all-inclusive.)

Shanklands Rainforest Resort (book through Cara Suites, *see* p.273, or any of the Georgetown travel agents). This, with Timberhead, is the best rainforest resort within fairly easy access of Georgetown. The birding is very good. Accommodation ranges from rustic camp facilities to luxurious self-contained cottages with carved balconies, porcelain baths, four-poster beds and great views out across the Essequibo. Flop on white-sand river beaches, explore the rainforest on foot or by canoe, or try the very English activities such as croquet on the lawn, badminton and golf putting. Prices range between $50 and $150.

Baganara Island Resort (book through Evergreen Adventures, 159 Charlotte St, Georgetown, ✆ 60605 / 65128, ✆ 51171; *everg@solutions2000.net*) is not to be confused with Baracara, though they both offers much the same facilities. This large, modern mansion lies on the banks of the Essequibo at its meeting with the Mazaruni. Rooms are comfortable with balconies and river views and the standard package of excursions and activities include trail walks, river trips, fishing, volley ball and wave-runner rental. Expect to pay $110 a day.

Baracara Island Resort (book through Whitewater Adventure Tours, *see* above) is a comfortable resort, on a beach-fringed island in the Mazaruni, visited on Whitewaters' jet boat day trips. A good place to come to with the kids.

The Interior

The forest begins less than 25 miles from Guyana, and rises over misty blue hills, dips into secret valleys, thick with lianas and dripping bromeliads, and thins into the Rupununi savannahs in the south and west. These are connected to the Gran Sabana in Venezuela. Guyana means 'land of many waters', and in the interior, her rivers and streams wind trhough green valleys, or ripple over smooth rainforest pebbles, rushing together to fill the sluggish arteries of the Essequibo, Mazaruni and Demerara Rivers. On their journeys, they plunge over the edge of 2 billion-year-old sandstone of the Guyana Shield. At Kaieteur, the 150m-wide Potaro pours as thick as strong dark coffee. At Orinduik, the Ireng River flows over steps and terraces of solid jasper.

The Kaieteur Falls

The Angel Falls may be the tallest and Iguazu the broadest, but Kaieteur is surely the most beautiful of all the waterfalls in South America. As it courses over the ancient sandstone that forms the Pakaraima mountains, the Potaro River swells from a tiny mountain brook to a broad and swift flowing, tea-coloured river, dark brown against the lush and tangled green of its rainforest surrounds. At Kaieteur, the mountains abruptly stop, and the Potaro crashes over the edge of a perfect rock amphitheatre in a thundering cataract of white and brown foam.

The Kaieteur Falls   ***Getting There***

A tough four- or five-day **overland trip** begins in Mahdia, reachable by air or 4x4 from Georgetown. A jeep ride takes tourists to the Potaro River, and a boat across it to the Amatuk Falls camp. From here a trail leads along the course of the river, through rainforest to the second camp at the Waratuk Falls. This marks the entrance to the mouth of the long gorge that leads to Kaieteur. The third camp is made at the base of the Mount Yaki at Tukiet. From here it's an uphill and slippery walk to the first viewpoint.

Roraima Airways (*see* p.272) and most of the tour operators (*see* p.274–5) in Georgetown offer round-trip **flights** to the falls, many of which also include a stopover at Orunduik. Expect to pay $90 for Kaieteur, and $140 for the two together.

Lethem and the Rupununi Savannah

The only settlement of any size in the Interior is Lethem, on the border with Brazil, whose muddy streets and dilapidated houses are strewn over the scrubby plain of the Rupununi savannah at the foot of two beautiful mountain ranges. The Kanuku, only a few miles to the south, are swathed in virgin forest, a nesting ground for harpy eagles, and Guyanan cock-of-the-rock which cavort here in the wet season (April–August), which is also when the harpies give birth. Most of Lethem's electricity comes from Kanuku, through a Chinese-built hydroelectric dam on the Moco Moco Falls. The Pakaraima Mountains to the north are less forested: savannah mountains with islands of trees, hiding the red jasper of the Orinduik Falls and rising towards the Venezuelan border to Mount Roraima. Karanambu Ranch (*see* p.279), a hospitable, well-run and excellent base for Guyanan wildlife trips, and an important centre for giant otter rehabilitation, lies on the Rupununi River, at the southern extremity of the Pakaraima Range.

If you are coming overland from Brazil or Venezuela, you will have to come through Boa Vista in the state of Roraima in Brazil to Bonfim, where there's a Brazilian passport control office, and then Lethem. There are buses several times a day, connecting to small ferries over the River Takutu. A dirt track runs to Georgetown. When trucks make it, they usually take just under a week. There are plans to improve the road, which is bad news for the forests the track cuts through at present.

Flights to Georgetown with Roraima Airways, or Trans Guyanan Air, several times a week, via the ugly goldmining settlement of Mahdia (about $60 one way). An extra $60–$100 will take you to the Kaieteur Falls on the way to Georgetown. A round trip to Lethem costs $110. Enquiries should be made to Shirley Melville at the airport shop.

Lethem

Lethem is struggling to become a hamlet, but despite its size, Lethem can be used as an alternative base to Georgetown for visits to the Interior. Trips can be arranged to Kaieteur and Orinduik, and planes can be caught to Karanambu and Dadanawa Ranches (*see* p.279). Locals offer tours of the Rupununi Savannah and nearby attractions.

Border control and entry formalities: Border control is very laid-back in Lethem. It's up to visitors to track down the customs and immigration officer, who stamps passports in his kitchen when he's not in Lethem police station (near the river crossing). Visas are sometimes issued on the spot, even though this is not strictly government policy. Be sure to get a passport stamp as your documents will be checked once again when you arrive in Georgetown. Those not carrying malaria prophylactics will be forced to have a blood test at Lethem airport before they are allowed to travel to Georgetown.

Accommodation options in Lethem are limited. There are only a few houses in 'town' anyway, and no street names or addresses. In the unlikely event of getting lost (only possible when it's pitch dark), knock on any door and ask a local.

Manari Ranch Hotel, 7 miles from Lethem, and **Pirara Ranch**, 15 miles from Lethem; book for both through Shirley Melville at the airport shop. Both are simple but comfortable, with horse-riding and boat trips and swimming in the creeks (*both moderate*). **Khan's Guest House** (Savannah Inn), next to the general store, is the most comfortable place in town, but the owners have a lot to learn about conservation. **Takutu Guest House** has basic, fan-cooled rooms and shared bathrooms, but is friendly, charming and full of fifties British kitsch (*both inexpensive*).

Shirley Melville, who runs the airport shop, is in the process of installing backpacker accommodation (hammock space and shared bathrooms and meals). This will cost about $5, not including food. Ask at the airport shop.

Tours Operators in Lethem

There are no tour companies in Lethem, only individuals.

Shirley Melville can arrange a variety of camping, fishing and pick-up tours of the Rupununi, Kanuku and Pakaraima mountains. She will also book Dadanawa and Karanambu Ranches.

Spanish and Portuguese also spoken. Ask at the airport shop. She is also an agent for **Shirley Humphries,** who organizes horse-riding tours of the Rupununi and Shiriri Hills and caves from a beautiful ranch house. $50–100 per day all-inclusive.

Kangaroo, ✆ (07) 2102, is so-called because he is always 'hopping from place to place'. Adventure and survival trips in the mountains or pick-up tours of the Rupununi. Good for groups on a tight budget. $25–$60 per day.

Lodges and Ranches in the Interior and Rupununi Savannah

Karanambu Ranch, book through Wilderness Explorers, Shell Beach Adventures, Wonderland Tours in Georgetown, or Shirley Melville in Lethem; around $120 per person per day, all-inclusive (flights extra). If you go nowhere else in Guyana, come here. The ranch is owned by Diane McTurk who rehabilitates giant river otters. The ranch is in creek country in the heart of the Rupununi, where the savannah grasslands, swamps and varzea forest meet. The Pakaraima mountains loom on the horizon. The diversity of habitats make it excellent birding and wildlife country. Rivers at Karanambu drain both into the Essequibo and the Amazon river systems (via the Branco River), and in the wet season the two are connected by Lake Amuku and a network of creeks and rivulets overflowing with Victoria lilies, a metre across. These are a favourite breeding ground for numerous water birds (*see* birding information, below), black and spectacled caiman and the last in the Rupununi for the increasingly rare pirarucu (called 'arapaima' here). Staying at Karanambu is very much staying *chez* Diane McTurk. She is a wonderful hostess, full of interesting stories and conversation. Food is excellent and plentiful and accommodation simple but comfortable in thatched *cabanas* with verandas and en suite bathrooms. There is a small library of natural history books and novels. Karanambu's indigenous guides are excellent, with very good birding knowledge and the eyes of hawks. Most excursions from the ranch are by boat, though horse-riding is also available.

Birding: Simoni Creek, the varzea forest surrounds, and Crane Pond are excellent birding areas, and in the wet season (June–August) are a nursery for breeding waterfowl. A select few of those are seen here include; egrets; jacanas; sharp-tailed, buff-necked and green ibises; white-necked, boat-billed and black-crowned night herons; white-faced tree duck; white-faced and black-bellied whistling ducks; azure and purple gallinules; pied and southern lapwings; stripe-backed bittern; roseate spoonbill, and jabiru stork. A selection of the birds to look out for in the savannahs around the ranch include great and grey potoos; king vulture; black and white hawk eagle; crane-hawk; Rio Branco antbird; band-tailed, least and lesser nighthawk; rufous nightjar; black-throated mango hummingbird; ruby-topaz hummingbird; long-billed starthroat; white-tailed and violaceous trogons; lineated woodpecker; Rio Branco and pale-breasted and yellow-throated spinetails. Birders looking to see the Rio Branco spinetail and/or antbird should arrange a boat trip along the River Ireng, which runs between Lethem and Karanambu.

Peacock bass fishing: Simoni Creek and the waterways around it offer the best Peacock Bass fishing facilities in the country. Fishermen should bring all their own gear.

Dadanawa Ranch, book through Wilderness Explorers, Shell Beach Adventures, Wonderland Tours in Georgetown, or Shirley Melville in Lethem; around $100 per person per day all-inclusive (flights extra). Dadanawa is the largest ranch in the country, covering some 2,000 square miles of wild savannah. The Kanuku Mountains hover on the horizon. Philip De Freitas, the friendly and hospitable owner, is an experienced tourist guide who takes tourists in jeeps or on horseback to remote parts of the Rupununi Savannah, and to the Kanuku

Mountains in search of harpy eagles and jaguar. He also takes a backwater trip to Georgetown via the creeks that lead into the Essequibo River and camping trips under the Rupununi stars.

Birding and wildlife: Like Karanambu Lodge, the creeks and savannahs around Dadanawa are great for wildlife (for select species *see* Karanambu, p.279), but the main reason to come here is for the Harpy Eagle Trek: Jeeps take tourists to Amerindian villages on the edge of the Kanuku Mountain rainforest, where guides who monitor the nesting sites are picked-up and camp is made, either in the village itself or further into the forest where jaguar prowl. A dawn trek leads to the nesting site. Though success cannot be guaranteed, previous visits have allowed numerous vantage points to observe the eagles and their chicks. There is good birding along the way, especially for cotingas and hummingbirds. Birds seen before include ornate hawk-eagle; Amazonian umbrellabird; crimson fruitcrow; purple-breasted cotinga; blue-tailed emerald; blue-chinned sapphire; amethyst woodstar; the beautiful tufted coquette humming-bird; pink-throated becard; Guianan cock-of-the-rock and Finsch's euphonia.

Rock View Ecotourism Resort; c/o Jacqueline Allicock, ✆ 65412, 🖷 55310; *caralodge@carahotel.com*; *http://members.tripod.com/~RockView,* or through Wilderness Explorers (*see* p.274) or Shell Beach Adventures (*see* p.275). Rock View is a luxury converted ranch house in the village of Rupertee, a few miles from the Amerindian village of Annai, on the edge of three of Guyana's premium wildlife habitat: the Rupununi Savannah, the forests of the Iwokrama Rainforest Reserve and the foothills of the Pakaraima mountains. The ranch offers horse-riding, nature tours, fishing, bird-watching and specializes in cultural exchanges, arts and crafts and painting. There is a craft centre with an emphasis on Amerindian art and design, where guests can learn how to make hammocks, straw, balata and leather goods. Apart from cultural trips to Amerindian villages, Rock View offer natural history excursions. Giant otters, Brazilian tapir, red howler monkey and many rare and endangered species of waterfowl can be seen on the Burro Burro River. The area has been little birded.The dirt road linking Lethem and Georgetown makes access to Rock View just about possible by 4x4. Shell Beach adventures call here on their Camel Trophy safari. Trans Guyana Airways and Roraima Air flights will land here on their way between Georgetown and Lethem on request.

Iwokrama Rainforest Reserve

This rainforest reserve and research centre is a shining example of why Guyana needs to preserve more of her forests: one in three visitors here see jaguar. The little-seen Guianian and brown-bearded saki monkeys are found in primary rainforest in Iwokrama, new species of birds, reptiles and amphibians, orchids and insects are found virtually every other week. The park comprises 360,000 hectares, half of which are designated a Wilderness Preserve, the other half set aside for research and development purposes, focusing on the sustainable use of tropical forest ecosytems and a nascent ecotourism programme. The Amerindian communities of Annai, Kurupukari and Sarama lie at its extremities. Indian petroglyphs can be seen at the beautiful Kurupukari Falls, and a hot, sweaty hike up Turtle Mountain affords wonderful views out of the rainforest canopy and savannah as far as the eye can see.

Iwokrama Centre for Rainforest Conservation and Development, 41 Brickdam, Starbroek, P.O Box 1074, Georgetown, ✆ 51504, 🖷 59199/71611, *iwokrama@guyana.net.gy*; *www.idrc.ca/iwokrama*; or book through Wilderness Explorers, Shell Beach Adventures, Wonderland Tours or Rainforest Tours. Stays in Iwokrama are very good value, especially if you book direct through the office in Georgetown (*see* above). Rustic accommodation, in timber cabins with thatched roofs is available for around $30 night, and hammocks can be slung up at numerous satellite camps. Camping at the centre with your own tent is only $10. Pick-ups from Lethem or Annai cost around $150 for a round trip. Boat hire is around $30 a day (with a guide), and trail guides cost around $2 per hour. The park entrance fee is around $15.

Birding: As a birding destination, Iwokrama is only beginning to be explored. Unusual species include crested and harpy eagles; grey-bellied goshawk; black-faced hawk; barred, lined and slaty-backed forest-falcons; Amazonian pygmy-owl; yellow-knobbed currasow; sun parakeet; tepui parrotlet; pearly-breasted and rufous-winged ground cuckoos and Capuchinbird.

Suriname

Few visitors, apart from the occasional Dutch tourist, ever make it to Suriname, and here, in part, lies its charm. Like Guyana, 90 per cent of the country is unspoilt and little explored wilderness, and its capital city, Paramaribo, a charming and elegant colonial surprise. Its tall Dutch houses and grassy squares don't feel like South America at all. Nor do the city's hinterlands, where paddy fields are tilled by Asian Indians and Javanese in conical hats, and buffalo lollop lazily under heavy wooden yokes along cracking roads. Only the Interior betrays the country's true identity; virgin forests and tropical savannahs stretch into Brazil to the south, and the other Guianas to either side. The coppery rivers that drain them are home to Amerindians, and communities of 'Maroons'; Africans who fled slavery on the coastal plantations in colonial times and re-established a tribal lifestyle in the then uncharted forests of the Interior. Both the coastal regions and the Interior overflow with wildlife: marine turtles nest on the mosquito-infested beaches, flaming red scarlet ibis breed on the mudflats and the forests of the Interior hide over 700 species of bird, and most of the Amazon's important mammals, including giant otter, the rare Guianan saki monkey and the even rarer oncilla. Despite its low profile, Suriname treats its visitors well. The capital has good hotels and restaurants, together with a handful of professionally run tour companies and is the best base for any trips around the country. Distances are relatively small. Trips to the Interior may require flights, but even these are short: Suriname is South America's smallest country.

Paramaribo

Poverty and a lack of government funds may be slowly peeling the white-painted wood and cracking the dark terracotta tiles of Suriname's capital, but none of this has detracted from Paramaribo's colonial charm. It remains one of the most picturesque of any of the Amazon region's cities. Streets and markets buzz with mopeds and the chatter of half a dozen languages; Dutch, English, Sranan Creole, Amerindian, Javanese and Hindi. Locals sit out on the brick steps of their wooden houses, watching the world go by. Paramaribo is the only feasible base for visitors wishing to visit the Interior (all of the country's tour operators are based here). Paramaribo is generally a safe and relaxed city, but care should be taken at night.

Paramaribo (no local code)

Getting There and Around

by air

Paramaribo's Johan Pengel international airport is 50km (40 minutes by taxi, about $30) from the city. There is an airport tax of $20 on international flights. Surinam Airways, Dr Sophie Redmondstraat 219, ✆ 432700, ✉ 434723, have regular flights to

Miami, Amsterdam, Guyane, Guyana and to Belém in Brazil as well as several Caribbean destinations. KLM Royal Dutch Airlines, J.C de Mirandastraat 9 bv, ✆ 472421, ✆ 477526, fly to Amsterdam. Internal flights, for destinations in the Interior leave from Zorg-en-Hoop airport, on the outskirts of town (10–15 minutes from the centre by taxi).

by road

Buses and collective taxis are few and far between and visitors are strongly advised either to hire a car or use a tour company. The few services that remain run as follows: buses leave from outside Hotel Ambassador on Dr Sophie Redmondstraat, between Walldijkstraat and Zwartenhovenbrugstraat (leave when full) for Nickerie (for the Guyanese border). Buses for Albina (for the border with Guyane) depart from the Meerzorg ferry dock next to the central market on Waterkant.

Le Grand Baldew, ✆ 474713, ✆ 421164, *baldew@sr.net,* run a **private collective taxi service** and have a weekly service to Albina and on to Guyane. They will pick you up from your hotel.

Car rental: All the following companies require an international driving licence: Avis, Fred O'Kirkstraat 11, ✆ 451000, ✆ 456392, *paragrp@sr.net;* De Paarl, Kankantriestraat 42, ✆ 403610, ✆ 465312; Ashruf, Heveastraat 29, ✆ 403151; Henha, Gomperstraat 4-6, ✆ 550323, ✆ 550468.

Pedal bike hire: Cardy Bike Rental, Heerenstraat 19 boven, ✆ 422518, ✆ 424505.

Paramaribo is easy to find your way around **on foot.** For longer journeys, taxis are cheap and plentiful and are easily booked through hotel receptions.

Airport taxis: For the international airport, airport shuttles are cheaper than taxis, and use comfortable minibuses. Call Garage Ashruf, Aidastraat 19, ✆ 454451, ✆ 455411; De Paarl Airport Service, Kankantriestraat 42, ✆ 403610, ✆ 465312, who will also meet incoming flights at the airport.

Water taxis: Boatmen hover around the quay, particularly near the Central Market, offering boat trips along the river to the pretty suburb of Leonsberg (site of the colonial riverfront views on many of Paramaribo's postcards) or the Paramaribo waterfront.

Paramaribo (no local code)   ***Tourist Information and Useful Addresses***

Tourist office: Suriname Tourism Foundation, Dr J.F Nassylaan 2, ✆ 410357/477892, ✆ 477786, *stsur@sr.net, www.sr.net/users/stsur, www.parbo.com/tourism.*

Changing money: Alhough most of the large hotels and tour companies accept Visa, there are at present no credit card cashpoints in Suriname, nor are any cash advances issued at banks. Bring Amex traveller's cheques in US dollars (though exchange rates are poor) or, better still, US dollars in cash. FINA Trust, Dr Sophie Redmondstraat 59, ✆ 472266, offer the best rates for cash or traveller's cheques. Centrale Bank Van Suriname, Waterkant 20, ✆ 473741, ABN/AMRO Bank, Kerkplein 1, ✆ 471555, Hakrinbank, Dr Sophie Redmondstraat 11–13, ✆ 477722.

Internet: CIM Centre, Dr J.F Nassylaan 43

Embassies and consulates: UK, Van't Hogerhuysstraat 9–11, ✆ 472558; **USA,** Dr Sophie Redmondstraat 129, ✆ 474401; **France,** Gravenstraat 5–7, ✆ 475222. Note that visas for Guyane (France) are issued in 24 hours. Nationals of other South

American countries (including Brazil, who need no visas for France itself) require a visa for Guyane. This can only be issued in their country of origin. **Brazil**, Maratakkastraat 2, ✆ 400200, **Guyana**, Gravenstraat 82, ✆ 477895, **Venezuela**, Gravenstraat 23–25, ✆ 475401. **Netherlands**, Rooseveltkade 5, ✆ 477211.

Maps: The best map of Suriname is the Canadian International Travel Map (ISBN 1 895907 705). It is not available within Suriname. The best Paramaribo map is the Hebri International Map of Suriname (with a Paramaribo street map on the reverse). This is available from the Hotel Krasnapolsky, most of the town's good bookshops (try Vaco on Domineestraat) or from the publishers Hebri International, Drakenstein 25–1121 HB Landsmeer, Netherlands, ✉ (31) 20 638 8608.

Photography: Slide film is impossible to find in Suriname. Bring plenty.

The Sights

Fort Zeelandia, Graven Straat at Zeelandia Weg (*free tours Sun 11am and 12pm*) on the banks of the Suriname River, is the best place to begin a walking tour of Paramaribo. The country began with forts like these; they served both as trading posts and as protection against the indigenous population. It now houses the **Surinam Museum**, devoted to indigenous pottery, and colonial flotsam and jetsam. Every Sunday morning men with caged songbirds gather on the huge grassy square called the Onafhankelijkheidsplein (probably more easily remembered as Independence Square) in front of the Parliament buildings for a competition. Two birds are judged by a referee, who scores the ornateness and beauty of their trills on a little blackboard. The **cathedral of St Peter and St Paulus,** Graven Straat at Monseigneur Wulfighestraat, is one of the largest wooden buildings in South America. The neo-Gothic exterior with its towering steeples is magnificent, but the interior, decked out in polished tropical hardwood, is even more splendid. It may be hard to get a glimpse as the cathedral is indefinitely closed for refurbishment. **The Reformed Church**, Kerkeplein at Wagenweg Straat, was the site of the proclamation of independence in 1975. It dates from 1835 and is worth a visit to see the beautiful copper chandeliers, the organ, which is nearly as old as the church, and the mahogany pulpit. Suriname has a long and strong Jewish heritage, and the impressive **Sedek Ve Salom Synagogue**, at Gravenstraat and Malebathrumstraat (*open Fridays from 6pm*) dates back to the early 18th century. The Ark (where the Torah scrolls are kept) and bimah (the pulpit) are beautifully carved. Suriname's religious groups seem to be more tolerant than many: the High German synagogue on Keizerstraat must be one of the very few in the world to have a mosque as a next door neighbour. These places of worship, as well as most of the numerous Hindu temples that dot the city can be visited; the best is the Shri Vishnu mandir out on the Koningstraat at Dr Samuel Kafiluddistraat. Please remember to remove shoes, and, in mosques and synagogues, cover your head.

Paramaribo (no local code)   ***Where to Stay***

Paramaribo's best hotels are well up to any international standards. Budget travellers will find little under $20.

luxury–expensive

Hotel Torarica, L.J Rietbergplein 1 (off Kleine Waterstraat), ✆ 471500, ✆ 411682, *torbc@sr.net*. The only four-star hotel in Paramaribo; large and well-equipped with souvenir shops, gym, pool, casino, tropical gardens, and an unpleasant zoo.

Zeelandia Suites, Kleine Waterstraat 1a, ✆ 424631, ✆ 424790, *zeelands@sr.net*, *www.vat.cq-link.sr*. Comfortable air-conditioned flats with Internet access (with your own laptop). Safe and central with very helpful management.

Residence Inn, Anton Dragtenweg 7, ✆ 472387, ✆ 424811, *resinpbo@sr.net*. In the luxurious confines of the former Soviet embassy; travel agency (Mets), a swimming pool and tennis courts. At the bottom end of this price range.

moderate

Stardust Hotel and Riverclub, Anton Dragtenweg at Condorstraat, Leonsberg, ✆ 451544, ✆ 452921, *stardust@sr.net*. Swimming pool, dancing, sauna, and tennis courts in the pretty suburb of Leonsberg.

Hotel Plaza, Domineestraat 39, ✆ 420350, ✆ 420345, *plazahot@sr.net*. Comfortable air-conditioned rooms and a restaurant, on the city's main shopping street.

Krasnapolsky, Domineestraat 39, ✆ 475050, ✆ 420139, *krasnam@sr.net*. Business-style hotel on the city's main shopping street with swimming pool and club.

Combi-Inn, Kleine Waterstraat 9, ✆ 426001/473991. Small hotel in the best part of town, next to a casino, with air-conditioned rooms.

inexpensive–cheap

Hotel Flair, Kleine Waterstraat 9, ✆ 422455/474794. One of the best cheap options in town, at the top end of the budget market. Clean, comfortable fan-cooled rooms with shared bathroom, in the best part of town.

Albergo Alberga, Lim A Postraat 13, ✆ 474286. Simple rooms near the Presidential Palace overlooking some of the city's most beautiful houses.

Surinam Museum, Commewijnestraat 18, ✆ 401080/497209. Rooms within the grounds of the Surinam Museum (not Fort Zeelandia).

YWCA (Wy-koo), Heerenstraat 14–16, ✆ 472089, ✉ 472072. Centrally located in a fine old wooden colonial building with a café serving delicious breakfasts.

Paramaribo (no local code) **Eating Out**

The multi-cultural cuisine of Paramaribo is one of the city's greatest charms.

Surinamese Creole

Local specialities include *heri-heri*, made with root vegetables, plantain banana and smoked fish; *pinda brafu*, a spicy chicken and peanut soup; *pom*, made from spiced chicken and grated *tayer*, and various spicy pasties, similar to West Indian patties. Try **Upstairs**, Kleine Waterstraat 1, ✆ 424631, which serves international and Creole dishes in a semi-open air restaurant above the Zeelandia Suites (*inexpensive*). **Muntje**, Verlengde Hoogestraate 32, is a real spit and sawdust place, popular with taxi drivers (*cheap*). Or there is **Tori Hoso**, Rust en Vrederstraat 76, ✆ 420234 (*inexpensive*).

European

Suriname's European restaurants have good international menus, and are one of the few places in the Amazon region where it is possible to uncork a reasonable bottle of (usually French) wine. **Cyrano**, Wagenwegstraat 46, ✆ 422886. A good French and Italian menu in one of the city's better restaurants (*expensive*). **Moulin Rouge**, Hofstede Crullan 8, ✆ 476205. French and European cuisine cooked by Arjen de Heer, who has a good local reputation (*moderate–inexpensive*). **Plantation Room**, Hotel Torarica (*see* above). One of the best hotel restaurants in town, with a varied international and local menu served in pleasant surroundings (*expensive–moderate*).

Indonesian

Javanese *warungs* (food stalls) are dotted about everywhere, and are one of the best options for cheap food in the city. There are a number on Waterkant, and many more in the Javanese suburb of Blauwgrond, a popular weekend eating spot for Surinamese. Sit-down restaurants in the city itself include: **Bali**, Ma Retraiteweg 5, ✆ 422325; **Jawa**, Kasabaholoweg 7, ✆ 92691; **Bandung**, Gemenelandsweg 76, ✆ 472602.

Chinese

There are many Chinese restaurants in Paramaribo; along many of the principal streets in the centre, and on Kleine Waterstraat. The **Phoenix**, Plutostraat 86, ✆ 453950, has an extensive menu. Other good places include **Oriental Food**, Gravenstraat 118, and **Fa Tai**, Magdenstraat 64 (upstairs).

Indian

There are countless *roti* shops, serving stuffed *rotis* (chappatis fried in ghee) with lamb, chicken, duck or vegetarian fillings, chickpeas, beans and egg. Try **Chris** or **Joosje** on Zwartenhovenbroogstraat 9 and 10. For a sit-down meal, try **Het Hofje**, Wagenwegstraat 10, ✆ 411290, or **Roopram**, Grote Hofstraat 4, ✆ 478816.

vegetarian

Most of the Asian restaurants serve some vegetarian options, and *rotis* come with optional chickpeas and vegetable curry fillings.

Tour Operators in Paramaribo

All of Suriname's tour companies are based in Paramaribo. STINASU by far the best for natural history and birding trips as they provide specialist biologist guides. Mets and Cardy are good for adventure tours in the Interior and trips to Maroon and Amerindian villages.

Cardy Adventures, Heerenstraat 19, Paramaribo, ✆ 422518, ✆ /✆ 424505. Trips to Maroon villages, around the Interior and to the turtle egg-laying beaches. Around $70–$100.

Independent Tours, Rooseveltkade 20, Paramaribo, ✆ 474770. Trips to Maroon villages in the Interior for around $70–$100.

Ma Ye Du, Matoelistraat 22, Paramaribo, ✆ /✆ 410348, *ma-ye-du@paramaribo.net*; *http://huizen.dds.nl/~mayedu*. Trips to Maroon villages in the Interior; between $70–$100.

Mets (Movement for Ecotourism in Suriname), Dr J.F. Nassylaan 2, Paramaribo, ✆ 477088/477093, ✆ 497062, *mets@sr.net*; *www.surinfo.org/mets*. Offer some of the best encounter trips with Amerindians and Maroons, combined with a stay at their forest camp at Palumeu (good for wildlife) or a visit to the Kasikasima Mountain in the south. They also offer an Aukaner (Maroon group) encounter trip to Tukanari island in Brokopondo Lake, where they have rustic lodges, and a range of other tours around the country.

STINASU (Foundation for Nature Preservation in Suriname), Cornelius Jongbawstraat 14, ✆ 471856, ✆ 421850, *stinasu@sr.net*; *www.surinfo@sr.net*. STINASU can provide accurate and well-researched conservation, natural history and birding information for much of the country, as well as specialist guides and tours to Brokopondo, Raleighvallen Nature Reserve and destinations throughout the country.

Around Paramaribo

After the Second World War, European and American colonial powers briefly considered Suriname as a contender for a new Jewish homeland: the country had a long Jewish heritage and was one of the first Jewish settlements in the Americas. In 1650 Portuguese Jews started sugar plantations and built an imposing synagogue. By 1694, some 570 Jewish colonists and 9,000 African slaves lived on the Casipora Creek at **Jodensavanna**. All that remains today of their settlements are a few ruined brick buildings, neglected graves, and the shell of the old synagogue. To get there, take the Brokopondo Road (via Domburg and Paranam) and turn left between electricity masts 32 and 33. Drive through Powaka and Carolina, where a bridge leads across the Suriname River. Jodensavanna is 3km further on, on the right. There is no public transport. Wild Coast Expeditions, Van't Hogerhuysstraat 10, Paramaribo, ✆ 404978, ✆ 424522, offer bespoke trips, stopping at various locations along the way.

Cola Creek is a popular weekend spot for Paramaribo's young, 50km south of the capital. Groups of huts for hanging hammocks are gathered together around a concrete canal filled by a black-water creek. Take the airport road to Zanderij village, and turn right towards the tiny hamlet of Kraka after reaching the village, and look out for signs to Cola Creek.

The Coastal Wetlands and Turtle Egg-Laying Beaches

Suriname's coastline is a labyrinth of mangrove forests, brackish swamps, mudflats and silty ridges, broken by the occasional sandy beach and tiny wooden village. The sea is soupy with mud washed westwards from the Amazon River, by the Guiana current. Few come to swim, but the coast is a paradise for animals. There are abundant ibis, herons and egrets as well as millions of migrant North American waders, and a whole host of other waterfowl. Turtles nest amongst the driftwood on the scruffy beaches and deer, peccary and even jaguar can sometimes be seen. Suriname has had the foresight to protect large areas of its coastline. There are currently seven parks or nature preserves; at Bigipan and Hertenrits near Nieuw Nickerie, Coppename, Matapica and Wia Wia near Paramaribo and Wanekreek and Galibi near Albina.

Four turtle species nest along Suriname's coast: green turtle, olive ridley, hawksbill and the giant leatherback, the world's heaviest reptile (the largest weighed 961kg), which has a mass of small mosaic-like bone plates in its leathery skin in place of armour. Turtles are easily disturbed, and will stop laying eggs altogether if torches are shone directly at them. Be sure to be as discreet as possible, and to wait until they have finished egg-laying before approaching. Turtle nesting sites are under increased threat, and Suriname's are crucial to the species' survival. The main beaches are **Matapica** and **Eilantani** (near Galibi), which is the most important nesting site for olive ridleys in the western hemisphere. Nesting takes place between February and early August. It is possible to stay for a while in the relaxed and friendly Carib village at Galibi.

Red and black **mangroves** are two of the few trees able to colonize tidal zones washed by salt and fresh water, and their labyrinthine roots and spreading branches are an important nursery for numerous Surinamese animals and hundreds of species of fish, including several species of sharks. There are two wetland sanctuaries on the Surinamese coast at **Coppename** and at **Wia Wia**, as well as other birding areas of international reputation and importance. Coppename was established as a game sanctuary as early as 1953, especially for herons and ibises, and put on the RAMSAR list as one of the world's most important waterfowl habitats in 1985. The Amazon River is responsible for the extraordinary fertility of both Coppename and Wia Wia. The tide washes Amazon mud here, nearly 1,000km from the river's mouth. The nutrients are recycled, the mud pumped rich with oxygen, and thousands of tiny crustaceans and molluscs, and over 300 species of fish provide ample fodder for the millions of birds that gather here: azure gallinule; scarlet, white and glossy ibis; boat-billed heron; reddish egret; boobies and magnificent frigatebird can be seen on and around the reserve. During the North American winter, legions of migrants arrive from Nova Scotia and New Brunswick. The reserve is also one of the few remaining habitats for the West Indian manatee, larger and even rarer than the Amazon manatee. Guianan piculet, the spectacular crimson-hooded manakin, Cayenne jay, Finsch's euphonia and the rare blood-coloured woodpecker live in the mangrove and coastal forests. Migrant waders can also be seen at Bigipan and Hertenrits (*see* p.288). Though human activities in the protected areas are limited by STINASU, and there is no fishing, the recent exploitation of crude oil by the State Oil Company, and the use of agro-chemicals have begun to threaten the unique ecosystems of both. The best trips to the turtle beaches and nature reserves are offered by STINASU (*see* p.286), who can provide English-speaking biologist guides.

Other Towns Along the Coast and Crossing to Guyana

The border with Guyane lies at **Albina**, two hours drive from Paramaribo. There is nothing to see or do here, and only a couple of shoddy hotels, but the ferry for Guyane leaves a few times daily. Be sure to get your passport stamped by the Military Police. Minibuses for Cayenne meet the ferry in St Laurent-du-Maroni, on the French river bank.

Devonshire folk won't feel much at home in **Totness**. The rain is warm here and there are no castles amidst the palms and rice fields. Signs of the English colonists are long gone and the tiny

Asian Indian village is worth visiting only because its name is so incongruous. **Niuew Nickerie**, on the border with Guyana, is no more interesting than Totness, though birders will be entranced by the saltwater swamps and lagoons of **Bigipan** and **Hertenrits**; home to many indigenous coastal birds and, between November and March, millions of North American migrant waders that winter here. Fishermen in the market, or boatmen in the community of Long May or Hertenrits, can take visitors there for as little as $30 per day, or trips can be arranged with STINASU (*see* p.286). Crossing to Guyana is straightforward; passenger ferries leave from Nieuw Nickerie itself whilst car ferries run from Southdrain, 10km further south. Both take about half an hour. Buses connect Moleson Creek in Guyana with Georgetown. Taxis for Southdrain can be caught on the corner of Gouverstraat and Sint Jozefstraat in Nieuw Nickerie. Before leaving, get your passport stamped by the Military Police in the Maynardstraat.

The Interior

The country south of Paramaribo rises gently to scrubby savannah before turning to thick Amazon rainforest, dotted with monoliths of dark sandstone. Only a few thousand people live here, most of them Amerindians and Maroons. Brazilian *garimpeiros* are, unfortunately, beginning to arrive, and, though they have so far caused little damage, their presence does not bode well for the future. Unless otherwise stated, all locations in the Interior must be visited with a tour company (*see* p.274 for a list). Though there are few mammals or birds that are unique to the country, Suriname's forests contain healthy populations of several threatened and endangered species, and are among the best places to find a number of the Amazon's more unusual animals like large, flat Suriname toads, which turn from egg to frog inside pockets on their mother's skin. The forests of the Guianas are one of the best places in South America to find the world's largest spider, the Goliath bird-eating spider, with inch-long fangs. Harder to see are oncilla, an endangered spotted or sometimes black cat.

Brownsberg Nature Reserve

The view from the edge of the Brownsberg plateau over the vast Van Blommestein (Brokopondo) reservoir is reason enough to come here. On a clear day, the silhouettes of the Nassau Massif hover on the horizon and the forest canopy below is alive with the movement of birds and the call of cicadas and parrots. Brokopondo looks natural until you catch sight of the 2km-high Afobaka dam and the tops of submerged trees; the valley was flooded in the 1960s without the consent of the local Maroon people. Brownsberg is the depressing grid-plan town to which the inhabitants of the 28 Saramaka and eight Aukener Maroon villagers were relocated. Only Tukunari Island remains of the original forest floor. Aukener Maroons still live here, and Mets (*see* p.286) who run a traditional-style lodge on the island, offer cultural exchanges. Brownsberg is pretty much the only park in the Interior which can be reached independently. The road which runs out beyond the international airport leads only here and Afobaka, so it is difficult to get lost. Be sure to take the Brownsberg fork (left hand side) at the hamlet of Berg en Dal. The 130km trip takes between two and three hours. There is one petrol station along the way, in Paranam. There is no public transport. STINASU maintain the simple lodges on the top of the Brownsberg plateau. There are three styles of accommodation; the most comfortable are the bungalows (about $40 per night). Communal huts with bunk beds cost around $10. Hammock space is only $7. In all cases, bring your own bedding, hammock, toilet paper, food and drink. Bookings must be made with STINASU before leaving (*see* p.286).

Birding in Brownsberg: The reserve encompasses some superb forest and a range of different habitats, including the shores of the vast Professor Van Blommestein Lake and the rainforests of the Mazaroni Top Hill, which reaches just over 500m. It also has the advantage of being reachable by private car. Over twenty species of antbird live here, including white-plumed and rufous-throated, together with the bizarrely wattled white bellbird whose cry is like a ringing bell; some spectacularly coloured tanagers; blue-backed, red-billed and opal-rumped tanagers; the rare marail guan; Guianan toucanet and red-and-black grosbeak.

The Raleighvallen Nature Reserve

The reserve is centred on clear, dark waters of the upper Coppename River, which crashes over the Raleigh Falls, past overhanging lianas in the wet season, and trickles over mossy green and dark grey boulders in the dry. The park lodge lies on Foengoe Island in the river, whose airstrip is good for birding. Toucans and araçaris are a common sight, and the drooping nests of weaver birds hang everywhere. Swimming with piranhas in the clear black-water pools is quite safe, if you don't have bleeding wounds, and makes for a good story back home. The lodge can arrange canoe trips upriver in search of wildlife, trail walks and fishing. The Moedervallen Falls, another series of rapids that are especially impressive in the wet season, are a short boat journey and half-hour's walk away. Long sandy beaches are exposed in the dry, and the river is wonderfully refreshing. Beware of eddies and electric eels. Longer excursions include a climb up the steep sides of the Voltzberg, a massive fragment of the Guyana Shield. It's a sweaty 7km-walk to the rock and a steep and slippery one-hour climb once you're there. The clear creek water along the way is safe to drink and the chances of seeing wildlife are fairly good.

Birding in Raleighvallen: Black currasow, Guianan cock-of-the-rock, blue and yellow, red and green, scarlet and chestnut-fronted macaws can all be seen here, together with birds listed under Brownsberg. Animals include black spider monkey, red howlers and weeping capuchins.

Amerindian and Maroon Villages

Amerindians: Scientifcally dated petroglyphic carvings, stone arrowheads and grinding grooves in the sandstone boulders of the Interior rivers indicate that there have been indigenous people in Suriname at least since 6000 BC. With slavery came European disease, and their numbers greatly diminished. Caribs and Arawaks (Arowaks in Suriname), once slaving agents for the colonial powers, are still dominant, at least numerically: 10,000 live along the coast. About 2,000 Trio, Wayana, Warrau and Wayarekule live in the interior. Trips to Amerindian villages can be arranged through tour operators (*see* p.286). Ask before taking pictures.

Maroons: The Zeeuwen Dutch began to use imported West African slaves on the coastal plantations after friction with the dominant Indian tribes, and with Portuguese Brazil, which objected to Surinamese Caribs stealing Indians for the Dutch. Men were packed into the holds of the ships bound for South America, together with far fewer women, intended only as 'breeding stock'. A brave minority fled the tyranny of the colonists and escaped into the forests of the Interior, where they re-established the African life that had been taken from them. The descendants of these slaves are the modern Maroons of the Interior. Over time separate communities have evolved since the days of the first escapees; Aukaners, Saramaka, Paramaka, Matawai, Kwinti and Boni, numbering around 35 000 individuals. Various agencies arrange visits to the villages (*see* p.286). The highlight is usually the dance show.

Kasikasima

The twelve sandstone rocks of the Kasikasima range rise sheerly above from the surrounding expanse of forest like worn teeth. Mets (*see* p.286) offer an eight-day trip beginning with a flight from Paramaribo to their camp at Palumeu, and continuing by dug-out for two days through unblemished forests. Expect to pay around $100 per person per day, all-inclusive.

Guyane (French Guiana)

The smallest of the Guianas is not officially a country at all, but a *département* of France, making it the wealthiest corner of the Americas outside the United States, and one of the only places in the Amazon selling decent food. Life is centered around the capital, Cayenne, and occasionally in Kourou, when an Ariane rocket, launched by the European Space Agency, brings animation to what is otherwise a very dull town. There are a few other hamlet-sized settlements along the coast and in the forested Interior. Guyane's geography is much like neighbouring Suriname and Guyana; over 90 per cent of the department is forested, drained by boulder-strewn rivers, whose rapids have helped to guard the forests over the centuries and populated by Amerindians and Maroons. About five per cent of the rest is savannah lying behind a narrow coastal strip, lined with mangroves and sandy beaches where marine turtles come to lay their eggs. The Iles du Salut, a small archipelago of three islands (Royale, St Joseph and the Ile du Diable), lie in an idyllic setting in clear waters 15km off the coast.

High labour costs, and relatively strict forestry regulations have impeded the expansion of logging that threatens neighbouring Guyana and, although the expansion of mining in the Interior is beginning to cause serious environmental concerns and indignation over human rights (indigenous peoples have not been consulted about the annexation of their lands), Guyane is, to date, the most untouched of all the Guianas. Biodiversity is high: Guyane boasts more than 1,300 species of trees; 170 mammals, including the large cats, giant otter, southern river otter and West Indian and Amazonian manatees, and 720 species of birds. Specialities include harpy and crested eagle, ornate hawk-eagle, Guianan cock-of-the-rock and the endemic Cayenne nightjar, known only from an isolated specimen discovered in 1917, but still thought to inhabit the little explored forests of the Interior.

Cayenne

Cayenne is an undistinguished French provincial town in a tropical setting, perched on the end of a small peninsula looking out towards France over a warm and muddy sea. A fire in 1888 destroyed much of the town's colonial architecture, and her narrow streets are lined with modern flats hiding behind plastic shutters and cafés serving icy cold Abbaye beer. Long beaches of yellow sand backed by lush rainforests spread outwards from Cayenne. They are nearly always empty; turtles nest here under the moonlight, but sightings are more reliable near Mana and Les Hattes (*see* p.295).

Cayenne (© 0594–)   ***Getting There and Getting Around***
                                                          by air

Cayenne's swanky new international Aéroport Rochambeau is 15km (10–15 minutes by taxi, about $30) from the city. Airport tax on international flights is FF200.

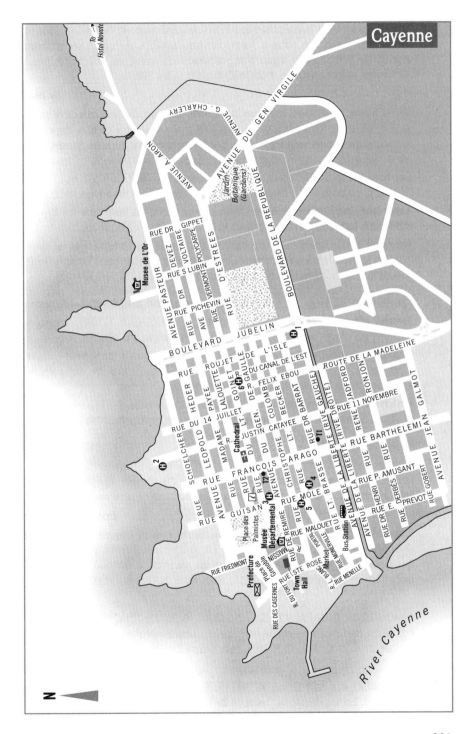

Cayenne

To Hotel Novotel

AVENUE G. CHARLERY

AVENUE DU GEN VIRGILE

AVENUE A. ARON

Jardin Botanique (Gardens)

AVENUE DE LA RÉPUBLIQUE

RUE DR GIPPET

DEVEZ

RUE VOLTAIRE

RUE S LUBIN

DR POLYCARPE

AVENUE PASTEUR

RUE PICHEVIN

RUE AVE VERMONT

RUE D'ESTREES

Musée de l'Or

BOULEVARD JUBELIN

BOULEVARD DE L'ISLE

RUE ROUJET

RUE HEDER

RUE PAYEE

RUE LALOUETTE

RUE GONET

RUE DE GAULLE

DU CANAL DE L'EST

R. FELIX EBOU

ROUTE DE LA MADELEINE

RUE DU 14 JUILLET

RUE SCHOELCHER

RUE LEOPOLD

RUE MADAME

LT. JUSTIN CATAYEE

DE GEN. DU COLOMBO

CHRISTOPHE BECKER

RUE DR BARRAT

RUE DR GAUCHE (RIVE GAUCHE)

RENE JADFORD

RUE 11 NOVEMBRE

RONJON

RUE BARTHELEMI

Cathedral

RUE FRANCOIS

RUE ARAGO

RUE MOLE

RUE BRASSE

RUE DE LA LIBERTE (RIVE DROITE)

AVENUE DE LA LIBERTE

AVENUE GOBERT

AVENUE JEAN GALMOT

AVENUE GUISAN

Place des Palmistes

Musée Departemental

AVENUES

RUE DE REMIRE

RUE P. AMUSANT

RUE DR HENRI

RUE E. DERBES

RUE PREVOT

RUE FRIEDMONT

Prefecture

Place de Grenoble

RUE NISSIM

Town Hall

RUE STE ROSE

Market

RUE MONNERVILLE

Bus Station

RUE LT. BRASSE

RUE MALOUET

RUE DES CASERNES

R. DU FORT

RUE MENELLE

River Cayenne

N

291

Air France, Aéroport Rochambeau and 17–19 Rue Lallouette © 298787, © 293636, fly to Paris (Orly) five times a week. Surinam Airways, Aéroport Rochambeau, © 293001, © 305786, fly regularly to Suriname and Guyana and to Belém in Brazil. Air Guyane, 2 Rue Lalouette, © 293630, fly daily to the Interior.

by road

SMTC **buses**, © 314566, only run in Cayenne and its suburbs. **Collective taxis**, © 270122, leave from opposite the Laussat Canal and serve Cayenne, the coastal towns and the frontier with Suriname at Saint-Laurent du Maroni, several times a day. For the Iles du Salut, stay overnight in Kourou as the only boat leaves early (*see* p.294).

Car hire: Europcar, ZI Collery and in the airport, © 351827/356279; ACL, 44 bld Jubelin, © 356636; Avis, 77 Rue de Lieutenant Goinet and in the airport, © 353414.

Aeroplane and helicopter hire: Guyane Aéroservices, Matoury (near the airport), © 356162; Héli-inter Guyane, Aéroport Rochambeau, © 356231, © 358256.

The centre of Cayenne is easily negotiable on foot. **Taxis** are the best option for longer journeys (as local buses are infrequent), and for getting to the airport. These are easily booked through hotel receptions, or call Varane Taxi, © 234654, © 232912.

Cayenne (© 0594–)　　　***Tourist Information and Useful Addresses***

Tourist office: FOTSIG, 12 Rue Lallouette, © 309629, © 312341, *ctgamgt@tourisme-guyane.gf*; *www.tourisme-guyane.gf.* Very helpful and efficient.

Changing money: Visa cashpoints in the airport and at banks throughout Guyane. Most hotels will change Amex traveller's cheques (the cards are not accepted anywhere). Bring French francs, traveller's cheques, or £ sterling.

Embassies and consulates: **UK**, 16 Av. Gaston Monnerville, © 311034; **Brazil**, 23 Ch. Saint Antoine, © 296010; **Suriname:** 38 Rue C. Colomb, © 300461.

Cayenne (© 0594–)　　　***Where to Stay***

Cayenne has plenty of comfortable modern hotels. Budget travellers are unlikely to find anything under $30 a night. Renting a flat is the cheapest option in Cayenne. Stays are usually for a minimum of a week. The tourist office has a complete list.

luxury–expensive

Novotel, Route de Montabo (a few kilometres east of Cayenne), © 303888, © 317898. A high-class beach hotel in the European business chain. The **Hostellerie des Amandiers**, Place des Amandiers, on the sea front, © 302600, © 307484, is more intimate and more central than the Novotel; excellent restaurant.

moderate

Central Hotel, Rue Molé at Becker, © 313000, © 307776/311296. is at the bottom end of the moderate market and offers clean, comfortable rooms. **Guyane Studios**, 16 Rue Molé, © 302511, © 304805, have central flats with small kitchens.

inexpensive–cheap

Neptima, 21 Rue Felix Eboué, © 301115, © 301478; basic but comfortable. **Hotel Le Badoel**, Lot les Heliconias, route de Bachel, © 305159, © 307777, is one of the cheapest places in Cayenne, but still over $30 a night for a double.

Asia, Africa and equatorial America all meet in Guyane's kitchen, where they mingle with French culinary panache to produce mouth-watering results; most delicous is the sea food. *Bouillon d'aouara*, eaten at Easter and Pentecost, or prepared in honour of important visitors, is a Creole dish of pulped savannah palm fruit, marine fish, crab and chicken, smoked with fresh vegetables. Shrimps are famous here and are prepared in a whole host of ways. Portuguese *bacalhau* (marinated cod) is a favourite starter, accompanied by *ti-punch* and a salad of greens and tropical fruit. Steaks are rare in more ways than one; the *viandes bois* ('woodland meat') is a pillar of the province's cuisine. Those who chew with a conscience might try *calalou*, a smoked dish of okra, meat, fish and spinach served with *couac* (manioc flour) or *boudin*, a blood sausage.

The smartest and most expensive restaurants include **Paris-Cayenne**, 59 Rue Lalouette, ✆ 317617, and **Le Patriarche**, Rue Voltaire at Samuel Lubin, ✆ 317644; both serve the finest French cuisine in the city accompanied by a good wine list and an intimate atmosphere. The **Hostellerie des Amandiers** (*see* above) offers delicious French and Guianese cuisine and a fine wine list, in one of the town's most highly regarded restaurants (and hotels). You can dine less expensively at **La Sarrasine**, 55 Rue Lt. Goinet, ✆ 317238, on wonderful sweet and savoury crêpes made with fresh tropical fruit, fine French cheeses and other delights to the palate. Good house wine. Or try **Porta Verde**, 58 Rue Lieutenant Goined, ✆ 291903, which serves Brazilian food, including an excellent *feijoada*. **Ko Fei**, Rue Lallouette, ✆ 312888, is one of the better cheap Chinese restaurants and **Les Palmistes**, Place des Palmistes, ✆ 300050, has good value, well-prepared Creole food in the centre of town.

Tour Operators in Cayenne
Cayenne (✆ 0594–)

Cayenne has only two professional tour companies. Both are well-established with a high standard of service and can arrange to take visitors to any corner of the province. English spoken.

Takari Tour, 8 Rue du Capitaine Bernard, ✆ 311960, ✉ 315470, *takari.tour@wanadoo.fr*. The most adventurous operator in Guyane; scheduled and bespoke tours to the Interior and the coast, including the Maroni River, Saül and around, turtle beaches at Les Hattes, Kaw Marshes, Ariane Rocket launchings and Iles du Salut. From about $100 per person per day.

JAL Voyages, 26 Av. du Général de Gaulle, ✆ 316820, ✉ 301101, *jal@ariasnet.fr*, *www.ariasnet.fr/jal*. Comfortable adventure and family orientated tours to the coast and Interior: five-day dug-out canoe trip along the Maroni River to Maripasoula; two-day river cruises in the Kaw Marshes and two-day trips to see giant leather back turtles lay their eggs.

Birding in Guyane

There are currently no specialist professionally-run birding trips to Guyane's interior.

GEPOG (Le Groupe d'Etudes et de Protection des Oiseaux en Guyane), 55 Rue Lieutenant Becker, ✆/✉ 294696. A private institution/ornithology club who organize amateur tours around the coast, run by keen birders and field biology students. They should be given plenty of prior warning by those wishing to explore Guyane's birding sites. No English spoken.

Guyane's most modern city, 60km west of Guyane, comes to life only when Ariane rockets blast their way out of the swamps and forest. The tourist office in Cayenne has details of take-off dates. Tours can be booked through Takari, JAL (*see* p.293) or Espace Amazonie (*see* below). At other times the town merits a visit only as a jumping-off point for the Iles du Salut.

The Iles du Salut

The Iles du Salut are dots of sharp rock, encrusted with crumbling chapels and prison buildings, and sprawling palm lost in the blue-green and shark-infested Atlantic off the coast near Kourou. Only the **Ile Royale** is accessible from the mainland. From here it is possible to visit the **Ile du Diable** and the **Ile St Joseph**, the most beautiful of the islands. Both lie a short distance away and, although the swim looks fairly easy, the waters are so treacherous and shark-filled that even boatmen are usually reluctant to take visitors there. They can be persuaded at the Ile Royale dock. The Iles du Salut were named by early colonists who fled here to escape the malaria and yellow fever that were ravaging their communities along the coast. Today the name hangs heavy with irony; between 45 and 65,000 convicts died on the islands' penal colonies. Two of the most famous internees, Alfred Dreyfus and Henri Charrière (author of *Papillon*), both imprisoned for crimes they did not commit, managed to escape this fate. The rocky-shored Ile Royale has many open wells and crumbling prison buildings now frequented only by agoutis, humming birds, macaws and by the occasional intrepid camper. Ile Saint-Joseph has a small beach and is wilder and seldom visited. Prisoners sentenced to solitary confinement were sent here. A daily ferry service links Kourou with the Ile Royale. It departs from the landing stage (Kourou old village) at 8am and returns at 6pm. Guided tours are given three times a week from the governor's house. Both of Cayenne's tour companies (*see* p.293) can organize visits to the islands. The tourist office, Place de l'Europe, ✆ 324884, offeres information on the Ariane Rocket and the Iles du Salut. Espace Amazonie, in Kourou, ✆ 323430, ✉ 325702, organizes tours to the Interior, the Iles du Salut and rocket launchings.

Kourou (✆ 0594–)   ***Where to Stay in Kourou and Iles du Salut***

Most of the half dozen hotels in Kourou are on or around Rue de Gaulle, the town's principal street. Out on the Ile Royale, the **Auberge Iles du Salut**, Ile Royale, ✆ 321100, ✉ 324223, has smart rooms and an excellent seafood and Guianese restaurant (*expensive*). In town there is the **Hotel des Roches**, Rue de Gaulle, ✆ 320066, ✉ 328315, with two reasonable restaurants (*expensive*). **Les Jardins d'Hermes**, 56 Rue Duschène, Kourou, ✆ 320183, ✉ 320917, in the old part of town, has air conditioned rooms and a good restaurant (*moderate*). The **Centre d'Acceuil**, Av. de Gaulle, ✆ 322540, offers inexpensive, if spartan, rooms with fans.

Sinnamary

The first population centre of any note west after Kourou is another dull village in beautiful surroundings. This is thought to be the birthplace of Madame de Maintenon, the morganatic wife of Louis XIV. **Iracoubo**, a tiny Amerindian village at the estuary mouth, has a 100-year-old wooden church with a huge fresco stencilled by a former convict. Fine crafts are made here and at Bellevue by the Galibi Indians, including pearl items, and artificial flowers made from feathers. Both **Morpio Creek**, 12km to the west of Iracoubo, and **Organabo Creek**, 30km to the west, are good for swimming and a little bird watching. Morpio has a palm-shaded rest area. Taxis can be hired in Sinnamary. The Sinnamary River estuary at the village of Iracacoubo, and the forests and savannahs surrounding Sinnamary itself, attract migrant and endemic waders and a host of other rare birds. These include king vulture; rufous crab-hawk; rufous-crowned elaenia; scarlet ibis ; mangrove cuckoo; ruby-topaz hummingbird; green-tailed goldenthroat; yellowish pipit and snail kite. There are no organized birding tours to or from Sinnamary.

Saint-Laurent du Maroni

This attractive 19th-century colonial town, 250km from Cayenne on the banks of the Maroni River and the border with Suriname, is most famous for its penal transportation camp. Cells and brickwork arches moulder in the tropical sun next to lovingly restored guard houses and refectories. Guided tours are available; ask at the tourist office, 1 Bvd Malouet, ✆ 342398. Collective taxis leave for Cayenne from the jetty at the end of Av. Général de Gaulle. The Saint-Maurice rum distillery, 2km to the south of the town, is the only rum distillery still in operation in Guyane. Morning tours are free and include plentiful samples. There is a handful of places to stay, including La Tentiare, 12 Av. Franklin Roosevelt, ✆ 342600, ✉ 341509, and the Le Relais des Trois Lacs, Domaine du Lac Bleu, out of town, ✆ 340505, ✉ 340276 (*both moderate*).

Around Saint-Laurent du Maroni

Noah's Ark, at Saint-Jean, 17km from Saint-Laurent, houses a small collection of animals that have been recaptured from smugglers. Guided tours are available. Boats leave there from the quay. **Tatou Creek** is a small forested resort some 27km from Saint-Laurent on the Paul Isnard road, with over 2km of trails, picnic sites, shacks for slinging up hammocks, and a small bathing area. The **Cascades de Voltaire**, a magnificent 200m-high series of waterfalls, lie at the end of a 3½km forest trail leading off the Paul Isnard road (get precise directions from the tourist office). Food and accommodation are available at the waterfall inn, ✆ (0594) 342716.

Mana is an old Cluniac mission village and former gold-rush hamlet, surrounded by yellow beaches and Indian settlements. It's a quiet place, ideal for doing nothing but watching the muddy sea and walking along the coast to look for nesting turtles. The best places to find them are near the Indian villages of **Awala** and **Yalimapo**, 16km from Mana, and the long sandy beach at **Les Hattes**, 4km further on again. The indigenous peoples of both villages offer good-value excursions both to the beaches and around the creeks and the headland, which are undisturbed and provide excellent birding. Bring plenty of insect repellent and ask around.

Mana, Awala and Yalimapo (✆ 0594–)   **Where to Stay**

Accommodation in Mana, Awala and Yalimapo is rustic. There are a number of cheap and dilapidated guest houses in Mana and the Cluniac Community offer beds (Communauté des Soeurs de Saint-Joseph de Cluny, 1 Rue Bourignon, ✆ 348062).

Tourist Camps and Forest Inns

Amazonie Détente, contact M. Villaréal in Kourou, ✆ 325288, ✉ 328252. A simple lodge with good food next to the Valentin Rapids, on the Mana River. Reservation required. Good for wildlife. Sleeping is in hammocks.

Chez Jeanne Tiouka, Plage des Hattes, Yalimapo, Awala-Yalimapo, ✆ 342982, ✉ 342071. Hammock accommodation under open-sided thatched roof shacks, very close to the Les Hattes turtle nesting beach. Cheap and cheerful.

Chez Judith et Denis Thibault, Av. Paul Henri, Yalimapo, Awala-Yalimapo, ✆ 342438. Great value. Indigenous-style thatched huts near Les Hattes.

Campement Itup, Awala Yalimapo, Association Yawo Yadélé, Rue Charles Claude, Awala, ✆ 343414, ✉ 343253. A simple indigenous run and managed lodge on the Coswine Creek near Awala. Good value; interesting trips and good birding.

East of Cayenne

The forests southeast of Cayenne spread towards the border with the Brazilian state of Amapá on the Oyapock River. Along the way they are interrupted by a broad marshy strip of land, cut by creeks and savannahs, interspersed with villages and contained by the Gabrielle and Kaw mountains. Though hunting has depleted their numbers, this is still one of Guyane's top coastal birding and wildlife destinations. The main highway from Cayenne, RN2, leads to Régina, one of the largest settlements in the area, passing Roura and Cacao on the way.

Roura, on the banks of the Roura River, is close to the Gabrielle Creek, which winds its way through varzea and gallery forest and marshland to the Mahury Estuary and the sea. The village is close to the Fourgassiés Waterfalls, which can be reached via the dirt road to Kaw. Mount Kaw affords wonderful views out over the forests and marshes lying between Gabrielle Creek and Approuague estuaries, and there is good birding in the terra firme forests. Irregular collective taxis leave from opposite the Laussat Canal in Cayenne. Getting here under your own steam is far less hassle; the drive takes about 40 minutes.

The tiny village of **Kaw**, reached by dirt track from Roura and a short canoe-ride across the Kaw river, is in the heart of the Kaw marshes, a wet savannah, which, though it has been hunted, is still teeming with wildlife, including plentiful black caiman, sloths and monkeys, including the rare, golden-pawed midas tamarins, which can be found in groups of two to six in dense viny habitats. Mount Kaw is even better for birds, with two major specialities, Capuchin bird and Guianan cock-of-the-rock.

Cacao, some 60km from Roura, is populated almost entirely by Hmon refugees from Laos. The Hmon are traditionally a mountain-dwelling people and must feel rather hot in Guyane, wrapped up in their beautiful sarongs, thick hats and robes. Their food is hot too; wonderful spicy soups and croustillades. There's a Laotian market every Sunday morning.

East of Cayenne (✆ 0594–)   ***Where to Stay***

Most lodges offer tours around the Kaw Marshes, and the forests around Roura.

Chez Madame Luap, Le Bourg, 97311 Roura, ✆ 270403. Simple lodge with views across the river. Second floor rooms are the best (*moderate*).

Camp Caïman, Route de Kaw PK 27, 97311 Roura, ✆ 376034. Organizes trips along the caiman-filled creeks, and around Mount Kaw. The lodge is rustic but comfortable. Reservation required.

Crique Gabrielle, Village Dacca, Roura, contact M. Marc Outsama, ✆/✉ 280104. In the wetlands north of Roura. Good for birds and butterflies. Reservation required.

Quimbé Kio, Le bourg, 97352, Cacao, ✆ 270122, ✉ 270148. Rustic but clean and well maintained modern lodge, with sleeping in hammocks or beds. There are plenty of activities organized from here, including kayaking, mountain biking and trail walks. Very good value at around $10 a night including breakfast.

They may be a long way from the Amazon but, if you fly into **Rio de Janeiro, Caracas** or **Lima** on your way to the forest, here are a few basics.

Rio de Janeiro (✆ 021–)

Metropolitan Rio sprawls inland, but the most beautiful areas fringe the ocean beaches south of the centre. Of these, Copacabana, Ipanema and Leblon all sitting under the gaze of the Christ of Corcovado mountain, are the most famous. These beaches offer the best places to stay. Ipanema and Leblon are safer and more upmarket than Copacabana.

Tips: There are two tourist offices (who supply city maps), and a bank in the airport.

Transport: Take taxis in Rio; a ride from the airport to Ipanema/Copacabana/Leblon will take less than half an hour and cost around $20. Buses are packed to the brim. Keep your camera hidden (especially on Copacabana beach), as robberies are not uncommon.

Useful website: *www.embratur.gov.br* has information on tourism across Brazil.

Where to stay: Caesar Park, Av. Vieira Souto, 460, Ipanema, ✆ 525 2525, @ 521 6000, w*ww.caesarpark-rio.com.* is one of Rio's top hotels, overlooking Ipanema beach (*lux–exp*). **Copacabana Palace**, Av. Atlantica 1702, Copacabana, ✆ 548 7070, @ 235 7330, *www.copacabanapalace.com.br*, is Rio's most famous hotel (*lux–exp*). **Sheraton Rio Hotel and Towers**, Av. Niemeyer 121, Praia do Vidigal, ✆ 274 1122, @ 239 5643, *www.sheraton-rio.com* has one of the world's most wonderful views (*lux–exp*). **Sol Ipanema**, Av. Vieira Souto, 320, Ipanema, ✆ 525 2020, @ 247 8484, *wwwsolipanema.com.br*, very comfortable with good beach views (*exp–mod*). **Marina Palace**, Rua Delfim Moreira 1117, Leblon, ✆ 540 5212, @ 294 1644, *hotelmarina@callnet.com.br* is in a safe area (*exp–mod*). **Praia Linda**, Av. do Pepê, 1430, ✆ 494 2186, has apartments and a restaurant on the Barra da Tijuca beach (*inexp*). **Ipanema Inn**, Rua Maria Quitéria 27, Ipanema, ✆ 523 6092, @ 511 5094, near Ipanema beach (*inexp*).

Where to eat: There are plenty of inexpensive and cheap eateries and juice bars near the beaches. Avoid salads in the cheaper restaurants. A selection of the better restaurants follows. **Claude Troisgros**, Rua Custódio Serrão 62 (in the Botanic Gardens), ✆ 522 8582. Masterful French food with a Brazilian twist from the eponymous chef (*exp*). **Alho e Óleo**, Barrão da Torre 348, Ipanema, ✆ 523 4842, Brazilian and international cuisine (*moderate*). **Capricciosa**, Rua Vinícius de Morais 134, Ipanema, ✆ 523 3394. Brazilians, especially Paulistanos, consider their pizza to be the best in the world. This is one of Rio's finer restaurants (*moderate–inexp*). **Celeiro**, Rua Dias Ferreira 199, Leblon, ✆ 274 7843, is Rio's best veggie restaurant serving exclusively organic products in a buffet of over 40 salads, quiches and tarts (*moderate–inexp*).

International Cities

Caracas (✆ 02–)

Venezuela's capital sprawls along the floor of a mountain valley 900m above sea level. The Atlantic Ocean and the airport are about 30 minutes drive away. It is an unpredictable, hectic, vibrant, and often dangerous place. The remaining colonial portions of the city lie to the west of the city, around the Plaza Bolívar. This is the most interesting part of the city for visitors. The cheapest places to stay lie here. The heart of the city, further to the east, is dominated by attractive Latin American modernist skyscrapers. The city's many clubs, salsa bars and museums lie here, as do the fine Botanic Gardens.

Tips: Caracas can be dangerous. Be careful, especially near the bus station after dark. The tourist office, **Corpoturismo**, is on the 37th floor of Torre Oeste in Parque Central, ✆ 507 8815, *open Mon–Fri 8.30–12.30 and 2–5*. The **Unidad de Atención al Turista**, ✆ 507 8607, in the same building on the 35th floor, offers advice in English. There are *casas de cambio* and banks in the airport for changing money.

Transport: Buses link Simon Bolivar International Airport with the centre of the city. A taxi will cost around $25. Both leave from outside the terminal building. Caracas has a clean, efficient underground railway system.

Internet: *www.venezuelaturistica.com.*. General tourist information.

Where to stay: **Gran Meliá**, Av. Casanova at El Recreo, Sabana Grande, ✆ 762 8111, *caracas@gran-melia.com.ve, www.solmelia.es,* has its own heliport (*lux*). **Hilton Caracas,** Sur 25, at El Conde, ✆ 503 5000/503 4203, ● 503 5003, is the city's most luxurious: aimed principally at business clientele (*lux*). **Best Western**, Centro Ciudad Comercial Tamanaco (CCCT), ✆ 902 8000, ● 959 6697, in one of the city's largest shopping complexes (*exp*). **Crillon**, Av. Libertador at Av. Las Acacias, ✆ 761 4411, ● 762 8969, is comfortable and chic (*mod*). **Hotel Kurasal**, Av. Casanova at El Colegio, in the Plaza Venezuela, ✆ 762 2822, ● 762 5715. Clean and safe if spartan.

Where to eat: There is a lot of choice in this city. Some of the best restaurants are in the El Rosal and Las Mercedes districts. You will find plenty of reasonably priced Italian eateries in the Sabana Grande. One of the nicest simple pleasures is stopping off in one of the many little street bars for hot pasties (*empanadas*) and thick, strong *café con leche*.

Lima (✆ 01–)

Even those that live here agree that Peru's capital is a place people are glad to leave. It sits in between an ugly desert and a misty sea and reeks of drying fish and exhaust. Try to catch a flight out as soon as you arrive. If you can't, we list a few hotel options. Taxis are cheap.

Tips: The government tourist office has closed. **South American Explorers**, Av. República de Portugal, Breña, ✆/● 425 0142, *montague@amauta.rcp.net.pe, www.samexplo.org,* are a wealth of information for excursions anywhere in the Andean countries. There are several banks at the airport and around town.

Transport: Take taxis, buses or collective taxis. Try to have the right change.

Where to stay: **Gran Hotel Bolívar,** Plaza San Martín, Centro, ✆ 428 7672, ● 428 7674. A fine old colonial hotel, with uniformed bell boys, and a model T Ford in reception (*expensive*). **Posada del Parque**, Calle Hernan Velarde 60, Alta Cuadra 1–2 de la Av. Petit Thouars, Barrio Santa Beatriz, ✆ 433 2412; ● 432 3011 is in a quiet suburb away from the centre (*inexp*). **Mochilero's**, Pedro de Osma 135, Barranco, ✆ 477 4506, *backpacker@amauta.rcp.pe*.The best for backpackers, and one of the few that doesn't double up as a whorehouse (*cheap*).

Where to eat: There is no shortage of places to eat in Lima. Most are chicken and burger bars. Those looking for something classier should take a taxi to the posh suburb of Miraflores, which has a few upmarket pizzerias and fish restaurants. This is a very small district, stretching back from an ugly beach, and is easily negotiated on foot.

It may look similar on the page, but the sound of **Brazilian Portuguese** is as different to Spanish as *The Girl from Ipanema* is to *La Bamba*. It is gentler, more feminine and far more confusing. Relax your mouth when you are in Brazil: consonants are softened here, vowels are lengthened, the mouth is opened more fully. 'R's become 'h's seemingly at random: ask a Brazilian which band Mick Jagger sings for, and they'll say: De Holeing Storns. 'O's become 'u's: Rio de Janeiro is pronounced 'Hi-u de Janair-u'. 'D's become 'j's before an 'i' and often before 'e's; 't's become 'ch's: This makes Brazilian Portuguese a 'Jifficult' language to pronounce, as you'll be repeatedly told. At the end of a word 'em' becomes 'eng': Santarém is pronounced 'Santareng'. The tilde (~) is most commonly used in *ão*, which should produce a sound like a nasal 'ow' in 'cow', without the final use of the lips that seals the word in English. If it appears at the end of a word – as in Maracanã, stress this final syllable and push it up your nose. The circumflex (^) opens the vowel: turning 'e's to open 'a's. Gardênia is pronounced Gardaynia. As in Spanish, the acute accent produces a stress. A cedilla (ç') produces an 's'.

Greetings

good morning	*bom dia*	no	*não*
good afternoon/evening	*boa tarde*	please	*por favor*
goodnight	*boa noite*	thank you	*obrigado/a*
goodbye	*adeus*		(for men/women)
see you later	*até logo*	excuse me	*com licença*
yes	*sim*	I am sorry	*desculpe*

Common Phrases

please help me	*você pode me ajudar, por favor*	where?	*onde?*
		how are you?	*tudo bem?*
do you speak English?	*você fala inglês?*	I'm lost	*estou perdido/a*
how much is it?	*quanto custa?*	I don't understand	*não entendo*
I am in a hurry	*estou com pressa*	what do you call this?	*como se chama isto?*
why?	*porquê?*		

Asking Directions

left	*esquerda*	the bus station	*a rodoviária*
right	*direita*	railway station	*estação ferroviária*
straight on	*em frente*	taxi rank	*ponto de táxi*
can you direct me to...?	*pode indicar-me o caminho para...?*	police	*polícia*
		hospital	*hospital*
the centre of the city	*o centro da cidade*	chemist	*farmácia*

Accommodation

a single room	*um quarto de solteiro*	with private bathroom	*com banho privativo*
a double room	*um quarto de casal*	bring me a towel	*me traga uma toalha*

Language

Restaurant

the menu	*o menu/cardápio*	the bill	*la conta*
breakfast	*café da manha*	is service included?	*o serviço está incluindo?*
lunch	*almoço*		
dinner	*jantar*		

Restaurant (cont'd)

a small, black coffee	*um cafezinho*	pineapple/orange	*abacaxi/laranja*
a tall glass of white coffee	*café com leite* or	apple/pear	*maçã/pêra*
	pingado (less milky)	grapes/banana	*uvas/banana*
tea	*chá*	papaya	*mamão papaya* (small)
chicken	*frango*		*mamão* (large)
ham	*fiambre*	guava	*goiaba*
pork	*porco*	avocado	*abacate*
I am a vegetarian	*eu sou vegetariano/a*	roasted/boiled/fried	*assado / cozido/frito*
fish	*peixe*	smoked/grilled	*fumado/grelhado*
tuna	*atum*	stew/baked	*guisado/ o forno*
garlic	*alho*	mixed (i.e. salad)	*mista*
rice	*arroz*	bread/butter/cheese	*pão/manteiga/queijo*
potatoes	*batatas*	ice	*gelo*
spinach	*espinafres*	salt/pepper	*sal/ pimenta*
broad beans	*favas*	beer	*cerveja*
peppers	*pimentão*	white/red wine	*vinho branco/tinto*
fruit	*frutas*	water	*água*

Time and Days of the Week

what time is it?	*que horas são?*	Sunday/Monday/Tuesday/	*domingo/segunda-*
when	*quando*	Wednesday/Thursday/	*feira/ terça-feira/*
tomorrow	*amanhã*	Thursday/Friday	*quarta-feira/ quinta-*
today	*hoje*		*feira/ sabado*

Money

can I have...?	*pode dar-me...?*	can you change...?	*pode trocar...?*
the bill	*a conta*	do you take traveller's	*vocés aceitam*
the receipt	*o recibo*	cheques?	*traveller's cheques?*
the change	*o troco*	a bank	*um banco*

Numbers

1/2/3/4/5/6/7/8/9/10	*um/dois/três/quatro/cinco/seis/sete/ oito/nove/dez*

In the Forest

tree	*árvore*	hammock	*rede*
river	*rio*	mosquito net	*mosquitero*
boat	*barco*	insect repellent	*repelente*
village	*aldeia*	torch (flashlight)	*lanterna*

A Few Animals

river dolphin	*boto*	caiman	*jacaré*
jaguar	*onça*	capybara	*capivara*
puma	*onça parda*	snake	*cobra*
bird	*pássaro*	sloth	*bicho preguiça*
parrot	*papaguayo*	monkey	*macaco*
macaw	*arara*	humming-bird	*beija-flor*
eagle	*aguia*	butterfly	*borboleta*
vulture	*urubú*		

Latin American Spanish is one of the easiest languages to get a basic grasp of. Words are pronounced pretty much as they are written and, outside Chile and Colombia people don't tend to rush through sentences like an express train. Understanding a little more than '*gringo*' and '*cerveza*' will greatly enhance your trip. Here are a few basics.

Vowels

a short 'a' as in 'bat'
u is silent after q and gue- and gui-; otherwise long 'u' as in 'flute'
e short 'e' as in 'bet'

i as e in 'be'
o is usually long as in 'note', also short as in 'hot'
y at end of word is as the Spanish 'i'

Dipthongs

ai, ay as i in 'side'
ei, ey as ey in 'they'

au as *ou* in 'sound'
oi, oy as *oy* of 'boy'

Consonants

c before the vowels 'i' and 'e', as an s
ch like 'ch' in 'church'
g before 'i' or 'e', pronounced as 'j' (see below)
h is silent
j the 'ch' in 'loch'
ll pronounce as 'y' or 'ly' as in 'million'

ñ ny as in 'canyon' (the ~ is called a tilde)
q like a 'k'
r usually rolled, which takes practice
v often pronounced as 'b'
z pronounced as 's'

Greetings

hello (informal/phone)	*hola*	yes	*sí*
good morning	*buenos días*	no	*no*
good afternoon	*buenas tardes*	please	*por favor*
goodnight	*buenas noches*	thank you	*gracias*
goodbye	*adiós*	excuse me	*disculpe*

Common Phrases

do you speak English	*habla inglés?*	where?	*dónde?*
can you help me, please?	*puede ayudarme por favor*	how are you?	*cómo está/cómo le va?*
how much is it?	*cuanto es?*	I'm lost	*estoy perdido/a*
why?	*porqué?*	I don't understand	*no entiendo*
		what do you call this?	*cómo se llama esto?*

Asking Directions

left	*izquierda*	Where is...?	*dónde está...?*
right	*derecha*	bus station	*la estación de autobuses*
straight on	*todo recto*	railway station	*la estación de ferrocarril*
square	*plaza*	police station	*la policía*
street	*calle*	hospital	*el hospital*

Accommodation

a single room	*una habitación simple*	with private bathroom	*con baño privado*
a double room	*una habitación doble* .	a towel	*una toalla*

Restaurant (*see* also pp.22–3)

the menu	*el menú*	the bill (check)	*la cuenta*
breakfast/lunch/dinner	*desayuno/almuerzo/cena*		

Restaurant (cont'd)

see also pp.22–3

a small, black coffee	un café solo	chickpeas	garbanzos
a tall, white coffee	un café con leche	lentils	lentejas
tea	té	fruit	frutas
chicken	pollo	orange/pineapple	naranja/ananas
ham	jabon	apple/pear	manzana/pera
pork	cerdo	grapes/banana	uvas/plátano
I am a vegetarian	soy vegetariano	guava	guiaba
fish	pescado	avocado	aguacate/palta
tuna	atún	roasted/boiled/fried	assado/cocido/frito
garlic	ajo	baked	al horno
rice	arroz	mixed (e.g. salad)	mixta
potatoes	patatas	bread/butter/cheese	pan/mantequilla/queso
onions	cebollas	ice	hielo
beans	frijoles	salt/pepper	sal/pimenta
peppers	pimentos	beer	cerveza
asparagus	espárragos	red/white wine	vino tinto/blanco
		water	agua

Time and Days of the Week

what time is it?	que hora es?	today	hoy
when	cuando	Sun/Mon/Tues	domingo/lunes/martes
yesterday	ayer	Wed/Thurs	miércoles/jueves
tomorrow	mañana	Fri/Sat	viernes/sabado

Money

can you change...?	puede cambiar...?	the bank	el banco
traveller's cheques	cheques de viajero	the exchange rate	qué es el cambio

Post Office/Internet

letter	carta	email	correo electronico
postcard	carta postal	Internet	Internet
by air mail	correo aerero	computer	computadora/ordenador

Numbers

1/2/3/4/5/6/7/8/9/10   un/dos/tres/cuatro/cinco
seis/siete/ocho/nueve/diez

In the Forest

tree	árbol	mosquito net	mosquitero
river	río	insect repellent	repelente
boat	barco/bote	torch (flashlight)	linterna
village	aldea	boots	botas de goma
hammock	hamaca		

A Few Animals

jaguar	jaguar/tigre (col)	sloth	oso perezoso
puma	puma/león (col)	monkey	mono
bird	pájaro	humming-bird	colibrí
parrot	loro	butterfly	mariposa
eagle	aguila	river dolphin	delfín del rio
snake	serpiente		

Glossary

buttress	A tree root that extends out from the trunk to support the tree.
campesino	Poor agricultural worker (lit. peasant), but without a pejorative connotation.
caboclo	Poor person of mixed blood.
canopy	The treetop layer of the rainforest ecosystem.
cerrado woodland	Thick woodland.
chaco	Scrubby, bleak grassland peppered with thorn bushes. Characteristic of Paraguay and parts of Bolivia.
CITES	The 1988 Convention on International Trade in Endangered Species, whose lists of endangered species were written as appendices to their report, and have been updated since.
cloud forest	A mountain forest that remains semi-permanently covered in mist; characterized by abundant epiphytic and moss growth.
deciduous	Seasonal or stress related leaf loss.
ecosystem	The total interactive, living and non-living components of a given area.
elfin forest	Stunted forest growing on a ridge top; usually gnarled, moist and mossy and at high elevation.
epiphyte	A plant that lives on another without parasitising it; usually hanging.
gallery forest	Lush forest bordering a seasonally flooded lake or river.
garimpeiro	gold rush itinerant miner.
igapo	Varzea (*see* below).
igarapé	A creek (often seasonally flooded).
jungle	Literally secondary growth forest, characterized by a tangled mass of young plants competing for light. Often used as a synonym for tropical forest.
maloca	Traditional longhouse used by the indigenous peoples of the Amazon,
mangrove	A group of wooded plants highly tolerant of immersion in salt water. Constitute a major coastal ecosystem in the tropics.
neotropics	The American tropics,
meseta	A table-top mountain.
montane forest	A generic name for warm mountain forests. Pre-montane forests covers the lower mountain slopes.
oxbow lake	A bend in the river that has become isolated and blocked at both ends, to form a lake.
pampas	Literally temperate grasslands in southern South and Central America. Often used for any predominantly grassland area.
paramo	Mountain shrubland found at high elevations in the Andes and Sierra Nevada de Santa Marta.
table-top mountain	An ancient sea bed whose hard sedimentary rock has been exposed over millions of years to form a flat topped mountain.
tropical rainforest	A synonym for tropical moist or wet forest, used in common parlance for any lowland tropical forest.
savannah	A predominantly grassland ecosystem with scattered trees and shrubs.
tepui	The Venezuelan term for table-top mountains.
terra firme forest	An area of forest not subject to flooding.
tropical moist/ humid forest	A seasonal tropical forest receiving not less than 10cm of rainfall. in any month for two out of three years and is frost free, with an average temperature of 24°C or more.
tropical wet forest	As above but with rainfall of 40–1,000cm.
varzea	Seasonally flooded riverine forests.

History

Robin Furneaux *Amazon* (Hamish Hamilton, 1971). A witty, anecdotal and easily digestable Amazon history.

John Hemming, *Red Gold* (Macmillan, 1987) and its sequel *Amazon Frontier.* A history of the Brazilian Amazon under the Portuguese. Very clearly written and thoroughly researched.

The **Latin America Bureau** publish a range of modern history, and current affairs books on Latin America, including their excellent In Focus, pocket-sized country introductions.

The Incas

Anthony Aveni, *Empires of Time* (Kodansha Int., 1995). Includes a fascinating explanation of how the Koricancha emple in Cusco functioned as a giant astronomical clock.

Von Hagen and Morris, *The Cities of the Ancient Andes* (Thames & Hudson, 1998). The best introduction to the pre-colonial archaeological sights of the Peruvian Andes.

John Hemming, *The Conquest of the Incas* (Harcourt Brace, 1973). Lively history, with accounts of Bingham's 'discovery' of Machu Picchu and other lost cities of Vilcabamba.

Michael Moseley, *The Incas and their Ancestors* (Thames & Hudson, 1993). Very readable.

William Sullivan, *The Secret of the Incas: Myth, Astronomy, and the War Against Time* (Crown, 1997). Controversial new theories about Inca astronomy and cosmology.

Natural History

J.C. Kricher, *A Neotropical Companion* (Princeton University Press, 1989). The best available introduction to the neotropical forests, their ecology and their plants and animals

L.H. Emmons, *Neotropical Rainforest Mammals* (Chicago University Press, 1990). Invaluable field guide to most mammalian neotropical rainforest species.

Dixon and Soini, *Reptiles of the Upper Amazon Basin* (Milwaukee Public Museum). Focuses on the lowland forests typified by the area around Iquitos in Peru.

Castner, Timme & Duke, *A Field Guide to the Medicinal and Useful Plants of the Upper Amazon,* (Feline Press USA).

Birding Field Guides

No single volume, even the weighty *Birds of South America,* covers the entire Amazon Basin. Most are usually available at the best rainforest lodges.

S.L Hilty and W.L Brown, *The Birds of Colombia* (Princeton University Press, 1986). The largest book in the series, with a species range useful for much of the region.

De la Pena & Rumbolli, *The Birds of Southern South America and Antarctica* (Harper Collins, 1999). Covers part of the Pantanal and the Chapada dos Guimarães.

Roberts, Ridgely & Tudor, *The Birds of South America, Vols I and II,* (Univ. Texas Press, 1994). So far only the oscine and suboscine passerines have been described, yet both these books are huge. When complete, the series will be the definitive work.

De Schauensee and Phelps, *The Birds of Venezuela* (Princeton Unviersity Press, 1978). Essential for the birds of the Gran Sabana and tepuis.

N. Wheatley, *Where to Watch Birds in South America* (Princeton University Press, 1995). Invaluable and expansive pocket guide, with comprehensive lists of species.

Conservation and Current Affairs

Marcus Colchester, *Guyana: Fragile Frontier* (Latin America Burueau, 1997). An exposé of the problems of logging and mining in Guyana and their effect on indigenous people.

Catherine Caufield, *In the Rainforest* (Picador, 1984). Not so current any longer, but the issues it explores are: dam building, logging and turning the forest to cattle ranching.

Forest Peoples Programme, World Rainforest Movement, *Undermining the Forest* (published 2000). A case study of the problems caused by mining in the rainforest, with an emphasis on indigenous peoples.

Joe Kane, *Savages* (Vintage, 1996). A personal account of time spent with the Huaorani of Ecuador, which explores their problems with the government and the oil companies.

George Monbiot, *Amazon Watershed* (Arrow, 1994). One of the first writers to explore the land rights issues and gold mining that lie behind the Amazon deforestation.

Jan Rocha, *Murder in the Rainforest* (LAB 1999). The story of the Yanomami Massacres in the 1980s and 1990s.

Indigenous Peoples

Stephen Hugh-Jones, *The Palm and the Pleiades* (CUP, 1979). An academic exploration of Northwest Amazonian Indian cosmology and ritual from a leading anthropologist.

Gerardo Reichel Dolmatoff, *Rainforest Shamans* (Themis, 1997). The great Colombian anthropologist's essays on the spirituality of tribal peoples of the Upper Rio Negro.

Phillip Wearne, *The Return of the Indian* (LAB, 1995). Essential background reading for those interested in contemporary indigenous issues.

Fiction

Robert Holdstock, *The Emerald Forest* (Penguin). The book of John Boorman's poetic film about a North American boy captured and adopted by an uncontacted Amazon tribe.

Peter Matthiessen, *At Play in the Fields of the Lord* (Vintage 1991). The clash of two men —one hired to kill Indians, the other to save them.

Peter Shaffer, *The Royal Hunt of the Sun* (Penguin). A play inspired by the conquest of the Incas.

Travelogues

Benedict Allen, *Mad White Giant* (Macmillan, 1985) The author stumbles into in the middle of the Brazilian state of Amapá with entertaining conseqences.

Wade Davis, *One River* (Pocket Books, 1998). A series of trips through the forests and the psychotropic plants of the Amazon mingle with accounts of the greatest US plant-hunter, Richard Evans Schultes. Unusual, inspiring reading.

Gerald Durrell, *Three Singles to Adventure* (Penguin). Not very conservationally correct, but amusing accounts of hunting for animals in the savannahs and forests of Guyana.

Percy Fawcett, *Exploration Fawcett* (Century, 1988). The edited diaries of the British explorer who charted the borders of the northern Bolivian Amazon in the early 20th century.

Martin and Tanis Jordan, *Out of Chingford and Up the Orinoco* (Frederick Muller, 1988). Two madcap Essex Londoners and an inflatable venture blindly into the Amazon .

Joe Kane, *Running the Amazon* (Pan, 1997). A kayak journey down the Amazon from source to sea. Pacily written and likely to become a mini-classic.

Alfred Russell Wallace, *A Narrative of Travel on the Amazon and Río Negro* (Dover, 1972). The most humane and readable account of the 19th-century British naturalists.

A List of NGOS (Non-Governmental Organizations)

Environment and Wildlife

Asociación Hombre y Naturaleza, Calle Tacuarembó 2065; ℗/✆ (03) 436968; in Warnes (30km from Santa Cruz) Av. Circunvalación lado Norte, Distrito 13, Rotonda salida a Montero; ℗/✆ (0923) 2239, *hynb@bibosi.scz.entelnet.bo, www.paisvirtual.com/ong/comercial/hynb/index.html.* Work in conjunction with the Spanish group **Amigos de Doñana** to protect areas of the Bolivian Amazon and Pantanal.

Conservation International, Call Box, Connecticut College, New London, CT, 06320, USA, ✆ 1 202 973 2219, ✉ 1 203 873 8514, *j.sweeting@conservation.org, www.conservationinternational.org.* Campaign to protect rainforests and develop community-based ecotourism projects in Third World countries, including Bolivia, Brazil, Guyana and Suriname.

Earthwatch, PO Box 403, Mt. Auburn St, Watertown, MA 0227, USA, ✆ 1 880 776 0188, UK ✆ 44 (0)1865 318831. Ecological and conservational research placements in 46 countries, including Brazil, Ecuador and Peru. Average cost is $1,600 for a 1–3 week team duration.

Frankfurt Zoological Society, Alfred-Brehm-Platz 16, D-60316, Frankfurt, ✆ 069 21234410, ✉ 069 439348. Protect giant otters in Peru in conjunction with **Munich Wildlife Society.**

Friends of the Earth, (offices worldwide) *www.foei.org.* Campaign on environmental/social issues, including conservation of primary forests, and banning of exportation of wild mahogany.

GreenNet, *www.fern.org.* Web-based resource for all things environmental.

Greenpeace International, (offices worldwide) *www.greenpeace.org.* Campaign to prevent the exportation of wild mahogany from the Amazon.

Human Rights Watch, (offices throughout the USA, in the UK and in Belgium). *www.hrw.org.* Leading human rights NGO who publish reports on governments worldwide.

Instituto Socio Ambiental, *socioamb@ax.apc.org, www.socioambiental.org;* publish The most up-to-date information about Brazilian indigenous people, environmental issues and political plans for the future of the Amazon.

The International Institute for Peace through Tourism, 360 Rue de La Montaigne, Montreal, Quebec, H3G 2A8, Canada, ✆ 1 514 281 1822; ✉ 1 514 848 1099, *www.iipt.org.* Brings together leaders from the tourism industry, general public, private sector, academics and NGOs.

Mamirauá Sustainable Development Reserve, Caixa Postal: 38, 69470-000, Tefé, AM, Brazil; *www.cnpq.br/mamiraua/mamiraua.htm, mamiraua@pop-tefe.rnp.br.* Protect the Mamirauá Forest Reserve and promote research in areas such as environmental education and ecotourism.

The Nature Conservancy Council, 4245 North Fairfax Drive, Suite 100, Arlington, VA 22203-1606, USA, ✆ 1 800 628 6860, *www.tnc.org.* Protect a number of Amazon National Parks.

Rainforest Concern, 27 Lansdowne Crescent, London W11 2NS, UK, ✆ (020) 7229 2093, ✉ (020) 7221 4094, *rainforest@gn.apc.org .* Work to protect forest reserves in Ecuador.

Rainforest Action Network; 221 Pine Street, Suite 500, San Francisco, CA 94104, ✆ 415 398 4404, ✉ 415 398 2732, *rainforest@ran.org, www.ran.org.* Campaign for rainforests worldwide.

World Rainforest Movement, Maldonado 1858, 11200, Montevideo, Uruguay ✆ 598 2 409 6192, mobile ✆ 598 2 408 0762, *rcarrere@chasque.apc.org, www.wrm.org.uy.* Highly respected NGO campaigning to preserve rainforests. Support forest peoples seeking to control the use of their lands and work with the United Nations.

WWF-International, 1250 24th Street, NW, Washington DC, 20037, ✆ 1 202 293 4800. *www.panda.org;* **WWF-UK,** Panda House, Weyside Park, Godalming, Surrey, GU7 1XR, UK, *www.wwf-uk.org .* One of the world's largest environmental and conservational agencies.

Responsible Tourism

The Ecotourism Society, P.O. Box 755, North Bennington, VT 05257, USA, ☎ 1 802 447 2121, ✉ 1 802 447 2122, *ecomail@ecotourism.org, www.ecotourism.org*. Publish and distribute ecotourism publications and organize workshops.

Centre for Environmentally Responsible Tourism, Indaba House, 1 Hydeway, Thundersley, Essex, SS7 3BE, UK ☎ 01268 795772, ✉ 01268 759834, *info@c-e-r-t.org, www.c-e-r-t.org*. Campaign for environmentally conscious tourism; provide useful guidelines for travellers.

Tourism Concern, Stapleton House, 277–281 Holloway Road, London, N7 8HN, UK, ☎ (020) 7753 3330, *www.tourismconcern.org*. Information about responsible tourism.

Community Support and *Campesinos*

Ashoka; 3rd Floor, The Wilson Building, 1 Curtain Rd, London, EC2A 3JX, ☎ (020) 7375 3989, ✉ (020) 7375 3988, *ashoka_uk@compuserve.com, www.ashoka.org*. Grass roots projects like local radio stations and ecotourism projects aimed at rejuvenating poor communities.

Health and Happiness, Travessa Dom Amando 697, 68005-420, Santarem, PA ☎ 91 523 1083, ✉ 91 522 5144, *fesperan@ax.apc.org*. Cultural, educational and health support for poor peasant communities near Santarém.

MST: Movimento Sem Terra, *semterra@mst.org.br, www.mstbrazil.org*. Brazilian land reform movement, fights for land equality and other basic social rights such as education. Largest social movement in Latin America and one of the most successful grass-roots movements in the world. Unjustly portrayed by the Brazilian press.

Indigenous Peoples

Co-ordinador de las Organisaciones Indígenas de la Cuenca Amazonica (COICA), Alemania 832 at Mariana de Jesús; (Casilla Postal 1721753), ☎/✉ (02) 553297, *coica@ecua.net*. Information on indigenous issues and concerns throughout all the countries of the Amazon Basin, compiled by indigenous peoples in a centre run by indigenous peoples. Connections throughout South America.

CONFENIAIE (Confederación de Naciones Indígenas de la Amazonia Ecuatoriana), Av. 6 de Deciembre at 159 Pazmino, Edificio Parlamento, piso 4, Of. 408, ☎ (02) 543973, ✉ (02) 220325. The very latest on indigenous issues in the Ecuadorian Amazon, from an indigenous perspective. Run by indigenous people.

Cultural Survival, *www.cs.org*. The leading US NGO campaigning for the protection of the rights of indigenous peoples worldwide.

FIUPAM (*see* foreword, p.1). An NGO set-up by Tucano Manoel Moura, for the promotion of dialogue and unification of indigenous peoples worldwide.

Forest People's Programme, 1c Fosseway Business Centre, Moreton-in-Marsh, GL56 9NQ, England, ☎ + 44 (0)1608 652893, ✉ + 44 (0)1608 652878, *info@fppwrm.gn.apc.org*. *See* p.100.

Survival International, 11–15 Emerald St, London, WC1N 3QL, UK, ☎ (020) 7242 1441 ✉ (020) 7242 1771, *survival@gn.apc.org, www.survival-international.org*. NGO that campaigns for indigenous people's rights.

General Information

Latin America Bureau, 1 Amwell Street, London EC1R 1UL, UK ☎ (020) 7278 28 29, ✉ (020) 7278 01 65, *www.lab.org.uk*. Publisher and information database for all things Latin American. Very good book list, particularly current affairs and politics.

Oneworld, *www.oneworld.net*. An online community of over 750 organizations, covering the whole spectrum of development, environmental and human rights activities.

Main page references are in **bold**. Page references to maps are in *italics*.

Index

The Forest Peoples Programme supports the response of forest peoples to the global forest crisis. It aims to secure the rights of peoples who live in the forests, and depend on them for their livelihoods, to control their lands and destinies. The programme seeks to create political space for forest peoples to exercise their right to self-determination and to sustain their forests.

The programme has five main goals:

⊚ to support an effective global movement of forest peoples.

⊚ to promote coordinated action on forests by NGOs of North and South in line with forest peoples' visions and concerns.

⊚ to promote the rights and interests of forest peoples in international forest policy and human rights.

⊚ to support genuine, community based, sustainable forest management.

⊚ to counter top down planning and official solutions to the deforestation crisis, which deny local people a decisive voice about resource use in their areas.

A publication list is available from the address below.

To support field projects that help forest peoples map, own and control their lands, **please send donations made out to:**

**Forest Peoples Programme,
1c Fosseway Business Centre,
Stratford Road, Moreton-in Marsh,
GL56 9NQ, UK**

.

Forest
Peoples
Programme

WHEN YOU'RE GOING SOMEWHERE THAT'S NOT YOUR HOME, IT'S BETTER TO GO WITH A LOCAL.

DAILY FLIGHTS TO RIO DE JANEIRO AND SÃO PAULO DEPARTING FROM LONDON - HEATHROW.

If you're looking for a reliable and efficient partner in Brazil, you've found it: VARIG. The only airline in Latin America that's part of the Star Alliance network, offers you flights to more than 78 destinations in Brazil and 11 countries in South America. You can also earn and redeem miles in the Smiles Programme, the most complete mileage programme of Latin America. Experience our international quality of services with Brazilian warmth.

VARIG Brazilian Airline. Number One in Latin America.

For further information or to make a reservation call your travel agent or VARIG 0845 603 7601
www.varig.co.uk

Cadogan Guides are available from good bookshops, or via **Grantham Book Services**, Isaac Newton Way, Alma Park Industrial Estate, Grantham NG31 9SD, ℗ (01476) 541 080, ℘ (01476) 541 061; and **The Globe Pequot Press**, 246 Goose Lane, PO Box 480, Guilford, Connecticut 06437–0480, ℗ (800) 458 4500/℗ (203) 458 4500, ℘ (203) 458 4603.